CRITICAL ACCOUNTS

Also edited by David J. Cooper and Trevor M. Hopper

DEBATING COAL CLOSURES

Critical Accounts

Edited by

David J. Cooper
Professor of Accounting
University of Alberta

and

Trevor M. Hopper
Peat Marwick McLintock Professor of Management
Accounting
University of Manchester

MACMILLAN

First published 1990

Published by
THE MACMILLAN PRESS LTD
Houndmills, Basingstoke, Hampshire RG21 2XS
and London
Companies and representatives
throughout the world

Printed in Hong Kong

British Library Cataloguing in Publication Data
Critical accounts.
1. Accounting
I. Cooper, David J. II. Hopper, Trevor M.
657
ISBN 0–333–44970–3

Contents

Notes on the Contributors

Bailey, Derek Lecturer in Accounting, University of Birmingham. His major research interests lie in accounting in socialist countries and accounting history. He has close contacts with accounting specialists in Poland and other socialist countries, and he is editor of an abstracting quarterly, *The Soviet and East European Accounting Bulletin*. He is also editor of a recent book, *Accounting in Socialist Countries*.

Booth, Peter Senior Lecturer in Accounting in the School of Accounting, University of New South Wales, Australia. His major research interest is in management control systems within not-for-profit organisations. He has published several articles on this topic. Recently he has concentrated upon power and accounting, of which the chapter in this volume is an offshoot.

Bougen, Philip D. Lecturer in Accounting at the University of Leeds and Visiting Associate Professor of Accounting, Rice University of Texas. His principal research interest is the use of accounting in industrial relations. He has published several articles in leading journals on this topic. His current interest is in the emergence of accounting systems.

Cocks, Neil Associate Professor in Accounting, Bond University, Gold Coast, Australia. Prior to this, he was at Griffith University and has held various positions as an auditor and a management accountant. His major research interests lie in applying Critical Theory to the study of the accounting profession, and the social psychology of portfolio investment behaviour.

Cooper, David J. Professor of Accounting, University of Alberta. He has held appointments at the Universities of Manchester, East Anglia, UMIST, British Columbia, California (Berkeley), Uppsala, and the Copenhagen School of Business. He has published extensively, predominantly on the organisational and social aspects of accounting. He is an Associate Editor of *Accounting, Organizations and Society* and joint editor of *Critical Perspectives on Accounting*. His current principal research interests are management budgeting in the

National Health Service and accounting regulation in the UK, USA, West Germany, and Sweden.

Davis, Jon S. Assistant Professor of Accounting at the University of Illinois in Champaign. His research interests include the behavioural impact of management control systems in organisations, experimental tests of economic models of the market for auditing and the impact of taxes upon investment.

Freedman, Martin Associate Professor of Accounting in the School of Management at the State University of New York at Binghamton. His publications and research interests lie in the measurement and reporting of the social costs of production, especially those dealing with occupational health and air and water pollution.

Gubbay, Jon Lecturer in Sociology at the University of East Anglia. A mathematics graduate from the University of Manchester. His research interest is in political economy, with particular concern for class structure and the economic activities of the state. He has published in this area and is currently doing research on the curriculum in higher education. He is a member of the Socialist Workers Party.

Hopper, Trevor M. Peat Marwick McLintock Professor of Management Accounting at the University of Manchester. He has also held positions at the Universities of Michigan (Ann Arbor) and Sheffield, and Wolverhampton Polytechnic. He was secretary of the Management Control Workshop for five years. His past research and publications have been on organisational approaches to management control. His current interests include management accounting history and the socio-economic consequences of management accounting within the public sector.

Jefferis, Keith Lecturer in Economics at Kingston Polytechnic, London and formerly a research student in the Co-operatives Research Unit at the Open University, Milton Keynes. He was awarded a PhD in 1988 for research on the economics of British worker cooperatives. His interests are the social and economic performance of worker co-operatives; the potential for changes to the labour process in co-operatives; and socialist methods of resource allocation.

Jones, T. Colwyn Senior Lecturer in Economic Sociology at Bristol Polytechnic where, since 1975, he has taught sociology to accounting undergraduates. His interests include 'the social construction of accounting' and 'accounting versus engineering rationales for investment in computer-aided manufacturing technology'.

Laughlin, Richard C. Lecturer in Accounting and Financial Management in the School of Management and Economic Studies at the University of Sheffield. His current research interests lie in accounting methodology as well as in exploring the social and historical base underlying accounting system design. He has published in these and related areas in a wide range of accounting, management and organisation journals.

Lowe, E. Anthony Professor Emeritus of Accounting and Financial Management at the University of Sheffield. He retired from his position at Sheffield in 1985. Subsequently he was a Research Associate at UMIST working on an ESRC research study of international accounting regulation. Tony Lowe has been a leading researcher for over three decades in management control, accounting methodology, and accounting education, and he has published widely in these and other areas. His current academic interests concern the social and political consequences of accounting and accountancy practice.

Macintosh, Norman B. Professor of Accounting and Information Systems at Queen's University, Canada. He researches and publishes widely in the area of behavioural accounting where he has developed several theories including a path-goal theory of financial controls, a technology-personal decision-style model of information systems, and a paradigm based on Jungian personality traits of managerial response to accounting and information systems. His book, *The Social Software of Accounting Systems*, has received wide acclaim.

McSweeney, Brendan Lecturer in Accounting and Finance, Warwick Business School, University of Warwick. Previously Senior Technical Officer of the Chartered Association of Certified Accountants. His major research interests include accounting and organisational change, and the organisational and social influences on accounting. His publications include the joint authorship of a book on accounting and multinational corporations, and many articles in academic, professional, and business journals.

Murray, Gavin Lecturer in Interdisciplinary Studies at the University of Kent at Canterbury. Gavin's teaching and research focuses upon the problem of ideology; his research interest in accounting concerns the practical strategies of accounts users and methodological debates within accounting. He believes that accounting is more intelligible as drama than it is as an attempt to establish scientific objectivity.

Neimark, Marilyn Associate Professor of Accountancy, Baruch College, The City University of New York. She received her PhD from New York University in 1983 and is a Certified Public Accountant. She is General Editor of *Advances in Public Interest Accounting*, a research annual published by JAI Press, and she writes extensively on the social and historical origins and consequences of accounting theory and practice.

Ogden, Stuart Lecturer in Industrial Relations at the University of Leeds. His research and publications include studies of accounting within industrial relations. He is currently researching the disclosure of information in collective bargaining.

Puxty, Anthony G. Professor of Accounting at the University of Strathclyde, Glasgow. Prior to this, he was a lecturer in the School of Management and Economic Studies at the University of Sheffield. He is the author/editor of four books and monographs, and some forty academic and professional papers. His major current research interest is the relationship between the accounting profession and the state.

Roberts, John Research Fellow at the Management Studies Group at Cambridge University. He received his PhD from the University of Manchester Institute of Science and Technology in 1982. Subsequent to this, he was a Research Fellow in the Department of Accounting and Finance at the University of Manchester and at London Business School. His research has focussed on issues of management control and the uses of accounting information, and he is currently concerned with understanding the organisational processes involved in the formulation and implementation of strategic decisions.

Robson, Keith Lecturer in the School of Management at the University of Manchester Institute of Science and Technology. He obtained a BA and MA in Accounting and Finance from the University of

Manchester and a PhD on the Accounting Standards Committee in its social context from UMIST.

Scapens, Robert W. Professor of Accounting at the University of Manchester. He is currently researching the role of accounting and accountability in large organisations. His publications inlcude *Management Accounting: A Review of Recent Developments* and papers in *The Accounting Review*, *Accounting Organizations and Society*, and various other journals.

Sherer, Michael Royal London Professor of Finance, University of Essex. His major research interests include the role of accounting information in the management control processes of public sector organisations and the efficacy of auditing as a means of accountability. His publications include two books on auditing and articles on the political economy of accounting.

Stagliano, A. J. Edward G. Sutula Professor of Accounting in the College of Business and Administration at Saint Joseph's University in Philadelphia. Formerly the Chairman of the Department of Accounting at George Mason University, he has also served on the faculties at the University of Maryland and the University of Illinois.

Thomas, Alan Lecturer in Systems at the Open Unversity, Milton Keynes, where he has worked on course teams in Systems Management, Systems Modelling, Control of Technology, and Third World Studies. He had been researching UK worker co-operatives since 1977, and from 1984 to 1988 he co-directed a major project on 'Creating Successful Co-operative Businesses'.

Tinker,Tony Professor of Accounting at Baruch College, City University of New York. He is the author of *Paper Prophets: A Social Critique of Accounting* and *Social Accounting for Corporations: Private Enterprise versus the Public Interest*. Together with David Cooper he is editor of *Critical Perspectives in Accounting*. He is an editorial board member of *Accounting, Organizations and Society*, *The Journal of Accounting and Public Policy*, and *The Employee Responsibilities and Rights Journal*. A graduate of Manchester University, Tony has taught at the Universities of Sheffield, Washington (Seattle), UCLA, and NYU. He has published in a variety of fields including sociology, finance, accounting, cybernetics, organisation theory, and systems theory.

Tomlinson, Jim Senior Lecturer in Economics, Brunel University. His main interests lie in the history of economic policy, and in industrial democracy. His six books include *The Unequal Struggle? British Socialism and the Capitalist Enterprise* (1982), *Monetarism: Is There an Alternative?* (1986), and *Employment Policy: The Crucial Years 1939–55* (1987).

Willmott, Hugh C. Lecturer in the School of Management, UMIST having previously been at the Management Centre, Aston University. He has published widely in sociology, political science and accounting journals. Together with David Knights, he has organised the UMIST/ASTON Labour Process Conferences and edited a series of volumes in this area including *Job Redesign* (1985), *Managing the Labour Process* (1986), *New Technology and the Labour Process* and *Labour Process Theory*. He is currently engaged in research into management control within the life-insurance industry and in an international study of the regulation of accounting.

Young, S. Mark Associate Professor of Accounting and Peat Marwick Faculty Fellow at the University of Colorado in Boulder. He received a PhD from the University of Pittsburgh. His current research interests are in the area of the impact of new manufacturing technology on control systems. His recent work has been published in *Accounting, Organizations and Society*, *Journal of Accounting Research*, and *Journal of Marketing Research*.

Acknowledgements

This book is a product of the First Interdisciplinary Perspectives on Accounting Conference held at the University of Manchester in July 1985. The editors would like to acknowledge the financial assistance given to the conference by the Economic and Social Research Council.

Every paper submitted was subjected to referees' comments and, if presented at the conference, written discussant's comments. Unfortunately, space precluded inclusion of the latter. Nevertheless, our thanks go to the necessarily anonymous referees and the discussants for their major contributions to developing the contents of this book. The discussants were Simon Archer, Peter Armstrong, Derek Bailey, Phil Bougen, Roger Bryant, Rob Bryer, Dave Collinson, Andrew Coulson, Laurence Harris, Tony Hope, Keith Hoskin, David Knights, Richard Laughlin, Anne Loft, Tony Lowe, Richard Macve, Jim McGoldrick, Brendan McSweeney, Gareth Morgan, Gavin Murray, Marilyn Neimark, Stuart Ogden, David Owen, Bob Perks, Mike Power, Tony Puxty, John Roberts, Mike Sherer, John Storey, Grahame Thompson, Tony Tinker, Jim Tomlinson, Stuart Turley, Richard Whitley, Hugh Willmott and Mark Young.

Neither the Conference nor this book would have been possible without the moral and administrative support of the editors' respective departments, the School of Management at UMIST, and the Department of Accounting and Finance at the University of Manchester. The final stages of editing were eased considerably by the administrative support provided by the School of Business at The University of Michigan (Ann Arbor), where Trevor Hopper was a visitor during 1987. The exemplary secretarial services of Mary Hardy require a special debt of gratitude.

1 Stimulating Research in Critical Accounts

David J. Cooper and Trevor M. Hopper

This intoductory essay is concerned to explore the form, diversity and reasons for an interest in critical accounts. It seeks to explain why increasing numbers of social scientists regard the terrain of accounting thought and accounting practice with interest, and why accountants have increasingly turned to a variety of alternative theories to make sense of accounting knowledge and practice, and to reform it. How is accounting implicated in deindustrialisation, deskilling at work, increasing rationalisation and bureaucratisation of society, environmental pollution and conflict in society? What understanding can be derived from theories of the control of work, of professional formation and change, of knowledge and power, and of processes of social structuring? This book explores some of these questions and this introductory essay provides a context for that exploration. The essay is in three independent parts. The first explains the origins of the book. The second part outlines the nature and diversity of the themes in the contributions. The third reflects on the rise of the critical accounting movement.

THE ORIGINS OF THE BOOK

Critical accounting arose both as an expression of attempts by scholars within accounting to apply fresh, typically nonfunctionalist, theoretical insights into the effects of accounting within organisations and society (for example: Burchell et al., 1980; Colville, 1981; Tinker, 1980); and because of an interest by radical social scientists, many of whom were not normally associated with the teaching and research of accounting, in examining a pervasive and increasingly significant set of social and economic practices (for example: Johnson, 1977; Thompson, 1978; Tomkins et al., 1980). Attempts to understand accounting through economic analysis, and more recently, psychology, have been augmented by the insights offered by sociology and

1

political theory. But although these studies and understandings began to permeate the accounting literature, notably through the vision of Anthony Hopwood, the editor of *Accounting, Organizations and Society*, it is clear that much of this work has had a marginal and eccentric status attributed to it by conventional accounting scholars, brought up in the traditions of positivism and economic understandings of accounting.

It seemed appropriate, therefore, to try and develop some coherence and interaction between the individual and diverse scholars who constituted critical accounting knowledge. We were not, and are not, concerned to develop a monolithic alternative to conventional accounting thought. Our interest lies in exploring the 'silences' in that thought and in identifying whether there is an opportunity for a more coherent set of alternative possibilities for accounting knowledge. We identified, with help from colleagues such as Anthony Hopwood and Tony Tinker, the possibility of commissioning and otherwise stimulating research in accounting for labour, alternative forms of accounting calculation, the organisation of accounting practice and the role of professions therein, and the application of interesting new theories of the roles of accounting in organisations and society. These possibilities were realised in a conference and the underlying themes also structure the contents of this book.

The *First Interdisciplinary Perspectives in Accounting* (IPA) *Conference* was held at the University of Manchester in July 1985. It stimulated a considerable response, both in terms of the volume of papers offered and the geographical diversity of their authors. Work was submitted from Japan, North America, Australia, and Continental Europe, as well as from the UK. Contributions came from sociologists, economists, historians, educationalists, and philosophers, as well as accountants and those who would seek not to be classified! The quality of the papers presented is illustrated by the fact that ten of them have been published in *Accounting, Organizations and Society* (Vol. 11, No. 2, 1986 and Vol. 12, No. 5, 1987), and a further eighteen are now published in this volume. Selection of the papers for inclusion was not easy. Our criteria for this volume was clarity and originality of argument and relevance to accounting thought and practice. We are extremely grateful for the colleagues and friends who helped review the papers, both for the conference and this book. Indeed, we regret that pressure of space forced us to forego publication of these reviews; many of them identified strengths, weaknesses, and points of departure for future work.

This book is neither an exposition nor a definitive statement of current knowledge within critical accounting. Rather, it offers a series of loosely connected articulations of critical accounts. It is critical of conventional accounting theory and practice and, through critical social science theory, it seeks to explain how the current state of affairs in accounting came about. From such a perspective it seeks to explore how accounting statements might be reconstituted to assess critical aspects of organisational and social performance. We hope that the book will be ultimately judged by the extent to which it stimulates others to develop and pursue ideas sketched in the contributions.

THE CONTRIBUTIONS: DIVERSITY AND THEMES

Editors tend to present collections of papers as if there were a unifying theme that provides overall coherence. Coherence may be desirable, but frequently the state of knowledge reflects incoherence and diversity. The contributions in this book and the other conference papers published in *Accounting, Organizations and Society* were chosen because they display both diversity and coherence. This tension is marked in the papers in Part One of this book on 'Major Issues in Theory and Policy', for example, with regard to their assessment of the potential roles for economic measurement within society. As Laughlin and Lowe indicate in Chapter 2, the papers in Part One, along with other critical accounting papers, display coherence in terms of their contrast to conventional accounting research, but diversity in the sources of that contrast. The chapter by Laughlin and Lowe outlines some of the major theoretical strands underlying critical theories currently being applied to accounting and it explains why these ideas are of relevance. The intellectual sources are various, as is liberally illustrated throughout this book and IPA Conference papers published elsewhere. Gramsci's ideas of power and hegemony are applied to accounting by Booth and Cocks in Chapter 19, and Lehman and Tinker (1987). The deconstructionism of Derrida and Adorno is used by Tinker and Neimark in Chapter 3 to critique analytical approaches to accounting thought. The interpretative and incremental organisation theories of March and Olsen, and Lindblom respectively, are applied by McSweeney and Sherer in Chapter 15 to critique conventional uses of accounting in improving organisational performance.

Despite these diversities, four related, if not entirely compatible, sets of work appear to predominate within the contributions. Work stimulated by Foucault, especially his arguments concerning the relationship between power and knowledge, his concern with forms of calculation and knowledge, and the effects of knowledge on discipline and domination, are utilised by Roberts and Scapens (Chapter 6), Murray (Chapter 9) and Cooper and Robson (Chapter 18). In addition, four other papers, (Loft, 1986; Hoskin and Macve, 1986; Whitley, 1986; and Thompson, 1987) presented at the IPA Conference directly explore these themes. Second, there is the Critical Theory of the Frankfurt School, with its emphasis upon language, communication, enlightenment, and emancipation. These ideas of communication, and the oppressing and potentially liberating roles of accounting, are explored by Macintosh in Chapter 8, and Laughlin (1987). Third, there is the 'post Braverman' labour-process theory illustrated in part by Young and Davis in Chapter 5, Knights and Collinson (1987), Armstrong (1987) and Hopper et al. (1987). Exploration of the role of management and accounting in the labour process offers to invigorate that important strand of social science theory. The papers in Part Two of this book, on Accounting and the Control of Labour, are representative contributions in this respect. Lastly, in the desire to reassess the failures and achievements of specific forms of socialism, the contributions of Bailey (Chapter 10) and, more explicitly, Tomlinson (Chapter 4), address the issue of the forms and measurement of accountability in society. This theme, namely the development of alternative forms of accounting calculation, forms the basis of Part Three of this book.

Whilst the sources may be diverse, certain themes run throughout. They include the rejection of the scientist as a neutral detached observer. Values and beliefs are seen as inextricable from the research process. For many of the contributors research is seen as social critique. In place of objectivism and determinism, there is an emphasis upon ideology, language, and the role of human agency. And above all, there is a desire to understand accounting holistically, in relation to social structures of power and domination. The belief in scientism, that accounting knowledge as a whole can be constructed by the sum of many small, objective micro-studies of a given reality, is rejected.

This rejection has brought distinct and fresh perspectives to accounting research, moving accounting scholars beyond conventional boundaries of their subject. Whilst there are undoubted dangers of theoretical eclecticism, a benefit has been a greater willingness of non-accountants to be involved in accounting research. This is demonstrated by the variety of source disciplines represented by authors in this volume.

The emphasis upon holistic social critique, and the attendant desire to recognise and illustrate accounting's involvement in prevailing structures of power and domination, has led to a questioning of the taken-for-granted in accounting thought and practice. There has also been a de-emphasis of the study of the technical and procedural, which has tended to dominate conventional accounting research. Whilst there is always a danger in moving away from the study of detailed accounting practices and embracing an abstract and disembodied conception of the subject and the practitioners of the craft, there is an important place for general analyses of the accounting profession's position within society.

A concern to understand and to analyse the accounting profession is evident in Part Four on 'The Accounting Profession and Power', and in several other chapters within this book. Willmott scrutinises the profession's claims for self-regulation and their definition of the public interest in Chapter 16. Puxty (Chapter 17) and Cooper and Robson (Chapter 18) scrutinise the functions of the accountancy profession, by exploring the sociological literature on professions and examining accountancy's position with regard to social classes and the state. An examination of the relationship between accounting, class and the state is also to be found in the study of social accounting by Jones in Chapter 14.

Young and Davis, and Roberts and Scapens, in Chapters 5 and 6 respectively, question whether the 'paper empires' of accounting controls are compatible with a humanistic conception of society. The desire to reconstitute accounting from a societal analysis downwards is not just a feature of the sociologically inclined contributions. Those contributions informed by economic theory, especially those in Part Three on accounting calculation, all emphasise the importance of a macro-approach initially. In the first two chapters in this Part, by Bailey and Gubbay, enterprise accounting is seen as a subset of (reconstituted) national accounts which provides a basis for formulating accounts designed to serve a wider conception of society instead of merely the business community. In a similar spirit, Freedman and Stagliano in Chapter 13 argue that to prevent environmental pollution and industrial hazards we need transnational schemes of social accounting.

Many of the chapters in this book display a scepticism towards accounting knowledge, as currently espoused and practised. There is a tendency to see accounting as a particular ideology and, through the language it utilises, as a mechanism for creating a socially undesirable prioritisation of criteria whilst simultaneously deflecting attention from alternative ones. This may be altogether too crude a conception, seeing accounting as a mythical monster, created by a society which it now entraps. As several chapters suggest, it is important to look at the antecedents and consequences of particular accountings, as well as exploring the assumed totality of a monolithic activity and knowledge. Accounting knowledge may not be all-pervasive and dominating, but instead be particular and partisan, but contestable. For example, Bougen and Ogden (Chapter 7), and Puxty (Chapter 17) note, as do others, the malleability of key accounting concepts over time, noting their ability to be transformed, or to disappear and reappear, in response to attempts to control broader social conflicts. Whilst one group may consistently use accounting's malleable property for its own ends, resistance may lead to unanticipated effects.

The claims of accountancy training (Booth and Cocks in Chapter 19), accounting textbooks (Bougen and Ogden in Chapter 7; Hopper et al., 1987), and leading accounting journals (Lehman and Tinker, 1987), to either constitute academic knowledge or modes of enquiry are similarly critically reviewed. These authors do not focus on the mechanisms which created these claims, rather they argue that such claims to knowledge and enquiry have the effect of producing, sustaining, and legitimising certain values and beliefs, not least when training and socialising accountants and managers. The consequences are significant. For example, Jones (Chapter 14) notes the lack of knowledge and/or interest in social accounting by practising accountants, who instead saw business interests as paramount. Such conclusions lead to a questioning of whether the accounting profession is the rightful reservoir of accounting knowledge and whether accounting knowledge, under the control of its practising arm, is able, from the perspective of society rather than the sectional interest of capital, to create and support reform at a social level. This, in turn, leads back to the examination of the accountancy profession's relationship to the public interest (Willmott,Chapter 16) and its specific class interests (Puxty, Chapter 17; Cooper and Robson, Chapter 18).

The desire to raise such questions may explain the strong historical element within many of the papers, for example, Loft, 1986; Hoskin and Macve, 1986; Bougen and Ogden, Chapter 7; Puxty, Chapter 17; Armstrong, 1987. If accounting is to be reconstituted, then it would appear that a reconstruction and reinterpretation of its antecedents is essential. Again, the historical contributions are distinct in that they seek to build upon the traditionally technical and procedural work of accounting historians, by applying the broader theoretical approaches outlined earlier. By so doing, they enable us to step outside of the assumptions that accounting is inevitable, neutral, disinterested, and always desirable. They permit us to see accounting as a feature of a particular form of society, waxing and waning in response to crises and contradictions, moulded not only by dominant powers but also by processes of resistance and accommodation.

For the editors the insights into accounting theory and practice offered by the contributions in this book are exciting and stimulating. But they demand of the reader a degree of theoretical eclecticism and a willingness to think through the implications of the analyses offered. Moreover, they display the theoretical and practical tensions and weaknesses within any developing tradition. We believe that an important quality of these interdisciplinary perspectives on accounting is their capacity, singly or in combination, to be self-critical and reflexive.

Theoretically, the problem of reconciling human agency and the subjective processes of knowledge creation within the existence of broader social structures is addressed in different ways by Murray, Roberts and Scapens, and Tinker and Neimark in Chapters 9, 6, and 3 respectively. The latter implicitly attack the eclecticism hinted at by Laughlin and Lowe in Chapter 2 who, by outlining a variety of approaches for researchers, implicitly argue for a pluralistic approach to methodology – though their own preferences are made clear. Tomlinson in Chapter 4, whilst focusing his critique upon political economy approaches to accounting, which he believes adopt a functionalist approach to their purposes, also seems to question the humanistic concerns about accounting measurement as expressed by Roberts and Scapens elsewhere in Chapter 6.

Meanwhile, radical and critical accountants, fighting deindustrialisation, plant closures, privatisation and unemployment, and seeking to articulate and justify alternatives, conduct short-run firefighting exercises, utilising and discrediting conventional accounting measures as and when it suits their tactics. The issues, techniques and methods examined in the economic measurement section of the book (Part Three, Chapters 10–15) are the source of such practical politics. But these immediate concerns are currently weakly linked to the more discursive and theoretical ones expressed elsewhere in this collection. Prescriptions remain unclear. Further investigation of possible forms of accounting and accountability and what role, if any, alternative and critical accounts might have in the types of societies sought by critical theorists are undoubtedly required. Whilst the insights of broad critique and analysis are essential in unlocking assumptions, providing understanding, and showing how accounting problems are inextricably linked to social and political issues, the need for medium-term and short-run accounting techniques for facilitating social change cannot be ignored. These then are some of the internal critiques of the book.

THE RISE OF CRITICAL ACCOUNTS?

Why such work should develop in the late 1970s and 1980s is difficult to answer, particularly by those involved in its propagation and development. No doubt part of the explanation concerns the 'internal' logic of theorising and academic activity. Critical theories may be seen to arise out of the problems of conventional theories and critical academic activity in the 1970s and 1980s in the social sciences, which now includes the growing but relatively youthful areas of management and accounting. Of course, other explanations may focus on individual personalities or institutional changes that facilitate and encourage such work. Whilst not ignoring these possibilities, we wish to focus on the 'external' forces which helped to give rise to an interest in critical accounts. Whether changes to these external forces will, in their turn, lead to the demise of the 'movement' remains to be seen.

The work in critical accounting may be a reaction to the politics of our time, especially the re-emergence of the so-called intellectual right, represented, for example, by the espousal of monetarism, individualism, self-regulation, the idolatry of markets, and a general distaste displayed towards public enterprise and collective action. The application of such notions in government, not just by espoused conservative ones, has produced in its wake a series of social problems in which accounting is implicated. Some of these problems are identified and illustrated in this book. For example, McSweeney and Sherer in Chapter 15 examine how the accounting profession has responded to and has been involved in the popularisation of specific conceptions of Value-for-Money audits in local government. The audits profess to evaluate the efficiency and effectiveness of specific services. However, the chapter notes the theoretical and technical deficiencies in such accounting, especially its inability to either define or measure effectiveness satisfactorily. The authors observe that the adoption of a simplistic and unitary conception of local government by such studies impinges upon the political processes of local authorities, elevates markets as neutral indicators of the value of social activity,and delimits alternative actions and criteria. Freedman and Stagliano (Chapter 13) examine how accounting neglects ecological issues and they trace the personal and environmental damage which this creates. Jones (Chapter 14) discusses the lack of concern by UK accountants in the social responsibility of enterprises. All three chapters illustrate the shortcomings of accounting measures and disclosures which rely exclusively on market models.

Roberts and Scapens, and Young and Davis, in Chapters 6 and 5, discuss the depersonalisation and alienation associated with accounting measurement and control systems. They argue that rather than serving humanity, contemporary accounting technology may be stunting its potential. Similarly, Macintosh in Chapter 8 is concerned with the ability of vested interests to rationalise and reinforce the status quo through the medium of published accounts; he illustrates this by scrutinising how accounting reports reproduce sexual stereotypes of women and their subordination to men in society. Jefferis and Thomas in Chapter 12 address how best to make an economic evaluation of co-operatives. Their concern stems from the desire for job creation and more egalitarian work experiences in a time of growing unemployment and repressive management methods. Other IPA Conference papers examined accounting's relationship to de-industrialisation (Williams et al., 1986; Bryer and Brignall, 1986) and its use by local authorities for evaluating plant closure decisions from a community perspective rather than that of the profit-maximising firm (Harte and Owen, 1987). All these contributions identify both accounting's repressive and emancipatory potential.

Recognising these potentials has led some researchers to question the role of the accounting profession in society. This questioning is also part of a political project to understand the effects of changing regimes of social regulation and the claims to knowledge used by accountants. In Chapter 17, Puxty is concerned to identify the consequences of the accounting profession's concern with information for decision-making and its links to class interests. In Chapters 18 and 16, Cooper and Robson, and Willmott undermine the self-conception of accountants as a professional body deserving of special privileges in society and both critically explore the roles accountants play within UK society. Their concerns are similar to those which informed Armstrong's contribution to the IPA Conference (1987).

The above does not exhaust the political issues inspiring the growing wave of critical accounting represented within this book. However, it is illustrative of the broader social concerns of its advocates, who not only critique accounting's role within society, but seek to materially alter accounting's mission and the content of accounting reports, in order to help reform or transform society. Integral to these concerns is a desire to open up alternatives to the status quo, both within capitalist and socialist societies.

For many of the contributors to this book the resolution of such practical problems is closely linked to a desire to utilise fresh theoretical approaches in social science research generally, and within accounting specifically. However, there may not be any necessary connection between the practical reformers and those concerned to revitalise our understanding of accounting through the application of ideas from the social sciences. Some of the reformers may utilise quite conventional theories whilst some of those using stimulating new interdisciplinary ideas may not have overtly political and practical concerns.

There is always the risk that the theoretical contributions are all one way, that accounting theory utilises, but does not add to social science theories. However, we believe that the new accounting has the potential to feedback into, and thereby enrich, its source disciplines and methodologies, rather than just being derivative of them. This book hopes to contribute to a critical mass that offers social science the study of particular practices which have social significance. In this way, we trust that critical accounting research will develop a maturity which may lead to a better set of accounts, a more coherent account of the activities and effects of accountants and accountancy practice, and a more enriched understanding of social and economic life more generally.

Bibliography

Armstrong, P., 'The Rise of Accounting Controls in British Capitalist Enterprises', *Accounting, Organizations and Society* (1987) pp. 415–36.

Bryer, R. A. and Brignall, T. J., 'Divestment and Inflation Accounting: An Unemployment Machine?' *Capital and Class* (1986) pp. 125–55.

Burchell, S., Clubb, C., Hopwood, A., Hughes, J. and Nahapiet, J., 'The Roles of Accounting in Organizations and Society', *Accounting, Organizations and Society* (1980) pp. 5–27.

Colville, I., 'Reconstructing "Behavioural Accounting"', *Accounting, Organizations and Society* (1981) pp. 119–32.

Harte, G. F., and Owen, D. L., 'Fighting De-industrialisation: The Role of Local Government Social Audits', *Accounting, Organizations and Society* (1987) pp. 123–42.

Hopper, T. M., Storey, J., and Willmott, H., 'Accounting for Accounting: Towards the Development of a Dialectical View', *Accounting, Organizations and Society* (1987) pp. 437–56.

Hoskin, K. W., and Macve, R. H., 'Accounting and Examination: A Genealogy of Disciplinary Power', *Accounting, Organizations and Society* (1986) pp. 105–36.

Johnson, T. J., 'The Professions in the Class Structure', in R. Scase (ed.), *Industrial Society: Class, Cleavage and Control*, (London: St. Martins Press, 1977) pp. 93–110.

Knights, D., and Collinson, D., 'Disciplining the Shopfloor: A Comparison of the Disciplinary Effects of Managerial Psychology and Financial Accounting', *Accounting, Organizations and Society* (1987) pp. 457–78.

Laughlin, R. C., 'Accounting Systems in Organizational Contexts: A Case for Critical Theory', *Accounting, Organizations and Society* (1987) pp. 479–502.

Lehman, C., and Tinker, A. M., 'The "Real" Cultural Significance of Accounts', *Accounting, Organizations and Society* (1987) vol. 12, No. 6.

Loft, A., 'Towards a Critical Understanding of Accounting in the U.K., 1914–1925', *Accounting, Organizations and Society* (1986) pp. 137–70.

Tinker, A. M., 'Towards a Political Economy of Accounting: An Empirical Illustration of the Cambridge Controversies', *Accounting, Organizations and Society* (1980) pp. 147–66.

Thompson, G. F., 'Capitalist Profit Calculation and Inflation Accounting', *Economy and Society* (1978) pp. 395–429.

Thompson, G. F., 'Inflation Accounting in a Theory of Calculation', *Accounting, Organizations and Society* (1987) pp. 523–43.

Tomkins, C., Rosenberg, D., and Colville, I., 'The Social Process of Research: Some Reflections on Developing a Multi-disciplinary Accounting Project', *Accounting, Organizations and Society* (1980) pp. 247–62.

Whitley, R., 'The Transformation of Business Finance into Financial Economics: The Roles of Academic Expansion and Changes in U.S. Capital Markets', *Accounting, Organizations and Society* (1986) pp. 171–92.

Williams, K., Haslam, C., Wardlow, A., and Williams, J., 'Accounting for Failure in the Nationalised Industries: Coal, Steel and Cars since 1970', *Economy and Society* (1986) pp. 167–219.

Part I
Major Issues in Theory and Policy

2 A Critical Analysis of Accounting Thought: Prognosis and Prospects for Understanding and Changing Accounting Systems Design

Richard C. Laughlin and E. Anthony Lowe[1]

This paper is concerned with developing our understanding about the design of accounting systems in organisations. It is based on the assumption and concern, shared by others (cf. Hopwood, 1978, 1979, 1983; Burchell et al., 1980; Scapens, 1984; Otley, 1984), about:

> how little we know about the actual functioning of accounting systems in organisations.
>
> (Hopwood 1979, p. 145)

Admittedly a number of recent studies have attempted to analyse some of the complex social factors which are deemed to be part of these designs (cf. Berry et al., 1985; Colville, 1982; Tomkins, 1982; Roberts and Scapens, 1985; Laughlin, 1984, 1986). However, despite these developments, much of accounting theory and theoreticians treat these efforts as largely marginal in the search to understand accounting practice. This paper is addressed to exploring the reasons for this situation as well as arguing a case for significant changes in the research perspective we adopt in looking at accounting systems design.

For the purposes of this paper it is important to define an accounting system as:

> A formal system with structural and behavioural characteristics

whose terms are expressed in fundamentally financial form, whose meaning is derived from the organisation of which it is an integral part.

This definition has four important characteristics. Firstly, that the accounting system is both organisationally based and, to the extent that all organisations are part of society, societally based, and its meaning is embedded in this context. Secondly, that the term 'organisation' refers to both micro- and macro-organisations, including society itself. Thirdly, that the accounting system needs to be considered through specified ontological, epistemological and methodological perspectives. Fourthly, that this definition of an accounting system refers to information transactions both internal and external to that organisation (that is, its 'behavioural and structural characteristics' (cf. Klir, 1969)). Thus both financial and management accounts constitute integral elements of an accounting system.

These underlying characteristics and assumptions provide the important bases for analysing the nature of current accounting thought, as others have already suggested (cf. Chua et al., 1981; Cooper, 1983; Hopper and Powell, 1985; Chua, 1986). Here we adopt a similar basis for analysing current accounting thought. However, the reason for using this common approach is not simply to create another classification but rather to critically analyse the underlying basis of accounting thought.

Our thesis is that the two dominant wings of accounting (management and financial accounting) have been addressed to the theory of the design of accounting systems, but that they have, in the main, been working (and usually implicitly) under inappropriate theories of organisations and society with inappropriate ontological, epistemological and methodological assumptions. This has resulted in very partial analyses concerning the functioning of accounting systems in organisations. The small minority of researchers who have actually tried to make amends for this theoretical ignorance have largely been unanimous in their rejection of the dominant set of assumptions under which much of accounting thought is based. This paper is intended to not only clarify these assumption sets but also to pose more clearly the alternatives available. We also make a case for a particular alternative set of assumptions for enabling us to understand accounting in practice.

The paper has three major sections and a conclusion. The first presents a classification of financial and management accounting as the two dominant wings of accounting primarily concerned with accounting practice. The second explores the organisational, societal, ontological, epistemological and methodological assumptions which underly the classified accounting thought discussed in the first section. The third section critically analyses the relevance of the dominant assumptions under which current accounting thought is situated in terms of its restrictive nature for understanding as well as changing the design of accounting systems in practice. Also a more meaningful basis is posed.

A SURVEY OF FINANCIAL AND MANAGEMENT ACCOUNTING THOUGHT

A Survey of Financial Accounting

There have been some attempts to classify and codify financial accounting (cf. American Accounting Association, 1977; Laughlin and Puxty, 1981) but one of the most interesting recent approaches has been by Davis, Menon and Morgan (1982). Davis et al. see the whole of financial accounting as consisting of four distinct 'images':

> They are those which treat accounting as a historical record, as a descriptor of current economic reality, as an information system, and as a commodity.
>
> (p. 309)

These four images can be seen to contain a number of subschools which together provide a summary of the major strands of thought in financial accounting. Table 2.1 presents this analysis and in the following paragraphs we briefly discuss the contents of each strand.

The 'historical record' image of financial accounting contains the more traditional understanding of external reporting practices as a historical picture along with a more recent development adopting similar thinking. This perspective views accounting as a recorder of organisation history in financial terms and has led some to attempt to codify and synthesise these practices (cf. Sanders et al., 1938; Paton and Littleton, 1940; Littleton, 1953; Grady, 1965). Although this image persists in professional policy making, in recent decades it has been attacked by those who argue for a closer alignment of accounting with economics which has led to the second image. However, the

TABLE 2.1   *Schools and Sub-schools in Financial Accounting*

Schools	Historical Record	Current Economic Reality	Information System	Economic Commodity
Sub-schools	Historic Cost Accounting Events Accounting	Income and Wealth Measurement Inflation Accounting	Information for Decision Models Behavioural Accounting Research Security Price Research Human Information Processing Information Inductance	Information Economics Agency Theory Approaches Social Welfare Considerations

work of Sorter (1969) and Johnson (1970), on events accounting, can be seen to be both a counter-attack and a further development of this original approach allowing a broader-based set of measures (of events) to form the content of information statements for external users.

The 'current economic reality' image has a primary concern for measuring income and wealth. Its initiators included economists and lawyers (cf. Canning, 1929; Sweeney, 1936; Bonbright, 1937; Alexander, 1950; Edwards and Bell, 1961) but also accountants who have led its further development (cf. Mattessich, 1964; Chambers, 1966; Sterling, 1970). There is now a large accounting literature on the alternative bases for the measurement of income and wealth more generally and a particular sub-school in accounting for changing prices.

The 'information system' image takes as its criterion decision needs or wants, and consists of a number of distinct subschools of thought: those who maintain that decision 'needs' are the key criterion for accounting choice; and those who see the decision-makers' 'wants' of greater significance (cf. Sterling, 1970). The latter sub-school has further subdivided into, firstly, those who have researched into aggregate market behaviour (primarily on the assumption of efficient markets) and, secondly, those who have investigated individual or small group behaviour (cf. Hofstedt, 1976). Furthermore, this second subdivision of researchers have pursued two approaches: a 'human information processing' approach (cf. Snowball, 1980) and an 'information inductance' approach (cf. Prakash and Rappaport, 1977) which investigates the processes involved in the sending of information.

The 'commodity' image sees financial accounting information as an economic commodity and attempts a supply and demand analysis in the context of welfare implications. The primary work in this area has been in terms of evaluating financial accounting from an information economics perspective (cf. Demski, 1972; Feltham, 1972; Demski and Feltham, 1976). Other theorists have extended this approach using agency theory concepts (cf. Watts and Zimmerman, 1978; Zmijewski and Hagerman, 1981; Leftwich, 1981; see Puxty, 1985 for a critical survey of this work). Similarly a growing number of accounting, finance and economic theorists have been involved with the welfare implications of financial accounting. This concern has led to the analysis of the regulatory process and the welfare implications of these activities (cf. Kelly-Newton, 1980; Laughlin and Puxty, 1983).

The above is not intended to be a comprehensive survey of financial accounting, but helps to indicate the main strands of thought as well as indicating how all of this work has been concerned with different theories about the design of organisational accounting systems.

A Survey of Management Accounting

Management accounting, following Bhaskar (1981) and Scapens (1984), has been labelled as 'quantitative' and 'behavioural'. This distinction is surely arbitrary but does offer a basis for a classification of theories about management accounting which can be used to trace the various developments and subschools of thought.

Table 2.2 presents in diagrammatic form the various sub-schools of thought over time. This Table is intended to clarify how certain ways of thinking about management accounting have persisted over time while other theories have developed. The overall impression is now one of an expanding set of schools of thought in management accounting more generally.

The 'quantitative' strand of management accounting has developed

TABLE 2.2   *Management Accounting Images and Developments*

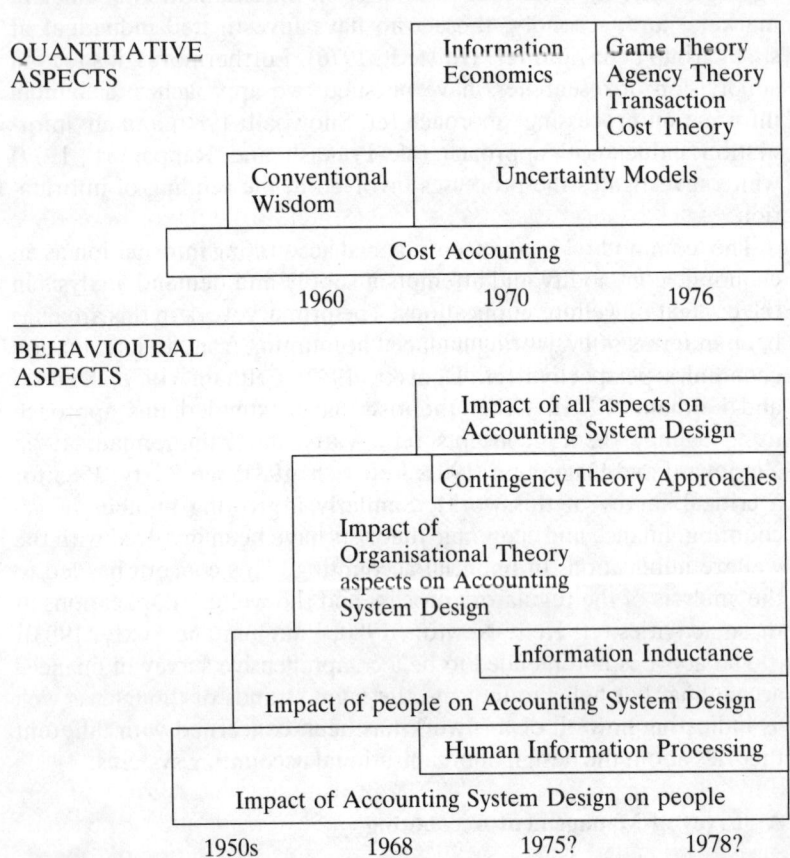

QUANTITATIVE ASPECTS		Information Economics	Game Theory Agency Theory Transaction Cost Theory
	Conventional Wisdom	Uncertainty Models	
	Cost Accounting		
	1960	1970	1976

BEHAVIOURAL ASPECTS

		Impact of all aspects on Accounting System Design	
		Contingency Theory Approaches	
	Impact of Organisational Theory aspects on Accounting System Design		
		Information Inductance	
	Impact of people on Accounting System Design		
		Human Information Processing	
	Impact of Accounting System Design on people		
1950s	1968	1975?	1978?

directly from cost accounting practice using a neo-classical economic theory of the firm. Before and during the Second World War the primary concern in this area of management accounting was with developing quantitative systems for the control of factory costs. These concerns remain but since around 1946 a stronger user-orientation in management accounting became more prevalent. This development in the quantitative area led to the need to expand the cost accounting function into what Scapens (1984) calls the 'conventional wisdom' which is so much a part of current textbook material. The concept of uncertainty was introduced into conventional models in the late sixties (cf. Jaedicke and Robichek, 1964; Jensen, 1968). These developments of the 'conventional wisdom' were further enhanced by the use of information economics (cf. Demski and Feltham, 1976) and some time later, 'game theory' (cf. Baiman, 1975 and 1979; Sundem, 1979), 'agency theory' and 'transaction cost theory'. An important consequence of these economic theory based developments in management accounting was to bring the design of accounting systems issues much more to the fore.

The 'behavioural aspects' of management accounting have their roots in the need to understand the relationship between management accounting systems and their human designers. Although this relationship has long been a concern of accounting thinkers, it became focused in management accounting with the work of Argyris (1952) and Stedry (1960) whose primary concern was with the impact of management accounting system design on individuals. More recently, human information processing explores these same concerns in a more analytical fashion. However, in the late 1960s, a new concern was emerging with respect to the impact of people on management accounting system design rather than the relationship of design to people (cf. Lowe and Shaw, 1968; Schiff and Lewin, 1970). More recently information inductance research has developed further the importance of both individuals and the organisational context (or individuals in the aggregate) to a more complete and sophisticated theory of management accounting system design. Contingency theory has been one such notable development (cf. Otley, 1980). A newer school of thought (cf. Hopwood, 1978, 1979, 1983; Burchell et al., 1980; Colville, 1981; Tomkins and Groves, 1983) regards (management) accounting systems as organisational phenomena whose nature cannot be determined solely in terms of current developments in organisation theory but rather is traceable to (un)certain social and historical phenomena.

Enough perhaps has been said to cover the main strands of thought. It is important to appreciate that all of these developments have been concerned, in differing ways, and under different assumptions, with the design of part of the accounting systems in organisations.

SOCIAL SCIENCE AND THE SOCIETAL AND ORGANISATIONAL ASSUMPTIONS UNDERLYING ACCOUNTING THOUGHT

Accounting theories, as with all theories, are not created in a vacuum. They depend on key underlying assumptions which mould and determine their nature. This section starts with an approach to exposing these assumptions using the framework suggested by Burrell and Morgan (1979), the heuristic merit of which has already been demonstrated in surveys of primarily management accounting (cf. Chua et al., 1981; Cooper, 1983; Hopper and Powell, 1985).

A Classification of Underlying Assumptions

Burrell and Morgan (1979) maintained that all social theory is '. . based on different sets of metatheoretical assumptions about the nature of social science and the nature of society' (p.x). These two variables (the nature of social science and the nature of society) can be seen as continuums with a range of bipolar characteristics at either extreme.

The nature of the social science continuum, according to Burrell and Morgan, is actually a scale containing four key variables about ontology, epistemology, human nature and methodology. Burrell and Morgan typecast these variables in terms of an overall 'subjective' and 'objective' label the details of which are contained in Figure 2.1.

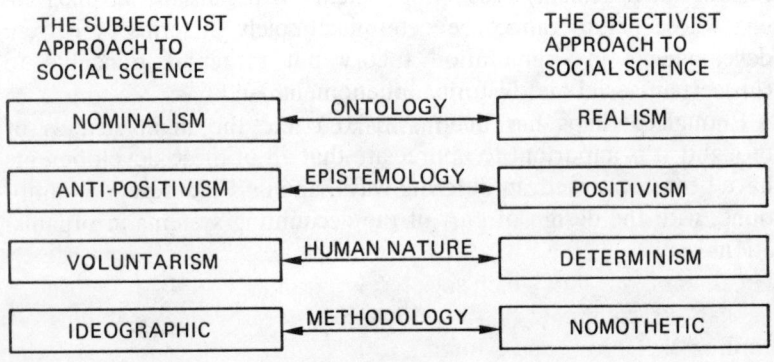

FIGURE 2.1 *Assumptions about the nature of social science from Burrell and Morgan (1979)*

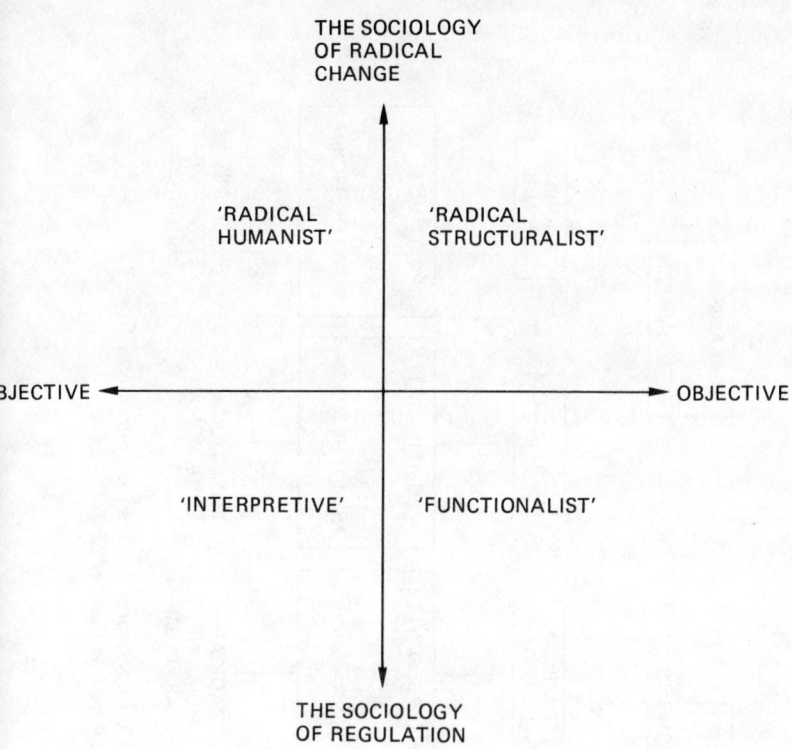

FIGURE 2.2 *The four paradigms of social theory from Burrell and Morgan (1979)*

In a similar manner the 'nature of society' assumption needs to be seen in terms of a continuum ranging from what Burrell and Morgan call a 'sociology of regulation' to a 'sociology of radical change'. The former assumes a certain unity, cohesiveness and basic 'goodness' in society which needs to be maintained and, possibly, marginally changed. The latter assumes that present societal configurations are far from optimal and are destroying rather than aiding human development and are thus in need of change.

These two variables together form a two by two matrix of underlying assumptions into which social theory can be classified. Figure 2.2 depicts the combined continuums and the resulting paradigms according to Burrell and Morgan with Figure 2.3 providing a fuller understanding of the nature of the paradigms in the light of the multiple nature of the social science continuum.

24

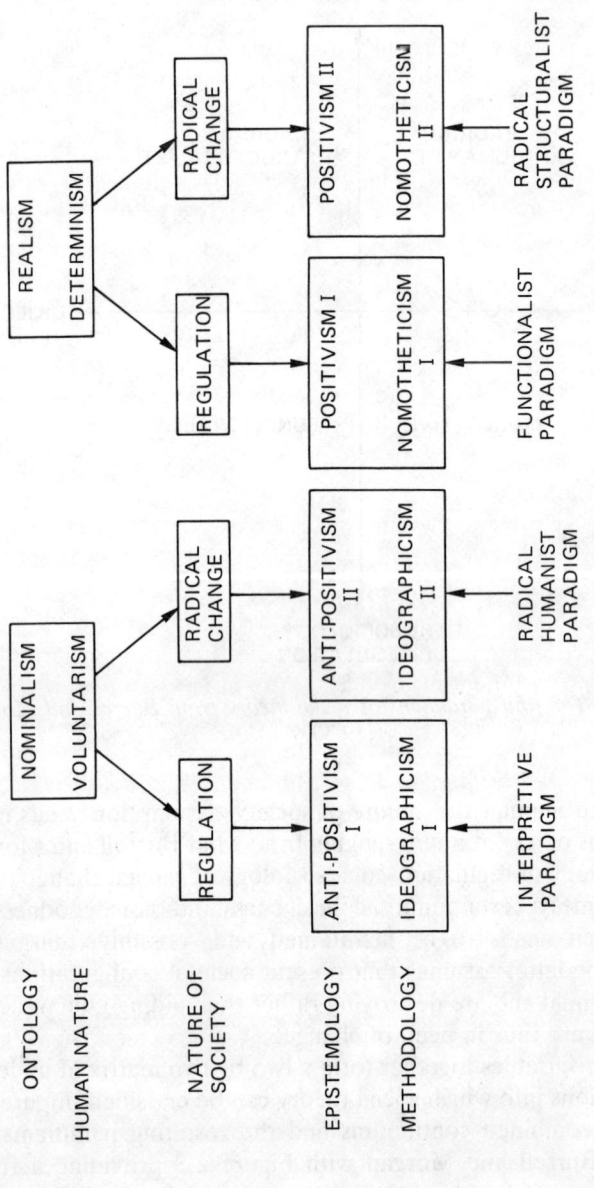

FIGURE 2.3 *Some insights into the nature of the four paradigms from Burrell and Morgan (1979)*

Organisation Theory in the Context of Burrell and Morgan's Framework

Burrell and Morgan amplify their framework by analysing the nature and content of organisation theory and their overall conclusion is that:

> most organisation theorists, industrial sociologists and industrial relations theorists approach their subject from within the bounds of the functionalist paradigm.

> (p. 28)

If this insight is true then it seems likely that not only organisation theory but also accounting theory will be working within the functionalist paradigm. We will try to demonstrate this general conclusion by introducing the summary of organisation theory put forward by Scott (1981) and showing how extant accounting thought falls into the classification he cites.

Scott (1981) provides a summary of the major developments in organisation theory over time analysing these developments in the context of certain underlying assumptions. He classified organisation theory in terms of two continuums as depicted in Figure 2.4. The open/closed continuum is rather a crude discriminator concerning the permitted and assumed uncertainty in the phenomena being investigated. The rational/natural continuum, on the other hand, is to do with certain predetermined views about the nature of organisational action. Different combinations of these continuums provide, for Scott, the key underlying assumptions behind the well-recognised schools of organisation thought as contained in Figure 2.4.

It can be argued that Scott has not fully appreciated the nature of the assumptions which underlies various theories of organisations. However, it is possible to set Scott's analysis in the context of Burrell and Morgan's more probing framework and Figure 2.5 depicts this relationship.

There are a number of points which need to be made to help clarify the rationale which has led to the contents of Figure 2.5. Firstly, it is important to appreciate again the continuous nature of Burrell and Morgan's framework: if particular approaches are positioned away from the extremes they naturally take on the characteristics of the paradigms to which they are closest. Secondly, concerning Scott's

	CLOSED SYSTEM MODELS	OPEN SYSTEM MODELS
RATIONAL MODELS	1900-1930 SCIENTIFIC AND ADMINISTRATIVE MACHINES (cf. Taylor, 1911; Fayol, 1949)	1960-1970? SYSTEMS AND CYBERNETIC CONCEPT (cf. Burns and Stalker, 1961; Woodward, 1965; Lawrence and Lorsch, 1967; Pugh et al., 1968, 1969)
NATURAL MODELS	1930-1960 HUMAN RELATIONS FORUM (cf. Roethlisberger and Dickson, 1939; Mayo, 1945; McGregor, 1960)	1970- AMBIGUOUS, COMPLEX CONFLICTING PHENOMENA (cf. March and Olsen, 1976; Pfeffer and Salancik, 1978)

FIGURE 2.4   *A historical 'imagery' of organisation theory (adapted from Scott (1981))*

rational and natural continuum: this concern, in Burrell and Morgan's terms, can be seen to be related to the ontological and human nature assumptions: 'rational' is more related to realism and determinism, whereas 'natural' relaxes these constraining assumptions and tends more towards nominalism and voluntarism. Thirdly, concerning Scott's open and closed continuum. This concern, in Burrell and Morgan's terms, can be seen to be related to the epistemological and methodological assumptions: closure relates to positivism and nomotheticism (see Figure 2.3); openness, on the other hand, is more akin to anti-positivism and ideographicism in Figure 2.3. Fourthly, Burrell and Morgan's nature of society assumption is, in fact, ignored by Scott who, like most other organisation theorists, shows little or no concern for this impinging variable in the underlying theories of organisations.

We can now see why the various cells in Scott's matrix are classified as in Figure 2.5. The rational/closed cell with its highly constrained

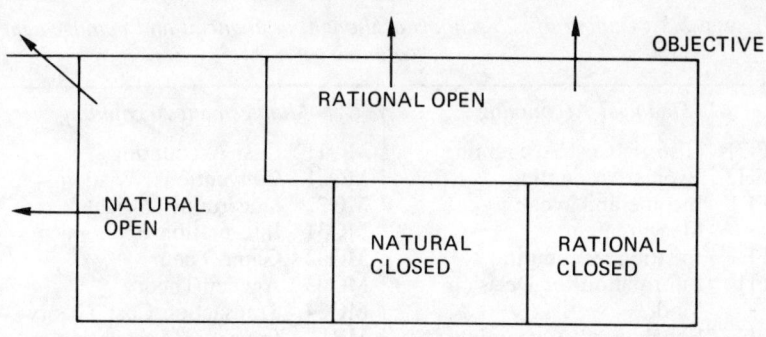

FIGURE 2.5 *Scott's analysis of organisation theory in the context of Burrell and Morgan's framework*

view about organisations seems naturally to feature in the extremes of the functionalist paradigm. In a similar manner the natural/closed cell is appropriately placed beside it, on the grounds that the 'naturalness' becomes highly constrained by the 'closure' assumptions. The rational/open cell seems most appropriately placed in the upper right hand part of the functionalist paradigm with the possibility, but not a current actuality, of moving upwards to the radical structuralist paradigm. In this case the 'rationality' constrains the 'openness' preventing a marked movement towards the subjective end of the Burrell and Morgan framework whilst still containing the latent potential to become critical of the current social order. The natural/open cell, on the other hand, seems to be appropriately positioned towards the left hand side of the functionalist paradigm with the potential for, and growing actuality of, moving sideways to the interpretive paradigm and upwards to the radical humanist paradigm. These paradigms, as we have already seen, give a greater credence to human agency in all its variegated forms and thus fits more closely with what Scott calls 'naturalism' with the 'openness' criteria avoiding any constraint around the meaning of this concept.

In general then, as Burrell and Morgan have already suggested, most of organisation theory is indeed situated in the functionalist paradigm. Yet as the above analysis indicates there are various schools of thought in organisation theory which have the potential, although not necessarily the present intent, except in the natural/open cell, to move away from functionalist thinking.

TABLE 2.3   *Coding of sub-schools of thought in financial and management accounting*

Financial Accounting		Management Accounting	
FH1	Historic Cost Accounting	MQ11	Cost Accounting
FH2	Events Accounting	MQ21	Conventional Wisdom
FE1	Income and Wealth Measurement	MQ22	Uncertainty Models
		MQ31	Information Economics
FE2	Inflation Accounting	MQ32	Game Theory
FI1	Information for Decision Models	MQ33	Agency Theory
		MQ34	Transaction Cost Theory
FI2	Behavioural Accounting Research	MB11	Impact of Accounting System Design on People
FI3	Security Price Research	MB12	Human Information Processing
FI4	Human Information Processing	MB21	Impact of People on Accounting System Design
FI5	Information Inductance	MB22	Information Inductance
FC1	Information Economics	MB31	Impact of Organisational Aspects on Accounting System Design
FC2	Agency Theory Approaches		
FC3	Social Welfare Considerations	MB32	Contingency Theory Approaches
		MB41	Impact of All Aspects on Accounting System Design

Underlying Assumptions Behind Current Theories in Accounting

As we have indicated throughout this paper, particular accounting systems only have meaning in and through the organisational context of which they are part. Thus their practical meaning as well as their theoretical roots are most obviously related to theories about organisations. Equally, as we have indicated above, theories of organisations are, in turn, dependent upon other underlying assumptions. Thus tracing accounting theories, in terms of their organisation theory roots and using the above analytical framework, allows us to identify these other possibly more important underlying assumptions.

Based on this rationale the following traces the schools and sub-schools of financial and management accounting in the context of Scott's survey of organisation theory. The argument is summarised in Table 2.3 and Figure 2.6. Table 2.3 is simply a coded version of the schools and subschools of financial and management accounting summarised in Tables 2.1 and 2.2. Figure 2.6 classifies this coded set

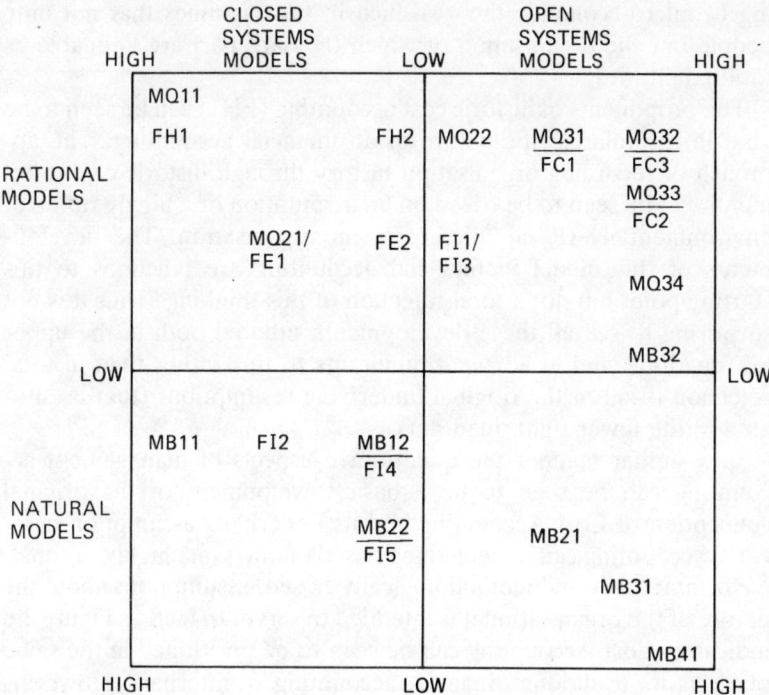

FIGURE 2.6   *Financial and management accounting sub-schools of thought in Scott's (1981) classification scheme*

in terms of the alternative models of organisations as suggested by Scott. In the following we will not go through the positioning of each and every subschool of thought, but rather trace the dominant patterns in each of the three key areas of financial accounting, management accounting (quantitative) and management accounting (behavioural).

The majority of subschools of financial accounting can be seen to be situated in the top two quadrants of Scott's framework due to the heavy reliance on the assumed rationality of the actions of the sending and, to an extent, receiving organisation. In fact only three financial accounting subschools (FI2, FI4 and FI5) can be seen to be situated in the bottom left quadrant which allows some level of user-defined rationality but creates a closure constraint around this in terms of naturalness permitted. These observations are to be ex-pected in some sense due to the close alignment of financial accounting to micro-economic theory which in turn assumes that not only people but the organisation of which they are part are definable as rational entities.

The proponents of historic cost accounting (FII1) can be seen to be vital in formulating the nature of all financial accounting. The approach of recording organisation history through historic cost statements can be seen to be based on an assumption of a highly rational, environmentally closed, picture of an organisation. The developments of this model in financial accounting are reactions to this starting point but not a total rejection of this thinking. Thus it is not surprising to see all these developments situated both in the upper left quadrant and in adjacent quadrants to this rather than in total rejection of all of the original underlying assumptions (that is, situated in the lower right quadrant).

In a similar manner the quantitative aspects of management accounting can be seen to be a basic development of the original conception of Cost Accounting and its underlying assumption base. Cost Accounting can be seen to be based on the same highly rational, environmentally and methodologically closed, assumptions about the nature of the organisation it is intended to serve. In fact, as Figure 2.6 indicates, Cost Accounting can be seen to be positioned in the same place as its traditional financial accounting counterpart. However, unlike the developments in financial accounting which have moved to adjacent quadrants, the new subschools in the quantitative aspects of management accounting have all been situated in the top two quadrants. This constrained movement should not be that surprising due to the heavy reliance on traditional and modern economic theory in this wing of management accounting which, as we have already suggested, sees organisations primarily as nexuses for defined rational action.

The behavioural aspects of management accounting start from a position in the bottom left quadrant and apart from a few deviations have progressively moved into the bottom right quadrant and largely out of the current classification. The early work of Argyris and others (MB11) can be seen to be situated in the top left point of this (bottom left) quadrant due to the very real constraints implicit in their work. Yet those who are increasingly callling for an analysis of accounting systems in terms of tracing the many underlying social roots (MB41) are working under minimal constraint and as such are situated in the bottom right corner of Scott's framework. They are, in effect, moving out of his classification due to their clear intention of going beyond present theories of organisations.

Figure 2.6 in the context of Figure 2.5 suggests, not surprisingly, that financial and management accounting seems to be basically functionalist and will remain so unless those working in the rational/open and natural/open cells in Scott's terms choose to develop their ideas into other Burrell and Morgan paradigms. Already this is happening (cf. Tinker, Merino and Neimark, 1982; Neimark and Tinker, 1986; Colville, 1982; Tomkins, 1982; Roberts and Scapens, 1985; Cooper and Sherer, 1984; Laughlin, 1986, 1987) partly by default and partly by intention. In terms of the problem focus of this study, however, there is still a place for a clearer explanation as to why this move away from functionalism is necessary. There is also a need for a better understanding of the direction in which to go if we are to come to terms with our practical concern. It is to these issues we now turn.

A CRITIQUE OF CURRENT ACCOUNTING THOUGHT AND SOME SUGGESTIONS FOR CHANGE

Figure 2.7 provides both a summary of the argument to date of this paper along with the basis for critically analysing the nature of current insights into the design of accounting systems.

The nature of accounting systems (at the practice plane) are set in a context and are given meaning through various theories (from the theory plane) which, in turn, are derived from certain assumptions (from the meta-theory plane). Operative accounting systems (at the practice level) are part of organisations which, in turn, are part of society. However, as soon as we try to understand and change any of these interconnected phenomena we are building a theory which, in turn, is reliant upon certain defined assumptions. Often these theories are implicit but they are nevertheless in being and mould what we understand to be an accounting system, an organisation or society.

In this section we, firstly, clarify what the assumption base of functionalism informs us is the nature of accounting systems, and secondly, critically analyse this, as well as suggest a more meaningful basis for future theoretical and hence practical advance.

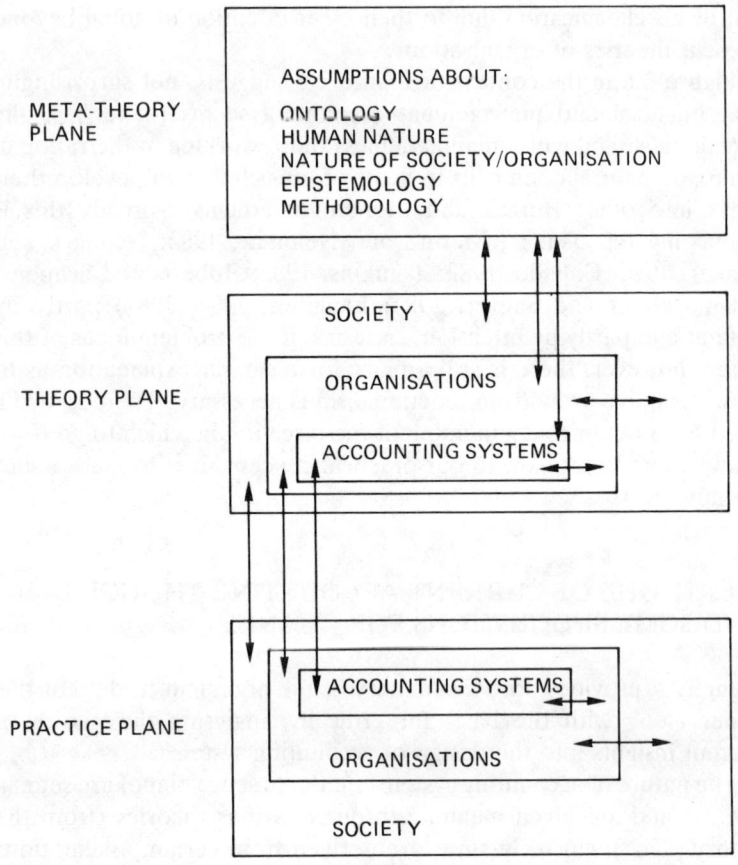

FIGURE 2.7   *The theoretical and practical interlinkages surrounding the design of accounting systems*

The Nature of Accounting Systems Design according to Functionalism

In the first part of this paper we have demonstrated that most accounting thought adopts the underlying thinking implicit in Burrell and Morgan's functionalist paradigm. We have purposely not discriminated between accounting theoreticians or practitioners in this conclusion: it is taken to refer to both groups on the grounds that both are either explicitly or implicitly using theoretical modelling processes in terms of their respective beliefs about the nature of accounting systems.

Our thesis is that both theoreticians and practitioners are working under functionalist assumptions which creates a highly technocratic, restrictive understanding about accounting systems design.

Insights from the functionalist paradigm are highly pragmatic, the overarching concern being to discover practical knowledge which can be put to general use in a real patternable world which needs but marginal change. More formally it works under: an ontological assumption of 'realism' which assumes that there is a real world 'out there' which is ordered and patterned and independent from any observational bias; a human nature assumption of 'determinism' which maintains that human beings are simply part of an ordered rule-conforming reality; a societal assumption based on a 'sociology of regulation' which assumes a certain unity, cohesiveness and 'good-ness' in the social world; an epistemological assumption of 'positivism' which assumes that knowledge equals patterns, regularities, general causal relations and universal laws; a methodological assumption of 'nomotheticism' which assumes that to understand the patterned universe requires systematic, careful, sophisticated approaches to allow the observer to expose the underlying causal order which is assumed to be there to be discovered.

These assumptions, in their purest form, restrict what is deemed to be an accounting system to a generalisable, technical, observable craft produced by some universal human designer for the mainten-ance of a current social order. Accounting systems are deemed to be objective phenomena which exist and, in some sense, have their being distinct from the designers and possess definable and generalis-able qualities. Parts of these qualities include some universal charac-teristics, or laws, whose nature is accessible through clearly defined observations. These qualities also include a particular defined func-tional purpose. To claim that the accounting systems designer has, in any sense, a position and significance in giving meaning to accounting systems design, in this purest functional form, is apparently unthink-able.

This extreme position encompasses all those who define the nature of accounting systems following the rational/closed assumptions of Scott (see Figures 2.5 and 2.6). But it also applies to those working under rational/open and natural/closed assumptions. Their respective different emphases are movements away from the more 'pure' rational/closed way of thinking, whether it be in terms of uncertainty analysis, or lack of generality in the actual design of the accounting system ('openness') or relative significance and variability of the designer or the context of the design process ('naturalness'). However, when combined with the 'rationality' or 'closure' assumptions they are restricted in their innovation and become very closely aligned to the 'purer' rational/closed way of thinking.

A Critique of Functional Thinking and an Alternative Basis for Understanding and Changing Accounting Systems Design

Our view is that accounting systems are more than functional, technical phenomena where both the designer and context have little part to play. Consequently there is a growing body of opinion calling for an abandonment of functional thinking, and adopting more directly alternative sets of metatheoretical assumptions. It is to these issues we now turn.

There is a growing number of studies which maintain that the technical aspects of accounting systems design mould and are moulded by a wide range of societal, organisational and personal factors (cf. Hopwood, 1978, 1983, 1985; Colville, 1981, 1982; Tomkins, 1982; Burchell, Clubb and Hopwood, 1985; Roberts and Scapens, 1985; Laughlin, 1984, 1986, 1987; Miller and O'Leary, 1987). The overarching view of these proponents is that most of our current knowledge about accounting systems design has failed to appreciate or uncover this important social dynamic which both moulds and is moulded by the more visible technical practices of accounting. Few, adopting this perspective, would dispute the comments of Burchell, Clubb and Hopwood (1985) when they claim that:

> little is known of how the technical practices of accounting are tethered to the social, of how wider social forces can impinge upon and change accounting, and how accounting itself functions in the realm of the social, influencing as well as merely reacting to it.
>
> (p. 382)

The studies which have been undertaken all have uncovered a complex and highly significant web of social factors which have a marked effect on the technical elements of accounting systems design. For instance Berry et al. (1985) traced the rudimentary nature of the UK coal industry's management control systems in both areas and collieries to important social factors concerning the dominance of the 'mining line' at these levels in the organisation. Colville (1982) and Tomkins (1982), analysing the accounting systems of a social services department and a police force, trace the social roots behind these different technical systems to important political and social factors. Laughlin (1984, 1986) traces the reasons for highly simple accounting systems in the Church of England to dominant social beliefs in this institution. Neimark and Tinker (1986) trace the origins of the management control system in General Motors to important social mechanisms to do with interorganisational and social conflict. At a more general level Burchell, Clubb and Hopwood (1985) trace the rise and fall of value-added accounting to a number of important social factors as do Miller and O'Leary (1987) in their study of the reasons for the emergence of cost accounting. In all these studies there is an increasing awareness that a variety of social factors have a large part to play in the technical design of accounting systems, and that these aspects of design have been seriously underresearched by those who look at accounting through functionalist eyes.

It is this assumption of functionalism, upon which most accounting research is based, it can be argued, which is the key reason for our present lack of understanding. Despite marked differences in their approaches, the above studies all, without exception, maintain that the domination of functionalist thinking and the assumption base upon which it relies creates unnecessary and inappropriate constraints around the research endeavour. Functionalist thinking has restricted the analysis of the social context and its interactions with the technical to elements which have readily observable qualities omitting relevant, often hidden, social factors which have a vital part to play in understanding and hence in designing accounting systems.

Although there is common agreement amongst this growing minority in their rejection of functionalist thinking, it would be wrong to see the alternative approaches which they advance as some homogeneous set. There are those who propound the merits of symbolic interactionism (cf. Colville, 1981), ethnomethodology (cf. Berry et al., 1985), structuration (cf. Roberts and Scapens, 1985), Marxian dialectics (cf. Neimark and Tinker, 1986), critical theory (cf. Laughlin, 1987), and those informed by the thinking of Foucault (cf. Burchell, Clubb and Hopwood, 1985; Miller and O'Leary, 1987). In fact, going back to the Burrell and Morgan framework (see Figure 2.2) there are those who, in some sense, fit into all three of the remaining paradigms along with those who consider their work cannot be accommodated within this classification schema but would concur with their rejection of functionalist thinking (cf. Chapter 3 by Tinker and Neimark in this book).

Despite the legitimate doubts concerning the ability of the Burrell and Morgan framework to capture a comprehensive picture of alternative approaches, it does help to focus the mind that choices have to be made as to different sets of key assumptions. It could be argued that the Burrell and Morgan framework is caught in a subtle form of what Bernstein (1983) calls the 'Cartesian Anxiety' whereby we are led:

> to a grand and seductive Either/Or. Either there is some support for our being, a fixed foundation for our knowledge, or we cannot escape the forces of darkness that envelop us with madness, with intellectual and moral chaos.
>
> (p. 18)

Although Burrell and Morgan are not setting up a framework which sets the functionalist paradigm as 'objective and true' and all the others as 'relative and false', they are posing the view that choices have to made on key assumptions, and once made, form the basis for alternative perspectives, on a relatively defined 'firm foundation'. Despite the view of people like Giddens and Foucault, whose ideas have been adopted by some of the new wave of accounting thinkers, who maintain that the opposites can be held in dynamic balance making the choice unnecessary and counterproductive, we would maintain that the key dimensions highlighted in the Burrell and Morgan framework are mutually exclusive, where choices are necessary in the formulation of any approach to research into accounting systems design. We conclude this section with exploring the implications of this thinking.

We see the key assumptions concerning ontology, human nature and society in the Burrell and Morgan framework as key in this respect: all are continuums whereby toward the middle of each is a distinctive mix of characteristics, but despite this there is still a dividing line between fundamentally different perspectives. For instance we would maintain that there is a fundamental ontological distinction between 'realism' and 'nominalism' in terms of perspective: either one believes, in the final analysis, that the world exists in some pure sense distinct from the observational bias of the observer, or one doesn't. As one approaches the mid-point in this ontological continuum, the mix in the various positions become blurred, but on probing we would maintain that observers hold a position on one side of the line or the other. Similar considerations apply to the human nature and societal assumption.

Given this overall assumption, we would argue that the emerging characteristics of accounting systems design suggest that the most fruitful way forward is to build a new foundation for accounting research upon a 'nominalist' ontological assumption, a 'voluntarist' human relations assumption, and a 'radical change' societal assumption. This would base accounting thought in the radical humanist paradigm of Burrell and Morgan's framework which generates a particular, and radically different, epistemology and methodology to functionalism. In fact the radical humanist paradigm is, it will be noted, the complete opposite to functionalism, sharing no common sets of assumptions. The reason briefly is that accounting systems are a social construct which are created by organisational actors who are free to both change the design and provide, implicitly, the meanings which guide the design. We would argue that in addition, and possibly more questionably, that accounting systems and their designers should be actively involved in critically analysing the current state of the organisation and society of which they are part, and looking for what changes they can bring into being in pursuing emancipation and development in our social world.

CONCLUSION

A number of endeavours have been undertaken in this paper. Firstly, we have attempted to provide a survey of the dominant lines of thought in financial and management accounting, as being the two theoretical areas whose primary brief has been addressed to the design of accounting systems in organisational contexts.

Secondly, an analysis of the underlying assumptions behind this thinking has been presented. Thirdly, the paper has provided a general and specific critique of this current theoretical situation in terms of its demonstrable inability to either adequately understand accounting systems design in particular organisations, or change and improve these designs.

With regard to the first and second of these points the paper has primarily relied on summaries and frameworks which are, to an extent, familiar to accounting thinkers. Relying largely on the framework put forward by Burrell and Morgan (1979) we concluded, as others have (cf. Chua et al., 1981; Cooper, 1983; Hopper and

Powell, 1985), that most accounting thought is primarily working under functionalist assumptions with realism as its ontology; determinism as to its assumption about human nature; positivism as its epistemology, and nomotheticism as its methodology, along with an acceptance of current societal configurations. Although this conclusion is unsurprising, given the previous analyses, the detail contained in the first part of the paper explores these issues possibly in greater depth and breadth including, as it does, the somewhat forgotten financial accounting domain. But in the end the paper is not about the merits of this classification schema *vis-à-vis* others. It is introduced only as an important contextual prelude to the more important evaluation which followed.

This evaluation has taken a number of forms in the latter part of the paper. In the first place an argument was advanced for the very restrictive nature, for both theoretical design and the reality these theories represent and affect, of using thinking based on functionalism. This basis with its concern for observable generalisations reduces our appreciation of the design of accounting systems to technical, context-free phenomena which, it was argued, is unnecessarily restrictive. In the final substantive section an argument was presented for developing a new theoretical approach for aiding our understanding of, and enabling change in, accounting systems design. These needs, it was argued, could most obviously be fulfilled by theoretical approaches based on the assumptions in Burrell and Morgan's radical humanist paradigm.

Undoubtedly the journey that this paper has travelled is complex and it may not be the pathway others would want to follow. We appreciate this but in the end would maintain that, unless there are fundamental changes in our theoretical approaches at a more general discipline level, then our ignorance of, and our actual incapability to change the design of, accounting systems in organisations will remain.

Note

1.   The authors would like to thank Gareth Morgan, Trevor Hopper, David Cooper and the participants at the Interdisciplinary Perspectives on Accounting conference for the critical, insightful comments on a previous draft of this paper.

Bibliography

Alexander, S. S., 'Income Measurement in a Dynamic Economy', in 'The Study Group on Business Income', *Five Monographs on Business Income* (New York, American Institute of Certified Public Accountants, 1950).

American Accounting Association, Committee on Concepts and Standards for External Financial Reports, *Statement on Accounting Theory and Theory Acceptance* (Sarasota, Florida: AAA, 1977).

Argyris, C., *The Impact of Budgets on People* (New York: The Controllership Foundation, 1952).

Baiman, S., 'The Evaluation and Choice of Internal Information Systems within a Multiperson World', *Journal of Accounting Research* (1975) pp. 1–15.

Baiman, S., 'Multiperson Analysis in Managerial Accounting: A Survey', Working Paper, Graduate School of Industrial Administration, Carnegie-Mellon University, 1979.

Bernstein, R. J., *Beyond Objectivism and Relativism* (Oxford: Basil Blackwell, 1983).

Berry, A. J., T. Capps, D. Cooper, P. Ferguson, T. Hopper and E. A. Lowe, 'Management Control in an Area of the National Coal Board: Rationales of Accounting Practices in a Public Enterprise', *Accounting, Organizations and Society* (1985) pp. 3–28.

Bhaskar, K. N., 'Quantitative Aspects of Management Accounting', in M. Bromwich and A. G. Hopwood (eds), *Essays in British Accounting Research* (London: Pitman, 1981) pp. 229–73.

Bonbright, J. C., *The Valuation of Property* (New York: McGraw-Hill, 1937).

Burchell, S., C. Clubb, A. Hopwood, J. Hughes and J. Nahapiet, 'The Roles of Accounting in Organisations and Society', *Accounting, Organizations and Society* (1980) pp. 5–27.

Burchell, S., C. Clubb and A. G. Hopwood, 'Accounting in its Social Context: Towards a History of Value Added in the United Kingdom', *Accounting, Organizations and Society* (1985) pp. 381–413.

Burns, T. and G. M. Stalker, *The Management of Innovation* (London: Tavistock Publications Ltd., 1961).

Burrell, G. and G. Morgan, *Sociological Paradigms and Organisational Analysis* (London: Heinemann, 1979).

Canning, J. B., *The Economics of Accountancy* (New York: The Ronald Press Co., 1929).

Chambers, R. J., *Accounting, Evaluation and Economic Behaviour* (Englewood Cliffs, NJ: Prentice-Hall, 1966).

Chua, W. F., 'Radical Developments in Accounting Thought', *The Accounting Review* (1986) pp. 601–32.

Chua, W. F., R. C. Laughlin, E. A. Lowe and A. G. Puxty, 'Four Perspectives on Accounting Methodology', Discussion Paper, University of Sheffield, 1981.

Colville, I., 'Reconstructing "Behavioural Accounting"', *Accounting, Organizations and Society* (1981) pp. 119–32.

Colville, I., 'Accounting Information Systems in a Police Force', Discussion

Paper, School of Management, University of Bath, 1982.

Cooper, D. J., 'Tidiness, Muddle and Things: Commonalities and Divergencies in Two Approaches to Management Accounting Systems', *Accounting Organizations and Society* (1983) pp. 269–86

Cooper, D. J., and M. J. Sherer, 'The Value of Corporate Accounting Reports: Arguments for a Political Economy of Accounting', *Accounting, Organizations and Society* (1984) pp. 207–32.

Davis, S. W., K. Menon and G. Morgan, 'The Images that have Shaped Accounting Theory', *Accounting, Organizations and Society* (1982), pp. 307–18.

Demski, J. S., *Information Analysis* (Reading, Mass.: Addison-Wesley, 1972).

Demski, J. S. and G. A. Feltham, *Cost Determination: A Conceptual Approach* (Ames, Iowa: The Iowa State University Press, 1976).

Edwards, E. O. and P. W. Bell, *The Theory and Measurement of Business Income* (Los Angeles: University of California Press, 1961).

Fayol, H., *General and Industrial Management* (translated by C. Stours, London: Pitman, 1949).

Feltham, G. A., *Information Evaluation*, Studies in Accounting Research, No. 5 (Sarasota, Florida: American Accounting Association, 1972).

Grady, P., *Inventory of Generally Accepted Accounting Principles for Business Enterprises*, Accounting Research Study No. 7 (New York: AICPA, 1965).

Hofstedt, T. R., 'Behavioural Accounting Research: Pathologies, Paradigms and Prescriptions', *Accounting, Organizations and Society* (1976) pp. 43–58.

Hopper, T. M. and A. Powell, 'Making Sense of Research in the Organisational and Social Aspects of Management Accounting', *Journal of Management Studies* (1985) pp. 429–65.

Hopwood, A. G., 'Towards an Organisational Perspective for the Study of Accounting and Information Systems', *Accounting, Organizations and Society* (1978) pp. 3–13.

Hopwood, A. G., 'Editorial', *Accounting, Organizations and Society* (1979) pp. 145–7.

Hopwood, A. G., 'On Trying to Study Accounting in the Contexts in which it Operates', *Accounting, Organizations and Society* (1983) pp. 287–305.

Hopwood, A. G., 'The Tale of a Committee that never Reported: Disagreements on Intertwining Accounting with the Social', *Accounting, Organizations and Society* (1985) pp. 361–77.

Jaedicke, R. K. and A. A. Robichek, 'Cost-Volume-Profit Analysis Under Conditions of Uncertainty', *The Accounting Review* (1964) pp. 917–26.

Jensen, R. E., 'Sensitivity Analysis and Integer Linear Programming', *The Accounting Review* (1968) pp. 425–46.

Johnson, O., 'Towards an 'Events' Theory of Accounting', *The Accounting Review* (1970) pp. 641–53.

Kelly-Newton, L., *Accounting Policy Formulation: The Role of Corporate Management* (Reading, Mass: Adison-Wesley, 1980).

Klir, G., *An Approach to General Systems Theory* (New York: Van Nostrand, 1969).

Laughlin, R. C., *The Design of Accounting Systems: A General Theory with an Empirical Study of the Church of England*, unpublished PhD Thesis, University of Sheffield, 1984.

Laughlin, R. C. 'Insights into the Cultural Base of Accounting Through a Case Study of the Church of England', Discussion Paper, University of Sheffield, 1986.

Laughlin, R. C., 'Accounting Systems in Organisational Contexts: A Case for Critical Theory', *Accounting, Organizations and Society* (1987) pp. 479–502.

Laughlin, R. C., and A. G. Puxty, 'The Decision-Usefulness Criterion: Wrong Cart, Wrong Horse?', *AUTA Review* (1981), pp. 43–87.

Laughlin, R. C. and A. G. Puxty, 'Accounting Regulation: An Alternative Perspective', *Journal of Business Finance and Accounting* (1983) pp. 451–79.

Lawrence, P. R. and J. W. Lorsch, *Organisation and Environment: Managing Differentiation and Integration* (Boston: Graduate School of Business Administration, Harvard University, 1967).

Leftwich, R., 'Evidence of the Impact of Mandatory Changes in Accounting Principles on Corporate Loan Agreements', *Journal of Accounting and Economics* (1981) pp. 3–36.

Littleton, A. C., *Structure of Accounting Theory*, Monograph No. 5 (Sarasota, Florida: American Accounting Association, 1953).

Lowe, E. A. and R. W. Shaw, 'An Analysis of Managerial Biasing: Evidence from a Company's Budgeting Process', *Journal of Management Studies* (1968) pp. 304–15.

March, J. D. and J. P. Olsen, *Ambiguity and Choice in Organisations* (Bergen, Norway: Universitetsforlaget, 1976).

Mattessich, R., *Accounting and Analytical Methods* (Englewood Cliffs, NJ: Prentice Hall, 1964).

Mayo, E., *The Social Problems of an Industrial Civilisation* (Boston: Graduate School of Business Administration, Harvard University, 1945).

McGregor, D., *The Human Side of Enterprise* (New York: McGraw-Hill 1960).

Miller, P. B. and T. O'Leary, 'Accounting and the Construction of the Governable Person', *Accounting, Organizations and Society* (1987) pp. 235–65.

Neimark, M. and T. Tinker, 'The Social Construction of Management Control Systems', *Accounting, Organizations and Society* (1986) pp. 369–95.

Otley, D. T., 'The Contingency Theory of Management Accounting: Achievement and Prognosis', *Accounting, Organizations and Society* (1980) pp. 413–28.

Otley, D. T., 'Management Accounting and Organisation Theory: A Review of Their Interrelationship', in *Management Accounting, Organisational Behaviour and Capital Budgeting* (London: Macmillan/ESRC, 1984).

Paton, W. A. and A. C. Littleton, *An Introduction to Corporate Accounting Standards*, American Accounting Association Monograph No. 3 (Sarasota, Florida: AAA, 1940).

Pfeffer, J. and G. R. Salancik, *The External Control of Organisations* (New York: Harper and Row, 1978).

Prakash, P. and A. Rappaport, 'Information Inductance and its Significance in Accounting', *Accounting, Organizations and Society* (1977) pp. 29–38.

Pugh, D. S., D. J. Hickson, C. R. Hinings and C. Turner, 'Dimensions of Organisation Structure', *Administrative Science Quarterly* (1968) pp. 65–91.

Pugh, D. S., D. J. Hickson, C. R. Hinings and C. Turner, 'The Context of Organisation Structures', *Administrative Science Quarterly* (1969) pp. 91–114.

Puxty, A. G., (ed.), *Reductionism ad Absurdum: Critiques of Agency Theories in Accounting*, Issues in Accountability No. 12 (Strathclyde, Scotland: University of Strathclyde, 1985).

Roberts, J. and R. W. Scapens, 'Accounting Systems and Systems of Accountability – Understanding Accounting Practices in their Organisational Contexts', *Accounting Organizations and Society* (1985) pp. 443–56.

Roethlisberger, F. J. and W. J. Dickson, *Management and the Worker* (Cambridge, Mass: Harvard University Press, 1939).

Sanders, T. H., H. R. Hatfield and U. Moore, *A Statement of Accounting Principles* (New York: American Institute of Certified Public Accountants, 1938).

Scapens, R. W., 'Management Accounting – A Survey Paper', in *Management Accounting, Organisational Behaviour and Capital Budgeting* (London: Macmillan/ESRC, 1984).

Schiff, M. and A. Y. Lewin, 'The Impact of People on Budgets', *The Accounting Review* (1970) pp. 259–68.

Scott, W. R., 'Developments in Organisation Theory, 1960–1980', *American Behavioural Scientist* (1981) pp. 407–22.

Snowball, D., 'On the Integration of Accounting Research on Human Information Processing', *Accounting and Business Research* (1980) pp. 378–81.

Sorter, G. H., An 'Events' Approach to Basic Accounting Theory', *The Accounting Review* (1969), pp. 12–19.

Stedry, A. C., *Budget Control and Cost Behaviour* (Englewood Cliffs, NJ: Prentice Hall, 1960).

Sterling, R. R., 'On Theory Construction and Verification', *The Accounting Review* (1970), pp. 444–57.

Sundem, G. L., 'A Game Theory Model of the Information Evaluator and the Decision Maker', *Journal of Accounting Research* (1979) pp. 243–61.

Sweeney, H. W., *Stabilised Accounting* (New York: Harper and Row, 1936).

Taylor, F. W., *The Principles of Scientific Management* (New York: Harper and Row, 1911).

Tinker, A. M., B. D. Merino and M. D. Neimark, 'The Normative Origins of Positive Theories: Ideology and Accounting Thought', *Accounting Organizations and Society* (1982) pp. 167–200.

Tomkins, C. R., 'The Use of Accounting Information in a Social Services Department and a Police Force: A Comparison of Two Case Studies', Discussion Paper, School of Management, University of Bath, 1982.

Tomkins, C. R. and R. Groves, 'The Everyday Accountant and Researching His Reality', *Accounting Organizations and Society* (1983) pp. 361–74.

Watts. R. L. and J. L. Zimmerman, 'Towards a Positive Theory of the Determination of Accounting Standards', *The Accounting Review* (1978) pp. 112–34.

Woodward, J., *Industrial Organisation: Theory and Practice* (New York: Oxford University Press, 1965).

Zmijewski, M. E. and R. L. Hagerman, 'An Income Strategy Approach to the Positive Theory of Accounting Standing Setting/Choice', *Journal of Accounting and Economics* (1981) pp. 129–49.

3 Displacing the Corporation with Deconstructionism and Dialectics

Tony Tinker and Marilyn Neimark

In 1932 Berle and Means observed that corporations were growing so large, and their ownership so diversified, that their managers could no longer be assumed to serve the interests of the shareholders; ownership and control were becoming disconnected. Their observations raised important questions of public policy: if management is autonomous from ownership, should that autonomy be allowed to persist? And if not, in whose interest should corporations be regulated, the shareholders or some broader social constituency? Berle and Means's concerns periodically recur in the social accounting, management and economics literature and in the political arena (for example, debates over US anti-trust policy, plant closings, and regulations concerning employment, employee health and safety, consumer product safety, pollution and so on).

These attacks on the autonomy of the corporation have not gone unchallenged. In this paper we critically examine one of the most recent of these challenges: transaction cost theory. In addition to providing a theoretical justification for the modern corporate form and the oligopolistic market structures that accompany its hegemony, transaction cost theory claims to offer a conceptual apparatus and research strategy for dealing with *any* problem that can be formulated, directly or indirectly, in contractual terms, and that its causal mechanism provides the driving force for the main institutional changes that have occurred both since and prior to the industrial revolution (Williamson and Ouchi, 1981).

In his review of Oliver Williamson's book *Markets and Hierarchies*, William Ouchi heralds transaction cost theory as a revolutionary new perspective that holds out the possibility of 'a unified social science . . . during our lifetime' (Ouchi, 1979A, p. 544). Ouchi also

44

writes that Williamson's book 'obsoletes the works by March and Simon, by Thompson, and by anyone who has attempted to understand the implications of bounded rationality, technology and uncertainty for the structure and functioning of organizations.' (ibid., p. 540) This grand theoretical synthesis encompasses a number of traditional disciplines: organisation theory (Williamson, 1980a; Ouchi and Jaeger, 1978; Ouchi and Johnson, 1978; Ouchi, 1977, 1978, 1979a, 1979b, 1980); economics (Klein et al., 1978; Goldberg, 1976; Dahlman, 1979; Williamson, 1975, 1976, 1979b, 1981); business law (Posner, 1979; Williamson, 1979a, 1979b, 1980b); labour economics (Williamson et al., 1975; Williamson, 1980a) and business history (North, 1978; Chandler, 1962, 1977, 1982; Williamson, 1981, 1982; Williamson and Ouchi, 1981). Accounting researchers are also appealing to transaction cost theory as a means of explaining the development of management accounting practices (Chandler and Daems, 1979; Spicer and Ballew, 1983; Kaplan, 1983, 1984; Johnson, 1980).[1]

Our critique of transaction cost theory is both epistemological and political, and is based on Derrida's deconstructionism and Adorno's negative dialectics. We differ from other criticisms of transaction cost theory (for example, Perrow, 1981, 1986), which are analytically based in that they focus on what transaction cost theory claims the corporation 'is'. In contrast, we focus on what transaction cost theory excludes in its portrayal of the corporation. We will argue that transaction cost theory serves to synchronise and focus thinking about corporations within specific patterns, thereby excluding some questions, elevating others, and otherwise cultivating a favourable disposition toward corporations. In taking this approach, we want to make it clear at the outset, however, that our target is not merely transaction cost theory, but the whole mode of theorising it represents. Transaction cost theory, with its sweeping claims for universal applicability and epistemological authority exemplifies the analytical thinking that dominates the social sciences, particularly those concerned with business organisations and accounting. Hence the implications of our critique extend beyond transaction cost theory to analytical theorising in general.

The critique proceeds in three steps. First, we sketch out the basic arguments offered by transaction cost theory to account for (and justify) the development of the modern corporate form. Next we introduce the theoretical bases for our critique: deconstructionism and negative dialectics. Finally, we will use the insights gained from these theories to critically examine the view of the corporation offered by transaction cost theory.

TRANSACTION COST THEORY

The intellectual roots of transaction cost theory lie in nineteenth-century social darwinism (see Tinker, 1982), and more recently, in Coase (1937, 1960), who introduced the role of transaction costs in explaining the origins of the corporation, and in Chandler (1962, 1977), who interprets the history of the corporation as a search for ever-greater administrative efficiency in the face of exogenous changes in markets and technologies. Williamson (1975, 1976, 1979a, 1979b, 1980, 1981, 1982), Ouchi (1980), and Williamson and Ouchi (1981) have expanded upon these earlier ideas to provide both a conceptual apparatus and a research strategy for dealing with institutional change in general and, of particular interest to us here, to explain and legitimate the origins and development of the modern corporation.

The modern corporation, according to Williamson, is the product of a series of organisational innovations that had the purpose and effect of economising on transaction costs in labour, capital and intermediate product markets (1981, p. 1543). Thus, in developments from early capitalism, the factory replaced contracting with independent producers (the 'putting out' system) as the dominant business structure; capitalist authority relations superceded inside contracting within the factory; large unitary, functionally organised firms supplanted small autonomous units; the functionally organised firm was followed by multidivisional organisations, in which operating activities were separated from strategic planning and resource allocation; next came multidivisional conglomerates; and most recently, the dominant organisational structure has been the multinational form, which transfers the transactional economies of the multidivisional form to the organisation of international activities. (Williamson, 1980, 1981)

Williamson sees little incompatability between the corporate quest for profitability and growth (through cost-economising and revenue-maximising activities) and the interests of employees, consumers, and other social constituencies. He assumes that the historical transformations in governance structures noted above were motivated by an efficiency objective that yields net social as well as net private gains. The modern corporation, for Williamson, is an economising rather than a monopolising entity. (1981, p. 1542) And, since economising on transaction costs is socially valued, it follows, Williamson claims, that the modern corporate form 'serves affirmative economic purposes' (1981, p. 1538).

The following section develops a blend of deconstructionist philosophy and negative dialectics that critiques transaction cost theory's portrayal of corporate development and suggests an alternative approach to organisational and management analysis.

DECONSTRUCTIONISM AND NEGATIVE DIALECTICS

Both Derrida's deconstructionism and Adorno's negative dialectics are immanent critiques of most conventional analytic philosophies. Although there are important differences between them, deconstructionism and negative dialectics share a number of affinities and it is these that are of interest to us here. (Ryan, 1982; Dews, 1986) The common basis of Derrida's and Adorno's critiques is found in their respective concerns with definition (Derrida) and identity thinking (Adorno), and their efforts to replace these closed systems of thought, and the ideological domination they represent, with new ways of thinking that focus on 'differances' (Derrida) and nonidentity (Adorno). Let us briefly look at each of these critiques and then consider their implications for our assessment of transaction cost theory specifically and social science theorising in general.

Deconstructionism

Derrida challenges conventional analytic philosophies by questioning their oppositional foundations, their implicit prioritisations, and their pretentions to providing a complete account of the truth or meaning of the world. (Derrida, 1976, 1978; Woods, 1979; Ryan, 1982) The interrelated terms, 'differance,' and 'undecidability,' capture the basic elements of this challenge.

The term 'differance' is a neologism composed of the French verbs to differ (in space or in kind) and to defer (in time). (Derrida, 1978; Ryan, 1982) By conferring a spatio-temporal dimension to definition, differance shows that meaning is never final or absolute, but is constantly being displaced by an endless series of comparisons with what is exterior to the object of interest. Thus, any entity or event that we attempt to describe is an effect of forces, histories and structures, which cannot be isolated or determined as self-identical in themselves. Consequently, 'no entity or event can be named "properly" or adequately, because to do so would require tracing out the web of referential roots, which produces it from an "outside" that is internal to the making of things.' (Ryan, 1982, p. 23) This approach to defining stands in sharp contrast to that adopted by analytic philosophies, for which it is standard practice to seek an exclusive and sovereign meaning by discovering those properties and attributes of a 'thing' that allows us to distinguish 'it' from what it is not. Thus, order stands in opposition to chaos, good to evil, subject to object, agency to structure, functional to disfunctional, and so on.

Accompanying these dichotomies is an implicit prioritisation: what is interior and included, is prior and superior to what is excluded and exterior. Hence, depending upon the theory, equilibrium is preferred to disequilibrium, science to non-science, optimality to suboptimality, modern to primitive, and so on. In each case, the second, 'other' term connotes something that threatens the reassuring and empowering values represented by and inherent within the first (Ryan, 1982). Deconstructionism consists of demonstrating that what is excluded as secondary and derivative is internally related to what is included and primary. This precludes a hierarchical or oppositional division and undermines a concept of self-identity (such as 'good') that is exempt from its differential relations with other terms (such as 'evil'). 'Good' and 'evil', in combination, are not a closed system which is dialectically related only internally. Collectively, and as individual terms, they are internally related to other terms and concepts in an unending chain of displacements.

Undecidability refers to the necessary incompleteness of axiomatic systems (whether in mathematics, as Godel showed, or in philosophy, as Derrida argues). Such systems are necessarily undecidable because they generate elements that can be proved to both belong to the system and not belong to it simultaneously (as 'evil' is an internally related part of a system called 'good'). (Ryan, 1982, p. 17)

In their various forms, analytic philosophies rest upon certain grounding assumptions (for example, those regarding the primacy of the Logos (reason), identity, subjectivity, and the clear correspondence of logical concepts to concrete objects) (Derrida, 1973). But for these grounding principles to serve as real foundations upon which philosophical systems can be constructed, they must 'stand on their own' and be absolutely self-sufficient (self-identical, in Adorno's terms) (Adorno, 1973; Held, 1980, pp. 204–218). They lose this foundational quality, however, and cease to be primordial grounds once they can be derived from something else. Deconstructionism demonstrates the limits of such metaphysical systems by showing their dependency on elements that are both inside and outside the system (Ryan, 1982, p. 18).

Science, then, cannot refer to an 'unmodifiable set of formal axioms which once and for all explain the absolute, decisive truth of the world'. Instead, it should be 'the attempt to discover undecidability, the limit at which present axioms cease to be complete and begin to require supplementation. Science does not mean the absoluteness of truth (in the vulgar sense of Althusser), but rather the persistently maintained possibility that any presently existing truth may prove not to be absolute.' (ibid., pp. 21–22) Understood in this way, deconstructionism can be seen to be not merely a critique, but more broadly as a way of thinking.

Negative Dialectics

Adorno's critique of identity thinking and his advocacy of non-identity thinking (that is, negative dialectics) closely anticipate deconstructionist ideas. According to Adorno, identity thinking, whereby the concept is presumed to be rationally identical with its object, is the normal mode of thinking in contemporary society. Identity thinking subsumes all particular circumstances, events, objects, and phenomena under general definitions and/or unitary systems of concepts. It corresponds to the closed, self-defining, self-identifying metaphysical systems discussed in relation to deconstructionism. Adorno tried to show that identity thinking – the normatively motivated closure imposed by analytic theorising – correctly registers but falsely affirms dominant ideologies (Adorno, 1973, pp. 58–70).

The consciousness which perceives the false identity constituted by concepts (that is, the non-identity relation between concept and object) is what Adorno calls 'non-identity thinking' or 'negative dialectics' (Rose, 1978). Adorno is not suggesting, however, that our concepts, and hence our understanding of reality, are entirely fictions. Rather, he is also concerned to expose the fallacies of subjectivism (that is, too great an emphasis on the role of the subject). For Adorno, the antimonies, illegitimate abstractions, and one-sided treatment of problems that characterise philosophical thought, all express aspects of the structure of society (Held, 1980, pp. 207). Thus, subject and object are mutually constituted by one another, but are irreducible to each other. 'They are internally related interdependent structures within which the cognitive process unfolds' (Held, 1980, p. 202).

While confirming the mediation of subject and object, however, Adorno's aim was also to demonstrate the priority of the object:

> An object can be conceived only by a subject but always remains something other than the subject, whereas a subject by its very nature is from the outset an object as well. Not even as an idea can we conceive a subject that is not an object, but we can conceive an object that is not a subject. To be an object also is part of the meaning of subjectivity; but it is not equally part of the meaning of objectivity to be a subject.
>
> (Adorno, 1973, p. 183, quoted in Held, 1980, p. 213)

Although we cannot grasp objects (the social world in which the subject is located) without concepts, objects do not dissolve into concepts. Concepts, on the other hand, disappear over time, 'as a result of their own inevitable insufficiency, into the flux and process of objects' (Held, 1980, p. 213). Reality always surpasses absolute comprehension, and for this reason, there can never be an absolute, complete, sovereign truth or theory, only provisional ones.

Both Derrida and Adorno see change as most effectively realised by targeting particular cases at the boundary or margin between the 'inside' and the 'outside' of an edifice of meaning. Their common aim is the displacement of sovereign systems of meaning. Displacement involves rupturing such an enclosed system and triggering its redefinition by deflecting attention along a trace of repressed associated meanings. But this process of redefinition itself is never complete and through time generates an ongoing unravelling of meaning, transmitted through an infinity of associations (Barnes, 1982).

In using Derrida's deconstructionism and Adorno's negative dialectics, the next section critiques the partiality of transaction cost theory in its choice of categories and its neglect of social structural conditions. We show that the theoretical categories of transaction cost theory are 'fictive' and 'ideological' in that they exclude from consideration the historical and social structural context of corporations. These categories reify and 'naturalise' socially created phenomena (such as the state, capitalist production relations, the various manifestations of the corporate form, and other social institutions), by reducing relations between human beings to relations between 'things': contracts, transactions, governance structures, markets, hierarchies, corporations, technological interfaces, and so on. On one level, this reduction reflects the 'truth' of social ideology and the commodification of social relations within capitalism. But on another level, by affirming and preserving the 'appearance' of capitalist society, it prevents us from comprehending its formative processes and historical mediations.

TRANSACTION COST THEORY

We begin our critique by examining what is a fundamental analytical dichotomy for Williamson: the efficiency versus market control (or power) explanations of the modern corporation.[2] Williamson concludes that the efficiency objective is historically the more important because a market control strategy alone is unlikely to succeed for long in the absence of specific structural conditions (high concentration with high barriers to entry) (Williamson, 1981, p. 1564). He argues that not only do most firms not meet these conditions, but they will be penalised if efficiency norms are seriously violated for long periods. Hence, although some of the structural changes that took place in the late 19th and early 20th centuries were motivated by efforts to achieve market power (for example, horizontal mergers), such strategies were only viable when they were accompanied by transaction cost economising innovations (such as vertical integration) (Chandler, 1982, p. 128).

Du Boff and Herman (1980) reveal the flaws in this market power versus efficient dichotomy. They argue that the fundamental objective of business enterprises in a capitalist system is neither market control nor efficiency for its own sake, but capital accumulation (they use the terms profitability and growth); and that this goal is compatible with and inseparable from both strategies. Vertical integration, for example, may reduce contracting costs, but it also imposes barriers to entry. Horizontal mergers may permit gains from scale economies, but it also increases market power. Moreover, Du Boff and Herman argue that market control on its own has been an effective strategy for ensuring profitability and growth for some enterprises for extended periods of time, by creating precisely those circumstances that Williamson insists are the prerequisites for its success. Du Boff and Herman give examples of large corporations whose market dominance ensured their profitability for many years despite inefficient administration and technological stagnation (for example, US Steel, Western Union, General Motors, Standard Oil).

Framing the research question in terms of management's motivations (efficiency versus market control) directs attention away from the social-structural conditions in which management behaviour originates and operates. Not only is market control versus efficiency a false dichotomy, it is underpinned in transaction cost theorising by an array of dubious theoretical categories of analysis that are both spurious and limiting. These include a focus on the polarity of markets versus hierarchies; the transaction as the basis unit of analysis; the contractual representation of social relations; efficiency as the criterion for assessing corporate (and social) performance; and on opportunism as the *sine qua non* of human behaviour. In the balance of this section we identify and critically examine these categories.

The Markets versus Hierarchies Polarity

Transaction cost theory presents a world in which the choice of governance structure is limited to a polarity of markets (composed of atomistic individuals) and hierarchies (that is, bureaucratic organisations, usually meaning corporations). Alternatives that fall outside this polarity are either excluded from the analysis (for example, democratically-organised state or community-based ways of organising social production); or are dismissed as non-workable (for example, worker cooperatives). (We will return to Williamson's discussion of cooperatives below.)

The Transaction is the Basic Unit of Analysis

The basic unit of analysis for Williamson is the transaction. A transaction occurs when a good or service is transferred across a technologically separate interface (1981, p. 1544). Williamson does not ask about the origins of these technologically separate interfaces; rather he takes them as given. In his paper on 'The Organization of Work' (1980), for example, he attempts to illustrate by an 'abstract assessment' of the transactional properties of alternative work modes that hierarchical modes (specifically, capitalist authority relations) are the most efficient. In doing so, Williamson assumes that the state of technology is constant, and that tasks are divided in the same way for each mode-of-work organisation. (The only differences between the modes he considers are the physical location of each task – centralised or dispersed geographically; the ownership of the means of production; and the output of intermediate and final stations.) Williamson fails to recognise that the technologically separate interfaces that he accepts as given depend upon prior design decisions concerning the mode-of-work organisation and hence, that the identity of the transaction is problematic. What constitutes a transaction depends, in part, upon the governance structure that it is supposed to explain.

Williamson is able to assume a constant technology because for him technology is an exogenous force to which the corporation must adapt (for example, in determining the absolute size of specific technological units). Consequently he fails to consider the possibility that organisations may actively strive to shape these forces in their own interest (capital accumulation, in the case of corporations). Such an analysis leaves no room for managers to selectively adapt technologies and workplace arrangement, or for corporations to intercept and shape scientific knowledge to erect barriers to entry, or to foreclose on technological options that are less compatible with maintaining private control over investment and the utilisation of labor (Du Boff and Herman, 1980). Williamson acknowledges that the choice of technology and internal organisation are not independent – technology, he writes, may render some forms of organisation inoperable. But he does not mention the alternative possibility, that organisation forms may restrict one's choice of technology (and may be designed to do so).

Formulating Social Relations as Contracts

The transaction cost approach construes social relations in contractual terms and then examines the comparative costs of planning, adapting, and monitoring task completion under alternative contractual frameworks (that is, governance structures) (Williamson, 1981, p. 1544). We can examine the consequences of viewing the employer-employee relationship in contractual terms by applying to it Williamson's first principle of efficient organisation design, Asset Specificity (ibid., p. 1548).

Williamson states that 'the normal presumption that recurring transactions for technologically separable goods and services will be efficiently mediated by autonomous market contracting is progressively weakened as asset specificity increases'. He approvingly quotes Alchian's comment that 'the whole rationale for the employer-employee status, and even for the existence of firms, rests on [asset specificity] . . . without it there is no known reason for firms to exist' (Williamson, 1982, pp. 112–113).

Let us examine the advantages of corporate governance over market governance when transactions supported by highly specific assets are involved. According to Williamson both suppliers and purchasers of highly specific assets will insist on contractual safeguards because such assets are not readily redeployed. Such contracts are costly to negotiate and write, and are difficult to implement. Placing such transactions under the internal direction of the firm avoids these costs and confers three execution advantages:

> First, common ownership reduces the incentives of the trading units to pursue local goals. Second, and related, internal organization is able to invoke fiat to resolve differences whereas costly adjudication is needed when an impasse develops between autonomous traders. Third, internal organization has easier and more complete access to the relevant information when disputes must be settled. The incentives to shift bilateral transactions from markets to firms also increases as uncertainty increases, since the costs of harmonizing a relation among the parties will vary directly with the need to adjust to changing circumstances.
>
> (Williamson, 1981, pp. 1548–1549)

The asocial nature of transaction cost analysis is vividly illustrated here. First, the technological separability of labour services from the means of production, that establishes the employer-employee relationship, is taken as given rather than being recognised as the historical outcome of social processes and social conflict.

Second, the source of increasing asset specificity is not questioned, although it is implied by Williamson's list of the contract execution advantages of internal organisation. Workers who are not tied to employers (because of the specificity of their skills and /or lack of ownership of the means of production) can more readily pursue goals which may conflict with employers' capital accumulation objectives; have access to, and may withhold or extract a high price for, information that may be needed to increase capital accumulation; and can 'hold their own' when differences arise. Clearly it is in the interest of employers to internalise the relationship if it will increase workers' dependence on the sale of their labour power and on the employment relation with specific employers. One way to achieve this dependency is to increase labours' asset specificity (through increasing the division of labour and/or by deskilling). Asset specificity is thus a tool in social conflict, a means of social control, a variable to be manipulated to change the relative bargaining strength of employer and employee.

Third, implicit in the term 'contract' is the notion of a reciprocity in exchange that is satisfactory to both parties, and is not a victory (whether total or partial) of one protagonist over another. Yet the history of employer-employee relations is one of ongoing conflict. These conflicts have frequently been overt and violent (as in the Homestead strike that Williamson refers to as an example of an efficiency-motivated organisational restructuring). Using the term 'contract' to describe these relations mystifies and obscures their nature. In his study of alternative modes of work organisation, Williamson acknowledges that the parties to the contract may have unequal bargaining strength, but he selectively focuses only on those resources that empower employees (for example, acquisition of firm specific skills and knowledge; collective organisation; ownership of physical assets); and not on the sources of the (usually greater) bargaining strength of employers (for example, ownership of the means and product of production; the support of the state and the legal system; the successful commodification of labour and the deskilling and replacement by technology of increasing numbers of workers; wealth) (Williamson, 1980a, p. 20).

Finally, in focusing on the bilateral nature of contracting, the interplay between government and business is de-emphasized. Williamson seems to approve of government intervention that reinforces 'natural' developmental processes, and to object to efforts that attempt to obstruct them. Thus, Williamson does not question the use of the state and federal governments to help Carnegie and Frick prevail over labour when they decided to de-unionise the company's Homestead mill in 1892. In his opinion de-unionisation was socially beneficial, since the defeat of the union allowed new institutional structures to be devised in the steel industry whose efficiency gains were diffused throughout society (Williamson, 1980, p. 32). On the other hand, Williamson apparently objects to anti-trust efforts. He wryly points out that: 'The natural growth of conglomerates, which would occur as the techniques for managing diverse assets were refined, was accelerated as anti-trust enforcement against vertical mergers became progressively more severe' (Williamson, 1981, p. 1557).

The Efficiency Criterion

The sole performance criteria applied by transaction cost theory is efficiency. Williamson sees no incompatibility between the corporation's quest for profits and the interests of employees, consumers, or society-at-large. Structural transformations are assumed to be primarily motivated by a socially-neutral efficiency objective rather than the result of distributional conflicts among capitals and /or between classes. The critical assumptions implicit in the transaction cost theory formulation of the efficiency criteria are that efficiency (that is, the production of increased outputs with given inputs) can be equated with cost economising, and that questions about distribution can be safely ignored. There is now an ample body of literature that suggests, however, that the marginalist notions of efficiency upon which transaction cost theory is based are flawed, and that questions of distribution and social conflict are central (Sraffa, 1960; Harcourt, 1972; Harcourt and Laing, 1971; Tinker, 1980.)

Williamson's study of alternative modes for organising work illustrates both his identification of efficiency with cost minimisation and the difficulty (indeed, impossibility) of trying to separate the quest for efficiency from distributional conflicts. Here, his efficiency criteria clearly refers to distributional conflicts over the costs of protecting property and property rights (for example, the costs of averting embezzlement, malingering, misuse and neglect of equipment, goal suboptimisation, work-quality declines). In the same article, Williamson criticises the efficacy of worker participation programmes. He offers as evidence Gunzberg's finding that although such programmes may yield social and psychological gains, they 'do not add to the value of goods and services, and can add to their cost' (Williamson, 1980, p. 35). The social priorities, allegiances and measurement biases of transaction cost theory are made clear here. Innovations that add to the value of goods and services (as measured by market prices) are clearly preferred over gains that are not mediated by the market.

Behavioural Assumptions

Transaction cost theory makes two behavioural assumptions – bounded rationality and opportunism – 'without which the study of economic organization is pointless'. The human beings that populate firms and markets are both 'less competent in calculation and less trustworthy and reliable in action' than the economic man of neo-classical economics (Williamson, 1981, p. 1545). Williamson considers, but dismisses the possibility that consciousness and behaviour – 'human nature as we know it – may be the product of the prevailing social system and is not immutable.

In attempting to account for the historical failure of worker cooperatives (and the transformation of many of the more successful ones into profit-making joint stock companies), despite the high efficiency ranking his analysis gives to the Peer Group mode of work organisation, Williamson resorts to the argument that democratically managed cooperatives fail because they are inconsistent with human nature (rather than their being inconsistent with capitalism's ideological hegemony). He writes that 'Organizing modes that are viable only among small communities of highly motivated members are scarcely interesting for purposes of organizing activity in society at large. Aspirations to improve the conditions of society are surely commendable but how extensively human nature can be reshaped is uncertain' (Williamson, 1980a, p. 22).

The existence of bounded rationality and opportunism are used to justify Williamson's third principle of organisation design, Hierarchical Decomposition: 'internal organization should be designed in such a way to effect quasi-independence between the parts . . . and incentives should be aligned within and between components so as to promote local and global effectiveness' (Williamson, 1981, p. 1550). The internal structure of multi-divisional, conglomerate, and multi-national corporations is thereby transformed by Williamson from a system for social discipline, control, exploitation and appropriation, into an expression of a fundamental organising principle.

Finally, let us briefly look at transaction cost theory's epistemological foundations. As we noted in the introduction, transaction cost theory's sweeping claims for its explanatory power are buttressed by claims for its epistemological authority. Like other analytical theories, transaction cost theory is grounded in a 'positivistic' epistemology that, although it aspires to the discovery of an invariant and immutable truth, offers criteria for theory assessment that are readily and regularly undermined because they fail to recognise both the social mutability of the reality that they seek to discover, and the part the social scientist plays in the social construction of that reality (Neimark and Tinker, 1986). Williamson and Ouchi (1981) claim that their theory is supported by 'ecological survival tests'. That is, they offer a hypothesis to explain the dominance of large multidivisional and multinational corporations, proposing that over time, only those governance structures that minimise transaction costs will survive. They then offer as evidence the persistence of the very organisational forms that their hypothesis was designed to explain. Refuting instances are explained away either as mistakes, or as special cases where efficiency has been sacrificed to serve special interests (Williamson and Ouchi, 1981, pp. 364, 389). And since the theory makes no claims for the speed of adjustment, the period of correction may be very long indeed (as in the cases of General Motors and US Steel, now USX), and the penalties for inefficiency need not be imposed on those responsible for them but on employees and communities.

In addition, transaction cost theory shares with all analytical thinking the implicit belief that the mind of the observer/scientist has privileged access to a vantage point outside the sway of socio-cultural developments from which to assess history as a whole (Held, 1980, p. 204). Because they lack self-reflection, transaction cost theorists have un-selfconsciously constructed a conceptual apparatus that 'correctly registers but falsely affirms dominant ideologies'. (ibid., p. 202) Transaction cost theory favours the status quo by affirming the efficiency and social value of the modern corporate form (in its multidivision, conglomerate and multinational manifestations) and oligopolistic market structure.

IMPLICATIONS AND CONCLUSIONS

Although we have focused in this paper upon a particular example, transaction cost theory, our critique has application to other totalising theories about organisations and accounting, especially those explicitly grounded in marginalist economics, such as agency theory, efficient market empirics, and information economics, but also to metatheoretical frameworks, such as that offered by Burrell and Morgan (1979) that purport to be all-encompassing (where would Derrida' deconstructionism or Adorno's negative dialectics fit in the latter's 2×2 matrix?). But deconstructionism and negative dialectics offer more than a mode of critiquing analytic theorising, they also offer a 'dialectical', way of thinking.

In what ways does dialectical thinking differ from the analytical mode, exemplified by transaction cost theory? Unlike analytics, dialectics does not 'hypostasise' the mind, and thus is aware of the social origins of consciousness, including its own. It makes no claims to universality or truth. It also takes as problematic the social relations, ideologies, and institutions that are reified and naturalised by analytic theorising, and seeks out their social-structural origins. Specifically, a dialectical approach to the origins and development of the corporation focuses on the complex and dynamic interrelationships within the social totality, between the quest for profits and growth (that is, capital accumulation), technological, social, and organisational innovations, and distributional conflicts (whether between or among classes, races, ethnicities, gender, or other social groups).

This approach to research represents a fundamentally different point of departure from orthodox analysis. At the risk of excessive specificity, some of the more important differences may be summarised as follows. Dialectics, in contrast with analytics:

(1) Employs a social and epistemological orientation that rejects logocentricism and theoretical monism, and stresses the role of science in demystification and radical change.

(2) Focuses on detecting what is excluded by extant social theories in order to uncover the implicit and hidden configurations of meaning that complement the identity of the object of investigation.

(3) Pursues an understanding of the general through adequate exposure and interpellation of the particular. For instance it:

(4) Focuses on individual cases and instances rather than working from highly abstract and empirically invulnerable categories.

(5) Accords a proper historicity to the phenomenon under investigation and stresses the dynamic and evolutionary processes by which meaning is acquired, rather than emphasising static, point-in-time equilibrating propensities.

(6) Uses measurement scales that are adequate to the particular phenomenon under study, rather than the much-remarked-on subjugation of qualitative to quantitative.

(7) Reflects social structural conditions in the construction of the object of enquiry (rather than rendering such conditions invisible, under the guise of the market, for instance, as occurs in neoclassical economics).

This list brings into sharp relief the differences between analytical and dialectical/deconstructionist approaches. The list is not exhaustive, there is considerable overlap between individual items, and not every item on the list applies with equal weight to every analytic theory. But the list does crystallise the points of difference between analytic and dialectical social science theories, and their applicability to interrogating the phenomenon of accounting for the corporation.

Notes

1. The accounting literature cited either draws directly on the transaction cost literature or appeals to its intellectual predecessor, Chandler's business history (for example, Chandler, 1962, 1977).
2. Chandler's *Strategy and Structure* (1962) was an important source for Williamson, and recently Chandler endorsed Williamson's transaction cost explanation of 'why the large industrial corporation came at the time it did, in what industries it did, and in the way that it did' (although he harbours some reservations concerning its wider applicability in explaining the strategy of growth through diversification) (Chandler, 1982, pp. 127, 124–9). Hence our criticisms of Williamson's work apply to Chandler as well.

Bibliography

Adorno, T., *Negative Dialectics*, trans. B. Ashton (New York: Seabury Press, 1973).

Barnes, B., and T. S. Kuhn, *Social Science* (New York: Columbia University Press, 1982).

Berle, A. A. and Means, G. C., *The Modern Corporation and Private Property* (New York: The Macmillan Company, 1932).

Burrell, G. and Morgan, G., *Sociological Paradigms and Organizational Analysis* (London: Heinemann, 1979).

Calabresi, G., 'Transaction Costs, Resource Allocation, and Liability Rules: A Comment', *Journal of Law and Economics* (1968) pp. 67–73.

Chandler, A. D., Jr, *Strategy and Structure: Chapters in the History of the Industrial Enterprise* (Cambridge, Mass: MIT Press, 1962).

Chandler, A. D., Jr, *The Visible Hand: The Managerial Revolution in American Business* (Cambridge, Mass: Belknap Press, 1977).

Chandler, A. D., Jr and H. Daems, 'Administrative Coordination, Allocation and Monitoring: A Comparative Analysis of the Emergence of Accounting and Organization in the U.S.A. and Europe', *Accounting, Organizations and Society*, (1979) pp. 3–20.

Chandler, A. D., Jr, 'Evolution of the Large Industrial Corporation: An Evolution of the Transaction-Cost Approach', in Jeremy Atack, ed., *Business and Economic History* (2nd series, vol. XI, 1982, Papers presented at the twenty-eighth annual Business History Conference) pp. 116–134.

Coase, R., 'The Nature of the Firm', *Economica* (1937) pp. 386–400. Reprinted in *Readings in Price Theory*, G. J. Stigler and K. E. Boulding (eds), (Chicago: Richard D. Irwin for the American Economic Association, 1952).

Coase, R., 'The Problem of Social Cost', *Journal of Law and Economics* 1960) pp. 1–44.

Dahlman, K. J., 'The Problem of Externality', *Journal of Law and Economics* (1979) pp. 141–62.

Derrida, J., *Speech and Phenomena*, trans. D. Allison (Evanston: Northwestern University Press, 1973).

Derrida, J., *Of Grammatology*, trans. Gayatri Chakravorty Spivak (Baltimore, Md: Johns Hopkins Press, 1976).

Derrida, J., *Writing and Difference*, trans. A. Bass (University of Chicago Press, 1978).

Dews, P., 'Adorno, Post-Structuralism and the Critique of Identity', *New Left Review* (May/June, 1986) pp. 28–44.

Du Boff, R. B., and E. S. Herman, 'Alfred Chandler's New Business History: A Review', *Politics and Society* (1980) pp. 87–110.

Goldberg, V. P., 'Regulation and Administered Contracts', *Bell Journal of Economics*, (1976), pp. 426–52.

Harcourt, G. C., and Laing, W. F., *Capital and Growth* (Harmonsworth: Penguin, 1971).

Harcourt, G. C., 'Some Cambridge Controversies in the Theory of Capital', *Journal of Economic Literature* (1972) pp. 369–405.

Held, D., *Introduction to Critical Theory: Horkheimer to Habermas* (London: Heinemann, 1980).

Johnson, H. T., 'Markets, Hierarchies and the History of Management Accounting', paper presented at the Third International Congress of Accounting Historians, London Business School, August, 1980.

Kaplan, R., 'Measuring Manufacturing Performance: A New Challenge for Managerial Accounting', *The Accounting Review* (1983) pp. 683–705.

Kaplan, R., 'The Evolution of Management Accounting', *The Accounting Review*, (1984) pp. 390–418.

Klein, B., R. A. Crawford, and A. A. Alchian, 'Vertical Integration, Appropriable Rents and the Competitive Contracting Process', *Journal of Law and Economics*, (1978), pp. 297–326.

Neimark, M. and A. Tinker, 'The Social Construction of Management Centre Systems', *Accounting, Organizations and Society*, (1986) pp. 369–96.

North, D. C., 'Structure and Performance: The Task of Economic History', *Journal of Economic Literature*, (1978) pp. 963–78.

Ouchi, W. G., 'The Relationship Between Organizational Structure and Organizational Control', *Administrative Science Quarterly* (1977) pp. 95–113.

Ouchi, W. G., 'The Transmission of Control Through Organizational Hierarchy', *Academy of Management Journal* (1978) pp. 248–63.

Ouchi, W. G., 'Review of O. Williamson, *Markets and Hierarchies: Analysis and Antitrust Implications*', *Administrative Science Quarterly* (1979a) pp. 540–4.

Ouchi, W. G., 'A Conceptual Framework for the Design of Organizational

Control Mechanisms', *Management Science* (1979b) pp. 833–48.

Ouchi, W. G., 'Markets, Bureaucracies and Clans', *Administrative Science Quarterly* (1980) pp. 413–28.

Ouchi, W. and A. M. Jaeger, 'Type Z Organization: Stability in the Midst of Mobility', *Academy of Management Review* (1978) pp. 305–14.

Ouchi, W. and J. B. Johnson, 'Types of Organizational Control and Their Relationship to Emotional Well-Being', *Administrative Science Quarterly* (1978) pp. 293–317.

Perrow, C., 'Markets, Hierarchies and Hegemony', in *Perspectives on Organization Design and Behavior*, A. Van de Ven and W. Joyce (eds), (New York: John Wiley, 1981) pp. 371–86.

Perrow, C., 'Economic Theories of Organization', *Theory and Society* (1986) pp. 11–45.

Posner, R. A., 'The Chicago School of Antitrust Analysis', *University of Pennsylvania Law Review*, (1979) pp. 925–48.

Rose, G., *The Melancholy Science: An Introduction to the Thought of Theodor Adorno* (New York: Columbia University Press, 1978).

Ryan, M., *Marxism and Deconstructionism: A Critical Articulation* (Baltimore, Md: Johns Hopkins Press, 1982).

Spicer, B. H. and Van Ballew, 'Management Accounting Systems and the Economics of Internal Organization', *Accounting, Organizations and Society* (1983) pp. 73–96.

Sraffa, P., *The Production of Commodities by Means of Commodities* (Cambridge University Press, 1960).

Tinker, A. M., 'Towards a Political Economy of Accounting: An Empirical Illustration of the Cambridge Controversies', *Accounting, Organizations and Society* (1980) pp. 147–60.

Tinker, A. M., 'Panglossian Accounting Theories: The Science of Apoligizing in Style', *Accounting, Organizations and Society* (1988) pp. 165–90.

Williamson, O. E., *Markets and Hierarchies: Analysis and Antitrust Implications* (New York: The Free Press, 1975).

Williamson, O. E., 'The Economics of Internal Organization: Exit and Voice in Relation to Markets and Hierarchies', *American Economics Review* (1976) pp. 369–77.

Williamson, O. E., 'Transaction Cost Economics: The Governance of Contractual Relations', *Journal of Law and Economics* (1979a) pp. 233–61.

Williamson, O. E., 'Assessing Vertical Market Restrictions: Antitrust Ramifications of the Transaction Cost Approach', *University of Pennsylvania Law Review* (1979b) pp. 233–62.

Williamson, O. E., 'The Organization of Work: A Comparative Institutional Assessment', *Journal of Economic Behaviour and Organization* (1980a) pp. 5–38.

Williamson, O. E., (ed.), *Anti-trust Law and Economics* (Houston: Dame Publications, 1980b).

Williamson, O. E., 'The Modern Corporation: Origins, Evolution, Attributes', *Journal of Economic Literature* (1981) pp. 1537–68.

Williamson, O. E., 'Microanalytic Business History', in *Business and Economic History*, Jeremy Atack (ed.) (2nd series, vol. XI, 1982, Papers presented at the twenty-eighth annual meeting of the Business History Conference) pp. 106–115.

Williamson, O. E., and W. G. Ouchi, 'The Markets and Hierarchies and Visible Hand Perspective', in *Perspectives on Organization Design and Behavior*, A. Van de Ven and W. Joyce (eds) (New York: John Wiley, 1981) pp. 347–70, 387–90.

Williamson, O. E., M. L. Wachter, and J. E. Harris 'Understanding the Employment Relation: The Analysis of Idiosyncratic Exchange', *Bell Journal of Economics* (1975) pp. 250–80.

Woods, D. C., 'Introduction to Derrida', *Radical Philosophy* (1979) pp. 18–28.

4 Accounting for Feasible Socialism: Accounting, Industrial Democracy and the Theory of the Firm

Jim Tomlinson

The purpose of this paper[1] is to discuss the character of accounting under a regime of 'feasible socialism'. This involves starting with a very general discussion of such socialism, in order to put in context the succeeding, more specific comments, on the character of firms under such socialism and the role of accounting this might entail.

The name 'feasible socialism' derives from Nove (1983). Feasibility may be in the eye of the beholder, but Nove's books seems a good starting point for discussing the organisation of socialist enterprises for three related reasons. First, his book is based on learning from the experience of the Eastern European socialist economies. Secondly, it does not set up any single principle of organisation for its 'feasible socialism', and linked to this, whilst it is based on a wide knowledge of economics literature, it is not part of any one theoretical school, unlike most economists' writings.

Plainly it is impossible to justify in the space of a few sentences that Nove's 'feasible socialism' is indeed that. Such a calculation of feasibility would require a complex set of issues to be dealt with in a length and manner impossible in the current context. However, at a minimum it may be said that Nove's socialism represents some of the major trends of Western European thinking on socialism in recent years. This is surely the case with his emphasis on the continuing role for markets, especially in consumer goods, under such socialism; his concern with democracy at the enterprise level as crucial to socialism, coupled with an appreciation of the problems this unavoidably entails; his eschewal of comprehensive planning as a plausible foundation for a socialist economy in already-advanced industrial countries.

Taken together these points make Nove's feasible socialism the best starting point for looking at the role of accounting under a prospective socialist regime.

However, before looking at Nove's arguments in more detail I want to make some general points about the notion of *socialist* enterprise organisation.

First, socialist enterprise organisation should not be seen as an 'end-state', a state of affairs to be realised and which is some sense will then be maintained. Rather I would want to focus on certain principles of social relations which can be seen as ways of assessing different actual or proposed forms of social organisation.[2] This means focusing on certain 'objectives', but 'objectives' seen as principles at stake in different forms of social relations, not as things attained which can then be ticked off before we pass on to achieving the next objective.

The point of making this very general point is to try and force certain issues out into the open, issues which often seem to be left implicit in discussions in this area. So it seems important to at least outline what these principles/objectives are, in the current context focusing on those relevant to enterprise organisation and the role of accounting. It will be apparent that these principles are far from 'original', but rather largely represent a particular gloss put on long-standing concerns of socialist politics.

SOCIALIST PRINCIPLES

First let us take democracy. Here it is important not to conflate democracy with socialism. It seems best to give socialism its traditional meaning of the supersession of private property in the means of production, but at the same time to accept that this can lead to alternative institutional arrangements, such as democratic or undemocratic (and most have in fact been the latter); competitive or co-operative; small- or large-scale, and so on. Then again, democracy is a specific mechanism, that is, the subjecting of decision-making agents to (effective) election and hence some degree of accountability (Hindess, 1983, ch. 2). Of itself it says nothing about the policy *outcomes* of democratised decision-making, that is, it is a mechanism whose effects cannot be derived from its democratic character. Socialists, like other political forces, will have desired outcomes, but democracy should be treated as one of those outcomes, not as a means to them.

Accountability might be seen as a more general socialist objective, because it embraces democracy as one possible (and probably crucial) form of accountability, but does not mean only that. In the case of individuals, subjection to democratic election may be a backdrop to making accountability effective, but may often be only the last resort. Accountability of *organisations* is plainly rather different, and may be exercised by withdrawal of custom from a firm, for example.

There seems to be no one way of defining the scope of democracy or accountability, that is, the set of other agents by whom agents of decision (human or non-human) will be elected, or accountable to. As Dahl (1970, pp. 64–7) has pointed out, an appealing notion like 'everyone who is affected by a decision should be party to making that decision' is wholly unworkable. At some remove almost everyone could be said to be affected by almost every decision. All one seems able to say is that socialism means the widest possible scope for democracy and accountability, and a willingness to devote considerable resources to its extension. The question of the boundaries to be drawn around units of accountability is impossible to decide in principle, separate from the specific unit under discussion.

Secondly there is the objective of 'generalisation of competence'.[3] This is the traditional socialist objective of attempting to breakdown the division of labour. Here I would wish to emphasise that this is very much not an 'objective' in the sense of something capable of final attainment. There will always be divisions of labour in production, namely, specialisms in forms of work, so that a Utopian notion of an end-state where there are no differences in tasks, and competences to perform them, is not at issue here. Also, especially in the current context, it is important that this notion of competence be seen to embrace not only 'technical' skills, but also organisational and managerial ones in the widest sense. (This issue is returned to in the final section.)

The first two principles are clearly related. As has rightly been pointed out, effective democratisation and accountability depends upon having agents able to exercise such functions, and currently this pre-condition is widely absent, (for instance, cf. Bullock, 1977). But there is also the link in the other direction, from expanding democracy to expanding competences. Just as it may be argued that universal suffrage is crucial to interpellating subjects as political citizens, so industrial democracy may have as a crucial *objective* the interpellation of subjects as 'organisational citizens', facilitating their acquisition of organisational and managerial skills. (This in turn may facilitate participation in other contexts – see Pateman (1970).)

A third general principle seems to be the desirability of a 'high standard of living'. This embraces both high 'production standards', that is, conditions of work, and high consumption standards. Obviously these may be in conflict; higher consumption standards may be purchased at the price of poor production standards, that is, for workers. Insofar as there is a trade-off here, socialists have rightly put an emphasis on production standards, particularly because the dominant neo-classical economic theory strongly downplays these in its celebration of consumer sovereignty. But equally, under conditions of industrial democracy, that is, where producers dominate the mechanisms of democracy and accountability *within* the firm, there is plainly a danger of consumption standards being sacrificed to production standards.

The standard of living is usually associated with consumption standards in a very narrow sense of income per head, or becomes very broad to embrace the 'quality of life'. In the current context, what seems important to emphasise is that the ease of availability, quality, reliability and safety of material products is a very important part of their value, and these qualities are equally significant for services, which make up an increasingly large part of total consumption. So enterprise organisation must be sensitive to these aspects of the standard of living.

Finally, as an objective, egalitarianism. This term seems a better way of posing this traditional socialist issue than 'equality', which both sounds like an end-state, and also seems to imply that there is somewhere a single scale upon which its attainment may be measured. Rather than this, egalitarianism emphasises a principle, but one which has no one dimension and is incapable of any 'final' achievement. In addition, it is important that this principle, like that of democracy, is not overgeneralised. This, for example, is a problem with Crosland (1956) and subsequent work in that tradition which tries to establish a single socialist goal of 'equality'. It has its effects in the socialist attempts to fit *every* policy into a framework of equality, with unhelpful consequences for the specification of the character of policy, in particular areas (Rose, 1980).

THE ECONOMIC REGIME

Nove envisages his feasible socialism having five different kinds of producing unit (pp. 197–210). These are state enterprises, centrally controlled and administered, consisting of large-scale industry, public utilities and finance. Secondly, the bulk of manufacturing would be 'socialised' enterprises, state-owned but with full autonomy and a management responsible to the workforce. Thirdly, there would be co-operatives, similar to socialised enterprises, but where the state would have no residual responsibility for the use or misuse of the means of production or debts incurred in their use. Finally, Nove sees a residual role for, on the one hand, small-scale private enterprise and, on the other, individuals working on their own account.

Nove's schema is not, then, one of a simple 'market socialism', in which all the complex problems of the existing socialist economies are dissolved by the pursuit of the market principle. Goods markets do play a substantial role in Nove's economy, but equally the state would retain vital functions in direct investment on major projects, monitoring other investments, running 'natural monopolies', and functions connected with foreign trade (pp. 207–8). However, the state has no role in Nove's schema in regulating or monitoring 'accounting standards' in any sense.

The concern of this paper is with Nove's socialised and co-operative sectors. These would cover the bulk of economic activity, and can reasonably be grouped together as a sector of 'industrial democracy', as both would have 'managers appointed by an elected committee, responsible to this committee – or to a plenary meeting of the workforce if the numbers are small enough to make this possible' (p. 206). *Vis-à-vis* this sector, apart from monitoring investment, the state would also have 'the vital task of setting the ground-rules' (p. 207). However, Nove does not say much more than this, and it is indeed a vital area and one of those where accounting practices will be of great importance. This is returned to below.

THE THEORY OF THE FIRM AND 'INFORMATION'

As already noted, Nove is not an adherent of any one school of economic theory, and this is apparent in his discussion of the socialist firm. However he does make sympathetic reference (for example, see p. 202) to the recent 'neo-classical' theories of the firm of authors like Williamson, and those theories clearly are important for two reasons. Firstly, they mark a sharp break with the dominant neo-classical treatment of the firm as a 'black-box', as a simple relay of impulses from input and product markets, with no important decision-making function (see Tomlinson, 1984). Secondly, a significant aspect of these new theories is their concern with 'information', which at least sounds as if it is relevant to accounting. Therefore it is helpful to make brief comments on this work in its implications for accounting.

Whilst it is no doubt an advance for neo-classical theory to take seriously questions of internal organisation, it does this in its own particular way. (These points are treated at greater length in Tomlinson, 1986). First, the theory stays within the traditional neo-classical notion of 'survival of the fittest', so that firms which are inefficient information users are driven out of business, whilst the efficient survive. Such a view has been devastatingly criticised in its application to profit maximising by Winter (1963, 1975). They point out the inapplicability of the biological metaphor to firms, where there is no mechanism whereby a characteristic which makes for survival in one context can be passed on, or adapted to survival in a different context. Such criticism would seem to apply to the attempts to use this metaphor in relation to efficiency in information usage.

Secondly, these approaches treat information as a 'good' which will be acquired like other goods, until the expected utility equals the cost of acquisition. The *locus classicus* of this type of argument applied to information is Stigler (1961). Whatever the logic of this kind of argument in talking about consumers' information, for example, information on secondhand car prices, it turns up profound difficulties when applied to production. If, for example, what is required is information about different production processes, then any simple cost-benefit calculus is very difficult to apply, Not only is the dispersion of prices, that is, costs of different production processes, likely to be unknown (as Stigler recognises, p. 219) but the acquirer of information doesn't know what she/he doesn't know. Secondly, the benefits of production information (for instance, the costs of a change in technology) are not parallel to the differences in car prices between garage X and garage Y, in that the distribution of any benefits from a lower cost technology is contestable.

Such uncertainty may be incorporated in more sophisticated approaches, like that of Arrow (1974), where investment in information is like investment in inventories. But this doesn't deal with either the question of the *distribution* of benefits from a change in technology, nor, more broadly, with the assumption made about the 'status' of that information.

Unsurprisingly perhaps, neo-classical economics treats information in a positivist manner. The acquisition of information is seen as giving a closer and closer approximation to the truth. If one is willing to expend sufficient resources, the world can be revealed in its naked actuality. Again, such a view is hardly adequate for discussions of, say, production costs. Cost figures are inherently the products of different kinds of *calculation*, and *calculative frameworks*, and these calculations have both conditions of existence and effects which are significant. But neo-classical economics tends to approach these in a prescriptive manner ('X is the correct way to calculate costs'), it is not equipped to analyse other aspects of their existence.

Hence the changes in the neo-classical theory of the firm do not fundamentally alter its relation to economic calculation and information. They retain the traditional neo-classical view that differences in forms of calculation (like other organisational differences) will 'come out in the wash' via the survival of the fittest in the market place. But, in addition, they unhelpfully treat information in a positivist manner which must understate the significance of economic calculation.

ACCOUNTING AND SOCIALISM

Discussion of the role of accounting under capitalism has often been the starting point for (at least implicitly) ideas about its role under socialism. Therefore it is important to look at these critiques, to see how far indeed they do lead into useful understandings of accounting and its role, understandings which can then be deployed in looking at the role of accounting under socialism.

Radical critics have attacked the character of capitalist accounting from two rather different perspectives. On the one hand, we have the view that accounting is (inextricably?) linked to the de-humanising and alienating organisation of society (Cherns, 1978). On the other hand, there is the view that capitalist accounting is based on neo-classical economics and as such represents the interests of the capitalist class (Tinker, 1980, Tinker et al., 1982).

Cherns's argument is that organisations (defined in a *very* general sense) are the major engines of alienation because they are based on 'segmentation and stratification, the essential features of bureaucracy' (p. 106). In turn, these features of organisation depend upon measurement and hence accounting *is itself* alienating: 'whatever at any time we cannot measure, we devalue' (pp. 108–109).

This thesis is tied to the view that most accounting takes monetary measures of organisation's output as appropriate: 'we know that these assumptions are quite false but we try to behave as if they were true' (p. 109), and the reforms which have tried to take this disparity into account have only papered over the cracks. Human resources accounting is analysed in this light – it takes the point of view of the organisation in evaluating humans, rather than that of humans evaluating organisations. However there are signs of hope – organisations can be non-alienating if designed on principles of self-expression, compensating particularism and assertions of identity, but their development is shackled by accounting practice (pp. 112–113).

A number of comments on this seem appropriate. First, there is the general status of the notion of alienation, which has been much debated of late and subject to withering criticisms which will not be repeated here (see, seminally, Althusser, 1970; also Rose, 1977). More specifically there is the clear affiliation between this argument and that of Sombart and Weber, on the theme that modern capitalism was founded on an ethic of rational calculation, most importantly expressed in double-entry bookkeeping. In part Cherns's argument is simply a 'radical' gloss on such ideas. Yamey (in Tucker, 1975) has pointed out that historically double-entry cannot bear the weight put upon it by Sombart. But more generally we may note that such a form of argument makes societies an emanation of a principle, which provides the essence of its functioning. Yet any attempt to demonstrate this must always gloss over the manner in which such principles become embodied in institutions and practices, and which in turn necessarily modify these 'principles'. This problem is illustrated by Cherns's uncritical acceptance of the view that scientific management at some (unspecified) stage in the past was the principle of all organisational development (cf., for instance, Nelson, 1974).

Perhaps the most crucial issue for 'socialist accounting' raised by Cherns is that of the status of measurement. The above critical points imply great scepticism whether one can see measurement as a 'principle' whose spirit determines and corrupts all organisation. But more prosaically one can pose the question, how could organisations be accountable in their functioning *without* measurement? Cherns raises the issue of measures of hospital efficiency, and the distortions of using bed occupancy to do this (p. 109). But he does not confront the issue of how, if the efficiency of a hospital is a matter of concern, we will have to try and *measure* it. Of course all measures have biasing effects, none is 'correct'. But this is a commonplace of the literature on, for example, health service planning, and cannot amount to a generalised critique of measurement as a principle.

In my remarks about socialist principles, I have emphasised the notion of accountability. This is hardly profound, but it is important to stress that accountability implies measurement. Further, a society with greater accountability would probably have greater measurement than today's. Of course these measures would be contestable and contested. But they would be a condition of accountability, not a route to alienation. (The link between measurement and accountability is commonly overlooked in radical critiques – for instance, critiques of the introduction of 'corporate management' into local authorities (Cockburn, 1977).)[4]

Cherns cites recent experiments in self-managed task groups as evidence of pressures towards the supersession of the alienating forms of organisation (p. 113). But whatever else ought to be said of these experiments, they do not displace measurement, but imply reorientation of measurement which maintains it as a crucial part of the experiments' functioning.

The criticisms by Tinker and associates of accounting focus on a critique of neo-classical economics. They see this economics as central to modern accounting, but argue that it is fundamentally flawed as theory (especially with reference to the Cambridge capital controversies) and epistemologically unsound, following Marx in seeing it as essentially dealing with only the appearances rather than the realities of capitalist society. Indeed accountants are pictured as less critical of neo-classical economics than many economists (Tinker et al., 1982, p. 187) and 'slaves of some defunct economist' (Tinker, 1980, p. 149).

Clearly it is the case that the growing formalisation of accounting over the last few decades has led to a great deal of economic theorising in accounting, and most of this has been neo-classical. But even if one shares the view that neo-classical economics is an intellectually unsatisfactory problematic, this kind of argument holds a number of difficulties.

First of all, it is far from clear that the practices of accounting are as closely related to neo-classical economics as this argument suggests. Tinker (1980, p. 147) sets up a simple dichotomy between seeing corporate profit as either a measure of a corporation's social efficiency (in accordance with neo-classical economics) or as a measure of the 'power of capitalists'. Yet it is not clear why accountants should be seen as committed to either of these highly simplified views. To calculate the profitability of a capitalist firm requires *no* view at all on questions of the *origin* of profit in the sense discussed by Tinker, it simply involves treating certain calculative frameworks as given.

Tinker's empirical example would seem to bear this out. He criticises a marginal productivity interpretation of a specific company's accounts, but this interpretation is his own, that is, one he ascribes to neo-classical economists. Secondly, he is unable to show how his preferred 'classical economic theory' could be translated into different accounting practices. His own discussion relies on a plausible but highly general assertion of the importance of the changing environment of the enterprise concerned, not on its practices, let alone its accounting.

Similarly the assertion that marginalism/neo-classical economics links into accounting via its 'individualism' and its focus on 'pseudo-objective' market prices seems equally too general to be helpful (1982, pp. 187–190). No doubt accountants have often taken too narrow a view of their responsibilities, but it is far from clear this can be linked to any philosophical commitment to individualism. Equally the focus of accountants on 'pseudo-objective' prices may be seen as at least explicable by the fact that to a greater or lesser extent *to the firm*, prices are 'objective'. To rue the political prejudices of accountants is one thing, but to reduce those to an entrapment by neo-classical economics does however seem to raise more questions than it answers. On these issues Cooper's (1980, p. 165) comment seems appropriate: 'I want to know more about the deficiencies of neo-classical economics for the prescriptions accountants have made and continue to make'.

Probably the most explicit and effective attempt by neo-classical economists to influence accounting practice has been in the area of cost accounting and decision-making, and it is these areas which would most justify the view that 'much of the progress made in accounting during the 20th century has been due to accountants accepting and adapting the theoretical framework given to them by economists' (Whittington, in Carsberg and Hope, 1977, p. 207).

Up to the 1930s most cost accounting was based on historic (*ex post*) procedures and average/unit costing. Then work by Edwards, Baxter and Coase applied marginal analysis to cost analysis in a manner which has been widely influential (see Edey and Yamey, 1974). But it is far from clear that the arguments here are marginalist in Tinker's sense of the word, that is, in terms of a theory of value. Whilst undoubtedly these writers adhered to such a theory, that is not the same as saying that the use of their concepts in accounting requires subscribing to such positions. For example, the idea that joint costs need not be allocated if the accountants' concern is with the marginal costs does not seem to imply any theory of value.

(Though such a procedure may actually cause problems for the organisation of the firm!) Much of the argument is based on the view that the notion of opportunity cost is vital to 'proper' accounting, though some have doubted whether such a notion is of much practical help to accountants (Gould, in Edey and Yamey, 1974; Amey, 1969). Overall, the thrust of such arguments is the importance of an evaluation by accountants of alternatives in resource usage – not prima facie a particularly marginalist objective.

Both Cherns, and Tinker and associates, criticise accountants for focusing on financial calculation. Clearly this is a valid criticism of existing accounting practice – but it has its limits. First, as everyone knows, financial accounting does not of course mean looking only at *market* prices. A large part of accounting practice in the UK is concerned with non-market prices of one kind or another – shadow prices are quite commonly used. More contentious is, of course, a technique like cost-benefit analysis. Cooper and Sherer (1984, p. 223) criticise this as 'where incommensurate dimensions are compressed into the single dimension of money and valued in relation to market prices'. Such criticism alerts us to a danger of cost-benefit analysis, but it is also problematic in its presumption that some alternative non-monetary calculation can be readily made, and that the only prices that can be used are *market* prices. In the absence of clearly superior alternatives, it could be asserted that there is a scope for an *expansion* of cost-benefit analysis, albeit with recognition (which in any case seems well accepted) of the problems of such measures. (My own favourite example being the lack of assessment of the enormous sums of money spent on keeping relatively small numbers of prisoners in highly secure prisons in the UK.)

More generally a critique of market-oriented accounting ignores the arguments for a continuation of a substantial role for markets under socialism. In the kind of feasible socialism of Nove, firms would continue to be separate financial entities, albeit the financial aspects would, of course, not exhaust the forms of accounting under such socialism (a point returned to below, under my next heading).

In summary, Cherns and Tinker do not provide very much help in speculating on the role of accounting under socialism. Both critiques are pitched away from accounting *per se*. Cherns focuses on general theories of organisation and the role of measurement. Tinker emphasises the role of economic theory in accounting. Neither directly focuses either on the functions of accounting nor on its subdivisions. These issues will now be discussed.

FUNCTIONS AND TYPES OF ACCOUNTING

The perceived functions of accounting partly depend upon the perceived functions of the management in the firm. Commonly in managerial ideology (or at least its formal rhetoric), management is seen as a technical practice, with accounting a technical tool for the management of the firm (see, for instance, CBI, 1983). Such a view is given superficial support by the clear advances in the technical sophistication of management over recent years. However this technical sophistication (including more complex accounting systems) may often provide simply more ammunition for groups within firms in which, for various reasons, the scope of bargaining and accommodation has actually increased not decreased (Batstone, 1977, pp. 214–7). (The economists' theory of the firm which comes closest to this view is that of Cyert and March (1965), albeit this insight is greatly clouded by an oversimple view about the scope and character of such bargaining.)

Under 'feasible socialism' such bargaining and conflicts within firms would of course continue. The firm under socialism would not belie Hopwood's (in Arnold et al., 1980, p. 224) assertion that 'the organisation is rarely an assembly of the agreed. Debate and deliberation are almost inevitable features of organisational life'. What is of interest is the ways in which the character and scope of conflict would be shifted, and what the role of accounting would be in such circumstances.

The notion of feasible socialism derives in part from the acceptance that firms could *never* be simply the relays of orders from a central planning authority. One way of thinking of this, popular amongst economists, is in terms of information. The information requirements to plan the incredibly large number of decisions which are made by all the producing agents in the economy are such that some degree of autonomy for those units is inescapable. 'Perfect computation' is as impossible a goal as perfect competition. The ideal of planning everything from the centre rests on the assumption that this would secure the triumph of the 'public purpose' (however arrived at) in production in the economy. The impossibility of such an ideal means we must accept that there will be conflicts between the objectives of individual firms and the 'public purpose'.

Of course the 'objectives of firms' should not be read in some 'simple maximising' framework, however exactly this is constructed.[5] So the conflict will not be a simple dichotomous one between, say, a firm trying to maximise average income per worker, versus the 'public purpose' trying to minimise production costs. Rather the 'public purpose', via a variety of 'agencies' (including competition in product and capital markets as well as agencies in the more usual sense), will attempt to regulate and bias the firm's decision-making in a number of directions.

So feasible socialism implies a set of regulatory bodies, some of which in *formal intent* might not be very different from such bodies as the Equal Opportunities Commission or the Commission of Racial Equality, as they impinge on employment practices. These bodies may be seen as imposing a form of social accounting or social audit on companies. However, as Medawar (1976, pp. 392–93) emphasises, there is a deal of differences between social accounting/social auditing and social accountability, the former being concerned with changing company reporting, the latter meaning processes whereby those with decision-making powers 'propose, explain and justify the use of those powers to those without'.

Although the distinction between 'social' and other forms of accountability is ultimately rather unhelpful, Medawar's point is a very important one. It implies a multiplication of the forms of 'external' accounting by the firm, and much more stringent scrutiny by external agencies of the firm's conduct. So auditing of the firm would be greatly enhanced under such a regime. Of course the audited accounts (in this broad sense) of the firm would still be in part a form of legitimation and rationalisation by the firm of its decisions (Burchell et al., 1980, pp. 17–18). In a sense this is the point – legitimation of the firm's activities would be much more important, as much more problematic, under feasible socialism. Legitimation and rationalisation may of course be obfuscatory and self-serving, but it does open up to some extent the managerial decisions of the firm, for legitimation can rarely be *pure* obfuscation – to some extent the 'goods' have to be delivered for legitimacy to be attained.

In Nove's feasible socialism, he envisages the credit-giving institutions as part of the nationalised, public sector. Now clearly, in some areas of the economy, this would be appropriate. In his terms, the externalities of some investment decisions would justify centralised decision-making. But if this were to apply to all investment decisions, then we would have central planning coming back via the back door. For the firm cannot make autonomous production decisions (what to produce and how to produce it) without having autonomous investment decisions. Hence I would argue that for large numbers of firms there would exist investment resources from institutions which functioned on a competitive basis. To be clear on this, the financial assets purchased by such institutions would not have any 'control' function in the firm, that is, they would be something akin to non-voting shares. Equally, the market would not function as a 'perfect market', but rather a diversity of institutions (publicly owned banks, pension funds, mutual societies and so on) would provide a diversity of assessments of the firms, and on this basis a diversity of types of funds as to loan period, security and so on.[6]

In relation to the co-operative sector, this diversity of financial institutions would provide the complete external financial framework of their activities, that is, there would be no state role in financing. For the socialised sector the matter would be more complex. These larger enterprises would raise issues of, for example, internalisation of externalities in investment decisions which would require a state role in the provision of finance. But, as already suggested, this would not mean a comprehensive planning of investment. Rather it would involve state provision of funds to some firms/activities on terms different from those provided by any other agency. An obvious example would be long-term funding for large-scale, risky projects which would not find ready investors elsewhere – that is, the state would 'socialise the risk' in the investment.

Both sectors (socialised and co-operative) would then produce external financial reports which would not be so different from those currently produced by capitalist firms – for instance, they would include measures of liquidity and profitability. But there would also be a distinction between accounts provided by socialised and co-operative enterprises. The former's role would be on a larger scale, and would involve the deployment of state resources of a substantial kind. Their activities would be of much greater significance for overall macro-economic and resource allocation decisions than the activities of co-operatives. Hence the state would have to lay down a more standardised and rigorous format for external accounts than would be necessary for co-operatives. To put the point summarily: both types of enterprise would have to account to external agencies of 'social audit' and sources of funds. But socialised enterprises would, as a consequence of their significance in the national economy, also have to be more accountable to the state as the agency of national economic management.

Firms would then be 'financially reproducing' in a framework of competition in both product and capital markets. So financial accounting would continue to be important. Of course, financial accounts produced by firms are not taken at face value by investing agencies today, and no doubt never could be. However a much greater public regulation of accounting standards would to some extent reduce the purely 'window-dressing' aspects of financial accounting, and this could also be helped by a much wider knowledge, both inside and outside companies, of accounting procedures, and hence a reduction in the capacity of firms to conjure up wholly misleading financial statements. (This last point is returned to at the end of this paper.)

The final and most contentious type of accounting is that of management accounting. This is the most contentious because for many people what is particularly at stake in feasible socialism is changes in the organisation of work, away from hierarchical forms of management with high levels of division of labour towards less hierarchical, more co-operative firms involving much greater task flexibility. In many views, management accounting is strongly implicated in current undesirable forms of work organisation, so its role under feasible socialism must be problematic. (See the papers in Part II of this book.)

Often the history of work organisation is told in much too simple terms. Most commonly there is a linear history of the development of scientific management which is seen as the realisation of the essence of capitalist production (Braverman, 1974; see Cutler, 1978). Alternatively there are complications of this theme, which see a twofold strategy by capitalism, but which holds to the same simplistic arguments of an unfolding history which emanates from simple principles (Friedman, 1977). Equally the relationship between scientific management and rigorous cost accounting can be presented as a relation of effect and necessary condition (Cherns, 1978, pp. 113–4).

Clearly the early formalisations of cost accounting did owe something to the scientific management movement (Parker, 1969). But, on the one hand, scientific management was both a much less simple and a much less successful strategy than is often implied, and on the other hand there is no reason to reduce the character of cost accounting to the circumstances of its birth. In the same way, National Income accounting, first developed to manage the economy, and especially to prevent inflation, in wartime, came later to be used for quite different principles, that is, measuring 'welfare' in different countries.

The point to be argued is that whatever the circumstances of its birth and past evolution, management accounting in a crucial sense (to be outlined) must be retained under feasible socialism. The thesis is that *some* of the functions of management accounting are independent of the capitalist/socialist framework. If we are talking of enterprises which involve a substantial division of labour, *whatever* the form of that division, or however it is arrived at, then problems of co-ordination of the production process will arise, and there will have to be managed, that is, organised so as to 'produce the goods'.

Equally, if we accept that there will be issues of how best to produce those goods, and competing views on the merits of different methods, some forms of costing and budgeting will be necessary. These costings may involve evaluations of such elements as the stress and other psychological costs, the potential physical dangers, and other costs not normally included in the corpus of management accounting. And in some way or another such variegated elements will have to be made roughly commensurable in order for *any* decisions to be made.

Therefore feasible socialism does not involve the abolition of management accounting. Management accounting has never had just one objective, and it would not do so under feasible socialism. It would both shape and be shaped by the organisations in which it functioned. For example, we can assume that feasible socialism would move as far as possible towards the abolition of management as a separate body of agents, whilst recognising the need to retain the function. This in itself would reduce the 'mystique' of costing and budgeting.

Such a view of management accounting, which seems to run in the opposite direction to much radical discussion of accounting, undoubtedly raises a number of problems.

Under feasible socialism, management accounting would have much more of an accountability function than at present, though it would retain its 'control' function. A difficulty here is that accountability may require formalisation (so that what is being done by managerial agents is explicable to others), but such formalisation may be purely 'formal'. We know that in currently existing firms, informal accounting is very important, and this is not something which can easily be changed (Hopwood, in Carsberg and Hope, 1977, pp. 256–7; see also Batstone, 1979).

Secondly, whilst accountability would require formalisation of accounting practice, it may well be that this is not a route to efficiency in the firm. Certainly there is evidence that tight financial control within firms is not often linked to financial success, but may well be the first sign of impending demise (Burchell et al., 1980, pp. 12–13). This is presumably partly because too rigorous a control system is likely to inhibit flexibility and worsen the atmosphere within a firm, with bad effects for its efficient functioning. If task flexibility is seen as an important aspect of feasible socialism, then it too may be hindered by very tight controls which might be desirable for account-ability reasons.

Thus the whole question of combining accountability with partici-pative management systems, plus task flexibility, is a crucial issue for accounting under feasible socialism – but very little work has been done in this area (Cooper, in Bromwich and Hopwood, 1981, pp. 181–2).

Some discussion has been generated in Sweden in the context of the movement towards autonomous work groups. In one view (Malmberg, 1980) such groups could be financially autonomous, and hence each one a profit centre. Whilst such a point is of interest, and is linked to the spreading of accounting competences, it leaves the organisational consequences of different accounting regimes unex-plored. It treats accounting as a kind of neutral instrument to be deployed to achieve organisational goals, and entirely subordinated to those goals. This ignores the problem of, for example, the exist-ence of large numbers of small profit centres for trying to develop co-operative relations within the firm as a whole. Small-scale ac-counting units may have positive aspects for purposes of democracy, but be problematic with respect to other objectives of feasible socialism.

EVERYONE THEIR OWN ACCOUNTANT

Finally, let us return to the objectives of feasible socialism as outlined at the beginning of this paper. It was argued there that one of those objectives is the 'generalisation of competences'. Clearly this is very important in the context of the internal organisation of the firm. A reduction in the extent of the intra-firm division of labour obviously requires that task competences be extended. Equally, a system of industrial democracy, that is, participation in some form or another by employees in management, has long been recognised to require training in the appropriate skills (Schuller, 1982). Clearly accounting is one such skill. So the 'generalisation of competences' may be seen as a *precondition* of any effective form of industrial democracy. But one may, to some extent, turn this on its head. Is not a major *purpose* of industrial democracy, of feasible socialism, generally, to generalise competences? Hence in looking at possible forms of such democracy we may argue that an *objective* is 'everyone their own accountant'.

Such a slogan requires some justification, as it clearly conflicts with a widely held view of accounting as a kind of excrescence on the body economic, to be got rid of under socialism. It should be clear from previous sections that this slogan is not based on any view of accounting as an 'objective knowledge', which everyone should possess. It is fully accepted that accounting is a conceptually-based apparatus, not an observational code. The point is that in some forms that apparatus is a necessary condition for feasible socialism, and that if this socialism is to be democratic, that apparatus should be part of the common stock of knowledge.

An analogy with language may help to make the point. We know that language is never neutrally descriptive; by language we are always interpellated into specific discourses and (at some remove) specific social relations. But this is not widely regarded as a reason for opposing language acquisition. Rather language acquisition is more often seen as a precondition for an effective effort to change discourse and social relations.

This analogy maybe extended further. Literacy, like language, is always inscribed in particular social relations. Prior to its generalisation, the possession of literacy was itself important to those social relations – the literate were also often the powerful, it was one condition of their power. The generalisation of competence in literacy has transformed that power relationship directly, as well as indirectly bringing others into challenge. (Note, for example, how modern political parties presuppose generalised literacy).

It has been rightly argued that the extension of accounting has often led to the growth of that accounting as part of an unchallengeable expertise (Hopwood, 1984). But in response to this point there are two strategies. One is to try and restrict the domain of accounting. This, the earlier parts of this paper have suggested, is both undesirable and unattainable. The alternative strategy is to challenge expertise by making *everyone* an 'expert'. If in the land of the blind the one-eyed is king, the best strategy is the general restoration of sight, not a reduction in the use of vision.

Notes

1. I am grateful to Stuart Burchell, Mike Sherer and Grahame Thompson for helpful comments.
2. This section is based a great deal on discussions in the Birkbeck seminar on 'Politics and the State'.
3. I owe this notion to Stephan Feuchtwang.
4. I owe this point to Stuart Burchell.
5. 'Simple maximising' has been applied not only to the capitalist economy (e.g. Tomlinson, 1984) but also to the state socialist (e.g. Granick, 1975, pp. 11–13, 88–128) and the 'market socialist' (e.g. Vanek, 1975).
6. This does not of course rule out a role for subsidies and other forms of intervention by central government, nor, of course, searching for means of breaking up the current homogeneity in the views of financial institutions, based on a small network of stockbrokers and merchant bankers.

Bibliography

Althusser, L., *For Marx* (New York: Viking, 1970).
Amey, L. R., *The Efficiency of Business Enterprises* (London: Allen and Unwin, 1969).
Arnold, J., B. Carsberg, R. Scapens, (eds), *Topics in Management Accounting* (Deddington: Philip Allan, 1980).
Arrow, K., *The Limits of Organisation* (New York: Norton, 1974).
Batstone, E., 'Management and Industrial Democracy' in *Industrial Democracy: International Views* (Warwick: Industrial Relations Research Unit, 1977).
Batstone, E., 'Systems of Domination Accommodation and Industrial Democracy' in T. Burns, L. Karlson, and V. Rus, (eds), *Work and Power* (London: Sage Publications Ltd., 1979).
Braverman, H., *Labour and Monopoly Capital* (New York: Monthly Review, 1974).
Bromwich, M. and A. Hopwood (eds), *Essays in British Accounting Research* (London: Pitman, 1981).
Bullock, *Report of the Committee of Inquiry into Industrial Democracy* Cmnd 6706 (London: HMSO, 1977).
Burchell, S., C. Chubb, A. Hopwood, S. Hughes, J. Napathiet, 'The Roles of Accounting in Organisations and Society', *Accounting, Organisation and Society* (1980), pp. 5–27.
CBI, *Response to the Government's Consultative Document on Draft EC Directive on Procedures for Informing and Consulting Employees (The 'Vredeling' Directive) and Draft EC Fifth Directive on the Harmonisation of Company Law* (London: CBI, 1983).
Campbell, R. W., *Accounting in Soviet Planning and Management* (Cambridge, Mass: Harvard University Press, 1963).
Carsberg, B. and T. Hope, (eds), *Current Issues in Accounting* (Deddington: Philip Allan, 1977).

Cherns, A. B., 'Alienation and Accountancy', *Accounting, Organisations and Society* (1978), pp. 105–14.

Cockburn, C., *The Local State* (London: Pluto Press Ltd., 1977).

Cooper, D. J., 'Discussion (of Tinker 1980)', *Accounting, Organisations and Society* (1980), pp. 161–6.

Cooper, D. J., 'A Social and Organisational View of Management Accounting' in Bromwich, M. and Hopwood A., *Essays in British Accounting Research* (Pitman: London, 1981).

Cooper, D. J. and M. Sherer, 'The Value of Corporate Accounting Reports: Arguments for a Political Economy of Accounting', *Accounting, Organisations and Society* (1984), pp. 207–32.

Crosland, A., *The Future of Socialism* (London: Dent, 1956).

Cutler, A., 'The Romance of Labour', *Economy and Society* (1978), pp. 74–95.

Cyert, R. and March, J., *A Behavioural Theory of the Firm* (New York: Prentice-Hall, 1965).

Dahl, R. A., *After the Revolution?* (New Haven, Conn.: Yale University Press, 1970).

Edey, C. and B. Yamey, (eds), *Debits, Credits, Finance and Profits* (London: Sweet and Maxwell, 1974).

Friedman, A., *Industry and Labour: Class Struggle at Work and Monopoly Capitalism* (London: Macmillan, 1977).

Gould, J. R., 'Opportunity Cost: The London Tradition' in C. Edey, and B. Yamey, *Debits, Credits, Finance and Profits* (London: Sweet and Maxwell, 1974).

Granick, D., *Enterprise Guidance in Eastern Europe* (Cambridge, Mass: Harvard University Press, 1975).

Hindess, B., *Parliamentary Democracy and Socialist Politics* (London: Routledge and Kegan Paul, 1983).

Hopwood, A., 'Accounting and Organisational Behaviour' in B. Carsberg, and T. Hope, (eds), *Current Issues in Accounting* (Deddington: Philip Allan, 1977).

Hopwood, A., 'The Organisational and Behavioural Aspects of Budgetting and Control' in J. Arnold, B. Carsberg, R. Scapens, (eds), *Topics in Management Accounting* (Deddington: Philip Allan, 1980).

Hopwood, A., 'Accounting and the Pursuit of Efficiency' in A. Hopwood, and C. Tomkins, (eds), *Issues in Public Sector Accounting* (Deddington: Philip Allan, 1984).

Malmberg, A., 'The Impact of Job Reform on Accounting Systems' in G. Kanawaty, (ed.), *Managing and Developing New Forms of Work Organisation* (Geneva: ILO 1980).

Medawar, C., 'The Social Audit: A Polemical View', *Accounting, Organisations and Society* (1976), pp. 389–94.

Nelson, D., 'Scientific Management, Systematic Management and Labour', *Business History Review* (1974), pp. 56–83.

Nove, A., *The Economics of Feasible Socialism* (London: George Allen and Unwin, 1983).

Parker, R. H., *Management Accounting* (London: Macmillan, 1969).

Pateman, C., *Participation and Democratic Theory* (Cambridge University Press, 1970).

Rose, N., 'Problems in the Theory of Fetishism', *Ideology and Consciousness* (1977), pp. 27–54.

Rose, N., 'Socialism and Social Policy: The Problems of Inequality', *Politics and Power* (1980), pp. 111–36.

Schuller, T., 'Learning and Democracy at the Workplace' in H. Glennerster, (ed.), *The Future of the Welfare State* (London: Heinemann, 1982).

Stigler, G., 'The Economics of Information', *Journal of Political Economy* (1961), pp. 213–25.

Tinker, A. M., 'Towards a Political Economy of Accounting', *Accounting, Organisations and Society* (1980), pp. 147–60.

Tinker, A. M., B. P. Merino, M. D. Neimark, 'The Normative Origins of Positive Theories: Ideology and Accounting Thought', *Accounting, Organisations and Society* (1982), pp. 167–200.

Tomlinson, J., *The Unequal Struggle? British Socialism and the Capitalist Enterprise* (London: Methuen, 1982).

Tomlinson, J., 'Economic and Sociological Theories of the Enterprise and Industrial Democracy', *British Journal of Sociology* (1984), pp. 591–605.

Tomlinson, J., 'Democracy Inside the Black Box? Neo-Classical Theories of the Firm and Industrial Democracy', *Economy and Society* (1986), pp. 220–50.

Tucker, K., (ed), *Business History, Selected Readings* (London: Macmillan, 1975).

Vanek, J., (ed), *Self-Management* (Harmondsworth: Penguin, 1975).

Whittington, C., 'Accounting and Economics' in B. Carsberg and T. Hope, *Current Issues in Accounting* (Deddington: Philip Allen, 1977).

Winter, S., 'Economic Natural Selection and the Theory of the Firm', *Yale Economic Essays* (1963), pp. 225–72.

Winter, S., 'Optimisation and Evolution in the Theory of the Firm' in R. H. Day and T. Groves, (eds), *Adaptive Economic Models* (New York: Academic Press, 1975).

Yamey, B., 'Accounting and the Rise of Capitalism' in K. Tucker, (ed.), *Business History: Selected Readings* (London: Macmillan, 1975).

Part II
Accounting and the Control of Labour

5 Factories of the Past and of the Future: the Impact of Robotics on Workers and Management Accounting Systems

S. Mark Young and Jon S. Davis[1]

Baley said, 'Come now, Daneel. The Third Law states: "A robot must protect its own existence, as long as such protection does not conflict with the First or Second Law." The Second Law states: "A robot must obey the orders given it by a human being, except where such orders would conflict with the First Law." And the First Law states: "A robot may not injure a human being or, through inaction, allow a human being to come to harm." A human being could order a robot to destroy itself – and a robot would then use his own strength to smash his own skull. And if a human being attacked a robot, that robot could not fend off the attack without harming the human being, which would violate the First Law.'

Isaac Asimov, *The Robots of Dawn* (1983, p. 38).

Just as 1984 was once viewed as being a time in the distant future, the science fiction creation known as a robot[2] has become a phenomenon of the present. The use of robots all over the world has become commonplace. Depending on one's definition (See Appendix I) there are approximately 7000 robots in use in the United States, 80 000 in Japan, and over 400 in the United Kingdom (Chase and Aquilano, 1985; Scarborough, 1981).

Currently, much is being written about the potential effects of robotics in the present manufacturing environment and in factories of the future (Scarborough, 1981; Smith and Wilson, 1982; Ayres and Miller, 1983; Chase and Aquilano, 1985). Research in robotics can be linked to the resurgence of interest on the impact of new technology and its implications for workers among social scientists including sociologists; political scientists (Braverman, 1974; Edwards, 1979; Burawoy, 1979; Kamata, 1982; Wood, 1982; Morris-Suzuki, 1984; Knights, Willmott and Collinson, 1985); management theorists (Argote, Goodman and Schkade, 1983; Schonberger, 1982, 1986), and accountants (Kaplan, 1983, 1984a, 1984c; Seed, 1984; Young, 1986).

While the literature offers conjectures regarding the changes brought about by robotics on manufacturing culture, little attention is paid to the role of the management accounting system in these changes. Proponents of the robotics revolution often expound benefits such as increased efficiency and the reduction of hazardous jobs[3] (Ayres and Miller, 1983). However, new technology, along with changes in management accounting systems, may give rise to changes in manufacturing culture that could further result in increased worker alienation.[4]

In this paper, we discuss the role that the management accounting system has played historically as a 'paper replica of production' (in Braverman's terms), designed to take the problem of manufacturing creation out of the hands of workers. As a result of this paper regime, the worker's task has become more discrete and simplified, focusing on manual rather than mental work. In response, the existing 'manufacturing culture', that includes group norms, rules, and rituals, has evolved to cope with, and resist, the further deskilling of their jobs, and the alienation that results.

Regardless of the kinds of work performed, laborers have retained one of their most important resources – their tacit skills (Manwaring and Wood, 1985) or private information regarding how best to perform tasks. These skills are protected principally by the culture of the shop floor. However, the introduction of robotics will disrupt the developed manufacturing culture by changing the sociology of the work group, stripping workers of their last resource via the transfer of their tacit skills to computer software. This software programs robots to perform the same tasks that workers performed. We argue that the changing nature of the work group and the stripping away of tacit skills lead to further alienation for those working alongside robots, and those whose function it is to monitor and coordinate robotic operations. The notion of the paper replica of production will achieve its penultimate form by eliminating large numbers of workers from the shop floor and by performing both the creation (through software and artificial intelligence) and execution functions of manufacturing.

The paper will proceed with an analysis of the role of management accounting systems in factories of the past[5] followed by an account of production-line culture as it has evolved as a response to the environment. Subsequently, the impact of both robotics and the concomitant changes in the accounting and control system on this culture will be assessed.

FACTORIES OF THE PAST

Management Accounting Systems and Manufacturing

In conventional thinking, a major function of the management accounting system is to provide measurements of selected types of organisational activities.[6] The resulting measurements are used by management to control and motivate behaviour, and to aid in assessing performance.

Another view is that measurement and accountability of behaviour serves to coerce and discipline individuals so that the interests of those with power can be met (Roberts and Scapens, Chapter 6). In business organisations these measurements or accounts serve management (or higher order stakeholders) by attempting to objectify the manufacturing environment in the hope of quantifying a complex process. This objectification process tends to drive the sociology of the work environment. Thus, accounting and information systems are neither neutral nor impartial, but can be used by management and other oganisational stakeholders to suit their own ends (Birnberg, Turopolec and Young, 1983; Hopwood, 1986).

An example of the use of accounting systems to serve management's purposes occurred with the rise of Scientific Management, popular at the turn of the century. This system attempted to increase the efficiency of workers by determining and setting work standards for as many aspects of the worker's task as possible. Each aspect of a worker's daily functioning was scrutinised, through time and motion studies, in order to increase efficiency.

In the era of Scientific Management, the standard cost accounting system facilitated the assessment of whether Taylor's time-and-motion studies were successful in transforming workers into more efficient producers (Epstein, 1978). The standard cost system generated accounting numbers from which work standards were developed. Chandler (1977) reports that the exclusive focus of these early cost accounting systems was on prime costs – direct materials and direct labour. The focus on direct labour proved to be crucial. The control problem and its emphasis on standard costs and piece-rates as controlling devices played a highly significant role in development of manufacturing culture.

An often overlooked, but extremely important, point to consider is the relationship between the standard costing system and the development of the piece-rate incentive system. Generally, piece-rate systems, as well as most other types of incentive schemes in manufacturing, are determined by a careful scrutiny of the standard costs involved in making a unit of product. The piece-rate paid the worker is a small percentage of its unit cost to produce (Horngren, 1982, p. 901). This point is crucial for a more complete understanding of the discussion of production-line culture, following in the next section.

Braverman (1974) suggests that Scientific Management facilitated the control of direct labour, separating mental and manual work through the creation of a 'paper replica of production'. This paper regime represented an accounting of physical events, moving the conceptual task of production, planning, design and record-keeping away from the shop floor to the management office. Braverman states (1974, p. 125),

> Thus in the setting of antagonistic social relations, of alienated labor, hand and brain become not just separated, but divided and hostile, and the human unity of hand and brain turns into its opposite, something less than human.

Scientific Management and the accompanying separation of the physical and mental elements of work removed the intrinsic satisfactions derived from the production process. Further, the management accounting and piece-rate incentive system associated with Scientific Management imposed a new rigidity on shop floor behaviour. These changes in the nature of work led to worker alienation. In response, workers developed methods of coping with and resisting the alienation from their work. These methods are embodied in aspects of 'manufacturing culture' as described in the section that follows.

The Nature of Production Line Culture in Factories of the Past

A significant body of research in industrial sociology examines behaviour on the shop floor (for example, Walker and Guest, 1952; Lupton, 1963; Roy, 1952, 1953, 1954; Whyte, 1955; Burawoy, 1979;

Knights and Collinson, 1985). Several of these studies, which vividly describe organisational culture, document the authors' experiences as workers on the production line. The possession of such phenomenological and historical data is crucial to our understanding of the work environment (Cooper, 1983).[7]

Of particular usefulness in understanding the work environment is the research performed by Roy (1952, 1953, 1954) and Burawoy (1979). This research, conducted in the same factory over a thirty-year interval, chronicles the evolution of production-line culture concomitant to environmental changes inside and outside the organisation. An historical investigation into the effects of Scientific Management on shop-floor culture provides a base on which to build predictions of cultural changes in the factory of the future. A brief review of Roy's work is of additional benefit; many of the terms that he coined or reported contributed to the formation of our lexicon of worker behaviour and culture on a production line.[8] Another study, by Roy (1959), is also reviewed because it clearly illustrates several dimensions of worker behaviour and culture not addressed in other research.

The Work of Roy

Between 1944 and 1945, Donald Roy studied shop-floor culture while he worked as a radial drill operator in a steel-processing plant. The most significant contribution of Roy's research was his graphic depiction of how workers restricted output and 'made out' under a piece-rate system. A multitude of techniques were observed, including *quota restriction*, which involved a culturally determined ceiling on production which labourers did not exceed when working on jobs with a high payoff ('gravy jobs'). Conversely, on jobs with a low piecework rate ('stinkers'), *goldbricking*, or using minimal effort to complete jobs was seen as an accepted practice. Other 'make-out' practices flourished: time records were manipulated so that over 100 per cent of standard output could be turned in (termed 'chiseling'), and kitties were established by workers where extra output could be kept and released when necessary. To successfully employ many of the 'make-out' practices, the co-operation of other shop groups was necessary. This co-operation was readily obtained in the face of unreasonable management practices and constant attempts to tighten standards.

Roy reported that the rationale for all of these practices was related to the piecerate standard-setting practices of the firm. Quota restriction was practiced because of the fear that time-and-motion men would lower the piecework rate if workers overproduced, and goldbricking was used by workers as a protest in the hope that piecerates would be raised. Likewise, chiseling and the establishment of kitties increased the opportunity for building slack in the face of tight standards. All of the 'make-out' practices observed by Roy served to protect workers from the alienating effects of Scientific Management and the paper regime.

Roy (1959) provides additional insight into the way that workers adapt to tasks devoid of intrinsic satisfaction. In this study, he researched the organisational culture in another factory setting where he was employed on a die-punching line with three other workers. The punching work, which consisted of placing a die and operating a lever, was boring and repetitive. In the face of such a task, Roy reports that the dominant source of job satisfaction was derived from informal social activity: there was frequent joking and verbal banter among the workers, occasionally punctuated with very brief rest periods entailing the consumption of food (for instance, 'banana time') and beverages (for example, 'coke time'). Through this inter-action, a complete but sensitively balanced sociocultural system evolved. This system was based on social status and included group norms and well-defined roles for individuals. However, the system's delicate equilibrium could be disrupted by small perturbations such as the violation of group norms.

Two key elements of Roy's work have relevance to the factory of the future. First, management was always battling with workers to get them to produce more. In response, workers developed both a social network to facilitate the fight against unreasonable manage-ment practices, and methods to use their knowledge and skills to time the flow of work that they produced. Workers knew how to manipu-late the system in order to cope with it. Second, Roy observed a sensitive sociocultural system whose functioning depended on the development of norms, rituals and games. Even the most tedious and boring of jobs could be coped with through this kind of group interaction.

The Work of Burawoy

Thirty years after Roy's work, Burawoy studied the same plant while working as a machine operator. Like Roy, he reports that the practice of 'making out' was widespread. Many of the techniques used in 1945 still existed on the production line of the 1970s. Quota restriction was still part of the shop-floor culture; as in 1945, workers still feared the spectre of standard increases. Burawoy also noted an apparent increase in the practice of keeping a 'kitty' (that is, banking excess output) over 1945 levels. To a lesser extent, goldbricking was also observed in 1975; the decrease being due to a reduction in the number of jobs with undesirable piece rates.

In contrast to the lack of change in individual gaming behavior noted over the thirty-year interval, strategies that required inter-group cooperation, such as 'chiseling', were much less common in 1975. This decrease was due to a distinct change in the production-line culture. Instead of the united front among workers in a 'war' against the time-study men and higher management observed by Roy, strategic alliances had to be bargained for in 1975. Burawoy hypothesised that this cultural shift from management-worker con-flict (and the resultant between-worker cooperation) to lateral be-tween-worker conflict and competition had several causes: (1) when compared to the pre-union 'whistle and whip' days of the past, the firm appeared magnanimous in the worker's view; (2) due to better union grievance machinery in 1975 and the increased size of the company (which insulated against market exigencies), employees were more fairly treated, and (3) management had used the system of 'making out' to its advantage, by encouraging competition among workers through the provision of a piece-rate and bonus system that was linked to specific production targets.

To summarise, while the major elements of Roy's observations prevailed in 1975, Burawoy noted a distinct change in the shop-floor culture. This insight is an enlightening aspect of Burawoy's work: the notion that management had simply legitimised 'making out', with workers 'consenting' to the rules of the game (however, see Knights and Collinson, 1985, for a critical review of Burawoy's study).

THE IMPLICATIONS OF ROBOTS ON THE WORKPLACE

Few will argue that robots will not bring any positive benefits to the workplace. It is widely acknowledged that perhaps the greatest benefit of robots is their ability to perform the most hazardous jobs, thereby reducing physical dangers for workers (Chase and Aquilano,

1985). However, with the introduction of robotics on the production-line, the existing manufacturing culture will be significantly
altered. In this section we address two of the consequent effects;
isolation and the deskilling of workers. Further, we consider the
concomitant effect on the management accounting system and a
resulting negative consequence for workers: increased alienation
from work.[9]

Alienation from Work

The distinction made by Israel regarding alienation is useful for our
discussion. Israel (1971) distinguishes between 'estranging processes'
– where conditions in the structure of the workplace induce alienation, and 'states of estrangement' – the resulting psychological
dispositions that result. In the review of Roy and Burawoy's work,
many of the behaviours, or states of estrangement, chronicled were
the result of particular estranging processes, the structural conditions
of production at the time. Robotics represents a new kind of estranging process; one that supercedes previous manufacturing technology.
While there are many ways in which alienation has been defined, we
consider two aspects of the construct: (1) estrangement from manufacturing culture and (2) participation in work that is not intrinsically
satisfying (Seeman, 1966), that is, work that requires little skill or
discretion.

In the Roy and Burawoy studies, it was evident that human
interaction was important for the development of group norms, rules
and culture. They presented convincing evidence that the satisfaction
derived from human interaction enabled workers to cope with alienation. Burawoy (1979, p. 81) makes it very clear, however, that these
are only 'relative satisfactions' and should not be construed as anything more than that. It is our contention that the introduction of
robots into the workplace will directly cause more alienation by (1)
disrupting the existing culture through reduction of the extent of
human interaction and isolation of workers, and (2) expropriating
from workers an extremely important resource, their knowledge
concerning the production process and their skill, resulting in work
requiring relatively less skill and discretion.

Isolation of workers

It is proposed that the robotics revolution will result in the complete
disruption of production-line culture and in the consequent alien-

ation of workers through increased isolation, displacement, or re-assignment to less fulfilling work. There is evidence supporting the proposition that workers remaining involved with post-robotic production report feelings of greater isolation. In a case study reporting worker reaction to the introduction of a robot in one factory (Argote, Goodman and Schkade, 1983, p. 33), robot operators reported decreased interactions with co-workers. For example, one operator said, 'I don't have time to talk with anyone . . . I'm isolated now'. Further support for the contention of increased isolation can be found in reports of premium payments, dubbed 'lonely pay', made to workers engaged in robot operation. Thus, it seems that much of the relative satisfactions derived from social interaction observed by Roy (1959) will be absent for workers who remain on the production line with work as intrinsically unsatisfying as Roy's die punching.

For workers who have been reassigned to other jobs (assuming that reassignment is possible), alienation will be generated through different means. To gain a competitive advantage in a world of heavily automated production, it will be necessary to channel resources into new product development rather than to development of new production techniques (since production will already be running with extreme efficiency).

With the advent of such an 'innovation economy', displaced workers will likely be assigned to information-production jobs (for instance, cf. Kaplan, 1984a; Morris-Suzuki, 1984) entailing such tasks as data entry. It seems unlikely that ex-production-line workers will be reassigned to jobs requiring specialised skills such as computer programming, given the extensive training required and the pre-existing labour supply of programmers. In some cases, however, unions are beginning to intercede at plants where robots are installed and to demand that shop-floor workers be retrained to perform all tasks covered by new technologies, including programming and maintenance of robots (Scarborough, 1981).

If unions are unsuccessful in their drive for retraining, one can conclude that, at best, the labourer's lot will not have changed much from the production line. Workers will still be facing ennui in their work.

The work of information production possesses some additional hazards capable of causing worker alienation. For example, if a job such as data entry (and other clerical work) is perceived by production workers as possessing less status than work on the production line, then job satisfaction could diminish. In addition, if the data entry performed by workers is done in relative isolation, it will be difficult for interaction with other workers to occur. Lack of interaction in this instance has several implications. Besides the alienating consequences of isolation, there will exist no opportunity for development of group norms such as quota restriction. Consequently management will be able to set standards for worker performance without cultural constraints. This will grant management a licence to pressure workers past their usual level of effort and may result in Tayloresque attitudes toward the worker. Kamata (1982) documents the alienation that he felt when subjected to working under similar conditions, when the cultural norm condoned a Tayloresque philosophy.

Workers' information and skills as a resource

Recently a significant literature has developed concerning Braverman's (1974) notion that workers are increasingly deskilled under new technology. For Braverman, deskilling has four characteristics: (1) the removal of a shop-floor worker's discretion concerning the planning and design of his or her work; (2) the division of work into smaller, meaningless tasks; (3) an increase in labour market demand for semiskilled and unskilled labourers to perform the increased number of meaningless tasks; (4) the replacement of the craft system with Scientific Management principles.

Braverman has come under criticism because of the simplicity of the relationship that he suggested (Zimbalist, 1979; Lee, 1982, Littler, 1982; Wood, 1982; Storey, 1983; Coombs, 1985; and Knights, Willmott and Collinson, 1985 in general provide excellent coverage of the debate). While a review of the debate goes beyond the scope of this paper, a particular critique of the concept of deskilling is germane. Specifically, Braverman's analysis fails to consider the existence of what Kusterer (1978) calls 'working knowledge' and what Manwaring and Wood (1985) call 'tacit skills' inherent in even the most menial tasks. Tacit skills (1) are acquired by a process of learning through experience; (2) incorporate different degrees of awareness, that is one can adapt one's skill to other unfamiliar situations and (3) have a cooperative component in that they lead workers to appreciate how their jobs relate to each other and to the production process. Under past production techniques and in most forms of new technology, tacit skills cannot be expropriated readily by management. However, with the introduction of robots on the assembly line, management gains access to the worker's tacit skills –

the last vestiges of the worker's knowledge concerning the production process. With the sharing of the worker's skills and information regarding the production process, it is proposed that he or she will have no value on the shop floor to a firm using robots.

Perhaps one way to view this problem is to frame it in agency theory terms. Agency research in management accounting (Baiman, 1982), has suggested that the private information of the worker (including tacit skills) is key when designing control systems including incentive contracts. Private information can include knowledge of one's productive capability, the number of units one can produce given certain parameters such as time, fatigue, response to incentives and one's skill level.

Empirical research on participation in standard setting and the creation of budgetary slack seems to be congruent with the notion of the importance of a subordinate's private information (Young, 1985). An agent's private information will always make him or her valuable to the organisation, because he/she has first-hand experience with the production process and is better able to make corrections and suggest improvements in the process. These abilities are tied to the skill level. Workers derive much of their pride on the job from their reputation in terms of skill, and gain much of their internal motivation and feelings of self-worth from how well they perform the task. Agency theory views the conflict between a worker and management (an agent and a principal) as one in which management attempts to obtain a worker's private information so that the process at hand can be improved. In return for parting with the information, the worker will be financially compensated via the employment contract. While much of agency research is modelled in a single period, an assumption appears to be that, in subsequent periods, the game will begin again under different informational and contractual conditions. Thus, workers will continue to obtain more new information in future periods, and new contracting devices will be used for trading on the information.

Certain elements of the worker's private information may be more easily acquired than others. For instance, management may be able to assess the number of units of a product that workers can make by observing their output over time. Management may also be able to infer something about the workers' skill level by observing their output, but the tacit skills of the workers will go undetected by simply observing output.

With the introduction of robots, it is not clear how long workers will be able to trade on their information. We argue that even their tacit skills are in jeopardy. The work of Morris-Suzuki (1984) offers a possible explanation by providing some clear insights into the relationships among workers' knowledge, their labour, and machinery.

Management knows that a major part of the value that workers bring to the shop floor is their information and knowledge about the production process. Morris-Suzuki suggests that, with current technology using robotics, it is computer software that drives the robotics systems, which in turn embodies workers' knowledge. Morris-Suzuki (1984, p. 109) paints a vivid picture of management's new-found ability to acquire information from workers:

> The picture is one of a worker, typically a highly-skilled spray painter, guiding the arm of a robot through the motions of a precise and complex task. The machine – a continuous path play-back robot – will then be able endlessly to replicate the exact movements of the human being. Almost certainly, the worker who has been selected to 'teach' the robot is the most experienced or the most efficient of this section of the factory's workforce. According to one's point of view, the picture may be seen as representing the ever-progressing triumph of technology, or the ultimate irony of automation – the mechanisation of a dreary and potentially dangerous job, or the moment at which years of carefully acquired skill are transferred to an inanimate object, and the human individual is simultaneously rendered redundant.

Once a worker's skill is transferred to the software package, there is a distinct physical separation of the worker from his or her knowledge.

Without the private information on which to contract, workers will clearly begin to lose their value in the eyes of the firm. More threatening to workers, though, is the notion that they are giving up or turning over those years of accumulated wisdom. Additionally, many robotics firms now envision that through the use of advanced software, robots will be able to learn how to perform tasks more efficiently themselves without the use of humans or human intervention (see O'Neill, 1984 for a recent example). With the advent of advanced software on the production line, the marginal value of a worker's private information will approach zero. Thus, there will be a decreasing incentive for the firm to contract with workers. Child (1985, p. 119) contends that, despite different orientations, the concept of factories without workers has been the goal of 'engineers and social visionaries' for years. Certainly this objective will be realised soon in some industries (O'Neill, 1984). Once the tacit skills of the job are taken from the workers they will face increased dehumanisation and alienation from their work.

From the observations made above it appears that Asimov's first law of robotics (quoted at the beginning of the paper) may be violated. That is, the human production-line work force will be injured through increased alienation. In the final section of this paper, the implications of the robotics revolution will be extended to accounting control systems.

Implications for Accounting and Control Systems

We have shown that the effects of robotics on manufacturing organisations will alter the nature of manufacturing culture. In addition, the management control system designed to account for and control production will be changed. In this section we discuss some aspects of these changes.

The traditional elements of control systems have been standard setting and their adjustment; measuring and reporting performance, and providing feedback. In the factory of the future, all of these facets of the control system will be modified.

For instance, the notion of work standards may be altered. With fewer workers and more robots on the production line, how will standards be determined? From management's point of view, standard setting may be based on the efficiency of the robot without concern for human shortcomings, that is, motivation, fatigue, boredom, illness, etc.). This approach has been suggested by Whaley (1982). He argues that such an output measure will simplify management's task of determining work standards by eliminating worker-input mechanisms such as participative budgeting and MBO. The implications are that opportunities for 'making out' as well as the building of slack into work standards will be eliminated, thus confirming our earlier contention that the introduction of robots will destroy the cultural insulation protecting workers.

Any management accounting system dependent to such an extent on the performance of robots in the standard setting process can only serve the function that Taylor originally intended. A more humanistic approach to standard setting in the factory of the future could be accomplished through techniques suggested by Japanese management theorists (Schonberger, 1982). One effective technique includes worker control of the pace of the production process. Furthermore, standards for workers could be different than those for the robots, and determined participatively.

Apart from dealing with normal activities on the production line, measures of workers' performance may include how well they monitor the robots under their control. For instance, the locus for the responsibility of quality control including robot dysfunction may reside with workers. Workers may be responsible for detecting errors in the production process or preventing errors from occurring. Their rewards may be based on the minimisation of errors in process and output. Thus, human workers may serve an integral role in the monitoring function of the management control system. As an example, O'Neill (1984) describes a factory in Japan that uses robots and workers to produce other robots and other small machines. In the daytime, nineteen workers are on the machining floor alongside robots. However, on the night shift, operations are performed entirely by robots, with only one worker in the control room to monitor performance. The monitoring function becomes extremely important in factories where dangerous substances are either inputs or outputs of the production process (that is, chemical plants and nuclear power plants). Such factories represent prime candidates for robotics installations because of the high rates of hazardous jobs.

Where workers do not participate on the production line, the measurement of robot performance will most likely occur through an integrated network of minicomputers connected to a mainframe computer (many of which will be attached to the robots). This is what Edwards (1979) and Hopper et al. (1986) label as technical control. Workers will again monitor printouts, and performance information will be recorded directly into performance reports.

For the most part, the function of feedback via traditional accounting reports will become obsolete, except for those workers monitoring machines. Task feedback for those workers will probably be obtained much more readily as soon as exceptions are found in the production process.

The robotics revolution in manufacturing may lead to broader implications for organisations. As the role of the management accounting system becomes more and more routinised and standardised at the operations level of the firm, greater emphasis will be placed on its use in the coordination of higher level activities and 'capital' within the firm and across multidivisional and multinational firms (Johnson, 1980).

Notes

1. We would like to acknowledge the helpful comments of Jake Birnberg, Anthony Hopwood, Charles Perrow, Mike Shields, John Storey, Tony Tinker, and Gerrit Wolf.
2. The word 'robot' is derived from the Czech word 'robotnik' meaning worker or serf. See Appendix I for the current definitions of robots.
3. Even with robots, physical dangers still exist for workers remaining on the shop floor. Already one death has been reported in Michigan in this nascent phase of the robotics revolution (Centers for Disease Control, 1984).
4. This paper focuses on those factories where workers and robots work together as opposed to factories that are fully automated with virtually no workers.
5. The term factories of the past has been coined and used in this paper to denote any factory facility where robots, CAD/CAM and other automation procedures are not in use.
6. However, Burchell, Clubb, Hopwood, Hughes and Nahapiet (1980), Hayes (1983) and Cooper, Hayes and Wolf (1981) suggest many other functions that the accounting system can serve in organisations.
7. Braverman (1974) is very critical of other methods such as attitude surveys when trying to assess the cultural milieu in a production line, but is very supportive of participant-observer studies.
8. In the discussion that follows, it is by no means our intention to romanticise factories of the past. We do not contend that the shop floor of the past provided ideal or even satisfactory conditions for production-line workers. It is our intention, however, to illustrate the kinds of behaviours that arise as a result of particular aspects of management accounting systems.
9. Apart from the possibility of increased alienation from work, the introduction of robots may have another negative consequence for workers, namely, increased job displacement. Projections of potential displacement vary, however, according to the results of the Carnegie Mellon University Robotics Survey (Ayres and Miller, 1981), 90 per cent of current robot users fall within the metal-working sector. Ayres and Miller (1981) note that based on the average weighted response of the percentage of jobs which robots could do, it appears that nearly half a million of these operatives (workers) could potentially be replaced by Level 1 (current generation) robots. The figure nearly doubles if Level 2 robots with rudimentary sensing capabilities were available. Extrapolating to all manufacturing, they concluded that the total potential displacement by Level 2 robots could total three million out of eight million workers presently employed in all manufacturing sectors. The time frame for this displacement was estimated to be at least twenty years. However, by the year 2025 it is possible that a third generation of robots may be developed, capable of replacing the entire operative manufacturing workforce (about eight per cent of the total workforce, or eight million workers). However, if modernisation of production through robotics succeeds in increasing sales through lowered production costs, the effects of displacement may be substantially reduced or

elimanated in the long-run through an increase in jobs in other sectors of the economy (Lublin, 1981; *Personnel*, 1981).

Bibliography

Aleksander, I., *Reinventing Man – The Robot Becomes Reality* (Harmondsworth: Penguin, 1983).

Argote, L., P. Goodman, and D. Schkade, 'The Human Side of Robotics: How Workers React to a Robot', *Sloan Management Review* (Spring 1983) pp. 31–41.

Asimov, I., *The Robots of Dawn* (New York: Ballantine Books, 1983).

Ayres, R. and S. Miller, *The Impacts of Industrial Robotics*, Report CMU–RI–TR–81–7, The Robotics Institute, Carnegie Mellon University, 1981.

Ayres, R. & S. Miller, *Robotics: Applications and Social Implications* (Cambridge, Mass: Sallinger Publishing Co., 1983).

Baiman, S., 'Agency Research in Management Accounting: A Survey', *Journal of Accounting Literature* (1982) pp. 154–213.

Birnberg, J. G., L. Turopolec, & S. M. Young, 'The Organizational Context of Accounting', *Accounting, Organizations, and Society* (1983) pp. 111–30.

Braverman, H., *Labor and Monopoly Capital* (New York: Monthly Review Press, 1974).

Burawoy, M., *Manufacturing Consent-Changes in the Labor Process under Monopoly Capitalism* (University of Chicago Press, 1979).

Burchell, S., C. Clubb, A. G. Hopwood, J. Hughes, and J. Nahapiet, 'The Role of Accounting in Organizations and Society', *Accounting, Organizations, and Society* (1980) pp. 5–27.

Centers for Disease Control – Weekly Report, Atlanta, Georgia, July 1984.

Chandler, A. D., *The Visible Hand: The Managerial Revolution in American Business* (Cambridge, Mass: Harvard University Press, 1977).

Chase, R. B. & N. J. Aquilano, *Production and Operations Management – A Life Cycle Approach* (Homewood, Ill.: Richard D. Irwin, 1985).

Cherns, A. B. 'Alienation and Accounting', *Accounting, Organizations and Society* (1978) pp. 105–14.

Child, J., 'Managerial Strategies, New Technology and the Labor Process', in D. Knights et al. (eds), *Job Redesign* (Aldershot: Gower, 1985) pp. 107–41.

Coombs, R., 'Automation, Management Strategies and Labour Process Change', in D. Knights et al. (eds), *Job Redesign* (Aldershot: Gower, 1985), pp. 142–70.

Cooper, D., 'Tidiness, Muddle and Things: Commonalities and Divergencies in Two Approaches to Management Accounting Research', *Accounting, Organizations and Society* (1983), pp. 269–86.

Cooper, D., D. C. Hayes, & F. Wolf, 'Accounting in Organized Anarchies: Understanding and Designing Accounting Systems in Ambiguous Situations', *Accounting, Organizations and Society* (1981), pp. 175–92.

Edwards, R., *Contested Terrain – The Transformation of the Workplace in the Twentieth Century* (New York: Basic Books, 1979).

Epstein, M. J., *The Effect of Scientific Management on the Development of the Standard Cost System* (New York: Arno Press, 1978).

Erickson, K., 'On Work and Alienation', American Sociological Association, 1985 Presidential Address, *American Sociological Review* (1986), pp. 1–8.

Hayes, D. C., 'Accounting for Accounting: A Story About Managerial Accounting', *Accounting, Organizations and Society* (1983), pp. 241–9.

Hines, C. and G. Searle, *Automatic Unemployment* (London: Earth Resources Research, 1979). Designed by Reg Boorer, FOE Publicity, Ltd.

Hopper, T., D. Cooper, T. Capps, E. A. Lowe, and J. Mouritsen, 'Financial Control in the Labour Process: Managerial Strategies and Worker Resistance in the National Coal Board', in *Managing the Labour Process*, H. Willmott and D. Knights (eds) (Aldershot: Gower, 1986) pp. 109–141.

Hopwood, A., *Accounting and Human Behavior* (Englewood Cliffs, NJ: Prentice-Hall, 1974).

Hopwood, A., 'Accounting and Organizational Action', Paper presented at the National Meeting of the American Accounting Association, New York, August, 1986.

Horngren, C. T., *Cost Accounting – A Managerial Emphasis* (Englewood Cliffs, NJ: Prentice-Hall, 1982).

Israel, J., *Alienation* (Newton, Ma.: Allyn & Bacon, 1971).

Johnson, T., 'Work and Power', in G. Esland, & G. Salaman, (eds), *The Politics of Work and Occupations* (Milton Keynes: Open University Press, 1980), pp. 335–71.

Kamata, S., *Japan in the Passing Lane – An Insider's Account of Life in a Japanese Auto Factory* (New York: Pantheon Books, 1982).

Kaplan, R., 'Measuring Manufacturing Performance, A New Challenge for Managerial Accounting Research', *Accounting Review* (1983), pp. 686–705.

Kaplan, R., 'Accounting Lag: The Obsolescence of Cost Accounting Systems' (Unpublished Manuscript, Harvard Business School, 1984a).

Kaplan, R., 'Yesterday's Accounting Undermines Production', *Harvard Business Review* (July/August 1984c), pp. 95–101.

Knights, D. & D. Collinson, 'Redesigning Work on the Shop Floor: A Question of Control or Consent?', in D. Knights et al. (eds) *Job Redesign* (Aldershot: Gower, 1985), pp. 197–226.

Knights, D., H. Willmott, and D. Collinson, (eds) *Job Redesign* (Aldershot: Gower Publishing, 1985).

Kusterer, K. C., *Know-how on the Job: The Important Working Knowledge of 'Unskilled Workers'* (Boulder: Westview Press, 1978).

Lee, D., 'Beyond Deskilling: Skill, Craft and Class', in S. Wood (ed.) *The Degradation of Work?* (London: Hutchinson, 1982), pp. 146–62.

Littler, C. *The Development of the Labour Process in Capitalist Societies* (London: Heinemann, 1982).

Littler, C., 'Taylorism, Fordism and Job Design', in D. Knights et al. (eds) *Job Redesign* (Aldershot: Gower, 1985), pp. 10–29.

Lublin, J., 'As Robot Age Arrives, Labor Seeks Protection Against Loss of Work', *Wall Street Journal*, 26 October 1981, p. 1.

Lupton, T., *On the Shop Floor* (Oxford: Pergamon Press, 1963).

Manwaring, T. & S. Wood, 'The Ghost in the Labour Process', in D. Knights et al. (eds) *Job Redesign* (Aldershot: Gower, 1985), pp. 171–96.

Morris-Suzuki, T., 'Robots and Capitalism', *New Left Review* (September/October 1984), pp. 109–21.

O'Neill, C. K., 'Robots Who Reproduce', *Across the Board* (June, 1984), pp. 30–9.

Osterberg, O., and J. Enqvist, 'Robotics in the Workplace: Robot Factors, Human Factors, and Humane Factors', in H. W. Hendrick and O. Brown, Jr., (eds), *Human Factors in Organizational Design and Management* (North-Holland, 1984), pp. 447–60.

Personnel (1981), 'The Robot in Industry: Friend or Foe of Workers?', pp. 51–2.

Roy, D., 'Quota Restriction and Goldbricking in a Machine Shop', *American Journal of Sociology* (1952) pp. 427–42.

Roy, D., 'Work Satisfaction and Social Reward in Quota Achievement: An Analysis of Piecework Incentive', *American Sociological Review* (1953) pp. 507–14.

Roy, D., 'Efficiency and "The Fix": Informal Intergroup Relations in a Piecework Machine Shop', *American Journal of Sociology* (1954) pp. 255–266.

Roy, D., 'Banana Time: Job Satisfaction and Informal Interaction', *Human Organizations* (1959) pp. 158–68.

Scarborough, H., 'Working with Robots is a Bore', *New Scientist* (28 May 1981), pp. 554–5.

Schonberger, R., *Japanese Manufacturing Techniques – Nine Hidden Lessons in Simplicity* (New York: Free Press, 1982).

Schonberger, R., *World Class Manufacturing* (New York: Free Press, 1986).

Seed, A., 'Cost Accounting in the Age of Robotics', *Management Accounting* (October 1984), pp. 39–43.

Seeman, M., 'On the Personal Consequences of Alienation in Work', *American Sociological Review* (1966), pp. 273–85.

Simon, H. A., *The New Science of Management Decision* (Englewood Cliffs, NJ: Prentice-Hall, 1977).

Smith, D. and R. Wilson, *Industrial Robots – A Delphi Forecast of Markets and Technology* (Dearborn, MI: Society of Manufacturing Engineers, 1982).

Storey, J., *Managerial Prerogative and the Question of Control* (London: Routledge & Kegan Paul, 1983).

Storey, J., 'Comments on Factories of the Past and of the Future: The Impact of Robotics on Workers and Management Accounting Systems', *Proceedings of the Interdisciplinary Perspectives on Accounting Conference*, University of Manchester, 8–10 July 1985.

Walker, C. and R. Guest, *The Man on the Assembly Line* (Cambridge, Mass: Harvard University Press, 1952).

Whaley, G. L., 'The Impact of Robotics Technology Upon Human Resource Management', *Personnel Administrator* (September 1982), pp. 61–71.

Whyte, W. F., *Money and Motivation* (New York: Harper & Row, 1955).

Wood, S., (ed.) *The Degradation of Work?* (London: Hutchinson, 1982).

Young, S. M. 'Participative Budgeting: The Effects of Participation and

Information Asymmetry on Budgetary Slack', *Journal of Accounting Research* (1985), pp. 829–42.

Young, S. M. 'Just-In-Time Manufacturing Systems, Management Control, and the Sociology of Work: Some Propositions', Paper presented at Workshop on Accounting and Technology, University of Limburg, Maastricht, Netherlands, 10–12 December 1986.

Zimbalist, A., (ed.), *Case Studies on the Labor Process* (New York: Monthly Review Press, 1979).

Appendix 1

DEFINITION OF A ROBOT

Currently there are two definitions of robots that are widely accepted. The Robot Institute of America (RIA) (1980) defines a robot as 'a programmable, multifunctional manipulator designed to move material parts, tools or specialized devices through variable programmed motions for the performance of a variety of tasks'. The second definition, more broad in scope, is used by the Japanese. An industrial robot in Japan is 'an all-purpose machine equipped with a memory device and a terminal, and capable of rotation and of replacing human labor by automatic performance of movements'. The Japan Industrial Robot Industry Association (JIRA) classifies robots in the following manner:

(1) Manual Manipulator – A manipulator that is worked by an operator.
(2) Fixed Sequence Robot – A manipulator which repetitively performs successive steps of a given operation according to a predetermined sequence, condition, and position, and whose set information *cannot* be *easily* changed.
(3) Variable Sequence Robot – A manipulator which repetitively performs successive steps of a given operation according to a predetermined sequence, condition, and position, and whose set information *can* be *easily* changed.
(4) Playback Robot – A manipulator which can produce, from memory, operations originally executed under human control. A human operator initially operates the robot in order to input instructions. All the information relevant to the operations (sequence, conditions, and positions) is put in memory. When needed, this information is recalled (or played back, hence its name) and the operations are repetitively executed automatically from memory.
(5) NC (Numerical Control) Robot – A manipulator that can perform a given task according to the sequence, conditions, and position, as commanded via numerical data. The software used for these robots is stored in punched tapes, cards, and digital switches. This robot has the same control mode as an NC machine.

(6) Intelligent Robot – This robot with sensory perceptions (visual and/or tactile) can detect changes by itself in a work environment or work condition and, by its own decision-making faculty, proceed with its operation accordingly.

For the purpose of this paper, we will use the term robot to refer to those fitting into categories 3–6, which is consistent with the RIA's definition. Clearly defining what is meant by a robot is especially important when analysing and reporting published statistics regarding robots.

6 Accounting as Discipline

John Roberts and Robert W. Scapens[1]

In this paper we want to present some empirical material drawn from our research into the uses and usefulness of accounting information in divisionalised companies. Our first difficulty in approaching this task was to find a suitable way of presenting accounting. The writers of management accounting textbooks, such as Horngren (1982), Drury (1985) and many others (see Scapens, 1984 for a summary) have traditionally presented accounting as a set of neutral, objective techniques available to managers, who are themselves viewed as a relatively homogeneous group of professional technicians for whom accounting information can serve as one of the principal mechanisms whereby they seek to integrate and co-ordinate their own actions and the actions of others. Recently, however, writers adopting a more critical stance have attempted to present accounting as an integral element in a system of domination whereby capital and its agents seek to realise and appropriate surplus value (Armstrong, 1985; Chua, 1986; Ogden and Bougen, 1985 – see also Chapters 7, 9, 10, and 19 in this volume). Here the role of individual managers is far from neutral – they are seen as agents of capital and yet they are controlled by means of the same information with which they seek to control others.

How then were we to reconcile these competing ways of presenting accounting and the role of management? The superficial attraction of our empirical research was the promise that a secure grasp of empirical reality would release us from the bonds of competing ideologies. In practice, however, we brought our own assumptions and beliefs to the work. Furthermore, the richness and complexity of the empirical material only compounded the difficulties of interpretation. Thus, rather than supporting one or other of the competing views outlined above, our empirical research seemed to imply the coexistence of dual uses of accounting information. Accounting information appeared to be used both as a means of integration and co-ordination and also as a instrument of domination. In this paper we want to use certain elements of Foucault's account of discipline (1979) as a vehicle for describing the less than easy and unstable co-existence of these dual uses of accounting information.[2]

The particular attraction of Foucault's work lies in the way that, in his exploration of the development and widespread adoption of disciplinary techniques, he is explicitly concerned to explore the interrelationship between the exercise of power and the formation of knowledge. The ways in which:

> Methods for the formation and accumulation of knowledge began to be employed as instruments of domination and increases in power began to produce an addition to knowledge.
>
> (Smart, 1983, p. 115)

Thus, rather than exploring the use of accounting information *either* in terms of the formation of a particular (technical) knowledge *or* as an instrument of domination, Foucault's analysis implies the necessity of exploring the use of accounting information in 'relations of power-knowledge'.

Foucault's account of discipline focuses on *how* power is exercised, and in giving this account he explicitly distances himself from conceptions in which power is treated as an individual possession or commodity, or is viewed in purely negative terms as coercion or physical force. Instead, Foucault develops a wholly relational view of power as 'a mode of action upon actions' (1982, p. 222). Such a focus draws him away from a study of the overtly powerful to an analysis of the 'micro-physics' of power relations; where the exercise of power is seen to be inherent in all social interaction; where power and resistance are in constant interplay; and where the reality of coercion is not allowed to obscure an understanding of the positive effects of power in the routine reproduction of particular forms of subjectivity and ways of life. Such a focus readily lends itself to the empirical material which we present below. This material explores the web of relationships between a small group of functional managers in a small division of a large multinational, multidivisional company.

ACCOUNTING AS A FORM OF DISCIPLINARY POWER

Given that we all live out our lives in a society where disciplinary power is pervasive, it is difficult to raise our knowledge of the mechanisms of discipline to the level of self-consciousness. Indeed, it is possible to argue that the very genesis of consciousness involves the introduction of a child to the mechanism of discipline. Thus, for writers like Mead (1934), we come to our first consciousness of self through taking over the attitudes of others towards us; we discover ourselves first as an object for others – as 'me' – and only then do we claim ourselves as a subject – as 'I' – in the space implied by the attitude of others. But even if the seeds of disciplinary power are latent in childhood, in the constitution of the self out of the interplay of the dialectic of seeing and being seen, for Foucault disciplinary power arises from mechanisms which actually dissociate the seeing/being seen dyad.

> Disciplinary power . . . is exercised through its invisibility; at the same time it imposes on those it subjects a compulsory visibility. In discipline, it is the subjects who have to be seen. Their visibility assures the hold of the power that is exercised over them. It is the fact of being constantly seen . . . that maintains the disciplined individual in his subjection.
>
> (1979, p. 187)

To know that one is observed by an eye that one cannot see, that one is seen without being able to engage that eye, to be dependent upon the judgement of that eye; these are the ways that invisibility becomes a source of power. One's own visibility gives knowledge to the other, but the other cannot be interrogated, cannot be reduced to a subject, never engages you as the subject. It induces a state of subjection.

Foucault sees Bentham's panopticon as close to the perfect mechanism of disciplinary power:

> The perfect disciplinary apparatus would make it possible for a single gaze to see everything constantly. A central point would be both the source of light illuminating everything that . . . must be known, a perfect eye that nothing would escape and a centre towards which all gazes would be turned.
>
> (1979, p. 173)

Although it seems a long way from a Victorian prison to Ferac International, a multinational multidivisional company, Foucault argues that the panopticon should be seen as political technology that may and must be detached from any specific use. He described this technology in terms of a hierarchy of levels designed to create visibility. For example:

> The disciplinary gaze did, in fact, need relays. The pyramid was able to fulfil, more efficiently than the circle, two requirements; to be complete enough to form an uninterrupted network – consequently the possibility of multiplying its levels and of distributing them over the entire surface to be supervised; and yet to be discreet enough not to weigh down with an inert mass on the activity to be disciplined.
>
> (1979, p. 174)

It is easy to see the organisation of Ferac International as a structure designed to secure visibility. Likewise, it is easy to see the flow of accounting information with its ability to span physical distance, as the principal instrument for realising this visibility. Thus, like light focusing in upon a retina, the apex of the hierarchy at Ferac was the main Board. A main Board director acted as Chairman for each of the Divisional Boards. Within the Engineering Products Division, which was the focus of our research, there were yet further subdivisions into four separate product divisions – most of our work took place with the managers of just one of these product divisions – the Plastics Division.

The reporting cycle within Ferac was as follows. Each month accounts were produced for all the functional areas. Within the Plastics Division, the functions comprised sales, production, new products, administration and marketing. The accounts were prepared by the divisional management accountant who also produced a written report interpreting the figures for each area. This report was complemented by a report written by each of the functional managers. These reports were then discussed at a meeting of the Plastics Division Management Committee, attended by the functional managers, the management accountant, and the Director and General Manager of the Plastics Division. Minutes of this meeting, together with the accounts, were discussed at an Engineering Division Board meeting, attended by the general managers of each of the product divisions, two divisional managing directors, and the divisional personnel and finance directors. Monthly, a single-page profit report from the divisional managing directors was sent to head office. Quarterly, a more substantial report, presenting various ratios, comparing actuals with budget, and providing revised forecasts for the coming year, was submitted to head office. Every six months, when Ferac International reported interim and final results, the whole company came under the gaze of the City and financial press.

This then was the formal management of visibility through accountability within Ferac International. However, it was not fixed or frozen. From our discussions with various people at Ferac, it appeared that the system of accountability was constantly evolving and constantly being refined. What people described to us was a process of divisionalisation which was in certain respects still incomplete. The advocates of divisionalisation would probably argue that organisational visibility should be structured in a way that coincides with market visibility – so that the internal definition of profit centres coincide with discrete businesses. However, within Ferac there appeared to be, at the time of our study, an inertia impeding such a structure: as if the habits of the old functionally organised, highly centralised structure continued to inhabit the new divisionalised structure.

Significantly perhaps, it was the finance group within the Engineering Division that had resisted decentralisation into the four subdivisions. Although there were a whole series of rationalisations justifying this resistance – mainly around staffing – it could be argued that finance personnel were concerned to protect their visibility and independence. Mirroring the split of the Engineering Division into four subdivisions, four divisional management accountants had been appointed within the finance function. These individuals, however, were located centrally, rather than in the divisions. The fear of the Finance Director was that:

> They would become too close to the division. It may have some advantages working that closely with the division; you get to know the division that much better and they may accept you that much better. But I think they could very easily just become the run-around for the division and lose their independence.

Without exception the divisional managers thought that the management accountants should be located with them. It was as if there was a contest going on over the bodies, and particularly the eyes, of the divisional management accountants; were they to be a resource for hierarchical surveillance, or a resource for divisional managers that could perhaps be used to resist such serveillance?

Although the move towards divisionalisation could, in part, be explained in organisational terms, it coincided with increasing external pressures on Ferac. These pressures came partly from the stock market and partly from customer markets: both of which appeared to be working as sources of discipline within the company. By all accounts in the 1950s and 1960s the Plastics Division, along with the rest of Ferac, had enjoyed a period of sustained profitable growth, selling almost everything they could produce. In the 1970s, however, their traditional markets began to be hit by the advent of alternative materials and methods of production, which began to erode their market share and profitability. Ferac's corporate response to this decline in its traditional markets was to use the resources it had accumulated to diversify into other areas. Momentum was added to this process by media attention to the safety of their traditional production activities. Unfortunately for Ferac, their attempts at diversification were less than successful, and the resulting decline in profitability coupled with the adverse media publicity precipitated a collapse of City confidence in the early 1980s and a major financial crisis during which institutional investors insisted on the appointment of a new Chief Executive to the main Board.

The context for our research then was an intensification of pressure on the management of the Plastics Division. There was intensified pressure for the control of cash flow and working capital coming down the hierarchy from the new Chief Executive. At the same time there was a pressure from customers for increased competitiveness on price and delivery.

Within this wider field of visibility created by accounting information in Ferac, we now want to examine the mechanisms whereby accounting works as a form of disciplinary power by focusing on the practices of, and form of relationships within, a small group of functional managers in the Plastics Division.

PENETRATING PRODUCTION

Our interview with the Production Manager began as follows:

> on the manufacturing side we are measured basically against our manufacturing performances for material, labour, overheads – and the overheads include efficiency and spends. Now, any deviation from these will class as a manufacturing variance. So our prime aim is to make sure that production is manufactured within those standard costs.

In contrast to production managers in other divisions of Ferac that we studied, who thought and spoke about production only in physical or material terms, what struck us immediately when we heard the above comment was the individual's financial literacy. He explained his ability to use the language of accounting in terms of habitual practice: 'What do you expect after ten years of monthly manufacturing accounts?' However, in this situation, it appeared that his ability to use the language of accounting was the result of a deliberate policy which had been pursued by senior management. As the Divisional Director explained:

> I certainly would claim responsibility for making the production management write a report on their variances for the monthly Management Committee. It's no use giving then a statement of variances; they'll just put it in the drawer unless they've got to come back and explain what's caused it. Before I made that change, what would happen would be that the financial variances would be handled by the Management Accountant. He would tell the Committee what the variances were. Full stop. You'd then get the operational people talking about machine efficiency and production of stock and quality problems and so on; but not saying that the reason we've got £5,000 adverse material spend is because of a certain batch which went wrong.

The form and regularity of accountability in the Plastics Division had been deliberately constructed so that the language of accounting penetrated or suffused itself into the activity of the Production Manager. How was this done and what were its consequences?

For the Production Manager the manufacturing variances were important as a set of records principally because he was held accountable in those terms:

> The important document is the manufacturing variances because that's the document I've got to explain. The other documents are for internal use where it will tell us the trend or the month, but they don't go any further than us.

For this individual it was through the language of accounting that his actions were made visible to distant senior managers. More significantly perhaps, it made these activities visible in a certain kind of way – it expressed senior managers' instrumental interest in production and their concern to maximise the return earned on the fixed and working capital used in production. Furthermore, production itself is understood through the language of accounting.

However, being held accountable in this way also has more personal implications for the individual manager. Tied up in the employment contract and the functional definition of an individual as a 'production manager' is a sense of compulsion which means that the individual is apparently unable to negotiate over the language and the practices through which he (or she) is judged. His continued existence as a production manager depends on his results. For purposes of accountability he is only recognised in terms of his functional utility. For the distanced senior managers he exists only as an object of use.

This sense of compulsion was expressed in two interesting ways in the course of the research in Ferac. As a person, the Production Manager retained some distance from the values of accounting, but as a functionary he felt bound by the language of accounting. For instance, he commented that:

> We've got one section of three men. Now we could probably reduce that to two men if we put in mechanical handling, but to do that would probably cost £50,000 so the payback is likely to be about ten years. You're never going to do that. It's heavy work with a lot of handling. Morally you're obliged to look at it and you say 'Bloody hell, it's a job that I personally wouldn't want to do.' We can't justify it morally, but we justify it financially.

Another vivid example of this split between the personal and the functional arose at a divisional management meeting. Before beginning his report the Production Manager announced that sadly one of the operatives had died. Everyone else at the meeting expressed regret. The meeting then moved on to the Production Manager's report where he said, 'We need another body in the machine shop'. For a moment the language of the personal and moral, and the functional and instrumental, confronted each other directly.

The essence of discipline as a technique of domination is a breaking, or a denial of the reciprocity of self and other as interdependent subjects. As people, managers could 'take the role of other' – that is, could put themselves in the place of others as subjects; but as functionaries they appear bound to see themselves, as if through the eyes of their superiors, as objects of use. As Foucault puts it:

> At the heart of the procedures of discipline, it manifests the

subjection of those who are perceived as objects and the objectification of those who are subjected.

(1979, pp. 184–5)

Of course maintaining his individual utility encouraged the Production Manager to see the activity of his subordinates in a similar way. In taking over the language of accounting, the manager discovered himself and those who worked for him as objects of use. He was disciplined through accountability; in addition, accounting provided him with the mechanism for disciplining his subordinates. Thus, the impact of being held accountable extended beyond management meetings and the writing of reports; the knowledge of being regularly held accountable structured the relationships of the manager on a day-to-day basis – as indeed it was intended to do.

What you've got to do is to get out on the shop floor and stop it before it happens.

I mean the superintendent could put on there [an accounting report] that results on one section were, let's say, £10,000 last month. And I would say 'Why?', and he would have to go through them and find out, and it would do him good to investigate that and to make sure that we identify the problem to rectify.

However, the extent of investigation would itself be influenced by the pressure from above.

A lot of it depends on what the bottom line really is. I mean, if the Director and I see from the bottom line that they've made a handsome profit, I'm not going to look at the manufacturing variances too critically. But if all of a sudden we're making £100,000 less and £90,000 of that is due to manufacturing variance, then you are going to say 'What the hell is going on here?'

Here, in a sense, a manager is describing the kind of taking the role of other that accountability induces. Producing good results avoids the attention of superiors, whilst conversely bad results bring the manager's actions under close scrutiny.

In these kinds of ways, for the Production Manager and his subordinates, the language of accounting, and the concerns and interests expressed in it, came to structure their own attention, actions and relationships. As Foucault describes:

> He who is subjected to a field of visibility, and who knows it,
> assumes responsibility for the constraints of power; he makes them
> play spontaneously upon himself; he inscribes in himself the power
> relation in which he simultaneously plays both roles; he becomes
> the principle of his own subjection.
>
> (1979, pp. 202–203)

But the field of visibility that accounting information creates is less
than total, and the Production Manager described to us a whole
variety of ways he sought to make use of the gaps in visibility. In a
sense what the manager seemed to be trying to do was to create space
for himself. As the above remark about the importance of the
'bottom line' suggests, his activities were seen by superiors only in
terms of financial results. Some of the Production Manager's activities could be interpreted as an attempt to create a disjunction between these results and what was actually going on on the shop floor.
   The manager justified his actions in terms of his own superior local
knowledge and his superior's lack of it.

> I don't think that they understand the minute detail because
> they've basically not been used to using the information. If we have
> a particularly bad month and it's out of tune with what you
> normally expect, then they expect a lot of work to be done to
> explain that month when you know very well that it's an oddball
> and it's going to come back next month.

However, it is precisely this superior local knowledge which can be
used by managers to create all sorts of invisible spaces through which
they attempt to shield themselves from the attention of their superiors. Local knowledge can be used as a resource for resistance
within the system of knowledge-power relations that accountability
establishes.
   Several examples of this space-creating activity were found in the
course of the research. For instance, attempts were made to create
space in the annual budgeting process.

> You see, you've got to be careful, as I see it, about trying to set
> targets which are realistic. And there's nothing worse than some-
> body setting a target for twelve months – I'm talking about the
> main company plan – setting targets which will give you good
> returns. And you know all the time that it's a tightrope and one

little waver on either sales or manufacturing and you've lost your target. So you need to have a relief valve in there.

The way this was done in the Plastics Division was through the standard costing system. Officially someone in the management accounting function sets the standards. But as one of the production superintendents explained:

George in Management Accounts actually does them, but he only goes off the information that we provide. Basically if we want to alter standard costs, I've got to justify it with the Production Manager. And if I get them through him, I'm 99 per cent certain of getting them on the computer. It would be the easiest thing in the world to put 50 per cent rejects on everything we're making into the standard costs. Now the Production Manager would say 'Hang on a minute, you can operate that plant at 3 per cent (rejects). But if we tell the Financial Accountant it's 50 per cent, it's 50 per cent. Well, what can they say? You just say, 'Well come down and show us how to make it at 3 per cent'.

Again specialised local knowledge becomes a resource for resistance, but there are limits to the margins that can be built in through such devices. On the one hand, the Production Manager could be costing himself out of the market. But, on the other hand, the margins may come through as favourable variances:

And straightaway they'll say 'Why have you got favourable variances?'. Well, it's because we're running better than standard allowance. And somebody then will say 'You'd better look at cutting your standard allowances then'.

In general terms, standard costing controls both for bad and suspiciously good performance. It creates pressure to normalise performance.

A further example of creating space involved avoiding changes to standard costs when new machinery is installed. This happened in the Plastics Division, and everyone knew it happened, but for a time it meant that no one could be quite sure how the accounting figures related to actual performance. As the Management Accountant explained:

My main argument was from a control angle really. The machine shop was always a bone of contention from the outset. We were always running quite high adverse variances. And we got to grips with that eventually and we introduced some new controls and eliminated some of the problem areas. And immediately that happened, they embarked on this project of introducing new machines and methods, so we really lost touch with just how we are performing now in the the context of the new situation.

Here you get a sense of the way that the balance of control shifts over time between accounting and production; with production having an interest in maintaining a certain obscurity which accounting seeks to clarify. However, the fact of this resistance should not obscure its form and character. The resistance took place not against, but within the language of accounting. Indeed the manager's ability to manipulate appearances through the figures actually provided him with an incentive to become thoroughly familiar with the language of accounting.

INTERFUNCTIONAL RELATIONS

In the above description of the penetration of production by the language of accounting we concentrated principally on the vertical dimensions of hierarchy. We now want to turn our attention to the impact of accounting and accountability on the form of interfunctional relations.

In a variety of ways Foucault talks of disciplinary power 'individualising'. He argues that individualising tendencies arise from disciplinary power as follows:

It [discipline] must also master all the forces that are formed from the very constitution of an organised multiplicity: it must neutralize the effects of counterpower that spring from them and which form a resistance to the power that wishes to dominate it: agitations, revolts, spontaneous organizations, coalitions – anything that may establish horizontal conjunctions. Hence the fact that the disciplines use procedures of partitioning and verticality, that they introduce, between the different elements at the same level, as solid separations as possible, that they define compact hierarchical networks, in short, that they oppose to the intrinsic, adverse force of multiplicity the technique of the continuous, individualising pyramid. They must also increase the particular utility of each element of the multiplicity.

(1979, pp. 219–220)

The functional division of managerial labour into sales, production, planning, accounting, and so on, is not just for the purposes of the accounts; it creates a set of actual divisions which are reproduced through accountability. In a sense, it is a way of partitioning, or separating, or dividing people.

Perhaps the most obvious *expression* of these individualising tendencies came in the way that each of the functional managers described how he was blamed by the others. Production people blame planning; planning blame production; sales blame high production costs; production blame sales for cutting margins, and so on. The interdependent character of the production process means that responsibility and costs do not necessarily coincide; unfavourable variances in one area could be explained in terms of the actions in another. In some respects this mutual blaming reinforces the pressures of accountability.

> You will always get criticism from the accountants. You will always get criticism from sales. I think the works has got to expect that because the accountant is always trying to screw you down on costs, likewise sales are always trying to screw you down.

But deeper issues are involved. Earlier in the paper we mentioned our belief that accounting is not the only source of discipline within the organisation. If the City and bankers were the ultimate source of discipline shaping the concerns of senior managers at Ferac, and through them vertically down the hierarchy into the management of the Plastics Division, then the market-place with competition on price and service also created a certain kind of discipline within the Plastics Division. This discipline, however, seemed to exert itself horizontally across the organisation. Within the Plastics Division this discipline was felt particularly strongly at the points of direct contact with customers, by those who dealt with orders or complaints and by salesmen; and less strongly by those in production. Whilst the discipline of accountability had a tendency to separate and vertically divide the functional activities, the market seemed to exert an integrative pressure, as competitiveness on price and service depended not just on each individual functionary fulfilling his/her separate tasks, but also upon the integration of those tasks – that is, upon the inter-dependencies between functions. In what follows we want to attempt to describe interfunctional relations in the Plastics Division in terms of an ever-present tension between the potentially contradictory pressures of the need for interfunctional co-operation and integration to satisfy market demand, and the individualising effects of hierarchical accountability.

Our best description of how these tensions express themselves in practice comes from the Production Planning Manager:

> Everybody is anxious to make sure his own specific reasons are right, especially at year end and half-year end. I have targets for raw materials, the works and production management have targets for their work-in-progress levels, which to some extent I can influence by the rate at which I'm putting orders onto them, and I'm responsible for the finished goods stock levels. Now obviously there's a mad scramble at the end of every month. I know that, as I'm at the end of the line of finished goods, I'm going to get a great surge of materials to stock in the last week of the month, because the Inspection want it off their books. Production like to clear their production line because it's easier to count when we do the stock audit, and of course the financial responsibility – they like to be patted on the back and say 'Great, you've done very well with your work-in-progress'. So it all finds its way into finished goods. Now in turn I increase the rate of dispatch operations. I get everything through the door that I can because that's the whole object of the exercise. But to balance that up, I've very often got to tighten things up on the raw materials front because I know that I'm going to be over the top on finished goods, so I've got to compensate somewhere else, because I'm responsible for both levels.

A wonderfully contradictory image of organisation comes through this account. In one sense it is a description of the individualising pressures created by accountability; each functional area is forced back into looking after itself and this means doing things which will allow them to give the best possible image of themselves to their superiors. The pressure is strongest when visibility is most acute; at the end of each month and particularly at half-year and year end when senior Ferac management are themselves visible to the City and investors. The paradox is that getting things right in your own area involves passing things onto other areas. The other image of organisation that comes through the above quote is of the interdependence of functional activities. The vertical divisions and separations that accountability creates are in a sense illusory or at least arbitrary. There was an unavoidable interdependence across the functional areas. The potential effect of trying to act independently in a system of interdependence is to weaken the effectiveness of the system as a whole. In the Plastics Division, at least, there seemed to be the possibility that each manager's individual attempt to construct the appearance of effectiveness through the accounts had the cumulative effect of disrupting the flow of the production system.

Understandably, perhaps, it was the Sales Manager with his closeness to customers who was most acutely aware of such disruption and its source. He commented:

Well, for good reasons at the end of the year we want to get the financial figures right and that means keeping work-in-progress and stocks down, which is great and it gets the figures right in December, and all wrong at the start of the year, because you're likely to start up in January starved of materials.

There was a recurrent argument in the Plastics Division between production and sales over cost versus standards of service, and at the time of the research these arguments had again surfaced. Sales staff were meeting increasing competition, such that service became an important factor. At the same time, however, there was increasing organisational pressure to reduce working capital. For the Sales Manager the net effect was that:

At a time when our service standards should be improving they are actually, for one reason or another, going downhill. We have lost orders this year because we have not been able to respond quickly to customer demands. Now the demands might have been outrageous but the customer is the guy who pays everyone's salary at the end of the day.

Overall it was indeed the customer who provided revenue, but it was senior managers who hired, fired, promoted, praised and blamed and who were felt to be the source of the most direct pressure, especially on production:

The Works Manager's greatest accountability is to the economy of his production, to meeting his financial targets – not ostensibly getting it right for the customer. He's going to plan his department to best suit his operations – long runs, most economical runs – and he's not going to be terribly worried about the service he's giving to customers.

Although it could be argued that in the long run low costs will benefit sales, at the time of the research at least the pressures generated through the accounting system were apparently weakening the business in the marketplace.

The above gives an illustration of how a hierarchical system of financial accountability can create an individualism which is potentially disruptive to the interdependence of production – and thereby harmful to the competitiveness of the business in the customer markets. It could be argued, however, that this tension simply needs to be managed or balanced, and indeed this was happening within the Plastics Division. Privately, between the Production and Sales Managers, there were agreements as to the real (as opposed to reported) costs and margins on particular orders. More formally, the value of the production planning function was described to us in terms of its role as a buffer between production and sales that would balance the demands for economic production with the demands for improved service. At another level, the regular monthly divisional management meetings served to emphasise collective responsibility – the whole 'management team' were jointly responsible for profitability.

However, despite or indeed as a result of those re-integrative devices, particularly divisionalisation, there was at least the suggestion (or perhaps the fear) of a more fundamental conflict of interest between the long-term future of the Plastics Division and of Ferac International as a whole.

I sometimes – very negatively – wonder whether Ferac are so concerned about our little division, because X million in their scale of things is of no account. Whilst we continue to turn in nice profits every year, great! Come the day when we ever go the other way, I don't think we'll last very long.

As a management group, as well as individuals, their survival was seen to depend upon their continued utility. Ferac was seen as having only an instrumental financial interest in the business, and this could cause them to act against the advice of local managers.

Well, if Ferac say you've got a Rolls-Royce product, you can sell that product at any price, screw your margins up, make the customer pay. The sales people don't agree. They say you can't put bigger margins on without losing the business.

As a small division of a large diversified company there is always the possibility, especially where production methods and materials are changing fast, that the 'centre' might define its interests in terms of short-term exploitation of high margins, rather than in securing the long-term future of the business. Whether the possibility is realised is perhaps less significant that the disciplinary impact which the knowledge of such a possibility has on divisional management – their survival depends on their continuing utility.

CONCLUDING REMARKS

In the introduction we contrasted the traditional view of accounting as a neutral form of knowledge with the Marxist-informed view of accounting as an instrument of domination and exploitation. Following Foucault, the above analysis of accounting practices has sought to illustrate something of the coexistence and interpenetration of accounting as a form of knowledge and a form of power relations. In adopting this focus, we were attempting to move away from a conception which treats power as an individual possession or commodity, or in purely negative terms of coercion, and towards a relational and positive conception of power.

Something of the difference between these two conceptions of power can be discerned in the discontinuities between the rationalisations and the practices of the individuals described above. Their sense of hierarchy and power seems to be of something external and superior to them. For them, power is located in senior management, the City or the market; to retain their jobs they must submit to this power. As people they would wish that more humane intentions would prevail, but superior power requires submission. At best they can use their superior local knowledge as a resource for resistance; to create a sphere of action that is invisible and thereby preserves a minimal sense of individual autonomy and independence.

Paradoxically, these rationalisations both conceal and reveal the mechanisms of disciplinary power. They conceal, in that the accounts of the working of power are projected away from the individuals involved. They reveal, in that power relations are in practice effective through the constitution of a certain form of subjectivity which these rationalisations reflect. We have sought to describe how accounting information creates a field of visibility within which people work as it were upon each other. Though enacted by individuals, the locus of the eye of authority is unclear, ambiguous and generalised. Thus, accounting information constructs a form of subjectivity through offering individuals a way of seeing themselves and others. In the name of an external power, individuals discover themselves and each other as objects of use.

Power is everywhere in the 'play of calculated gazes' which constitutes this field of visibility. Power and resistance are both aspects of the workings of disciplinary power. But as illustrated above, resistance can draw individuals further into the language and categories of accounting, and the fact of resistance perhaps conceals from sight the more positive productive power which accounting practices organise: the way it penetrates structures, and constantly refines relations of production; the way it partitions and divides – individualises – so that, in their concern to gain praise and avoid blame in the routines of accountability, individuals constantly undermine the conditions for collective resistance, and in practice act in ways which serve to discipline each other. Yet in such individualising effects we sense not only the strengths, but also the limitations of disciplinary mechanisms, for in the above case at least, the forces which perpetuate hierarchy also inhibit and weaken the potential for interfunctional co-operation.

Notes

1.   The authors gratefully acknowledge the support of the Economic and Social Research Council for funding the project on which this paper is based.
2.   In our previous work (Roberts and Scapens, 1983, 1985, 1987) we have made extensive reference to the work of Giddens. Consequently, some comment on the relation between Giddens and Foucault seems appropriate. There is a strong similarity in their respective work insofar as both are seeking to develop a relational conception of power. For Foucault, however, this is part of his concern to develop an analysis of the production of particular forms of subjectivity, whereas for Giddens it is part of his concern to give an account of human agency within a theory of structuration. But at this point their work clearly divides (see Giddens, 1982 and 1984; Cousins and Hussain, 1984). However, Foucault's focus on the microphysics of power relations, his complementary

analysis of resistance, and his emphasis on the individualising effects of disciplinary power (Knights and Roberts, 1982) seemed to make his work particularly appropriate for the empirical analysis of relationships within a divisionalised management group attempted in this paper.

Bibliography

Armstrong, P., 'Changing Management Control Strategies: The Role of Competition Between Accountancy and Other Organizational Professions', *Accounting Organizations and Society*, (1985) pp. 129–48.

Chua, W. F., 'Radical Developments in Accounting Thought', *Accounting Review* (1986) pp. 601–32.

Cousins, M. and A. Hussain, *Michel Foucault* (London: Macmillan, 1984).

Drury, C., *Management and Cost Accounting* (Wokingham: Van Nostrand Reinhold, 1985).

Foucault, M., *Discipline and Punish: The Birth of the Prison* (Harmondsworth, Middlesex: Peregrine, 1979).

Foucault, M., 'The Subject and Power', an afterword by Foucault in H. L. Dreyfus and P. Rabinow, *Michel Foucault: Beyond Structuralism and Hermeneutics* (Brighton, Sussex: Harvester, 1982).

Giddens, A., *Profiles and Critiques in Social Theory* (London: Macmillan, 1982).

Giddens, A., *The Constitution of Society* (London: Macmillan, 1984).

Horngren, C. T., *Cost Accounting*, 5th Edition (Englewood Cliffs, NJ: Prentice-Hall, 1982).

Knights, D. and Roberts, J., 'The Power of Organisation or the Organisation of Power', *Organisation Studies*, (1982) pp. 47–63.

Mead, G. H., *Mind, Self and Society* (University of Chicago Press, 1934).

Ogden, S. and P. Bougen, 'A Radical Perspective of the Disclosure of Accounting Information to Trade Unions', *Accounting, Organizations and Society*, (1985) pp. 211–24.

Roberts, J. and Scapens, R., 'Accounting Systems and Systems of Accountability – Understanding Accounting Practices in their Organisational Contexts', *Accounting, Organizations and Society*, (1983) pp. 443–56.

Roberts J. and Scapens, R., 'Towards an Understanding of Accounting in the Social Process of Control in Organisations', *Working Paper*, University of Manchester, 1985.

Roberts J. and Scapens, R., 'Two Case Studies of Accounting and Control in Divisionalised Organisations' in J. Arnold, D. Cooper and R. Scapens, *Management Accounting: British Case Studies* (London: Chartered Institute of Management Accountants, 1987).

Scapens, R. W., D. T. Otley and R. J. Lister, *Management Accounting. Organizational Theory and Capital Budgeting* (London: Macmillan, 1984).

Smart, B., *Foucault, Marxism and Critique* (London: Routledge and Kegan Paul, 1983).

7 Joint Consultation and the Disclosure of Information: an Historical Perspective

Philip D. Bougen and Stuart Ogden

Disclosure of accounting information to employees, as has been argued before (Ogden and Bougen, 1985), is most appropriately viewed as a managerial strategy designed to contribute to the managerial task of exercising control over labour. The need to exercise control over labour stems from the fact that contrary to consensual interpretations of the labour-capital relationship, industrial relations is characterised by fundamental and irreconcilable conflicts of interest. This is most visible in the buying and selling of labour power but also continues into the labour process itself. Although in the labour market the wage may be and usually is defined specifically, the amount and quality of work rarely is. Rather than agreeing to expend a given amount of effort, employees 'surrender' their capacity to work, their labour power, and it is the function of management to transform this capacity into actual productivity in the labour process. However, while employers usually want to be able to use their labour forces in as flexible a way as possible and as a resource to be manipulated, employees want to exert some control over the way they are used to prevent or minimise their insecurity and exploitation. Consequently, one of management's major tasks is concerned with attempting to ensure that labour as a factor of production can be rendered as susceptible to control as other factors of production. Although management pursues this endeavour within a general framework of domination and subordination of labour, the power advantages it enjoys over labour never fully guarantee that the exercise of control is non-problematic. In the light of this, management has continually engaged in developing and adapting a variety of strategies to enhance their control over labour. Exclusive reliance on traditional strategies of coercion has long been seen as inappropriate

(Fox, 1974) and in the search for effective strategies of consent, disclosure of information has been seen to have a valuable role. It offers management the opportunity to secure compliance from employees for managerial decisions, and to enhance the legitimacy with which they are viewed. However, the way in which disclosure of information is most effectively pursued remains largely a matter of debate. This is reflected in the fact that disclosure of information continues to occur through a variety of forms, such as employee reports, collective bargaining and joint consultation. This suggests that, as a managerial strategy, there is considerable discretion in how management utilises it, and that as yet no consensus appears to have emerged as to the best way of implementing it. The choice management makes as to which particular form to adopt for disclosure purposes is likely to be influenced by a number of organisational and environmental variables, amongst which will be the range of other management strategies currently being employed within the organisation, and the nature and extent of employee resistance. The choice will also reflect management's assessment of the net value of any particular form of disclosure practice, since each may carry different sets of trade-offs for management.

One of the most striking aspects of current disclosure practice is the popularity amongst managements of joint consultation (Smith, 1976; Knight, 1979; Cressey et al., 1981). How far it will prove, for management, to be a successful vehicle for the disclosure of information remains to be seen. However, by considering some case study evidence from an earlier period, it will be suggested that management's utilisation of joint consultation for disclosure purpose is likely to prove problematic.

JOINT CONSULTATION AND THE DISCLOSURE OF INFORMATION

Definitions of joint consultation usually begin by identifying it as a form of workers' participation (Armstrong, 1969; Clegg, 1979; Marsh, 1979), the essential feature of which is that employee views may be expressed, discussed and possibly taken into account before management makes a final decision on an issue. It is this which distinguishes joint consultation from mere communication, since the latter simply entails transmission of information, while joint consultation 'suggests opinions are sought which may influence a decision before it is made'

(Goodman, 1984, p. 104). However, the discretion management has as to whether to act or not upon employee advice and attitudes underlines the essential feature of the consultative process, which is to leave management's prerogative to make decisions formally intact.

Another aspect of joint consultation that is continually stressed is its separateness and distinctiveness from collective bargaining. Armstrong (1969) sees collective bargaining as entailing 'competitive bargaining, power-conscious relationships' whereas joint consultation involves 'discussions between partners, in the belief that there can be a wide community of interest between managers and managed' (p. 120). Marsh (1979) highlights this distinction, with the proposition that 'consultation is non-competitive and integrative in nature, whereas negotiation is competitive and concerned with temporary and unsatisfactory compromise, consultation therefore being equipped to resolve conflict and negotiation merely to contain it'. In order for consultation to perform this role, it is necessary not only to separate it from the process of collective bargaining, but also to exclude from its agenda contentious issues such as pay which are normally subject to negotiation. Indeed, Hawkins (1979) discusses joint consultation under the heading of alternatives to collective bargaining, arguing that the 'atmosphere of consultation must remain as non-controversial as possible in order to preserve the fiction that there is no real conflict of interest between employer and employee' (p. 40).

The use of joint consultation for purposes of disclosing information largely accounts for the recent renaissance it has enjoyed in British industrial relations, a phenomenon which confounds the conventional wisdom that joint consultation has exhausted its usefulness, either because it had been eclipsed by bargaining activities or had fallen into disrepute because it could only sustain its distinctiveness by dealing with trivia. Joint consultation first came into prominence in the First World War and was particularly promoted by the recommendations of the Whitley Committee in 1917 (Clegg and Chester, 1956), but the widespread adoption of joint consultation committees did not survive long, being 'swept away in the depression of the early twenties'. (Clegg, 1979, p. 151). A resurgence of interest was occasioned by the onset of the Second World War, notably in the engineering industries (Marsh, 1965; Clegg, 1979), but again the extensive adoption of joint consultation did not long survive the cessation of hostilities (Marsh and Coker, 1963; Clegg, 1979). In contrast to the impact of recession and unemployment which led to its demise after the First World War, the main factor explaining its disappearance after the Second World War was the growth in the importance of shop stewards and the increase in plant level collective bargaining, both of which were closely associated with the persistence of full employment (McCarthy, 1966; Clegg, 1979). These developments very quickly led to pressure within joint consultative committees for consultation over issues to be translated into negotiation of them. This compromised the integrity of joint consultation which depends on the maintenance of clear boundaries between negotiation and consultation. McCarthy (1966) has summarised this experience as follows: 'plant Consultative Committees . . . cannot survive the development of effective shop floor organisation. Either they must change their character and become essentially negotiating Committees carrying out functions which are indistinguishable from the formal process of shop floor bargaining, or they are boycotted by shop stewards and, as the influence of the latter grows, fall into disuse' (p. 3). Thus the dynamics of joint consultation under the conditions of full employment which supported the growth of workplace bargaining by shop stewards were that it was either effectively transformed into an arena for negotiation, or was reduced to discussing trivia – the 'tea and toilets' syndrome – or abandoned together. This became the conventional wisdom, with the practice of joint consultation, let alone the theory, being seen to be in 'disarray and decay' (Clegg, 1979).

Such pronouncements on the demise of joint consultation were perhaps premature, since subsequent surveys carried out in the late 1960s suggested that not inconsiderable numbers of joint consultative committees continued to operate (Clarke et al., 1972; Government Social Survey, 1968; Marsh et al., 1971; Parker, 1974, 1975). The evidence of these surveys indicated that the idea of joint consultation, at least amongst management, was still actively supported. As the 1970s progressed there was a manifest resurgence of interest in joint consultation, and consultative committees sprung up where they had withered or were sown afresh (Brown, 1981; Beaumont and Deaton, 1981; Marsh, 1982; Daniel and Millward, 1983). One of the major explanations for this renaissance, is the utility of joint consultation as a means for disclosing information.

Although interest in communicating information to employees has waxed and waned, it has always been regarded by management as an important ingredient for achieving good industrial relations. The contemporary interest management has shown in the disclosure of information is partly a product of the public debate occasioned by the

Bullock Report (Bullock, 1977; Elliott, 1978; Hawes and Brookes, 1980); and the need to accommodate Trade Union demands. Since the 1970s Trade Unions have argued for the need to extend the scope of their bargaining activities to strategic corporate decision-making, placing particular emphasis on long-term planning and investment decisions, both of which have stimulated a greater awareness of the significance of and need for information (Ogden, 1982; Batstone et al., 1983).

However, while the arguments for disclosing information to individual employees are clear-cut, the advantages to management in disclosing information to Trade Unions are more circumscribed. On the one hand, disclosure may provide benefits in terms of modifying Trade Union behaviour in collective bargaining, particularly in wage negotiations, in ways favourable to management, and of promoting conditions conducive to more effective integrative bargaining (Foley and Maunders, 1977; Palmer, 1977). On the other hand reservations have been frequently expressed about the potential for Trade Unions to 'misuse' disclosed information, which may lead to more rather than less militancy in wage bargaining, or to challenges to management proposals for change rather than co-operation with them (CIR, 1972; Craft, 1981). Management's continuing scepticism about the balance of advantage has resulted in only limited disclosure of information to Trade Unions. The cost to management, however, has been to forego the opportunity of reaping the benefits deemed realisable through a policy of fuller disclosure. It is this impasse in disclosure practice in collective bargaining that has led to a re-awakening of interest by management in joint consultation, and a re-evaluation of its capacity to act as a medium for pursuing policies of disclosure of information. (Elliott, 1978; Cressey et al., 1981; Dowling et al., 1981).

Joint consultation has a number of attributes that make it attractive to management as a medium for disclosing information. Firstly, joint consultation offers opportunities for active discussion of information which not only provides opportunities for management to clear up any misunderstandings and reinforce management's message, but also to pursue positive endorsement from employees of management's account of affairs as represented in the information. In contrast, direct provision of information to employees through, for example, employee reports, offers no similar scope for employee legitimation of management activity: it simply constitutes a one-way transmission of information in which employees are passive recipients of information.

Secondly, joint consultation enables management to maximise the role of information disclosure as a means of consensus-building. Joint consultation with its emphasis on co-operation, constructive and integrative discussion of issues of 'common interest' and joint problem-solving, provides a tailor-made context for the effective deployment of information designed to 'educate' workers about the business activities of the enterprise and the problems confronting it. Further, in joint consultation the disclosure decision is formally one of managerial prerogative, not one of joint agreement as would be the case in collective bargaining. Management is entitled to unilaterally determine the type and amount of information to be disclosed and to vary this as circumstances merit, and to evaluate the relevance and validity of employee responses to it. In contrast to collective bargaining, this leaves limited scope for employees to influence these issues, and with even less control over the decisions which the information is relevant to.

In the light of the above discussion it can be argued that there is a complementarity between management's purposes in disclosure of information and the role of joint consultation. Both are premised on perspectives which owe much to a unitary view of the enterprise: both emphasise the objective of encouraging and promoting greater employee identification with and involvement in the enterprise; both explicitly exclude any significant role for Trade Unions; both attempt to minimise the influence of collective bargaining on employer-employee relations; both emphasise the importance of maintaining managerial autonomy in decision making; both are concerned with consensus building rather than conflict resolution: both are initiated and controlled by management.

How far disclosing information through joint consultation will prove to be a successful management control strategy remains to be seen, since no detailed evaluation of contemporary developments has yet been undertaken. However, on the basis of historical evidence presented below it seems likely that the strategy will encounter problems: namely the inappropriateness of the unitary assumptions underlying the managerial preference for joint consultation; and the contradictory dynamics of the consultative process itself.

JOINT CONSULTATION: AN HISTORICAL PERSPECTIVE

Our interest in providing an historical view of the relationship between joint consultation and information disclosure is threefold.
Firstly, by having access to case-study material spanning a ten-year
experience of joint consultation within one company, from the
scheme's inception in 1920 to its abandonment in 1930, an appreciation may be gained of the dynamics of joint consultation enabling
identification of a number of issues and problems which emerged
over time. It will be argued that these have relevance for contemporary discussions over the use of joint consultation as a medium for
disclosure of information. Secondly, the historical dimension of the
material casts some light on attempts which have been made to trace
a cyclical managerial interest in joint consultation, and indeed in
other forms of so-called enlightened managerial practice such as
profit-sharing (Ramsay, 1977). This cycle of control theory suggests
that in periods of high employment and volatile industrial relations,
management has a pressing incentive to adopt strategies designed to
diffuse workplace tension and to present, at least superficially, some
visible concessions to labour's demands. The measures in question
are usually designed to be placatory and involve enhanced possibilities for worker participation; but they are also designed to be
temporary. However, our particular historical evidence suggests that
such a theory requires qualification. The company which is the
subject of the case study initiated its exploratory discussions with its
workforce into joint consultation and profit-sharing in 1920, which is
consistent with the cycle of control theory: but it continued to
operate these measures beyond the onset of economic recession and
the decline of Trade-Union militancy. For this company at least, the
perceived merits of joint consultation and profit-sharing went beyond
the purely placatory interest suggested by the cycle of control theory.
Further, our evidence suggests that the adoption of strategies such as
joint consultation and profit-sharing by companies may be determined as much by their own internal considerations and problems as
by the macro-economic variables, particularly the level of employment, emphasised by the cycle of control theory.

Thirdly, although the industrial relations implications of Joint
Consultation are well understood, little research had been done on
the use of accounting information in such a context, a shortcoming
this case study seeks to remedy.

The focus of the case study is to examine the use management made of joint consultation as a vehicle for the disclosure of information and to assess how far the disclosure strategy followed proved successful. This will entail considering the reasons for embarking on the policy of disclosure, the ways in which it was implemented, the amount and type of information disclosed, and the employee response to it.

The evidence for the case study is based on the detailed minutes of the Joint Consultative Committee and the writings of leading directors of the company who discussed the company's experience of joint consultation in a number of publications. As regards the latter, a word of caution is merited, since such material can be described as retrospective accounts of what occurred, and is of course based on a management perception of motives and events.

This is compounded by the lack of any equivalent documentary evidence providing workers' accounts of events. However, we have tried to cast as critical an eye as possible on the material that is available.

The company which forms the basis of the case study was the Hans Renold Company, founded in Manchester, England in 1879 by a Swiss engineer and craftsman. Sir C. G. Renold (Managing Director of the company during our period of analysis) described his father as follows:

> Mr Renold was a man of dominating personality with a passion for workmanship and orderliness. On this basis he established a strong personal leadership of his employees. His methods were autocratic and paternal but nothing that contributed to good work was too good for his workpeople.
>
> (Renold, 1950, p. 13)

This commitment to quality workmanship, efficiency and factory order was reflected in substantial inducements being offered to employees for appropriate performance. The company was characterised by a shorter working week and higher wages than the district engineering norm; good working conditions; and numerous in-house training programmes. All of these factors contributed to a tradition of long-service employees with a strong, 'closely-knit' culture based upon tradition, precedent and personal familiarity.

The company attached a great deal of importance to organisational stability and its significance for industrial relations, but could do little to avoid the disruptive effects brought about by the experience of the

First World War. It was in response to this that the early impetus towards joint consultation can be discerned, as the following statement illustrates:

> It was towards the end of 1916 that the Directors of the company felt the need for closer contact with their work-people. Conditions were in a state of flux. Products and processes were changing; departments were being re-organized; unskilled labour was replacing skilled; numbers were increasing bringing in many strangers and there was a growing flood of wage awards and Government directions to be applied. All the old familiar landmarks were going and if a general breakdown of works morale was to be avoided some means of talking things over between management and workers was essential.
>
> (Renold, 1950, p. 18)

This account also suggests that there was an awareness that the hitherto successful paternalistic style of management control was likely to become more strained within this more volatile organisational climate. In an attempt to respond to some of these imperatives, management introduced a Welfare Committee whose terms of reference were to discuss factory amenities such as industrial clothing and canteen facilities. The worker representatives for the committee were to be *chosen* by departmental superintendents and to consist of both trade unionists and non-unionists. What happened next can best be appreciated in the following:

> A provisional committee from amongst the nominees was formed to worked out a constitution.
> Everything seemed set fair, but an unexpected complication arose. No sooner had the provisional committee got to work than the Management received a notice from hitherto unknown individuals to the effect that:-
> 'A Committee of Stewards has been established
> in the shops at Renold Works by members of the
> Amalgamated Society of Engineers for looking
> after their interests as Trade Unionists.'
> Evidently the trade unionists nominated by the superintendents had not been the right ones! Probably a movement to establish shop stewards had already been on foot sponsored by the left-wing element in sympathy with the Rank and File Movement then

spreading throughout the country; the action of the Management merely brought it out into the open.

Whatever the reason, the Management, from having no organized body of its workers with which to communicate, was now faced with two, chosen on different bases and not recognizing each other. It was in a quandary.

(Renold, 1950, pp. 19–20)

Management's immediate response was to allow both bodies to operate in parallel, the Welfare Committee as a joint management and labour consultative arena to discuss matters of common interest; the Shop Stewards Committee as a trade-union negotiating group.

The emergence of the Shop Stewards Committee reflected a fairly rapid unionisation of the company's workforce: whereas before the war it had largely been a non-unionised shop, by 1920 the Shop Stewards Committee 'had in fact come to represent practically the whole of the employees below management level' (Renold, 1950, p. 24). The increasing importance of the Shop Stewards Committee coupled with employee dissatisfaction with the operation of the Welfare Committee resulted in its formal abandonment in 1920 at the request of employees, and its functions were taken over by the Shop Stewards Committee. The reason for its failure as given by Renold are interesting:

The workers' side considered that the committee was an unreal body and maintained that it needed a much wider scope and more real powers if it was to be effective.

and

On the other hand the Management felt that its explanations did not 'get across', or have any real effect or the understanding of the workers as a whole.

(Renold, 1950, p. 24)

This resulted in management being left with no joint consultation procedures independent of the negotiating and bargaining arrangements of the Shop Stewards Committee. This led management to manufacture a new framework for relaunching consultative procedures which took the form of a Profit Sharing Scheme. This gave a much broader focus to joint consultation than had previously been the case, and made the Company's financial performance the central agenda item. Management believed that worker interest in this scheme was likely to be greater since it offered the prospect of extra financial rewards. Furthermore, it gained legitimacy by appearing to build on a request for some sort of Profit Sharing Scheme made by the Shop Stewards during the war when the level of production had been extraordinarily high due to munitions contracts. It seems that earlier lessons had been well learnt.

Before proceeding to discuss the case study material in detail it is important, if only briefly, to consider the environmental conditions which surrounded the case study experience. The early impetus for the joint consultation arrangements occurred at a time of extreme social and political unrest, both in the country at large and in the engineering industry in particular (Hinton, 1973). At Renolds, this was reflected in growing uncertainty and dislocation: new products, new employees and rapid unionisation of the workforce were all occurring. The rise of joint consultation in these circumstances would appear to accord with the 'cycle of control' explanation offered by authors such as Ramsay (1977). However, the 'cycle of control' explanation is less applicable to the subsequent period. Although generally the use of joint consultation dramatically subsided with the onset of recession and the rise of unemployment, precisely the opposite occurred at Renolds, suggesting that the main factors explaining management's continued use of joint consultation were largely organisationally specific.

JOINT CONSULTATION AND PROFIT SHARING IN THE HANS RENOLD COMPANY

The main consultative committee was the Profit Sharing Committee which met monthly, and consisted of two Directors (Renolds himself, and Jenkins, Finance Director and later General Sales Manager) and a senior manager, and eighteen elected members of whom seven were from the monthly staff, one from the foremen and ten from the shop floor. Each year the Profit Sharing Committee accounted for its activities to a general meeting of all employees, reporting on the company's financial performance, and the results of the profit sharing scheme.

A detailed description of the mechanics of the Profit Sharing

Scheme are beyond the scope of this particular paper. However, a number of central features can be highlighted:

(1) The mechanics of the Profit Sharing Scheme computations relied heavily upon the introduction of a detailed budgetary and standard costing system. Comparisons of actual cost incurrence against standard, and the recording of any resulting cost savings, were essential for the workings of the scheme. The Directors of the company had been clear that any financial rewards to the employees had to be self-financed by cost savings.

(2) However, the scheme was not confined to cost considerations. Rather than merely comparing actual costs to standard, to arrive at some measure of employee performance, selling prices obtained in the final market for the products were also central to the scheme. Each department within the factory was allocated a proportion of total expected revenue which acted as the basis for comparison with actual costs. In effect, departments were treated akin to profit centres rather than cost centres. Management deemed the introduction of sales revenue into the computations as essential because in the deflationary environment of the 1920s they expected prices to fall. This provided management with the opportunity to channel cost savings into financing lower selling prices rather than into bonus payments under the profit sharing scheme. One implication of this however was that the direct relationship between employee effort and reward was substantially diluted, since revenue considerations were beyond the control of employees.

(3) The time period chosen for measurement proved to be problematic since the distributable profit under the scheme was computed on a monthly basis. This was chosen to capitalise on the scheme's potential to provide feedback data for managerial control purposes, and to strengthen in the employee's mind the relationship between effort and reward for motivational purposes. However, using so short a time period for measurement purposes served to exaggerate the well known accounting problems (Thomas, 1969, 1974) of trying to identify economic activities with one specific time period when both their origin and effect are experienced over a number of periods. By basing the scheme on the assumption that each month should stand by

itself, this introduced a volatility and indeed, at times, randomness, into the accounting numbers generated. This served to isolate the formal performance measures from employees' own perceptions of what seemed to be happening in the factory.

(4) The scheme was also characterised by the inclusion of an item of 'wages of capital' which was intended as a reward paid to the owners on the basis of capital employed, for their risk-taking and entrepreneurship, and was charged to the income statement of the profit sharing scheme as an expense of the period before the distributable surplus was computed. It therefore did not conform to the accounting treatment of rewards to capital as appropriations of the profit of the period, but was instead more akin to the economic concepts of normal profits and super-normal profits, with distributions under the scheme only being provided under the latter circumstances. The introduction of this concept served both to reduce the distributable surplus available under the Profit Sharing Scheme and to reinforce the notion that capital as well as labour contributed to producing the surplus and required rewarding.

THE MANAGERIAL INTEREST IN JOINT CONSULTATION AND PROFIT SHARING

Three major themes can be distinguished as to the benefits management perceived from entering into the consultative arrangements. Firstly, the Profit Sharing Scheme was seen as a vehicle for joint consultation and more specifically as a medium for the dissemination of information about company financial performance. This was valued by management as a means of introducing workers to, and educating them about, company activities. C. G. Renold, addressing a mass meeting of workers in December 1920 at the inception of the scheme, when answering a question as to what the workers could get out of the profit sharing scheme commented:

In the first place, a first-hand knowledge of business problems, and of the conduct of this business in particular. This should give you all a conviction that you are getting a square deal and are not working to enrich other people at your expense.

(Committee Minutes, 18.12.20)

This emphasis continued throughout the life of the scheme.

To this end the disclosure of information was extensive. Jenkins, the finance director, writing at the time, suggested the following types of information:

Financial Data

Capital employed
Distribution of capital employed within the company
Cost – Volume – Profit Relationships
Value added and Distribution
Sales Revenue and Distribution
The Controllability and Non-Controllability of specific costs
Distribution and Transportation Costs
Changes in Stock levels – and Investment in Stocks
Details and importance of Cash flow
Breakdown of Product cost
Existence of Reserves and their purpose
Depreciation policy
Output – total and per worker
Cost of new equipment installed
Cost of tools and equipment used per period
Cost of raw materials consumed
Numbers employed
Amount of bad work produced
Average wage per employee – by Grade of Labour
Average wage per employee – by Department

Other Data

Organisation Structure
Responsibilities and Duties of each Manager
Corporate objectives and prospects
Managerial policy relative to objectives
Success or failure of managerial actions
Reasons for success or failure of managerial actions
Justification of managerial actions to employees
Impact of environmental pressures on performance
Product range
Economic justification of technological change
Employment prospects

(Jenkins, 1925, pp. 304–306)

The above list of items is important in that it indicates the particular perspective the company adopted on disclosures. Management was not interested in a policy of selective information disclosure for tactical purposes, but rather preferred instead to pursue a policy of 'full' disclosure. The objective for management was one of promoting a management–labour discourse which attached primacy to managerial definitions of problems, and to problem evaluation in terms of financial criteria (Batstone, 1979, Ogden and Bougen, 1985). The full provision of accounting information provided management with an allegedly neutral basis for agenda construction and the basis for debate in the joint consultation arrangements. In this context management, rather than simply appealing to or asserting common interests, saw accounting information as providing a solid platform upon which co-operation could be built in joint consultation.

Secondly, following from the above, there clearly was the belief by management that once workers had been acquainted with the 're-alities of the business world' and had been exposed to the harshness and complexity of the trading conditions confronting the Company, then there would be greater commitment and co-operation from the workforce. This conviction was prominent in the writing of the Directors. For example:

The first step towards establishing a greater degree of common understanding and mutual co-operation by which alone progress can be made, lies in affording opportunities in every possible direction for the education of the worker in the financial conditions which govern industry and ultimately control its progress.

(Jenkins, 1925, p. 303)

There was a genuine belief by management that the 'reasonable' worker, when informed of the realities of the situation as perceived by management, would not only recognise the legitimacy of the company's structure and its actions but also endorse them as the best means of providing material rewards for the employees.

Thirdly, quite apart from the benefits management expected to flow from developing a more co-operative, business-orientated attitude amongst the employees, more tangible advantages resulted from the operation of the scheme. The Profit Sharing Scheme was specifically structured around the introduction of a sophisticated budgetary and standard costing control system. Evidence of this was provided by C. G. Renold himself. In 1929 he addressed the International

Management Institute at Geneva, where he gave a detailed account of the development of budgetary control systems at the Renold Company over the preceeding ten years. Although he makes no specific reference to the Profit Sharing Scheme, it is apparent that the budgetary control system discussed at the meeting possessed many features of the accounting system which provided the basis for the monthly determination of distributable profit under the Profit Sharing Scheme. Cost classifications; account headings; the basis of responsibility allocation; time period of feedback, and the process of budget reviews were all closely integrated into the data requirements of the Profit Sharing Scheme. Indeed, at the Second Annual General Meeting of the Profit Sharing Scheme, C. G. Renolds in discussing the scale (standards) which underpinned the scheme, commented,

> the scale, like the annual accounts, is not special to the Profit Sharing Scheme. It is used by management for control purposes and the setting of selling prices.
>
> (Committee Minutes, 23.3.23)

There is little doubt that the introduction of the new accounting control system afforded management the opportunity to undertake a detailed analysis of work methods and production techniques, thereby allowing areas for cost savings to be identified and efficiency improvements to be made. This entailed the widespread application of scientific management techniques including an intensification of the use of work study and extensive redefinition of job content involving wholescale deskilling by substitution of machines for skilled labour, and by the greater division of labour. In addition to this restructuring of the labour process, the management accounting control system made actual performance more visible and easier to monitor (Burchell et al., 1980). Furthermore, the accounting records produced by the new system were quickly elevated to a quasi-divine status, being blessed by the attribute of inherent precision and promoted as being independently and unequivocally determined. This constitutes a more latent form of control which is as important as any manifest control function (Crawford, 1984; Hopwood, 1984). For example, as the Profit Sharing Committee were informed by C. G. Renold as regards the division of selling prices into standard costs for the operation of the scheme,

> the method of making the divisions was not guesswork but was

founded on facts and figures which could be checked in detail later.
(Committee Minutes, 4.8.20)

Consequently, the control system itself was presented as being above disagreement and beyond dispute.

In operating the Profit Sharing Scheme, management was clearly determined that it should in no way interfere with or prejudice the exercise of managerial authority. The scheme offered no rights to the employees to formally exercise any influence over management decision-making. This was made explicitly clear to the employee representatives at an early stage and was adhered to and reinforced in all subsequent discussions. The employee representatives were allowed access to substantial quantities of information, and were given every opportunity to question management about company policy in these areas, but managerial decision-making prerogatives were to remain intact. Indeed formal changes were made in the rule governing the Profit Sharing Scheme during its operation in order to ensure this. For example, the changing of selling price standards originally stated that:

> particularly allocations made against it shall be so made only with the approval of the Board of Directors and with the agreement of the Profit Sharing Scheme Executive Committee.

This was changed to,

> and with the previous knowledge of the Profit Sharing Scheme Executive Committee.
(Committee Minutes, 25.10.20)

JOINT CONSULTATION IN PRACTICE

The operation of the Joint Consultation and Profit Sharing Scheme did not prove to be as straightforward as management had expected, and from management's perspective a number of developments occurred which proved problematic in terms of the objectives they sought to achieve. The first of these relates to the extent which the worker representatives did not blindly consume the information provided by management, but rather critically questioned it. Although initially the worker representatives were unfamiliar with the technical language of accounting, this did not prevent them from utilising their own local and intuitive grasp of any particular situation to ask management some searching questions about the company's account of the same situation. One area where this occurred was over the monthly reports. As indicated above, the choice of a monthly time period as a basis for evaluating performance placed particular stress on the ability of the accounting system to accurately record economic transactions. When the accounting interpretation of performance was at odds with the employees' own perception of affairs, they were not inhibited in drawing attention to the inconsistency. For example:

> The only comment on the accounts by the Committee was one of surprise at the remarkably good result in the Motor Cycle Department, where definite trouble had to be contended with, and the exact reverse in those departments which were supposed to be running smoothly. Mr. C. G. Renold admitted that the results were somewhat confounding and said that an attempt to get a really reliable picture of the position period by period was extremely difficult.
>
> (Committee Minutes, 23.4.23)

A second development which proved embarrassing for management was the extent to which the worker representatives experienced a learning process through the operation of the scheme. This not only resulted in reinforcing their unwillingness to consume information uncritically, but to them challenging the way in which management used and interpreted accounting data. Worker representatives were able to raise complex accounting problems, which still concern the profession, when the specific adoption of one accounting convention rather than others available seemed to work against the employee interest in profit measurement. So, for example, in determining the value of assets to compute the capital employed for the Wages of Capital charge, employee representatives challenged management's valuation. For example, one employee representative

> argued that the real valuation of an asset was its earning capacity and, judged from this point of view, he had a feeling that many items were not worth their book value.
>
> (Committee Minutes, 9.10.22)

Another example concerned the occasion the company was forced to scrap a large quantity of defective manufactured parts. The conventional accounting treatment would be to write off any such costs net of any revenue received to the accounting period in question. However, the problems normally associated with such a convention were greatly aggravated in this instance because the accounts were computed on a monthly basis. How this was resolved was clearly of interest to the employee representatives since they were very aware that the best course of action from their point of view was a full write off in one period which would avoid prejudicing bonuses in future periods, and that the opposite was desirable from management's point of view. Consequently fierce debate occurred when management reported that they were indeed intending to spread the cost over several periods. Interestingly, too, in the course of these debates the actual cost involved was also disputed by the employee representatives.

Employee representatives on the committee also exhibited the capacity to use information management had disclosed for purposes not anticipated by management. For example, management had consistently disclosed the quantities of total sales and the sale prices achieved which had gone to overseas subsidiaries and markets. With the depressed domestic market, management aimed to increase such exports, and to this end launched a major overseas marketing campaign, which involved reducing selling prices to overseas subsidiaries as a way of enabling them to stimulate demand. Although this was presented to the committee as evidence of an aggressive marketing initiative by the company, the employee representatives were quick to realise that the transfer of goods at less than the standard selling price allowed for in the profit sharing scheme would undoubtedly reduce the likelihood of budgeted profit being achieved. Rather, profit would accrue to the subsidiary companies whose results were not included in the scheme for profit sharing. As one of the employee representatives noted

It had been stated by the Finance Director that Foreign Sales on Period 3 other than through the subsidiary companies were made at a margin above the minimum selling value of 6% or 7%, whereas those made to subsidiary companies were at 11.3% below minimum selling value. Mr Parish asked the reason for the wide difference between the prices at which we sold for export to subsidiary companies and to others; was it that sales could not be effected in the markets covered by the subsidiary companies at any higher prices or that the difference (or more) was expected to be made as profit by the subsidiary companies.

(Committee Minutes, 8.10.23)

The net effect of this line of enquiry was that ultimately a proportion of the overseas companies' profits were brought into the Profit Sharing Scheme for distribution purposes.

What these examples demonstrate is the employee representatives' ability to learn about relevant areas of accounting practice, and to use that knowledge to challenge managerial definitions and practices in pursuit of their own interests. Even though management retained the right to make the final decision, and could (and did) ignore employee views, the arguments deployed by the employee representatives were not entirely without effect as the case of transfer pricing demonstrated.

On occasions the employee representatives also used the absence of accounting data to dispute the viability of management-proposed courses of action. For example, when management attempted to justify the use of outside contractors for joinery work inside the factory, an employee representative argued,

They were in a position to see what was going on and it was their belief that much of the work that was done by outside concerns could not possibly be done as well nor as cheaply by the inside staff. No proof had been supplied that this is not so.

(Committee Minutes, 22.4.24)

One major consequence of the learning capacity demonstrated by the employee representatives was that as the scheme progressed management was forced to systematically and continually explain and justify their actions. In the early years of the scheme this was willingly done, with strict reference to improvements in the financial performance of the company in terms such as cost savings, larger sales, and more revenues. But gradually, management's basis for justifying decisions changed. Rather than rely on the alleged neutral and objective accounting data which was presented to the committee, management resorted to the more subjective appeal of exhorting the employee representatives to trust them and their judgement, since the constant need to justify their decisions to the Profit Sharing Scheme was becoming both time-consuming and seemed to be having some undesirable effects upon the effectiveness of decision-making. C. G. Renold explained the problem as follows:

> In all discussions of policy the Directors had to consider two points of view viz: the needs of the business having regard to outside influences – competition, etc – and also how far the policy decided upon could be explained and justified to the Committee. He said there were a great many things the Board would be able to accept and act on with less explicit evidence than was considered necessary to go to the Committee. The Directors were dealing all day long with general questions of management and were able to act, to a certain extent, on general impressions which was quite a sound basis of action among persons who were in close touch with the things and with one another, but these impressions could not be expected to satisfy a Committee like the Profit Sharing Committee which was comprised of individuals who were not in such close touch. The problems of guiding the business through the present very difficult trade situation were as much as the Directors could handle and to have, at the same time, to give their attention to other aspects which they would not have to do were it not for the need to explain matters to the Committee did involve a very real extra strain.
>
> (Committee Minutes, 26.1.25)

The above quotation bears eloquent testimony to the interrogatory skills of the shop-floor representatives, particularly as regards their demands for consistency between accounting descriptions of events and managerial decision-making. C. G. Renold's explanation interestingly also acknowledges the reality that managerial decision-making did not always adhere to principles readily justifiable in terms of accounting criteria.

Although on occasion, management could not always exercise control over the agenda or the direction of discussion, nevertheless the extent to which matters of strategic import to the company were discussed was entirely at management's discretion. This is nowhere more vividly demonstrated than over the merger of the Company with the Coventry Chain Company in 1930. The Directors had written into the Profit Sharing Scheme rules in 1927 a provision that, in the event of a reconstruction of the company (which a merger would in effect be), the scheme would automatically terminate.

Although this was justified at the time as necessary to avoid jeopard-
ising the company's attractiveness to prospective merger partners, no
further mention was made in the Profit Sharing Committee's minutes
until the merger with Coventry Chain was announced. This is all the
more surprising since the period 1927–30 was generally one of intense
merger and takeover activity, as companies attempted to insulate
themselves from the uncertainty of financial and product markets by
strengthening both their asset and market base. Moreover, in Tripp's
(1969) history of the company he reports that the idea of a merger
between the two companies was first seriously considered by C. G.
Renold in 1919, and that it 'occupied much of his time for the next
ten years' (Tripp, 1969, p. 141). The absence of any initiative by
management to discuss the merger in the Profit Sharing Committee
indicates that there were issues of strategic corporate import which
were not considered suitable for the purposes of consultation with the
employees, a fact thrown into sharper relief by the 'full' disclosure
policy the company pursued.

CONCLUSIONS

Although it is not the intention to provide an overall assessment of
the success or otherwise of the Joint Consultation Scheme, since
there are no readily available indicators to evaluate its own specific
contribution to industrial relations in the company, what can be
discussed are the particular problems and issues which arose during
its period of operation. These can be best understood by placing
them in the context of the objectives both parties sought to achieve
by participating in the Joint Consultation Scheme.

For management, the primary objective in introducing joint consultation was to construct a forum for management-employee discussions separate and distinct from the collective bargaining
machinery. The purpose of creating such a forum was to generate an
atmosphere of co-operative problem-solving and to secure the benefits management believed would accrue by educating the workforce
into a corporate view of the problems facing the organisation. A
policy of full information disclosure to employees was an integral
aspect of such a strategy. There can be no doubt that the Joint
Consultative arrangements facilitated the introduction of new
work methods and formal control systems, and that the efficiency

improvements these generated contributed significantly to sustaining the Company through the difficult period of the 1920s. Renold himself commented,

> The period of fifteen years between 1913 and 1928 has seen a revolution in our manufacturing processes, clerical and statistical methods, and in our organisation . . . The 1,807 people in 1928 . . . produced in value nearly two-and-a-half times as much per individual as the group of 1,256 people in 1913
>
> (Renold, 1928, p. 599–602)

How far management succeeded in inculcating employees into a managerial view of corporate activity is more open to question. This was largely due to a persistent employee scepticism of management's intentions which was fuelled by a number of considerations. Firstly, the fact that the scheme itself was introduced at management's initiative did little to assuage employee suspicions that this was nothing more than a managerial response to hostile environmental contingencies, and did nothing to alter the existing decision-making arrangements within the company. Despite the rhetoric of management's appeal for co-operation, the inequality of power relations between management and employees, both on a *de facto* basis because of the inferior bargaining position, and on a *de jure* basis because of the formal preservation of managerial prerogatives as regards decision-making encompassed within joint consultation, always left employees at a disadvantage in terms of their capacity to influence decision-making. The scheme was not perceived as, nor as intended to be, a discussion between equals. Management to some extent acknowledged this, as they felt the need to buttress employee willingness to participate in joint consultation by offering a financial incentive to do so through the Profit Sharing Scheme. Workers' compliance was never volunteered: rather it was recruited by management. Secondly, such scepticism was reinforced on those occasions when employee representatives challenged management's accounts of company activities, either on the basis of their own local knowledge or on grounds of competing interpretations of accounting information. Such challenges served to undermine the veracity of management's attempts to explain and justify their actions in terms of the accounting calculus, which became particularly pertinent when managerial interpretations explicitly affected bonus payment calculations under the Profit Sharing Scheme.

However, employee scepticism was not the only obstacle to management's success in utilising accounting information as a basis for explaining and justifying managerial actions in a way convincing to employees. Not only were employees capable of challenging the accuracy of accounting descriptions when it contradicted their own local knowledge of events, but also on occasion the technical appropriateness of the accounting measures management employed. Furthermore, management encountered the tactical problem of employees using disclosed information for purposes not anticipated by management. However, perhaps the major difficulty for management was the increasing burden of always having to justify their actions in terms of improving company performance as measured by accounting criteria. Having entered into a discourse with employees that exclusively relied on the alleged neutrality, objectivity and rationality of accounting performance measures as the only legitimate basis for appraising company performance, management found it increasingly demanding when decision-making owed more to their own subjective and intuitive judgements rather than the straightforward application of the principles of applied economic rationality. On such occasions, management infringed employee expectations of consistency and undermined their faith, which management had taken pains to create, in the notion of decision-making on the basis of rational expertise.

For those employees who directly participated in joint consultation the benefits were largely perceived in terms of the opportunity to receive from, and discuss .with, management, information which would not have been otherwise available. However, for the bulk of employees, the possibility of enhanced financial reward through the Profit Sharing Scheme was the principal motivation for the continued support of the consultative arrangements.

How far the evidence of one case study, particularly when set in an historical context, is applicable on a more generalised basis is of course tentative. However, it is clear from recent survey evidence that management see a similar potential in joint consultative arrangements as a potent medium for disclosing information for the same reasons that informed its adoption by the Renold's management. For example, Cressey et al.'s evidence (1981) demonstrates that management's commitment to disclosure of information through consultative procedures is sourced by a desire to educate the workforce in the business realities confronting the enterprise; to explain why management was adopting a particular course of action, and to ensure that information disclosure was exclusively a matter of managerial discretion. Dowling et al.'s evidence (1981) also corroborates this. In summarising their findings they commented:

> The general intention to promote participative practices on a non-adversial basis, separate from negotiation, and to retain managerial autonomy in decision-making, illustrates the strong preference of companies and their managements that participation should in no substantial way lead to changes in existing authority relations in industry. As such, many of the so-called participation schemes identified in the survey may be seen as essentially offering greater opportunities for employees to influence management policies and decisions mainly in a consultative sense. At the same time, they offered management the opportunity both to explain their difficulties and the possibility of adding a greater legitimacy to the actions they took in response to those difficulties. (p. 20).

Not all companies, however, subscribe to such ambitious objectives. Some companies, in responding to what Cressey et al. term the 'obligation to discuss company strategy with employees' are intent on minimising disclosure, and have little concern for utilising information as a means of persuading employees of the rationale for managerial actions. However, where companies are seeking this objective, the case study evidence suggests that management is unlikely to avoid the problems associated with disclosure in the context of collective bargaining, even if they are experienced in a more muted form. Even in the context of joint consultation, the disclosure of accounting information is unlikely to yield a willing compliance from employees to, and support for, managerial decision-making.

Bibliography

Armstrong, E. G. A., *Industrial Relations: An Introduction* (London: Harrap, 1969).
Batstone, E., 'Systems of Domination, Accommodation and Industrial Democracy' in T. R. Burns, L. K. Karlsson and V. Rus, (eds.) *Work and Power* (London: Sage Publications Ltd, 1979).
Batstone, E., A. Fenner, and M. Terry *Unions on the Board* (Oxford: Basil Blackwell, 1983).
Beaumont, P. B. and D. R. Deaton 'The Extent and Determinants of Joint

Consultative Arrangements in Britain', *Journal of Management Studies* (1981) pp. 49–71.

Brown, W., *The Changing Contours of British Industrial Relations* (Oxford: Basil Blackwell, 1981).

Bullock Report, *Report of the Committee of Inquiry on Industrial Democracy* (London: HMSO, 1977).

Burchell, S., C. Clubb, A. G. Hopwood, J. Hughes, and J. Nahapiet, 'The Roles of Accounting in Organizations and Society', *Accounting, Organisations and Society* (1980) pp. 5–27.

Clarke, R. O., D. J. Fatchett, and B. C. Roberts *Workers' Participation in Management in Britain* (London: Heinemann, 1972).

Clegg, H. A., *The Changing System of Industrial Relations in Great Britain* (Oxford: Basil Blackwell, 1979).

Clegg, H. A. and T. E. Chester, 'Joint Consultation' in A. Flanders, and H. A. Clegg, (eds) *The System of Industrial Relations in Great Britain* (Oxford: Basil Blackwell, 1956).

Commission on Industrial Relations (CIR), *Report No. 31 – Disclosure of Information* (London: HMSO, 1972).

Craft, J. A., 'Information Disclosure and the role of the Accountant in Collective Bargaining', *Accounting Organisations and Society* (1981) pp. 97–107.

Crawford, A., 'Cost Accounting, Work Control and the Development of Cost Accounting in Britain, 1914–1925', Paper presented to the European Accounting Association, St. Gallen, Switzerland (April 1984).

Cressey, P., J. Eldridge, J. MacInnes, and G. Nams, *Industrial Democracy and Participation: A Scottish Survey* (Department of Employment Research Paper, No. 28, 1981).

Daniel, W. W. and N. Millward, *Workplace Industrial Relations in Britain* (London: Heinemann, 1983).

Dowling, M. J., J. F. B. Goodman, D. A. Gothing, and J. D. Hyman *Employee Participation: Practice and Attitudes in North West Manufacturing Industry*, Department of Employment Research Paper (No. 27, 1981).

Elliott, J., *Conflict or Co-operation* (London: Kogan Page, 1978).

Foley, B. and K. T. Maunders *Accounting Information Disclosure and Collective Bargaining* (London: Macmillan, 1977).

Fox, A., *Man Mismanagement* (London: Hutchinson, 1974).

Goodman, J., *Employment Relations in Industrial Society* (Oxford: Philip Allan, 1984).

Government Social Survey, *Workplace Industrial Relations* (London: HMSO, 1968).

Hawes, W. and P. Brookes, 'Change and Renewal: Joint Consultation in Industry' *Department of Employment Gazette* (1980) pp. 353–61.

Hawkins, K., *A Handbook of Industrial Relations Practice* (London: Kegan Paul, 1979).

Hinton, J., *The First Shop Stewards Movements* (London: Allen and Unwin, 1973).

Hopwood, A. G., 'Accounting and the Pursuit of Efficiency', in A. G. Hopwood and C. Tomkins, (eds) *Issues in Public Sector Accounting* (Oxford: Philip Allen, 1984).

Jenkins, H. G., 'Financial Publicity and the Employee', in J. Lee, (ed.) *Pitman's Dictionary of Industrial Administration*, vol. I (London: Pitman, 1925).

Knight, I. B., *Company Organisation and Worker Participation: the results of a survey* (London: HMSO, 1979).

McCarthy, W. E. J., 'The Role of Shop Stewards in British Industrial Relations', *Donovan Commission Research Paper 1* (London: HMSO, 1966).

Marsh, A. I., *Industrial Relations in Engineering* (Oxford: Pergamon Press, 1965).

Marsh, A. I., *Concise Encyclopedia of Industrial Relations* (Aldershot: Gower Press, 1979).

Marsh, A. I., *Employee Relations Policy and Decision Making* (Aldershot: Gower Press, 1982).

Marsh, A. I. and E. E. Coker 'Shop Steward Organisation in the Engineering Industry', *British Journal of Industrial Relations* (1963) pp. 170–90.

Marsh, A. I., E. O. Evans, and P. Garcia, *Workplace Industrial Relations in Engineering* (Engineering Employees Federation, Kogan Page, 1971).

Ogden, S. G., 'Trade Unions, Industrial Democracy and Collective Bargaining', *Sociology* (1982) pp. 544–63.

Ogden, S. G. and P. D. Bougen 'A Radical Perspective on Disclosure of Information to Trade Unions', *Accounting Organisations and Society* (1985) pp. 211–44.

Palmer, J. R., *Use of Accounting Information in Labour Negotiations* (New York: National Association of Accountants, 1977).

Parker, S., *Workplace Industrial Relations* (London: HMSO, 1974).

Parker, S., *Workplace Industrial Relations* (London: HMSO, 1975).

Political and Economic Planning, *British Trade Unionism* (PEP, 1955).

Ramsay, H., 'Cycles of Control: Worker Participation in Sociological and Historical Perspective', *Sociology* (1977) pp. 481–506.

Renold, C. G., 'Workshop Committees', in A. W. Kirkaldy, (ed.) *British Labour: Replacement and Conciliation 1914–21* (London: Pitman, 1917).

Renold, C. G., 'Relations in the Workshop', *Manchester Guardian*, 30 November 1927.

Renold, C. G., 'The Nature and Present Position of Skill in Industry', *The Economic Journal* (1928) pp. 593–604.

Renold, C. G., 'Budgetary Control in the Organization of Hans Renold Ltd.', Paper Issued to the International Management Institute, Geneva, Switzerland, 1929.

Renold, C. G., *Joint Consultation Over Thirty Years* (London: Allen and Unwin, 1950).

Smith, R., 'Keeping Employees Informed: Current UK Practice on Disclosure', *Management Survey Report No. 31* (British Institute of Management, 1976).

Thomas, A. L., *The Allocation Problem in Financial Accounting Theory* (Florida: American Accounting Association, 1969).

Thomas, A. L., *The Allocation Problem: Part Two* (Florida: American Accounting Association, 1974).

Tripp, B. H., *Renold Limited 1956–1967* (London: Allen & Unwin, 1969).

8 Annual Reports in an Ideological Role: A Critical Theory Analysis

Norman B. Macintosh

Under the peculiar logic of accountancy, the men of the nine-teenth century built slums rather than model cities because slums paid

(Keynes, 1933)

Accounting, as Keynes observed more than sixty years ago, occupies a significant position in the functioning of society. In organisations and in society alike, what is accounted for shapes participants' views of what is important, sets the agenda, and determines how institutions function (Burchell et al., 1980; Macintosh, 1985). This is not a new view; accounting authorities have long since argued that accounting is critical to decisions involving economic planning, industrial regulation, wage and price determination, taxation, and international flow of money (Paton and Littleton, 1940; Solomons, 1978). Recently, there has been a resurgence of the idea that the symbolic, non-rational roles of accounting, including ceremony, power distribution, value clarification, and political manoeuvreing, should be the subject of research (Ansari and McDonough, 1980; Cherns, 1978; Davis et al., 1982; Boland and Pondy, 1983; Markus and Pfeffer, 1983; Meyer, 1983; Schreuder, 1984; Matthews, 1985; Parker and Guthrie, 1986). This paper reports the results of a critical theory analysis of a case study of IBM's annual reports in terms of their construction and reconstruction of an ideology of an inferior role for women in the computer workplace.

Several studies have investigated accounting in its ideological role.[1] This is an important item on the agenda of relating accounting to critical societal processes. Cherns, (1978), for example, illustrated how accounting promulgates an ideology consistent with capitalistic objectives to the exclusion of other important values. Cooper (1980) argued that the current stock of accounting theories and accounting information acts as an ideology that: legitimises the prescriptions of neo-classical marginalist theories of economics; provides a valid economic rationale for the way organisations distribute funds; supports those groups who are currently powerful in society; and obscures the question of whether or not the existing society is socially desirable. Burchell et al. (1980) pointed to the ideological function of accounting information in legitimising particular corporate activities and in rationalising past actions. Davis et al. (1982) argued for a new image of accounting which includes its ideological role in reflecting and shaping important societal superstructures. Cooper and Sherer (1984) concluded that research into the ideological function of accounting would illuminate the relationships between accounting and the distribution of power and resources in society, and could lead to new types of accounting systems which are more appropriate to the needs of an entire society. While it may be carried out intentionally or unintentionally, the ideological function of accounting is an important area for investigation (Willmott, 1983; Hopper and Powell, 1985).

THE METHODOLOGY OF CRITICAL SOCIAL THEORY

'Critical theory' (or 'critical philosophy' as it is sometimes referred to) was chosen as the analytical methodology for this study. Critical theory is aimed directly at investigation of societal and institutional ideologies and so is ideally suited for the research problem of this paper. Laughlin (1983 and 1987), for example, demonstrated its potential in his study of the ideological role of accounting systems in the Church of England, and the relationship of the accounting system to the life-world and steering mechanisms of the Church. He concluded that critical theory holds great potential as a general methodology for first, understanding accounting systems and second, changing them in organisational contexts.

Critical theory was developed by a group of philosophers, known as the 'Frankfurt School', including Horkheimer, Gadamer, Adorno, Marcuse, and Habermas.[2] Critical theory takes a stance between philosophy and historical sociology. It argues that most societies are permeated with 'objective illusion'. This objective illusion stems from ideologies which individuals and groups (that is, agents) have a hand in creating, or at least legitimising, but subsequently come to treat as the handicraft of others. The consequence of this is that agents suffer from self-inflicted delusion (that is, false consciousness) and a fettered existence (that is, coercion). Critical theory aims to effect a transition of society to a state where agents are free from false consciousness (that is, enlightened) and liberated from self-imposed coercion (that is, emancipated). The transition, critical theory contends, can take place only through introspection and self-reflection.

'Ideology', the essential concept in critical theory, is used in the sense of a world view held by agents in a society. Agents have more than just a bundle of randomly collected beliefs, attitudes, life goals, and artistic endeavours. Rather, they have a coherent social knowledge whereby each piece fits into a package in which the parts are related, albeit in a complex way, to each other. This package is called an ideology and has a characteristic structure, deals with central issues of human life, is shared widely by all agents, is central to agents' concept of society, and has a deep influence on their behaviour. In this sense, it is a form of consciousness which legitimises social practices and institutions. Ideology is seen as a major social force in the process whereby society produces and reproduces itself.

In addition to its descriptive meaning, ideology also is conceived of within critical theory to have a pejorative sense. Here ideology is thought of as a false form of consciousness whereby individuals delude themselves about their personal true interests, their position in society, and society in general. In this case, the aim of critical theory is to demonstrate to agents that they are deluded. This is accomplished by showing them why they hold particular beliefs and attitudes, how these lead to false consciousness, and how society imposes 'surplus repression' on its members by frustrating their preferences more than is needed for society to maintain and reproduce itself. Ideology in the pejorative sense involves the criticism of consciousness that incorporates false beliefs, functions in a reprehensible way, or has a tainted origin.

Critical theory also defines ideology in a positive sense. Here the critical theory, itself a form of ideology, includes the actions agents take to understand how they are deluded, to sort out what their real interests are, to rid themselves of false consciousness, and to free themselves from self-imposed coercion. In this positive sense, critical theory provokes self-reflection and hence induces enlightenment and emancipation.

From the critical theory perspective it is not enough merely to investigate social institutions and practices in order to achieve a complete theory of a society. It is also necessary to identify and analyse a society's ideology (in the descriptive, pejorative, and positive senses) in order to understand the beliefs or social knowledge agents hold about their society. This means, paradoxically, that a full-fledged critical theory must include an account of itself if it is to produce an exhaustive understanding of this knowledge. The logic is that a critical theory is itself part of the objective domain of the belief system of any society. (This contrasts with natural sciences such as particle theories of physics, where the theory itself is not a particle in motion). So critical theory is at least partly about itself and so must be reflective and self-referential.

The self-reflective nature of critical theory calls for a unique type of evidence for its confirmation. Whereas scientific theory relies on empirical observation and experiment for corroboration, a critical theory must be 'reflectively acceptable'. A critical theory is acceptable only if the agents to whom the theory is addressed would freely agree to the ideas in the theory under conditions of perfect information, full freedom, and thorough consideration of the views expressed about freedom and coercion. (Perfect information in the sense that the information available is believed to be true by all parties. Full freedom in the sense of full implementation of normative expectations as to equality, order, and consensually acceptable rules.) Such conditions are labelled the 'ideal speech situation'.

Paradoxically, then, a valid critical theory must contain its own criteria of confirmation. Confirmation, however, is paramount to the theory. It acts as the grindstone to set free the utopian kernel of beliefs and values of any society, a kernel embedded in the false consciousness of both privileged and disadvantaged agents. The goal of a critical theory is to present the possibility to agents in society that they can explicitly recognise their true aims and can form correct views about their real interests.

WOMEN IN THE WORKPLACE

The specific ideology selected for analysis for this paper is that of the role of women in the computer workplace. This is seen as a particularly important issue, given the dominant role given today by organisations to harnessing the new information technology. Women today comprise over forty per cent of the workforce of Western capitalist nations. Yet throughout history they have been routinely underprivileged through consignment to the secondary sector where low-paying, specialised, deskilled jobs and insecurity are the order of the day (Mitchell, 1971; Davies, 1975; Barron and Norris, 1976; Hamilton, 1978; Rubrey, 1978; Clegg and Dunkerley, 1980). Why this is so has been the focus of much inquiry.

A widely accepted view is that this inferior position is the result of a major ideological theme of Western society whereby women are considered a 'reserve army' labour pool to be called upon to fill the voids whenever males are unavailable, particularly in times of crisis. The roots of this ideology stem from the fourteenth century in Britain, when peasant women in the feudal era were obliged under the Statute of Labourers (1349) to work in the fields due to the shortage of men as a result of the Black Plague. With the development of capitalist agriculture and the dissolution of feudal society, the peasant families were pushed off the land to produce a class of landless ex-peasants who swelled into urban centres in the hopes of selling their labour power. Wages for men were set at a rate sufficient only to sustain themselves, not their families. Women, in order to survive, were forced to work as servants, prostitutes, or in factories for only half of what men could make. Women also carried the brunt of their family domestic labour. The end result for women was a labour process which embedded them in a doubly exploitive situation – work and home – where their low wages reflected their auxiliary role in the labour commodity system (Braverman, 1974).

For the next few centuries women became a readily dispensable industrial reserve army to be pulled in or tossed out of work as required by the owners of the shops and factories (Adamson et al., 1976; Humphries, 1983). The past three centuries witnessed a large rise in female employment, a period of stabilisation, and another rise after the Second World War (Shorter, 1976). The world wars of the twentieth century gave rise to a surge in standardisation, mechanisation, and deskilling of production work, in large part so that it could harness the low-skilled reserve army of women available to work, and could then, at the end of hostilities, with the tacit consent of the unions, purge them from the labour force (Adamson et al., 1976; Clegg and Dunkerley, 1980; Tinker and Neimark, 1987). This ideology of a 'reserve army' of cheap labour, reinforced by the myth that women are well-suited in temperament (passive, patient and careful) and in physical abilities (graceful and dextrous with their hands), and thus perfectly suited to boring repetitive work, made it easy for employers to create a dual labour market which relegated women to the specialised, deskilled and low wage sector (Braverman, 1974).

Just as women entered the factories in increasing numbers in the eighteenth and nineteenth century, they were recruited into the office in the late nineteenth and early twentieth centuries, particularly during wartime economies. The office originally had been the purview of men. The post of office secretary was a prestigious job. It entailed administrative work such as composing important letters, recording and payment of accounts, dealing with routine meetings with suppliers and customers, and managing all correspondence on behalf of the owner. In addition to the mundane clerical chores, men were apprenticed in these jobs in preparation for advancement in the executive hierarchy, partnership, and even ownership.

With the advent of mechanisation, however, office work was reshaped in a pattern which paralleled that of the factory – specialisation, deskilling, low wages, and the employment of women (Scott, 1982). The men staked out the higher, skilled, thinking positions while the new deskilled jobs became the purview of women. Social domination, as before, proved to be accompanied by economic ascendency as male incumbents in the thinking positions enjoyed considerably higher salaries than their female counterparts in the manual jobs. The pattern developed in the factory had repeated itself in the office.

The increase in female white-collar work at the end of the nineteenth century, however, featured a new variation of the traditional theme. This change was driven by an enormous increase in the quantity of paperwork necessitated by the huge expansion of the economy, in particular in the industry, commerce, and government sectors. The ever-increasing volume of paperwork required a permanent battalion of foot soldiers for which the reserve army of women were ideal recruits. Once again the work was specialised and deskilled as clerical chores were separated from administrative work (Scott, 1982). Copy work, for example, previously done by the male secretary or hired out to educated women from middle-class and artisan families to do at home, could be done by women in the office, thanks to the invention of the typewriter. Stenography and filing, along with typing, became components of a full-time job in the office. Men moved out of secretarial work into sales, advertising and administration, and women were hired to fill the specialised, deskilled and low-paying white-collar service jobs. By 1910, over eighty per cent of these jobs in the US were filled by women, compared to an insignificant fraction a mere thirty years earlier. The outer office, a clean and respectable place to work, became, and remains today, the purview of women.

Mechanisation of housekeeping chores during the twentieth century also influenced women's lives in important ways. Society at home, as at work, had been dominated by fundamentally exploitive patriarchal relationships which did not change over the past few centuries. Until recently, most women have remained, through the institutions of marriage and family, tied to their largely reproductive and housekeeping roles. The host of labour-saving devices which came on the scene in the past couple of generations did give a softer look to women's subordination as mechanisation reduced sharply the tedium and physical activities. Paradoxically, however, it also tied women more closely to their traditional role of home-maker as they became new consumers of this ever-expanding range of domestic products. Mechanisation throughout history has not been an emancipatory force for women, on the contrary, it has relegated a large proportion of them to a 'double ghetto' at work and at home.

A CASE STUDY

IBM's annual reports were selected for a case study of their ideological theme regarding women in the computer and information system workplace for obvious reasons. IBM, the largest of the new information-technology firms, operates globally, employs nearly 375,000 people, and anticipates industry-wide sales of over one trillion dollars by 1993. IBM's expertise spans the entire spectrum of the new information technology, ranging from computerised typewriters and word-processing stations to satellite and ground stations, as well as frontier military and space products. In 1984, IBM was selected in a nation-wide poll as the best-managed company in the USA. As the leading firm in the key industry of the new era, and with a huge stake in continued growth, IBM's image of the role of women in the workplace may prove critical to the historical evolution of women's struggle for a more equitable stake in the workplace.

The research problem was to identify and analyse the ideological message contained in IBM's annual reports, as they shape and legitimise the role of women in the computer- and related information-workplace. For this purpose, a panel of twenty judges, graduate students in economics and management, examined a sample of pictures (with captions) from IBM's annual reports. Seven annual reports from 1957 through 1982 were selected at random. From these reports all pictures, eighty in total, showing people involved in using, designing, manufacturing, installing, and repairing information-technology products were included. The judges first identified every person in each picture as either male or female and then categorised each of them in terms of one of three types of work: (1) creative-thinking; (2) technical-supervisory, and (3) routine-repetitive (or routine-menial).

The results of the judging shown in Table 8.1, indicate that males in the pictures dominated the creative-thinking and technical-supervisory categories, while females dominated the routine-repetitive group. These data were compared to IBM's actual employment data for US locations for the years 1981, 1982, and 1983 shown in Table 8.2. While the categories in Table 8.1 and 8.2 are not strictly comparable, the pictures and captions in the annual reports indicate 70 per cent for males in the creative-thinking category compared to 85 per cent for males in the 'managing and professional' categories in Table 8.2. While for the routine-repetitive category in Table 8.1, females are depicted in 64 per cent of the cases, compared to 85 per cent females in the 'office/clerical' group in Table 8.2. It is of interest to note that the pictures and captions in the annual reports are more 'progressive' than is the case for IBM's actual employment situation. Either way, however, the picture portrayed in these accounting reports is one whereby a majority of females work in the routine-repetitive jobs, while the majority of men work in thinking-creative jobs.

It is important to note, however, that IBM's annual reports over the last decade included many photographs of women in thinking-creative and in technical-supervisory jobs. The reports also include photographs of males doing routine-menial work. And none of the photographs in the 1984 Annual Report depicted women in routine-menial jobs, while the cover features a woman marketing representative talking with a male customer. Further, a cursory examination of recent pictures in professional accounting magazines, advertising by other computer suppliers, and academic textbooks (particularly MIS texts) indicates that IBM, by comparison, is considerably more progressive than these other organisations and institutions in terms of depicting an equal-opportunity role for women during the information era.

TABLE 8.1 *Results of Judges's Classifications*

Category	Male	Female	Total
Type I (routine-repetitive)	239 (36%)	403 (64%)	642 (100%)
Type II (technical-supervisory)	460 (66%)	238 (34%)	698 (100%)
Type III (creative-thinking)	172 (70%)	71 (30%)	243 (100%)
Undecided			17
			—
			1 600

A CRITICAL THEORY ANALYSIS

Against this background, a critical theory analysis of the role of women in the computing and information systems workplace might proceed as follows. Under conditions of perfect information, full freedom, and thorough consideration, it seems plausible that agents in society, both male and female, would opt for a world where members of both sexes had equal opportunities to and participated equally in all segments of the computer- and related information-technology workplace. Now the ideology, in the descriptive sense, expressed in IBM's annual reports, differs distinctly from this normative world view. It contains a false form of consciousness and so deludes some of the agents involved. What is required, then, is reflectively acceptable action which will alert agents to their delusion, help them identify their real interests, and free them from false consciousness and self-imposed coercion.

Four possible major types of coercion for females can be identified in the IBM case. The first is the 'society of happy slaves' who are genuinely content with their chains. Under these conditions, social control is so effective that members are prevented from even forming desires which cannot be easily satisfied. This would be the case if the women in the menial and routine jobs resist, due to ideological delusion, understanding their plight, and cannot see that they are under the influence of social opiates (for instance, clean, modern working conditions; considerate bosses; company bowling leagues and picnics; short working hours; pension plans, and so on) that bind them to the present organisation of society. In this instance the women actually believe the descriptive ideology and are bonded to a set of false modes of gratification. Consequently they are immune

TABLE 8.2 IBM Employment Data
Employment Data for US Locations 1981–1983

	Total Employees	Male	Female	Total Minority	Black	Asian	American Indian	Hispanic
Managers								
'81	28 017	25 282	2 735	2 665	1 704	410	89	461
'82	29 478	26 390	3 088	2 831	1 781	468	81	501
'83	30 543	26 878	3 665	3 018	1 862	537	84	535
Professionals								
'81	61 937	53 061	8 876	6 603	3 047	2 452	78	1 025
'82	68 423	57 209	11 214	7 815	3 526	2 981	97	1 211
'83	73 831	60 755	13 076	8 826	3 986	3 355	118	1 366
Technicians								
'81	42 597	38 648	3 949	5 678	3 445	659	126	1 448
'82	42 554	38 308	4 246	5 836	3 471	724	140	1 501
'83	41 171	36 985	4 186	5 684	3 350	706	130	1 498
Marketing								
'81	19 437	14 533	4 904	2 811	1 817	442	56	496

'82	520	53	461	1 755	2 789	5 123	13 816	18 939
'83	525	51	505	1 765	2 846	5 334	13 717	19 051
Office/Clerical								
'81	1 564	125	436	5 069	7 194	21 296	11 936	33 232
'82	1 640	132	443	5 325	7 540	22 320	12 273	34 593
'83	1 660	142	452	5 376	7 630	22 694	11 949	34 643
Craft Workers								
'81	252	16	39	553	860	821	6 056	6 877
'82	324	18	55	603	1 000	988	6 191	7 179
'83	331	22	63	625	1 041	1 125	6 147	7 272
Operatives								
'81	1 158	52	369	2 139	3 718	7 311	8 767	16 078
'82	1 190	57	403	2 137	3 787	7 392	8 226	15 618
'83	1 128	51	407	2 107	3 693	7 045	7 806	14 851
Total								
'81	6 406	542	4 810	17 780	29 546	49 918	158 398	208 316
'82	6 895	578	5 537	18 606	31 616	54 383	162 856	217 239
'83	7 043	598	6 025	19 073	32 740	57 133	164 264	221 397

SOURCE: IBM *company records*

from emancipation. Critical theory here can at least invoke the principle of 'free assent' and point out that an opiate mode of gratification is appropriate only if the women themselves would have agreed, under an ideal speech situation, that the current state of affairs is in their own true interests.

The second case, known as 'ideological delusion', occurs when individuals in society are fully satisfied and show no signs of hidden frustration, because their social institutions are so powerful and effective that they cannot even formulate desires which are not available to them under the present institutional framework. The result, nevertheless, is delusion, shallowness and a dull, impoverished existence. Here a critical theory can extract, from the cultural tradition, standards of the good life and then compare these to the current state of existence of the deluded members. Even though parts of the good life may be utopian, and thus unattainable, critical theory can enlighten agents about how much more of their traditional good life remains to be realised. In the case of women in the computer and information systems workplace, a critical theory analysis enables them to compare their existence in the menial-routine segment with society's ideal that all individuals, regardless of sex, should have an equal opportunity to attain and hold jobs in the other segments. Even though this ideal may not be available, they will understand that the impediment is society's patriarchal ideology.

The third brand of coercion comes into play when individuals realise they are suffering, but have either no theory or a false one. Here critical theory aims to make agents aware of the source of their coercion. For women in the computer and information workplace, it is necessary for them to understand that the source is the patriarchal ideology which permeates much of organisational life. This understood, they can either set aside false biological theories (such as, women are physically more dextrous and so better suited to this type of work, and by nature more adaptable to repetitive boring work, than are their male counterparts) or, if they have no theory, fill the vacuum with a critical theory. Either way they come to realise the true source of their frustration. In both instances, critical theory is committed to the existence of the 'true' causal relationship between a powerful social institution and the agents who are suffering under it.

The fourth type of coercion occurs when the agents know full well what they want – an abatement in coercion and suffering – and they know which social institution is the prime cause. What they do not know, however, is that they could act in a legitimate and rational way, one which is compatible with the pursuit of their real interests, in order to relieve their suffering. Here critical theory shows them what can be done by confronting head-on the particular social group that fosters, promotes, and has every reason to resist the abolition of the patriarchal society. And it makes clear that active engagement by agents in society is required in the form of women's movements lobbying for legislation, making sure laws are followed, and confronting the coercing agents.

The critical theory, it should be underlined, must be aimed not only at women in the workplace, but also at their male counterparts. The goal in this instance is first to reveal to male agents their major 'objectification mistake'. Objective illusion occurs when any particular interest group produces a realm of social 'objects' and then fails to recognise it as a result of their own doing. If the society is to reproduce itself, of course, most agents must make this objectification mistake. This ideological form of consciousness, it is important to understand, serves to legitimise the social institution and its resultant action.

In the case of the ideology depicted in IBM's annual reports, it seems highly plausible that one group in society (the males) are entwined in an objectification error. The pictures clearly suggest that the majority of women work in (and should work in) the routine-menial segment. The normal explanation for this is that this is a physical (that is, natural) fact. A count of the actual number of females in public information issued by IBM regarding 'Equal Opportunity and Affirmative Action Programs' confirms that males dominate the managerial and professional positions and women dominate the office and clerical jobs (see Table 8.2). Thus it is easy for males to make the objectification error by merely pointing to the statistics and concluding that 'this is the way the world is as I experience it'.

This line of reasoning, however, obviously fails to recognise that the working world is dominated by males, and that this domination requires an ideology which legitimises it and serves to reproduce social relations at work whereby women are disadvantaged. This ideological delusion, of course, works to the benefit of the male members of the workforce. It seems better, within the current social order, to be a member of the dominant group. Ideological delusion helps this group to have as much normative ideological power as possible.

Critical theory here can become the self-consciousness of a successful process of emancipation and enlightenment for the male group. The first step is to extract from them their views about the good life in terms of their notions of freedom, truth, and rationality as embedded in their normative knowledge of the world. The normative kernel for most males would be a workplace where all individuals and groups are permitted equal access to all segments of the workplace. The next step is to confront the male group with the discrepancy between their ideal of the good life and the realities of the workplace. This makes it possible for them to see that it was subjectively rational for them to acquire a patriarchal ideological form of consciousness. They then have a chance to realise how this seems to allow them the personal development, expression, and satisfaction of their basic desires within their normative framework, yet is really self-destructive because it frustrates members of the dominated group from developing and satisfying these same desires. Once this is understood, both the advantaged and disadvantaged groups are enlightened, and the emancipatory process can take place whereby the underlying genuine human wants, needs, and aspirations of the entire society can be separated and recovered from their mode of expression in the patriarchal ideology.

In the case of women in the computer and information system workplace then, a critical theory analysis attempts not only to expose the false consciousness of both groups, but also through a reflective process, to bring all agents into a new set of social relations whereby males and females can participate in the computer and information systems workplace in accordance with the essence of society's normative views about freedom, truth and rationality.

Critical theory, of course, is not without limitations. One feature that comes into question is its emphasis on ideology and legitimation of the current social structure of a society. The result is a narrow range of interest which all but ignores the historical roots of the current social order. Thus it can lead to an inadequate account of the development of social classes and class conflicts (Bottomore, 1984). As a consequence, critical theory may place undue weight on the emancipatory possibilities inherent in unmasking the cause of coercive social arrangements, at the expense of ignoring the historical roots of the current social status quo.

In the case of women in the computer workplace, it can be argued that it may be idealistic to presume a desire on the part of males to want to work for the common good of people of both genders. The males, with the aid of critical theory, may perceive the discrepency in chances for females relative to males, but will merely carry on as before because they benefit more from the existing social order than from a normative society. At best, then, critical theory can be used to undermine the legitimacy of the dominant male position, thereby making it more difficult for this ideology to work effectively. So critical theory is seen as a tool to aid the subordinate group in the battle over which ideology will dominate, the patriarchal world view or the equality for all ideology, rather than as a guarantee of betterment.

Another criticism, closely related to the above, argues that critical theory pays too little attention to economic processes of capital accumulation and to the role of the state in managing a viable equilibrium, at least in Western capitalist nations, amongst capital, labour, and the middle classes (Gramsci, 1971; Althusser, 1971; Wellman, 1983). As a consequence, it downplays the importance of what Weber and others saw as the ever-increasing rationalisation of social life as embodying an ideology of the main tendencies of capitalist development (Bottomore, 1984). While critical theory places primacy on the subjective nature of social relations, it tends to deprecate the importance of objective empirical forms of social coercion and domination. Many sociologists would argue, following Marx's later writings, that emancipation is only possible when a widespread class consciousness, one that exists in a more positivistic sense outside any one individual, emerges and is used by the subordinate class to attack the dominant class and its world view. From this latter perspective, women in general will not be free merely by understanding the source of their oppression, but rather they must take collective action to become free from the structural male domination. Thus the primacy of subjectivity, excessive idealism, the exclusion of the historicity and economic foundations of social life, and an excessively philosophical tenor are limitations inherent in critical theory analysis. Nevertheless, critical theory offers the researcher one valuable way to describe accounting in action and to be critical in the sense of analysing accounting from a perspective beyond markets and established value systems (Matthews, 1985).

CONCLUSION

A major aim of this paper was to investigate the role of accounting in shaping and supporting important societal ideologies. This type of research demonstrates how accounting reports can play an important part, wittingly or unwittingly, in shaping important social relations. Accounting reports are seen as more than neutral objective documents providing investors with economic information about the financial affairs of the entity. They are, in and of themselves, phenomena that can be analysed and interpreted as texts to reveal their essential and significant social meaning (Tinker and Neimark, 1987). They are a permanent expression of those social issues which top management regard as important and wish to communicate to shareholders and the public, and so are a record of the entity's historical social consciousness. Accounting as social action is an important arena for investigation.

Investigations of accounting in its social role, however, require a different type of analytical methodology than, say, incremental economics. The nature, grounds of, and knowledge created by critical theory differ in essential ways from economics-based accounting theories. The former contends it is subjective and reflective while the latter asserts itself objective and positivistic. And while economics-based accounting efforts espouse a separation of theory and methodology, critical accounting tends to recognise them as integral parts of the reflective process (Schreuder, 1984). So rather than develop testable hypotheses based on theory, and devising objective tests to support or falsify them, critical accounting aims to bring basic attitudes, beliefs and behaviour patterns to full consciousness in order to change them if they appear undesirable or false. It holds the potential to take the current appreciation of accounting-systems design to new important levels (Laughlin, 1983 and 1987).

Critical theory investigations can be used, for example, to expose the role accounting plays in masking contradictions and tensions amongst classes in society.[3] The women in the pictures performing the menial-routine jobs appear happy, contented and natural. Yet a critical theory analysis unmasks the contradictions and tensions between a male-dominated managerial class and a female-dominated working class, and exposes how accounting reports serve to mystify these unequal arrangements. Similarly, Tinker's (1980) reconstruction of the accounts of Delco Company Ltd. exposed the contradictions between the European owners and the native workers who performed the underground production work. And Tinker and Niemark's (1987) deconstruction of General Motors annual reports over a period of sixty-one years revealed ideological themes that treated women as a reserve army of production workers to be called up or discharged as circumstances dictated. Critical accounting research is a valuable way of exposing ideological themes for what they are, and for helping to bring undesirable social class tensions and contradictions to the surface, where they can be treated as problematic.

The above research also points to the emancipatory possibilities of a critical theory analysis of accounting. When ideology is embedded in accounting reports but goes unnoticed, accountants, practitioners and academics alike take them for granted, and come to see the socially created reality as an external, objective fact. In doing so they prevent themselves from correctly perceiving the situation that they helped to establish and thus they alienate themselves from that reality by coming to treat it, not as something they created, but rather as 'the way things are'. Critical research is aimed at producing enlightenment by enabling accountants to determine more precisely their true interests and purposes (Neimark and Tinker, 1987). It holds out the possibility of freeing accountancy from socially repressive actions and ridding it of ideological illusion. Critical accounting investigations have special standing as guides for human action.

The research reported here, for example, exposes an ideology embedded in IBM's annual reports of an interior role for women in society. This ideology, if believed to be undesirable, can be confronted and changed. While the subjective and reflective nature of the methodology of critical analysis is a troublesome feature, its strength lies in the potential it holds for the emergence of powerful insights which can be shared and then incorporated into the wider collective conscience of society. As Parker and Guthrie (1986) point out, such analysis serves to identify social determinants of meanings attributed to social disclosures, to recognise the non-neutrality of the annual report, and to expose the role of corporate disclosures in legitimating the private interests of special privileged groups.

A final aim of this paper was to demonstrate that accounting research can benefit from analytical methods that go beyond viewing accounting as an information-providing activity to be analysed and understood within the terms and meaning of the theory of incremental economics. Incremental economics is deeply embedded in the history of intellectual accounting thought and dominates accounting research, literature and teaching. Yet, as this paper demonstrates, intellectual activity in accounting need not be limited to one paradigm. Accounting researchers can usefully look to advances in social theory and intellectual thought, such as critical theory, that have taken place in the past couple of decades. When other social sciences such as political science, sociology, and philosophy have gone beyond structural-functionalism as their major paradigm, why should accounting continue to look to it as the major source of intellectual nourishment? To continue to do so can only lead to further estrange accountants, accounting researchers, and accounting itself from the conditions of social order which they help to construct and then treat as an independent, objective, external reality.

Critical theory investigations into accounting, such as the study reported here, hold potential for a more emancipatory type of accounting action than has been the case historically. Not all accounting inquiry need have the structure of critical theory, but the construction of an empirically informed critical theory of accounting seems a legitimate aspiration for further accounting research. Accounting is part of a wider enterprise of social philosophy, and studies such as this one may even provide a logic of accountancy whereby 'men of the twentieth century build model cities instead of slums because model cities "pay"'.

Notes

1. In this paper ideology is used in the sense that it is a principal aspect of any social superstructure. The ideology serves as its system of beliefs to order, support and sanction social and political order (Bernstein, 1971; Giddens, 1971). The important operative aspect of an ideology, however, lies in its rhetorical element as it is used to motivate, justify, and mobilise action to accomplish specific programs and realise strategies (Geuss, 1981). Ideology, then, is an illusive aspect of social life, but one that can be invoked as a powerful means to legitimise, accomplish, and sustain both general and specific social ends.
2. The explanation and discussion of critical theory in this paper follow closely the expositions of Geuss (1981) and Bottomore (1984). It is recognised that the critical theory of the Frankfurt School is a complex phenomenon, and has been interpreted and expounded in a variety of ways.
3. Class is used here in the sense of an individual's position within the social relations of production in terms of first, whether or not the individual controls the labour power of others in, say, a supervisory way, and second, whether or not the individual owns the means of production (Wright, 1978).

Bibliography

Adamson, O., C. Brown, J. Harrison and J. Price, 'Women's Oppression under Capitalism', *Revolutionary Communist* (1976) pp. 2–38.

Althusser, L., *Lenin and Philosophy* (London: New Left Books, 1971).

Ansari, S. L. and J. J. McDonough, 'Intersubjectivity – The Challenge and Opportunity for Accounting', *Accounting, Organizations and Society* (1980) pp. 129–42.

Barron, R. D., and G. M. Norris, 'Sexual Divisions and the Dual Labour Market', in D. L. Barker and S. Allan (eds), *Dependence and Exploitation in Work and Marriage* (New York: Longman, 1976).

Bernstein, R. J., *Praxis and Action* (Philadelphia: University of Pennsylvania Press, 1971).

Boland, R. J. and L. R. Pondy, 'Accounting in Organizations: A Union of Natural and Rational Perspectives', *Accounting, Organizations and Society* (1983) pp. 223–4.

Bottomore, T., *The Frankfurt School* (London: Tavistock Publications Ltd., 1984).

Braverman, H., *Labor and Monopoly Capital* (New York: Monthly Review Press, 1974) pp. 70–84.

Burchell, S., C. Clubb, A. G. Hopwood, J. Hughes and J. Nahapiet, 'The Role of Accounting in Organizations and Society', *Accounting, Organizations and Society* (1980) pp. 5–27.

Cherns, A. B., 'Alienation and Accounting', *Accounting, Organizations and Society* (1978) pp. 105–14.

Clegg, S., and D. Dunkerley, *Organization, Class and Control* (London: Routledge and Kegan Paul, 1980).

Cooper, D. J., 'Discussion of "Towards a Political Economy of Accounting Reports"', *Accounting Organizations and Society* (1980) pp. 161–6.

Cooper, D. J. and M. J. Sherer' 'The Value of Corporate Accounting Reports: Arguments for a Political Economy of Accounting', *Accounting, Organizations and Society* (1984) pp. 207–32.

Davies, R., *Women and Work*, (New York: Arno Press, 1975).

Davis, S., K. Menon, and G. Morgan, 'The Images that Have Shaped Accounting Theory', *Accounting, Organizations and Society* (1982) pp. 307–18.

Geuss, R., *The Idea of a Critical Theory: Habermas and the Frankfurt School* (Cambridge University Press, 1981).

Giddens, A., *Capitalism and Modern Social Theory* (Cambridge University Press, 1971).

Gramsci, A., *Selections from the Prison Notebooks*, (London: Lawrence & Wishart, 1971).

Hamilton, R., *The Liberation of Women: A Study of Patriarchy and Capitalism* (New York: Allan and Unwin, 1978).

Hopper, T., and A. Powell, 'Making Sense of Research Into the Organizational and Social Aspects of Management Accounting: A Review of Its Underlying Assumptions', *Journal of Management Studies* (1985) pp. 429–65.

Humphries, J., 'The Emancipation of Women in the 1970s and the 1980s: From the Latent to the Floating', *Capital and Class* (1983) pp. 6–28.

Keynes, J. M., 'National Self-Sufficiency', *Yale Law Review* (22, 1933) pp. 755–63.

Laughlin, R. C., 'The Need for and Nature of a Critical Theoretical Methodological Approach to the Design of Enterprise Accounting Systems,' a paper presented to the Accounting Methodology Workshop (EIASM, Brussels, 1983).

Laughlin, R. C., 'Insights into the nature and application of a critical theoretic methodological approach for understanding and changing accounting systems and their organizational contexts', *Accounting, Organizations and Society* (1987), pp. 479–502.

Macintosh, N. B., *The Social Software of Accounting and Information Systems* (Chichester: John Wiley, 1985).

Markus, M. L. and J. Pfeffer, 'Power and Design and Implementation of Accounting and Control Systems', *Accounting, Organizations and Society* (1983) pp. 205–218.

Matthews, M. R., 'Justifying the Implementation of Social Accounting: Three Approaches', a paper presented at the Annual Convention of the American Accounting Association (Reno, Nevada, August 1985).

Meyer, J. W., 'On the Celebration of Rationality: Some Comments on Boland and Pondy', *Accounting, Organizations and Society* (1983), pp. 235–40.

Mitchell, J., *Women's Estate* (Harmondsworth: Penguin, 1971).

Parker, L. D. and J. E. Guthrie, 'Corporate Social Disclosure Practice: A Comparative International Analysis', working paper, Griffith University and University of New South Wales, Australia, 1986).

Paton, W. A. and A. C. Littleton, *An Introduction to Corporate Accounting Standards* (New York: American Accounting Association, 1940).

Rubrey, J., 'Structured Labour Markets, Worker Organization, and Low Pay', *Cambridge Journal of Economics* (1978) pp. 17–36.

Schreuder, H., 'Positively normative (accounting) theories', in A. G. Hopwood and H. Schreuder (eds), *European Contributions to Accounting Research* (Amsterdam: Free University Press, 1984).

Scott, J. W., 'The Mechanization of Women's Work', *Scientific American* (September 1982) pp. 167–87.

Shorter, E., 'Women's Work: What Difference Did Capitalism Make', *Theory and Society* (1976) pp. 513–28.

Solomons, D., 'The Politicization of Accouting', *Journal of Accountancy* (1978) pp. 65–72.

Tinker, A. M., 'Towards a Political Economy of Accounting: An Empirical Illustration of the Cambridge Controversies', *Accounting, Organizations and Society* (1980) pp. 147–60.

Tinker, A. and M. Neimark, 'The Role of Annual Reports in General Motors: 1917–1976', *Accounting, Organizations and Society* (1987) pp. 71–88.

Wellman, A., 'Reason, Utopia, and the Dialectic of Enlightenment', *Praxis International* (1983).

Willmott, H., 'Paradigms for Accounting Research: Critical Reflections on Tomkins and Groves' "Everyday Accountant and Researching His Reality"', *Accounting, Organizations and Society* (1983) pp. 389–405.

Wright, E. O., 'Race, Class, and Income Inequality', *American Journal of Sociology* (1978) pp. 1368–82, 1386–97.

9 Power/Accounts and Ideology

Gavin Murray

And knowledge, rightly honoured with that name –
Knowledge not purchased by the loss of power
                                                    (Wordsworth, *Prelude*)

THE PROBLEMS OF MANAGEMENT ACCOUNTING RESEARCH

Management Accounting Research exemplifies the more general problems of social research. These general problems are methodological ones and they have received considerable attention in the specifically accounting literature. Burrell and Morgan (1979) suggest a 2 × 2 classification which identifies four approaches to accounting research in organisations. Each of these approaches is in opposition to the other three. One aspect of Burrell and Morgan's classification is a distinction between subjective and objective research paradigms; subjectivism begins from the premise that knowledge is founded upon subjective experience which it defines and illuminates, while objectivism begins from the premise that the subject is constituted by structures of knowledge. This distinction is essentially concerned with different conceptions of the power of the subject: subjectivism conceives of the subject as active power while objectivism conceives of the subject as passive power. Boland and Pondy (1983) rightly claim that such classifications fail to appreciate the interaction between the subjective and the objective. They also insist that research which recognises this interaction must focus on action in organisational settings. Hopwood (1983) has also insisted upon this but has noted the paucity of such empirical studies of accounting in action.

There is now considerable support for the proposal that accounting should be understood as action in an organisational situation (Flamholtz, 1983, Markus and Pfeffer, 1983, Hayes 1983). The general thrust of this argument is that situated action rather than abstract

173

technical sophistication has shaped the development of accounting. Cooper (1983) has argued that research into the dysfunctions of accounting by means of organisationally grounded studies should be encouraged. Yet unless the interaction of subjective and objective is made the focus of attention in management accounting research, then an exploration of the conflict between objective accounting discourses and subjective experience will be impossible.

But there have been few studies of the interaction of subjective and objective poles reported in the accounting literature. In this context it is plausible for accountants to assume that this interaction is unproblematic; this seems to be the assumption in Boland & Pondy's conception of a genuine union of rational and natural systems. Empirical studies are needed which provide an understanding of the various modes of interaction that are possible between subjective and objective poles of experience.

PROBLEMS OF SOCIAL RESEARCH

If management accounting research does focus upon the interaction of rational and natural systems, then it will be able to inform social research in general in an important way. Burrell and Morgan's distinction between the 'radical humanist' and the 'radical structuralist' orientations in social research captures the general oppostion within social research between those who give priority to economic conditions and those who claim that discursive structures constitute experience.

Marxism is, of course, a term which now includes both orientations to research, in particular it includes those who believe that discursive structures strongly influence the activity of most members of society, and those who believe that the majority have not been incorporated into these structures.

Abercrombie et al. (1980) point to a passage in *The German Ideology* which is capable of two opposing interpretations:

The ideas of the ruling class are in every epoch the ruling ideas: i.e., the class which is the ruling material force of society, is at the same time its ruling intellectual force. The class which has the means of material production at its disposal, has control at the same time over the means of mental production, so that thereby, generally speaking, the ideas of those who lack the means of mental production are subject to it. The ruling ideas are nothing more than the ideal expression of the dominant material relationships, the dominant material relationships grasped as ideas; hence of the relationships which make the one class the ruling one, therefore, the ideas of its dominance. The individuals composing the ruling class possess among other things conciousness, and therefore think. Insofar, therefore, as they rule as a class and determine the extent and compass of an epoch, it is self-evident that they do this in its whole range, hence among other things rule also as thinkers, as producers of ideas, and regulate the production and distribution of the idea of their age: thus their ideas are the ruling ideas of the epoch.

(p. 64)

Abercrombie et al. identify the ambiguity in this passage as follows:

It is possible to formulate *two* interpretations of the passage, one stronger than the other. In the weak version, Marx and Engels can be interpreted as saying that the intellectual life of a society is dominated by the ruling class, so that an observer will necessarily perceive only the ruling ideas and will not be able to apprehend the culture of subordinate classes simply because that culture does not have institutions to give it public expression. More strongly, it can be argued that the command exercised by the ruling class over the apparatus of intellectual production means that there cannot be any subordinate culture, for all classes are incorporated within the same intellectual universe, that of the ruling class. So, in the first interpretation there are a variety of cultures present in a society, but only one is ever publicly noticeable, while in the second there is only one dominant culture, in which all classes share.

(p. 8)

For Burrell and Morgan the ambiguities of Marx reflect a more general opposition within social research, one which opposes Marxists who give priority to economic conditions to structuralists such as Foucault, who understand the subject as the product of incorporation into discursive structures.

For Foucault the subject is a site for power/knowledge:

The working hypothesis will be this: power relations (with the struggles that traverse them or the institutions that maintain them) do not only play with respect to knowledge a facilitating or obstructive role; they are not content merely to encourage or to stimulate it, to distort or to limit it; power and knowledge are not linked together solely by the play of interests or ideologies; the problem is not therefore that of determining how power subjugates knowledge and makes it serve its ends, or how it imprints its mark on knowledge, imposes on it ideological contents and limits. No body of knowledge can be formed without a system of communications, records, accummulation and displacement which is in itself a form of power and which is linked, in its existence and functioning, to the other forms of power. Conversely, no power can be exercised without the extraction, appropriation, distribution or retention of knowledge. On this level, there is not knowledge on the one side and society on the other, or science and the state, but only the fundamental forms of knowledge/power

(*Annuaire du College de France, 1971/2*, in Sheridan, 1980, p. 283)

Particular sites of power/knowledge have a status accorded to them by the discursive economy; that is, 'upon a definite relation of forces that is established, at a determinate, historically specificiable moment, in war and by war'. Foucault intends to escape both from the liberal conception of power (that is, a contractual conception), and a Marxist conception (that is, a conception of power in terms of its function in the maintenance of the relations of production and class domination). He found the alternative hard to define:

On the Right, it was posed only in terms of constitution, sovereignty, etc., that is in juridical terms; on the Marxist side, it was posed only in terms of the State apparatus. The way power was exercised – concretely and in detail – with its specificity, its techniques and tactics, was something no-one attempted to ascertain.

('Truth and Power', in Gordon, 1980, pp. 115–6)

Foucault's alternative, which derives from Nietzsche, is a technical and strategic model rather than a legal or class model, and one that operates at a micro level. It finds no use for either 'ideology' or 'dialectic'. Foucault cannot make use of either because it is the struggle within dispersed discourse which, in his view, produces truth, not a relation between discourse and extra-discursive experience.

A CASE STUDY

Accounting research like social research in general must resolve this theoretical dilemma. This might be done by a philosophical thought experiment but empirical research might also be able to show how the dilemma might be resolved. It is the aim of this paper to revisit Gouldner's *Wildcat Strike* (1965) in order to point out how this case study can inform our research methodology.

The Story of a Wildcat Strike

The Oscar Centre Gypsum mine employed 225 people in 1948. The main product was various forms of gypsum wall board which is produced in a continuous strip and is sliced into sections by a mechanical knife. During 1949 new board-making equipment was installed. The installation of this equipment was the work of a new manager – Vincent Peele – who had been sent to the plant on the death of the previous manager. Peele was not only responsible for the new technology but also for a new management strategy.

Under the previous manager, there was a pattern of informal accomodations; authority was recognised as necessary in order to effect the smooth running of the plant, but it was regarded as a means to an end not something which is exhibited for its own sake. Gouldner calls the order at the plant, prior to Peele's arrival, the 'indulgency pattern'; he describes the stability of this order as resting upon:

> a set of shared expectations which the men in one group had concerning their own rights and privileges and the degree to which those in the other group conformed to these expectations in their daily activities. . In a word, a word frequently used by workers themselves, their most salient expectation was "leniency", . . . most workers expected that they were there "to do a job", and that there should be "no constant check-up on you" . . . Workers defined their main role obligation as working or producing. Their obedience obligations to superiors were residual or auxiliary, at best these were thought of as legitimate demands only insofar as they were necessary to do a particular job.
>
> (*Wildcat Strike*, pp. 17–18)

Peele had been directed to make the plant more profitable. In part this was to be achieved by the new technology and in part by introducing more discipline into the plant. Peele's management style is illustrated by the dismissal of a miner for the theft of dynamite, which he intended to use for fishing, a practice which does not seem to have been unusual before Peele's arrival. Peele also enforced the absenteeism rules: men who were absent without reasonable cause were laid off. Management also began to talk of the need to 'put the bit in the workers' mouth'.

The technology and strategy changes coincided with general changes in the economy. Unlike the period during the war when demand exceeded supply, the postwar situation favoured buyers rather than sellers; there was increased fear of unemployment and there was widespread discussion of recession.

At this time the union regional director, Garten, was replaced by a man called Sundino. The move was welcomed by the union because, as someone put it: 'Garten was good, but Sundino was quicker'. The miners welcomed the fact that when Binder, the company's labour relations director, says something 'Sundino jumps right in before Binder can think, he got him cornered'. Thus the tone of union/management relations became more combative; this was welcomed by workers as tit-for-tat aggression. It also created a situation in which Sundino needed a victory to demonstrate the effectiveness of the combative style.

It was in the context of these management initiatives and fears of recession that the union submitted a wage claim. The union/management contract stipulated that only 'a major change in the area rates of the industry or a change in the cost of living' could justify renegotiation of the contract. There was no recognition that changes in technology or management strategy could warrant changes in the contract. Workers were not sure that changes which directly affected them and created great uncertainty were the proper concern of union/management negotiations, because of the informal status of plant custom and practice.

In response to the union claim of 30 cents that company made an offer of 2.5 cents. During the negotiations the men from the plant walked out. However the walkout proved to be short-lived: the company made an offer of 12.5 cents which was accepted, and work resumed. However the agreement did little to dissolve the resentment and uncertainty in the plant because the main issues had not been discussed. Wages were not the central concern, workers resented the enforcement of formal rules that had previously been used only within the context of the indulgency pattern.

The management expected opposition to their strategy and this caused them, when faced with grievances from the workforce, to assume that these grievances were symptoms of a strategic opposition to control rather than a series of concrete and piecemeal problems. Management did not deal with the specific issues because they took them to be symptoms of a general challenge to their 'right to manage'. Because the management saw the issues as matters of principle they refused to resolve them by means of a flexible response.

The union attitude to this situation was divided. One member of the union negotiating committee, a man called Issaboss, sought to represent the workforce's frustration and resentment. Others, led by a man called Byta, preferred to benefit from the management's strategy by developing the bureaucratic relationship between union and management. However, the management's response to grievances led to a breakdown in the formal procedures and this bureaucratic approach was ineffective.

Gouldner refers to this split as one between 'traditionalists' and 'market men'; the traditionalists, he argues, were expressing resistance to the violation of the indulgency pattern. The market men, led by Byta, were attempting to establish the union as part of the formal structure of control in the plant. Byta's group avoided contentious issues, such as the opposition to 'working foremen', in order to avoid straining their credibility with the management group. They claimed that disputes were the result of misunderstandings which they were in a position to resolve if the dispute was talked over. They emphasised the need for formal procedures, but they admitted that the formal grievance procedure had broken down. They blamed the company for this: 'The company wouldn't pay attention to the grievances. They wouldn't fulfil their promises'. However Byta's complaints about management practice did not cause him to doubt the formal processes, in fact he seems to have adopted, at times, the management view that the workers were either stupid or had been misled by radical political ideals. Byta's faction within the union were discredited because of the failure of the formal system to reduce tension. While Byta associated himself with the power of the formal rules, Issaboss associated himself with the tacit expectations of his peers. It was on the basis of this power that he was able to attain a position of leadership.

The tension continued to grow in intensity over the next two years. Management continued to insist upon the 'right to manage', despite the resentment of the workforce. Two years after the first walkout,

Peele was succeeded by a new plant manager called Landman, a change which coincided with the demotion of several supervisors.

Three months later the wildcat strike occurred. It lasted ten days. The strike was not unforeseen: both unions and management seem to have been aware of its inevitability. Two events seem to have triggered the unstable situation: firstly, Byta accepted, on behalf of the men, the transfer of an order from the parent plant which was on strike; secondly, there was open conflict in the plant between a union official called Tenzman, and a production engineer called Spiedman.

Shortly before the strike there were complaints about Spiedman, who, it was claimed, was trying to speed up changes on the line by using 'working foremen'. Byta attempted to resolve this issue with management but it was Tenzman who was responsible for keeping watch on the issue on behalf of the union. Spiedman was not a member of any of the groupings within the plant: he was an isolated individual who worked on projects at a number of plants. Furthermore he was an old enemy of Tenzman. Spiedman seems to have assumed that the 'inequality pattern' was still viable. He expected sensible accommodations to be made to technical problems which would permit the development of new production techniques. These accommodations had in the past permitted him to pursue a technical and instrumental style. This assumption was no longer valid. The strike was triggered when Spiedman instructed Tenzman's foreman to remove Tenzman from that part of the plant in which Spiedman was working.

After several weeks of negotiations between the company and the union, the strikers accepted a settlement. The settlement specified that:

(1) management was not to run the board machinery faster than related machinery allowed,
(2) that the union and the company work out a practical understanding concerning 'working foremen',
(3) that union stewards must obtain permission before leaving their department.

Forms of Power

Gouldner makes reference in *Wildcat Strike* to a balance of power. He points out that:

the degree of bureaucratization was explainable only in terms of a balance of power, of the relative strengths of opposing groups.

(*Patterns of Industrial Bureaucracy*, p. 154)

What are the forces in this balance of power? For Gouldner, who follows Weber's modes of authority, they are the 'traditional form' sustained by the practice of a peer group, and the 'bureaucratic form' in which loyalty is given not to peers but to formal and impersonal rules. Gouldner's three forms of bureaucracy can be interpreted as the result of different degrees of incorporation. In 'mock' bureaucracy neither management nor workers are incorporated: both groups perform according to the rules only when an important third party is present. In 'representative' bureaucracy, both groups have incorporated the rules. In 'punishment centred' bureaucracy, only one group has incorporated the rules.

It might be expected that Gouldner would develop this classification so as to show how the balance of powers resulted in a particular form of bureaucracy. But he prefers a natural, some might say mystical, functionalism:

Wherever bureaucratic patterns are found to be relatively entrenched, it must be assumed that their 'career' has resulted in a net balance of gains . . . the consequences which are brought about by bureaucratic methods of administration must be examined if their survival is to be understood. Here the problem is not one of motives or opportunities, or intentions or powers; it is rather a question of the practical results which sustain bureaucratic patterns once initiated.

(*Patterns of Industrial Bureaucracy*, p. 158)

Gouldner's functionalism marks the abandonment of critical discussion in favour of a belief that current activity is the best of all possible worlds. Such a strategy cannot provide an adequate analysis of the conflict exhibited in the wildcat strike. It must not be assumed that this strike resulted in a net balance of gains.

A more adequate analysis can be accomplished by taking it for granted that the problems discussed in the case study do concern 'motives and opportunities, intentions and powers'. The appropriate powers are identified by Gouldner: they are the traditional, *de facto* power of practice and the bureaucratic, *de jure* power of formal rules.

When the circumstances are so structured that traditional power contradicts bureaucratic power, then the force of circumstance has two contradictory aspects.

Because of the ever-present possibility of such contradiction it is useful to regard circumstances as possessing two distinct powers. This leads to a bipolar conception in which each pole is a distinct form of power. I shall refer to the bureaucratic pole as the 'canopy' and to the traditional pole as the 'core'. In this bipolar model, ideology is a dirempt state in which these two component powers conflict with one another so as to produce contradiction and doubt.

Action requires a resolution of powers. In some ways this resolution is similar to the resolution of mechanical forces, but in many ways such an analogy is misleading because each social force, may, taken in isolation, be assumed to provide a standard. In such cases one power may be 'closed' to the influence of the other. In such circumstances, doubt cannot be resolved but only ignored by the subordination of one force to the other. I shall refer to the dominated power as 'subordinately open.' If action is to resolve the two powers constructively, then the poles must be 'reciprocally open'.

MODES OF ACTIVITY

Distinct modes of activity result from this bipolar analysis. They can be shown on a diagram in which the powers are represented by orthogonal axes. The vertical axis represents the core and the horizontal axis the canopy. The negative portion of the axes represents 'closure' and the positive portion 'openness'.

Four modes of activity are identified in the diagram; these will be discussed below. Unfortunately the diagram conflates the two forms of openness mentioned above: in the case of Anarchy, the canopy is subordinately open, in the case of Legitimacy, the core is subordinately open, but in the case of Praxis both powers are reciprocally open. The different forms of openness require a more sophisticated scheme for adequate representation; however, such a scheme is an unnecessary complication for the present purpose.

Legitimacy is the mode of activity dominated by the canopy. Any doubt which may be caused by the contradiction between core and canopy is excluded or concealed. In the mode of Legitimacy, knowledge is power, it is the mode of activity of unilateral and legal control. In order for knowledge to exercise power it must be recog-

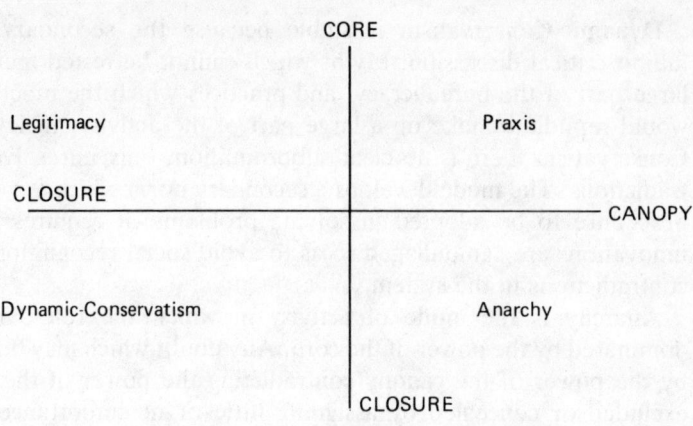

FIGURE 9.1　*Modes of Activity*

nised. It cannot be recognised by the core, because it denies the legitimacy of the core, so it must achieve recognition from the legal rules of other groups. Each group recognises the others so as to meet their common need for legitimacy. Each group acquires power by participating in a pluralistic discursive economy; each has its own domain and status which is recognised by the others, and each pursues a strategy which has as its aim an extension of its own domain and an increase in its status. In this mode, knowledge forms a strategy for the exercise of power in a discursive economy.

The identity of knowledge and power is a general norm which is taken for granted in the Legitimate mode of activity; so as not to confuse this norm with the specific norms constituted by the rules, I shall refer to it as a 'secondary norm'.

Dynamic-Conservatism is the mode of activity in which the role-bargain is maintained as a double standard. Dynamic-Conservatism is a term that was coined by Donald Schon (1971) to refer to social systems with 'a tendency to fight to remain the same'; the standards in such systems do not change, the only features that change are those informal practices that belong to neither standard. Because both core and canopy are closed, it is probable that they will be contradictory, therefore any action which complies with one standard will contravene the other. As a result every action will be open to criticism. In these circumstances action is made possible by the development of a secondary norm which inhibits criticism.

Dynamic-Conservatism is stable because the secondary norms inhibit critical discussion. Myths which cannot be tested make up a large part of the bureaucracy, and practices which the practitioners would repudiate make up a large part of the activity. In Dynamic-Conservatism there is no clear subordination, only unresolved contradictions. The mode develops a secondary norm which governs the procedure to be adopted in solving problems; it requires that all innovations are camouflaged so as to avoid social recognition of the contradictions in the system.

Anarchy is the mode of activity in which the role-bargain is dominated by the power of the core. Any doubt which may be caused by the power of the canopy contradicting the power of the core is excluded or concealed by assigning little or no importance to the symbolic structure other than as a subordinate instrument. Anarchic activity is only constrained by bureaucratic rules to the extent of ensuring that adequate rationalisations are provided for its actions. The secondary norm of this mode is that symbolic structures are the instruments of spontaneous actions.

Praxis is the mode of activity that occurs when both poles are reciprocally open; this enables both the modification of practice by reference to bureaucratic rules and the modification of bureaucratic rules by reference to practice. Praxis does not accept either pole as a standard, its secondary norm is a pragmatic one which calls for the recognition of doubt and its resolution by an alignment of core and canopy.

Argyris and Schon (1978) refer to this mode as 'Double-Loop Learning' because there is in this process a:

> double feedback loop which connects the detection of error not only to strategies and assumptions for effective performance but to the very norms which define effective performance.
>
> (*Organisational Learning*, p. 22)

The modes of activity described above provide an alternative scheme to the types of bureaucracy defined by Gouldner. In what follows I shall apply this scheme to the events of the gypsum plant with the aim of bringing out aspects of the story which Gouldner's analysis conceals.

AN ALTERNATIVE ANALYSIS OF THE WILDCAT STRIKE CASE

The 'indulgency pattern' was, as Gouldner pointed out, a system of expectations. These expectations comprised two different forms of power: firstly, there were the explicit rules which established the formal control system in the plant; secondly, there were the qualitative standards of practice embodied in the workforce. Mediating between these standards was the informal practice of 'leniency'. This informal expectation exerted greater control over conduct than the formal rules because these rules were invoked or ignored at will. This is not to say that the rules were superfluous; they and the qualitative standards combined together to control the activity of the plant. However, the way in which they combined was not simple: despite being an interdependent whole, the two orders contradicted one another.

The 'indulgency pattern' is an example of Dynamic-Conservatism. When changes in the environment, both in the level of demand and in technology, threatened management with a loss of status, they decided to change this mode of activity.

The way in which management might be expected to introduce changes is to elaborate the existing pattern of work, but there are two problems with this approach. Firstly the plant has a mode of activity which is comprised of two 'closed' orders; secondly, if management is to begin from the existing pattern then they must acknowledge the current contradictions, but they cannot publicly accept dual standards, for if they were to do so they would be recognising that the activity of the plant was not unilaterally controlled by them.

Therefore management's only alternative was to extend bureaucratic power and insist upon a shift in the mode of activity from Dynamic-Conservatism to Legitimacy. Management's attempt to bring about this extension resulted in a defensive response from those in the plant who had not incorporated the bureaucracy. This defence attempted to assert that the qualitative standards of the workforce were the only proper standards of control, in other words that Anarchy was the only acceptable mode of activity.

The workforce had to insist upon the priority of the core over the canopy, of standards of practice over standards of legitimacy. The aggression of management's unilateral attempt to change the mode of activity provoked a resentment which found expression in Sundino's combative style.

The initial moves towards Legitimacy and Anarchy are difficult to arrest because they tend to be self-confirming. The mode of Legitimacy which management insists upon is self-confirming because all opposition was perceived as a manifestation of an insurgent strategy, informed by an alien philosophy. This led management to personify the workers as adversaries and insurgents and therefore they were reluctant to treat complaints seriously. This caused the breakdown of the formal system which management insisted was the basis of order in the plant. This, in its turn, caused the workforce to regard the formal system as useless to their interests and therefore no more than an instrument of management. The dynamically-conservative mode of activity, because of its inherent limits of control, broke down; it was replaced by a win/lose conflict between alternative modes of activity.

The series of events which led up to the wildcat strike began with management's decision to respond to the fall in aggregate demand by extending the scope of the 'right to manage'. An analysis of the organisation is thus related to a broader economic analysis. A change in aggregate demand, whether as a result of deliberate policy or not, gave rise to a change in intergroup relations within the plant. The change in demand creates a split in the plant between those who insist upon Legitimacy and those whose only defence in Anarchy.

This split does not coincide with the management/union distinction. One group among the union leadership chooses a Legitimate mode of activity which matches the management mode, while another group rejects this and adopts an Anarchic mode which matches the workers' mode.

The two events which triggered the strike can be seen in the context of this conflict. Byta's acceptance of the order which had been redirected from the strikebound parent plant confirmed his incorporation into the discursive economy, and challenged the workforce to relinquish their commitment to peer group values; it discredited Byta as a leader. The naive action of Spiedman suggests that he was unaware of the polarisation that had taken place in the plant. He proceeded on the assumption that the informal values of Dynamic-Conservatism were still operative. The outcome was that he both offended the values of the workforce and failed to ensure that he was covered by those rules which would have legitimated his action.

THE SIGNIFICANCE OF THE CASE FOR SOCIAL RESEARCH

The above analysis suggests that power is not simply discursive or extra-discursive. It suggests that it is heterogeneous because it can derive from both aspects of a particular circumstance. There are four distinct modes of activity each of which corresponds to a particular relation between discursive and extra-discursive powers.

If the analysis is valid, it shows that Foucault's identity of power/ knowledge does not always reflect the facts, and conceals those modes of activity which do not correspond to his assumption that all members of society are sites which have been incorporated into the discursive economy.

The analysis also redirects attention within Marxism to the concept of 'Praxis'. Marx was always concerned with the unity of Thought and Being in Praxis but in the dispersion of his thought into many abstract doctrines, this central concern has been lost sight of. The power/ knowledge analysis of Gouldner's case suggests that Praxis becomes a normative criterion for social research both for those who accept the 'dominant ideology thesis' and those who do not.

THE SIGNIFICANCE OF THE CASE FOR MANAGEMENT ACCOUNTING RESEARCH

The revised analysis of the case provides accounting researchers with a scheme which, by accepting both the passive and active powers of the subject and emphasising the interaction of these powers, enables the use of accounting procedures to be critically described. Accounting researchers may thus put to one side those idealistic schemes which either make objectivism and subjectivism exclusive (Burrell and Morgan), or which assume a union between objectivism and subjectivism (Boland and Pondy).

Gouldner's case and the proposed analysis are offered as a sketch for organisationally grounded research projects in accounting. It is surely the paucity of such projects which is the major constraint on the development of a critical management accounting.

The potential usefulness of a theory which will keep in focus the interaction of powers is evident in a recent piece of research by Hopper et. al., (1986). This records the resistance to the extension of technical control by means of information technology. They report that while *prima facie* an NCB mine control room provides a means of impersonally gathering data, it was apparent that the control room was in some instances the focus of a struggle for control. In one pit, the colliery manager was concerned to limit access to the control room in order to limit the manipulation of data. Yet in their discussion of managerial strategies of control, no attention is paid to the resistance offered to managerial strategies in concrete situations. The study lapses into an interesting, but abstract account which conceals the resistance highlighted in the control room example. Yet it is this resistance which will influence the concrete activity of control and, in turn, further management strategies.

Such abstractions are an ever present lure for accounting research. If they become the norm, the result may be a systematic repression of the contexts in which accounting works. A repressed analysis can only seek to expose the defects in the abstract apparatus of accounting, and may create within accounting research those symbolic fictions which Meyer argues entail a systematic disconnection with organisational reality. The alternative is for accounting research to recognise the heterogeneous powers which operate in organisations, and to keep its focus of attention upon the interaction of these powers as they shape the development of accounting and organisational practice.

This focus already exists in accounting research; there is a growing recognition that the relation between discursive structures and concrete practice requires a critical analysis in terms of ideology (Meyer, 1983, Cooper, 1983). But the bipolar model goes further than a critique of ideology, by placing the emphasis at the locus at which incorporation is resisted, and by defining an adequate mode by which resistance may be resolved, it encourages accounting research to participate, in a critical way, in the situated development of accounting practice.

Bibliography

Abercrombie, N., S. Hill, and B. S. Turner, *The Dominant Ideology Thesis* (London: George Allen & Unwin, 1980).

Argyris, C. and D. A. Schon, *Organisational Learning: A Theory of Action Perspective* (Reading, Mass.: Addison Wesley, 1978).

Berry, A. J., T. Capps, D. Cooper, P. Ferguson, T. Hopper, and E. A. Lowe, 'Management control in an Area of the NCB: Rationales of Accounting Practices in a Public Enterprise', *Accounting, Organisations and Society* (1985), pp. 3–28.

Boland, R. J. and L. R. Pondy, 'Accounting in Organisations: A Union of Natural and Rational Perspectives', *Accounting, Organisations and Society* (1983), pp. 222–34.

Burrell, G. and G. Morgan, *Sociological Paradigms and Organisational Analysis* (London: Heinemann, 1979).

Cooper, D., 'Tidiness, Muddle and Things: Commonalities and Divergencies in Two Approaches to Management Accounting Research', *Accounting, Organisations and Society* (1983), pp. 269–86.

Foucault, M., 'Truth and Power (An Interview)', in C. Gordon, (ed.), *Power/Knowledge: Selected Interviews and other Writings 1972–1977* (Brighton: Harvester Press, 1980).

Foucault, M., *Annuaire de Collège de France, 1971/2*, quoted in A. Sheridan, *Michel Foucault: The Will to Truth* (London: Tavistock Publications Ltd. 1980).

Gouldner, A. W., *Patterns of Industrial Bureaucracy* (London: Routledge & Kegan Paul, 1955).

Gouldner, A. W., *Wildcat Strike* (New York: Harper & Row, 1965).

Hayes, D. C., 'Accounting for Accounting: A Story about Managerial Accounting', *Accounting, Organisations and Society* (1983), pp. 241–9.

Hopper, T. M., D. J. Cooper, T. Capps, E. A. Lowe, and J. Mouritsen, 'Financial Control in the Labour Process: Managerial Strategies and Worker Resistance in the National Coal Board', in H. Willmott and D. Knights (eds) *Managing the Labour Process* (Aldershot: Gower Press, 1986) pp. 109–41.

Hopwood, A. G., 'On Trying to Study Accounting in the Contexts in which it Operates', *Accounting, Organisations and Society* (1983), pp. 287–305.

Markus, M. L. and J. Pfeffer, 'Power and the Design and Implementation of Accounting and Control Systems', *Accounting, Organisations and Society*, (1983), pp, 205–18.

Meyer, J. W., 'On the Celebration of Rationality: Some Comments on Boland and Pondy', *Accounting, Organisations and Society* (1983), pp. 235–40.

Schon, D. A., *Beyond the Stable State* (London: Temple Smith, 1971).

Part III
Alternative Accounting
Calculations

Part III
Alternative Accounting Calculations

10 Accounting: Tool of Business or Tool of Society?

Derek Bailey

The frame of reference adopted for the conduct of the pursuit of intellectual enquiry into accounting is more or less as expressed in Wheeler (1971):

> three issues . . . which I believe are of utmost importance to accountants, the future of accounting, and the formulation of accounting theory.
>
> First, the relationship between information systems and accounting need to be explored . . . I take a much more limited view of accounting as a special form of an information system limited to data expressed in monetary terms . . .
>
> Second, the relationship between accounting and our business system needs to be clarified. There is a distinct symbiotic relationship between accounting and business . . . Accounting, however, is not the handmaiden of business, and it is not the role of accountants to preserve any particular institutions or specific economic system. Accounting is a universal type of information system which is needed in every known form of economic system and by all resource-using people or organisations within those systems. . . . We need to expand our horizons but not so much in terms of a larger role within the business firm but rather to a larger role within society by giving more attention to our possible service to nonbusiness organisations and to society in general.
>
> Third, the relationship between accounting and society needs to be developed. Accounting theory has developed with a theoretical foundation in the theory of the firm and the economic concept of business income. . . . We have, however, failed to develp a comparable foundation in macro-economics.
>
> Accounting needs to expand to provide one vital type of information for all decision-makers in our changing society in order to

facilitate the operation of all institutions of that society toward the attainment of the goal of the maximisation of human welfare. Here, the emphasis is on accounting as one type of information system utilised by all segments of society . . .

Progress in the development of accounting theory will be dependent upon the careful definition of the scope and purpose of accounting.

(pp. 26–30)

Although these observations were formulated at the time of the critique of corporate business ideology mounted during the late nineteen-sixties by the progressive coalition within the Democratic Party of the USA, it continues to be valid as a statement for the advancement of the boundaries of intellectual enquiry into accounting. It may be typified as an expression of 'constitutional radicalism' and contrasted with both 'moderate opportunism' and 'ideological extremism'. These observations are founded upon the contention that accounting, as an academic discipline, ought not to have as its centre of gravity considerations flowing from the practice of business accounting in the conditions of private ownership in the means of production.

NEUTRAL ACCOUNTING?

A class society is an unjust society: socially generated wealth is privately appropriated and unequally distributed. Correspondence between the distribution of wealth and the satisfaction of needs is lacking and the more unequal the distribution of wealth, the greater the disparity between the satisfaction of wants and the satisfaction of needs.

In industrial societies, business enterprises exercise a major role in the generation, appropriation and distribution of wealth. In its social structure, the business enterprise is a microcosm of society. But, apparently, the infelicities associated with an inequitable distribution of wealth are dissolved in the course of the preparation of the accounting statements. It may be conceded readily that accounting is a highly subjective process based on opinion and judgment, and in which the elements of indisputable fact are relatively few (Arthur Andersen, 1972). Nevertheless, it may be presumed that the accounting statements have been prepared with disinterested impartiality (the hallmark of the professional), avowed by an accountant and attested by an auditor as providing 'a true and fair view' of the affairs of the business enterprise.

How has such an agreeable accommodation been obtained? To answer the question it is necessary to consider the purpose fulfilled by accounting.

ACCOUNTING IN THE BUSINESS COMMUNITY

What does accounting stand for and what does it do in the business community? To grapple with this problem Paton (1963) began with 'a brief consideration of the general significance of accounting in the economic processes' and observed: 'Accounting is a means by which the complex data of the market, as they attach to the particular business, are translated into effective managerial criteria' (p. 7). Consequently, 'the important unit of organisation with which accounting deals is the private business enterprise' (p. 16). That is, the practice of accounting is circumscribed by the institution of private property in the means of production.

Paton made explicit the perspective adopted in the conduct of accounting. 'It is the function of accounting to record values, classify values, and to organise and present value data in such a fashion that the owners and their representatives may utilise wisely the capital at their disposal' (p. 7). He emphasised: 'the accounts are kept . . . of the business enterprise . . . from the standpoint and in the interests of the private owners' (p. 16). He drew the inference: 'the function of accounting and explanations of accounting principles and procedures must be stated immediately in terms of the needs and purposes of the owners of the individual business' (p. 17).

Similarly, Scott (1973) argued that 'in a competitive system accounting must always remain . . . dependent upon the market' (p. 206), although with the mechanism of the market becoming less effective in the changing economic situation 'accounting has been developed to supplement and supplant it' (p. 283).

In providing rationalisations of the practice of accounting Chambers (1971) declared: 'But I do not believe that any worthwhile theory of accounting or any worthwhile practice can emerge otherwise than from the examination of the exigencies of men engaged in the calculating, choosing, and dealing characteristic of the marketplace' (p. 77).

Both Paton and Scott (as well as others such as Sombart, 1922; Seidler, 1967, and Chambers, 1971) recognised that there existed a connection between accounting and the institutional framework of capitalism. Some members of an earlier generation of accounting specialists, such as Paton and Scott, speculated that accounting might well be different in a socialist society. However, more recently, accounting theorists have tended to presume the universality of the capitalist economy both temporally and spatially. As Hendrikson (1977) remarked: 'Most statements of environmental postulates include an assumption that exchanges in the economy take place in markets and that market prices have significance for accounting' (p. 110). That is, there is either an implicit or explicit assumption of the prevalence of the institutional arrangements of capitalism.

Such an assumption may well be natural for accounting specialists working within the confines of a robust market economy, such as Australia or the USA. The ready acceptance of such an assumption is not so easily understood for accounting specialists in a country such as Britain, where there are markedly different traditions. For decades Britain possessed a mixed economy in which public expenditure comprised up to two-fifths of the national product, and large nationalised corporations undertook both commercial and social obligations. Moreover, mixed economies are characteristic of many countries (for example, Mexico, Nigeria, Pakistan, Sweden and Turkey).

As has been remarked by Goldberg (1965): 'The existence of a point of view is fundamental for accounting, the one thing often being regarded from different points of view with very different accounting results' (p. 47). He cautioned 'anybody who postulates rationality should make it clear in what sense he makes use of it, for it may mean different things to different people'. For, as has been observed in Andors (1977), 'the notion of "efficiency" or "rationality . . . has no meaning until the underlying basis of social values has been comprehended' (p. 217).

SEWELL BRAY'S UNIQUE CONTRIBUTION

In attempting a realignment of the accounting perspective, it may be helpful to distinguish between privatised accounting (that is, accounting records prepared from the point of view of the business community) and socialised accounting (that is, accounting records that attempt to recognise a wider social interest). It is not a part of the present purpose to question the legitimacy of privatised accounting for the uses to which it has been harnessed by the business community. Instead, it is to question the universal validity of privatised accounting for providing a representation of business activities to the general public.

Accountability by business enterprises has been confined traditionally to a subset of the business community (that is, the financial institutions and other significant investors), although the published accounts are used increasingly as a medium for projecting a pleasing corporate image. The concept of socialised accounting implies a recognition of a responsibility for a wider public accountability. For its realisation there is required a new approach to the presentation in the published accounts. It was Bray who attempted to persuade the accountancy profession of the merits of a reform of business accounts.

From 1946 to 1955 Sewell Bray worked at Cambridge with Richard Stone who successfully incorporated the double entry principle into the design of a practical system of macro-economic accounts. Bray provided Stone with 'the opportunity of discussing weekly with an accountant who was on the same wavelength the accounting problems that arose in the formulation and defence of national accounting systems' (Forrester, 1982, p. 141). Bray (1946) considered that 'A mature system of national accounting must ultimately call for some aggregation of private accounting results, and there must be no impediments occasioned by lack of uniformity in private accounting practices' (p. 483).

During the late nineteen-forties Bray proposed a formal structure for the final accounts of a business enterprise that would be consistent with Keynesian economic concepts and with the tenets of accounting. It would be compatible also with the structure of the macro-economic accounting system being developed by Stone. Moreover, it would be 'general, reasonable, reliable and readily adaptable to the empirical facts of both actual and imputed transactions of exchange' (Bray, 1951, p. 11). As Bray remarked, 'it is one thing to have a formal balance pattern of symbols and quite another to tie these symbols to economic realities so that we frame our structure in terms of a useful, universal and invariant design which lends significance to those realities wheresoever they may be found' (p. 49).

Bray's proposals

To achieve this purpose Bray proposed that the existing final accounts used in the determination and appropriation of profit should

TABLE 10.1 *Bray's Formal Structure of Accounts (simplified)*

Activity Account

Operating outgoings	Operating incomings	
Operating surplus _____	_____	
_____	_____	

Income Account

Current financial outgoings	Operating surplus	
Entity income _____	_____	
_____	_____	
Transfers of income	Entity income	
Available product _____	_____	
_____	_____	

Outlay Account

Consumption expenditure	Available product	
Saving _____	_____	
_____	_____	

Resting Account

Capital outgoings	Capital incomings	
_____	(including depreciation) _____	
_____	_____	

---

be superseded by four new accounts to be entitled 'activity account' or 'operating account', 'income account', 'outlay account' and 'resting account'. Bray described the function to be performed by each of the proposed new accounts (See Table 10.1).

Activity account:

'It is the purpose of this account to define the operating surplus arising from real activity. . . . the outgoings in this account should be immediately classified in terms of production, selling and distribution, and administration and management' (ibid., p. 72). 'Total operating incomings, minus the total associated operating outgoings, should be expected to give the operating surplus resulting from the economic activity to be carried to the income account' (ibid., p. 76).

Income account:

'It is the function of the income account to measure the product available for outlay' (ibid., p. 83). . . . all items of current incomings and outgoings of a purely financial, as distinct from activity, order will pass through this account in definition of the income of the enterprise. Thereafter we pass through this account the transfers of income which properly find their place in the product available to other entities . . . The final balance on the enterprise income account finds place as product available for outlay, and as such is passed to the fundamental outlay account' (ibid., p. 84).

Outlay account:

'It is this account which marks the point of outlay decision over product; it records the effect of decisions to consume and to add to wealth' (ibid., p. 15). It will be comprised of one credit, available product, and two debits, consumption expenditure and saving' (ibid., p. 71). However, Bray considered that 'it is convenient to regard enterprise consumption as zero' (ibid., p. 84), but did not produce any arguments or evidence to support that statement. The closing balance on the outlay account represented saving by the enterprise and would be passed to the resting account.

Resting account:

'It is the resting account which establishes the relation between saving and asset formation. The individual enterprise resting account will contain a number of financial incomings and outgoings of a capital order which, on aggregation over the whole economy, will cancel out' (ibid., p. 84).

The structure of the final accounts proposed by Bray was based on 'the fundamental economic concepts of production, consumption, wealth and adding to wealth, which are the genuine sources for accounting notions of income, spending, capital and saving' (Forrester, 1982, p. 72). In explanation of the basic economic concepts, Bray quoted Stone (1975): 'An economic system embraces three basic forms of activity which we may term production, consumption and adding to wealth. Production may be defined as bringing into being goods and services on which members of the community or the community as a whole, through its elected representatives, set a valuation. Consumption may be defined as the using up and wearing out of the fruits of production and adding to wealth may be defined as the preservation of the fruits of production for consumption or for contributing to consumption later on'.

The nature and extent of Bray's specific contribution to the origin of the conception of double entry macro-economic accounts is uncertain. Stone was aware that a restructuring of business accounts would be advantageous for the provision of reliable data for the compilation of macro-economic accounts. No doubt it was with the encouragement of Stone that Bray advanced his proposal for the redesign of business accounts. Meanwhile, at Oxford, Hicks (1952) had proposed the recasting of business accounts into a standard form comprising production account, income-expenditure account and the saving-investment account. The production account and the saving-investment account corresponded to the activity account and the resting account, respectively, in Bray's classification. The three stages of the income-expenditure account corresponded to the structuring of Bray's income account and outlay account. The three accounts of Hicks's standard form comprised 'the bricks from which the system of social accounts is constructed.' (Hicks, 1952, p. 232).

A simplified basic accounting structure for business enterprises incorporating a profit and loss account (comprising operating, non-operating and appropriation sections), and a capital reconciliation statement, was proposed in 1951 in the report on 'Some Accounting Terms and Concepts' prepared by a committee of accountants and economists appointed jointly by the Institute of Chartered Accountants in England and Wales and the National Institute of Economic and Social Research. During 1946–51, Stone, Hicks and Bray worked together as members of a technical working subcommittee in the preparation of the proposals incorporated into the published report.

Bray's research activities were made possible by the consistent financial and moral support provided by the enlightened Society of Incorporated Accountants and Auditors. This support was withdrawn summarily when, in 1957, the Society was absorbed into the less enlightened Institute of Chartered Accountants in England and Wales. It is probable that Bray's advocacy of restructured and standardised business accounts was regarded as an attempt to promote the state surveillance of business enterprise by stealth and, for that reason, received no recognition in the higher councils of the ICAEW. Moreover, following the election of a Conservative Government, there occurred during 1952–54 a profound change in the political climate as the system of wartime controls enmeshing the economy was dismantled.

In 1982 a leading member of the accountancy profession dismissed the research concerns of Bray as 'an interest in areas of accounting thought that are now largely dead' (Forrester, 1982, p. 7). Such an epitaph is consistent with the perception of accounting as essentially utilitarian in the provision of a service to the business community.

Stone was awarded the Nobel Prize for his pioneering work on the design of a system of interlocking macro-economic accounts incorporating the principal of double entry. During the decades following the discussions at Cambridge with Bray, the work of Stone has gained worldwide recognition. The names of Luca Pacioli and Richard Stone may be bracketed together as the two outstanding European contributors to the development of accounting theory and practice.

YUGOSLAVIA'S CONTRIBUTION TO ACCOUNTING PRACTICE

In Britain there was no support for Bray's advocacy of restructured and standardised business accounts. For example, neither the nationalised corporations nor the co-operative organisations seemed to have attempted experiments based on Bray's proposals. In general, Bray's proposals were ignored by other capitalist and socialist countries. The socialist countries established at the close of World War Two used the Soviet prototype of a socialist economy as a model for the restructuring of their own economies on a socialist foundation. The adoption of the Soviet model of a centrally planned and administered economy – the command economy – meant that the design of a macro-economic accounting system did not become a problem urgent for solution.

However, in one country the final accounting statements did come to be redesigned in a manner that, although not identical with, did bear a resemblance to the recommendations advanced by Bray. That country was Yugoslavia.

Following the rupture of relations with the USSR and its allies in 1948, Yugoslavia abandoned the command economy model and evolved a system of workers' self-management for the nominally socially owned and autonomous enterprises. For the operation of the system and the realisation of workers' self-management over the

TABLE 10.2 *Yugoslav Structure of Final Accounting Statement (simplified)*

Statement of Determination of Operating Income	
Material costs	Revenues
Depreciation	
Operating income _____	_____
_____	_____

Statement of Allocation of Operating Income	
Taxes	Operating income
Net income _____	_____
_____	_____

Statement of Allocation of Net Income	
Personal incomes	Net income
Accumulation _____	_____
_____	_____

Statement of Allocation of Accumulation	
Transfers to business fund	Accumulation
Transfers to reserve fund _____	_____
_____	_____

distribution of the enterprise, there was introduced a restructured accounting statement. 'From an economic point of view, it can be thought of as representing a conscious, self-governing creation and allocation of that portion of national income which is formed by and within the enterprise . . . in terms of flows of the values created, through the production process, into the various funds corresponding to different categories and levels of consumption (including amortization, investment, etc.)' (Vanek, 1972, pp. 108–9). For its representation (see Table 10.2) the income statement summarising the activities of the enterprise came to be subdivided into a sequence of four interlinked accounts for:

(1) determination of operating income;
(2) allocation of operating income;
(3) allocation of net income;
(4) allocation of accumulation.

The function performed by the first account is similar to that envisaged by Bray for the activity account. That is, it is used to determine the operating income of the Yugoslav enterprise although the remuneration of its personnel is not entered into the account. Consequently the operating income determined bears some approximation to the concept of added value and does not correspond to Bray's concept of operating surplus.

In the second account there is recorded the allocation of the operating income of the enterprise. A portion of the operating income is absorbed by, in the main, financial outgoings (for instance, taxation, insurance premiums, interest) and the remaining balance represents the enterprise's net income. The net income so determined approximates to Bray's concept of available product as increased by the remuneration of the personnel. (Under Bray's proposal, wages and salaries would be entered into the activity account.)

In the third account is shown the division of the net income between consumption (for example, gross personnel remuneration) and saving (that is, accumulation). The function performed by the account is similar to that envisaged by Bray for the outlay account although he considered the consumption expenditure of the enterprise to be zero.

In the fourth account is shown the manner of utilisation (for example, expansion of the business fund through the acquisition of real assets) of the saving (that is, accumulation in Marxian terminology) achieved. Unlike Bray's proposed resting account, the total capital incomings and capital outgoings are not shown. For example, depreciation is excluded.

The structure of the Yugoslav income statement illustrated in Table 10.2 may well have been inspired by Marx's conception of the manner of distribution of the 'proceeds of labour' in the 'co-operative society based on common ownership of the means of production' in the period immediately following its emergence from capitalist society (Marx, 1951).

For the evaluation of the performance of the Yugoslav enterprise, there are utilised both worker-orientated and business-orientated indicators. For example, Article 143 of the Associated Labour Act, 1974 enumerated eight indicators (see below, Table 10.3) for the appraisal of the enterprise's performance with respect to its business activities and the workers (Turk, 1982):

TABLE 10.3 *Indicators of Yugoslavian Enterprise Performance**

$\dfrac{\text{operating income}}{\text{total workers}}$	added value per worker
$\dfrac{\text{net income}}{\text{total workers}}$	amount available per worker for personal income and accumulation
$\dfrac{\text{personal incomes and related benefits}}{\text{total workers}}$	overall satisfaction of worker's needs
$\dfrac{\text{net personal incomes}}{\text{total workers}}$	satisfaction of basic interests of the worker as a consumer
$\dfrac{\text{operating income}}{\text{business assets}}$	efficiency in use of business assets
$\dfrac{\text{accumulation}}{\text{operating income}}$	proportion of operating income saved
$\dfrac{\text{accumulation}}{\text{net income}}$	proportion of net income reinvested in the enterprise
$\dfrac{\text{accumulation}}{\text{business assets}}$	rate of growth of business assets

* In Yugoslavia there is no generally accepted single synoptic indicator for assessing the overall socio-economic efficiency of the enterprise.

TOWARDS ACCOUNTING RECONSTRUCTION

In the capitalist countries accounting has been developed to meet the needs of the business community in which there is private ownership of the means of production. The accounting statements prepared for their purposes are not necessarily either appropriate or relevant for other potential users who do not subscribe to the objectives of capitalist business. The force of the argument was appreciated by Bray and Falk (1974) in a consideration of the problems of the transition from a managerial capitalist economy to a worker-managed economy. With respect to accounting in a worker-managed enterprise they observed, 'In the profit and loss account there would be no distinction between personal incomes of workers and profits. To calculate the income of the enterprise, the cost of materials and services, and depreciation, would be deducted from the receipts from sales. Out of income would be paid interest, allocations to reserves, the balance being the personal incomes of workers'. They added that 'Special corporation tax laws would be needed . . . because of the lack of distinction between workers' personal incomes and profits' (p. 16).

In the model of simple reproduction in the capitalist economy, it is assumed that only socially necessary expenditures are incurred on non-human resources so that the enterprise's entire contribution to the net social product is divided between wages and profits (Marx, 1954).

In the corporate economy, the executives of the enterprise operating in conditions of imperfect competition are able to appropriate to their own purposes some part of the collectively generated stream of profits. The opportunity so to do is limited by the need for, and is conditional upon, an acceptable (that is, to the financial institutions) apparent rate of return on the capital advanced being disclosed in the published accounts. Given these conditions, then, part of the profits realised in the marketplace is absorbed within the enterprise as discretionary expenditures. That is, the socially necessary costs of production come to be supplemented by optional or discretionary expenditures.

As Marx (1954) observed: 'When a certain stage of development has been reached, a conventional degree of prodigality, which is also an exhibition of wealth, and consequently a source of credit, becomes a business necessity to the "unfortunate" capitalist. Luxury enters into capital's expenses of representation. Moreover, the capitalist gets rich . . . at the same rate as he sqeezes out the labour-power of others . . . therefore . . . always lurking behind it . . . the most anxious calculation, yet his expenditure grows with his accumulation' (p. 594).

Marx's perception of business behaviour has been re-expressed by Cowling (1982): 'managerial corporations will seek to minimise the direct costs of production, and therefore wage costs, and will choose price-output levels which maximise profits. Thus by way of wages, productivity and prices the managerial capitalist system will act to exploit labour . . . The fruits of such exploitation will appear in the profits produced but also in various elements of overhead costs' (p. 92). In advanced economies the proportion of discretionary expenditures to the total expenditures incurred by the enterprise is steadily increasing.

From the preceding argument it follows that:

realised profit	>	reported profit	⩾	minimum acceptable profit

and:

realised profit	−	discretionary expenditure	=	reported profit

Consequently the utility of the statement of reported profits as a tool of analysis needs to be examined. Williamson (1974) has pointed to 'a serious question as to whether studies of monopoly power based on reported profit provide an accurate estimate of the effects of monopoly'. And 'Hill (1979) has even suggested that the gross profit rate may be superior to the net as an estimate of the true rate' (Armstrong, Glyn and Harrison, 1984, p. 459).

According to the Marxian analysis of the capitalist economy, some part of the economic surplus generated through the business enterprise is consumed externally. Its external consumption is reflected in the accounting records by various kinds of transfer payments, such as for rent, interest and dividends. Some of these transfer payments are treated as charges against, and others as appropriations of, profit. From the Marxian point of view, the accounts of the business enterprise contain a jumble of heterogeneous items that prevent wages and profits, as defined by Marx, from being properly distinguished. Surplus value, in the transmuted form of profit, is understated. Therefore, the business accounts cannot be used analytically without their prior reconstruction.

Notwithstanding this conclusion, as Godelier (1972) has observed: 'The economic categories of wages, profit, interest on capital, etc., express quite well the viable relations of the capitalist system and as such they have pragmatic utility, being of service in management and the taking of decisions' (p. xxv). Business accounting is equally valuable for the same purposes. But for accounting to gain consideration as an embryonic social science rather than as merely a technical tool of business management, there would seem to be required a restructuring of the income statement.

How is the task to be performed? As a preliminary step it is useful to consider Marx's study of the functioning of the capitalist economy. Marxian economic deals with economic phenomena at two distinct levels:

(1) in the value domain, attention is directed to the creation of surplus value by labour and 'surplus value and the rate of exploitation are the key variables' (Desai, 1974, p. 38).

(2) in the price domain, attention is directed to the observed data so that 'profits and the rate of profit on capital are the key variables' (Desai, 1974, p. 38).

At the macro-economic level the mass of surplus value is equal to the mass of profits. 'Net profits correspond in a static view to labour used in producing the goods and services consumed by capitalists; in a dynamic setting to capitalist consumption plus 'accumulation' (= net investment)' (Kuhne, 1979, p. 137). But value and surplus value belong to the plane of underlying essences imperfectly represented by observable appearances (Sowell, 1986). That is, 'surplus value is produced but never appears as such; it appears as profit' (Fine and Harris, 1979, p. 24). Hence, 'Marxian theory employs two separate accounting systems in terms of values and prices' (Desai, 1974, p. 66). The accounting system in terms of values probes beneath the surface of economic phenomena to represent the system of productive relationships. The accounting system in terms of prices looks at the surface of economic phenomena to represent the system of exchange relationships.

A Marxian accounting in terms of prices is not identical with business accounting. For the purposes of the former, the income statement may be restructured as follows:

> sales revenue
> *less* socially necessary expenditures   _____
> economic surplus
> *less* external redistribution of economic surplus
>   (i.e. rent, interest, dividends, etc.)   _____
> corporate income
> *less* internal consumption of economic surplus
>   (i.e. discretionary expenditures)   _____
> saving   ========

A further elaboration of the restructured income statement is shown in Table 10.4.

From a socialist perspective it might be postulated that the maximisation of use-values per unit of labour effort would serve as a general indicator for economic action, as the maximisation of return on capital does for the business community of capitalism.

TABLE 10.4 *Restructured final accounts*

Income Account

Section I Value created by productive labour

Socially necessary costs (transfer of embodied values) i.e. materials
    utility services
    depreciation
Operating income
(Value created by productive labour = net product to society) _____
	Sales of goods and services

_____	_____

Section II Economic surplus

Other socially necessary costs (attributable to living labour) i.e. wages of necessary labour Economic surplus (Marxian profit) _____	Value created by productive labour
_____	_____

Section III External redistribution of economic surplus

Rent Rates Interest Taxation Dividends Corporate income (Net income to enterprise) _____	Economic surplus
_____	_____

Section IV Internal consumption of economic surplus

Managerial discretionary expenditure Saving _____	Corporate income
_____	_____

Investment Account

Real asset formation Lending Changes in monetary balances _____	Saving Depreciation Net finance
_____	_____

In certain circumstances, use-values may be regarded as being reflected in exchange-values. That is, provided there is an absence of imperfections in the operation of the market mechanism (such as, no exercise of monopoly power within the home market and raw materials not obtained on onerous terms from Third World countries) and an equitable distribution of incomes across society. Capitalism corrupts the operation of the market mechanism; it does not destroy its relevance for advanced societies. From the data of the reconstructed income statement the ratio would be:

$$\frac{\text{sales of goods and services}}{\text{wages of necessary labour}}$$

The rate of exploitation becomes:

$$\frac{\text{economic surplus}}{\text{wages of necessary labour}}$$

Profitability could be perceived from the point of view of society rather than that of the business community. For this purpose there could be made a distinction between private profit and public profit. Private profit represents the return to the entrepreneur as traditionally recorded in the accounting records. For the present purpose, public profit may be defined as the sum of external redistribution and saving, so that public profitability may be expressed as:

$$\frac{\text{external distribution and saving}}{\text{operating capital employed}}$$

The concept of public profitability was devised originally to meet the criticisms by Third World countries of the evaluation of the performance of public corporations made by the World Bank and other financial institutions of capitalism.

Other ratios may be conceived such as:

$$\frac{\text{real asset formation}}{\text{operating assets}}$$

to indicate economic progress in the expansion of productive capacity.

ACCOUNTING AND SOCIETY

At the beginning of the chapter there was cited the proposal by Wheeler (1971) that accounting, as an information system limited to data expressed in monetary terms, should be expanded to facilitate the progress of society towards the goal of the maximisation of human welfare. Lasserre (1967) considered the goal could be approached by means of 'the achievement throughout the community of the highest permissible ratio of satisfactions to sacrifices' expressed as:

$$\frac{\text{satisfactions}}{\text{sacrifices}} = \frac{\text{satisfactions}}{\text{goods and services}} \times \frac{\text{goods and services}}{\text{factors}} \times \frac{\text{factors}}{\text{sacrifices}}$$

Satisfactions represent the total amount of satisfaction which the population derives from its consumption. Sacrifices represent the total amount of sacrifices accepted by the population to obtain the factors of production.

Lasserre considered the three sub-ratios represented:

first sub-ratio	the effectiveness of economic activity in meeting the requirements of the community as consumers;
second sub-ratio	the efficiency of the economic activity;
third sub-ratio	the costs of production in terms of 'rare and irreplaceable resources and, above all, in arduous effort' (ibid., p. 78–9).

The three sub-ratios would be directed to different, although interconnected aspects of socio-economic performance. The first sub-ratio of effectiveness finds reflection in social indicators. The second sub-ratio of efficiency is reflected traditionally in accounting indicators. The third sub-ratio of economy finds reflection in technical indicators. Lasserre considered that for the first two sub-ratios, maximisation 'is achieved mainly by seeking means of raising the numerator to the highest possible level for any given denominator' (ibid.), and for the third sub-ratio, maximisation 'involves reducing the denominator to the lowest possible level for any given numerator' (ibid.).

It is a prospective approach to the assessment of socio-economic performance that would accord with the objectives of the Green

Movement. Its supporters have argued for an enlargement of public accountability and the adoption of socially responsible behaviour by business enterprises. For the realisation of these objectives there has been devised the concept of the sustainable economy. That is, business enterprises in undertaking economic activity should recognise explicitly the constraints imposed by non-renewable resources and by the indispensability of ecological life-support systems.

In the context of the sustainable economy, it is not possible for the profit indicator to be the supreme arbiter in the determination of the manner in which economic activity is to be undertaken. As has been observed 'market-place values, necessarily expressed in balance sheet money terms, do not measure poverty or the quality of life. Nor are they a good guide to environmental costs' (Thomas, 1986, p. 23). On the other hand, 'Modern societies obviously need some measure of profitability' (Porritt, 1984, p. 123). As Nove (1983) observed: 'It is the appropriation of profits by capitalists that offends, not profits as such' (p. 210).

The business enterprises constitute an intermediate sector and not the final sector in the totality of socio-economic activities. Therefore it is desirable to examine the implications of the exercise of managerial preference over the composition of discretionary expenditures for the realisation of social goals. The ratio of discretionary expenditures to necessary expenditures tends to rise in advanced economies. Williamson (1974) suggested that the preference has been exercised by managers in favour of the achievement of their own goals of enhanced salaries, security, status, power and prestige, and by spending on staff and emoluments. The restructured income statement makes explicit the exercise of managerial expense preference and, therefore, the scope for the rearrangement of expenditures to achieve desired social goals. To this end the restructured income statement could be extended as indicated in Table 10.5. It could assist in encouraging a realistic appreciation, rather than an utopian delusion, of the financial scope for socially desirable economic action by the business enteprise.

The business enterprise may be conceived as directing its efforts to the achievement of the greatest amount of 'value created by productive labour' and a level of saving that makes possible a certain rate of real asset formation (and, hence, a certain potential rate of economic progress). Provided that a minimum level of saving was achieved, other goals could be pursued. Consequently, there is required a vector of performance indicators to make explicit these

TABLE 10.5

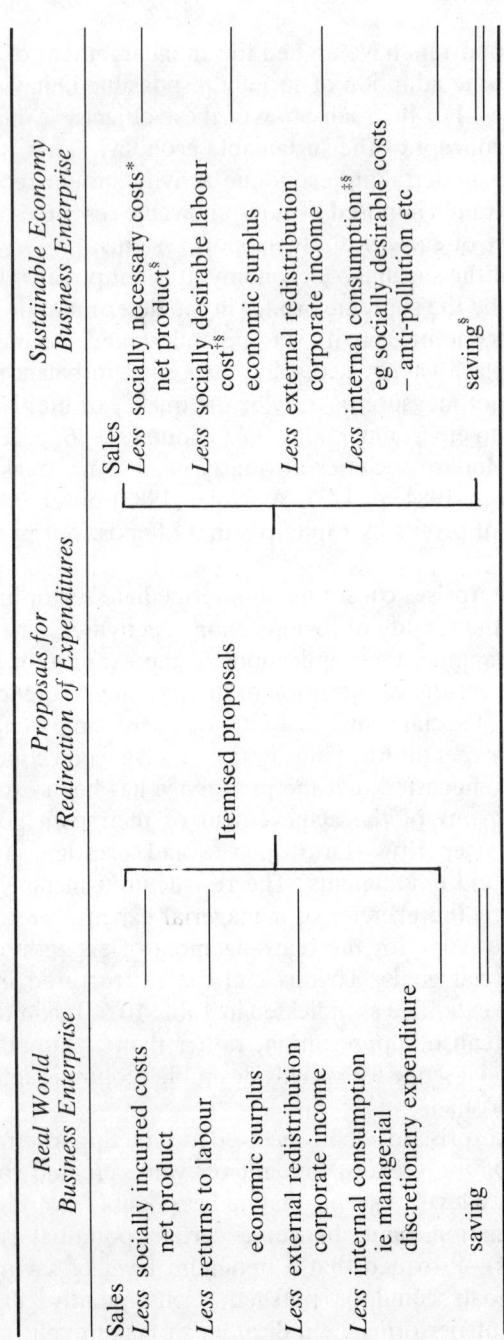

Real World Business Enterprise	Proposals for Redirection of Expenditures	Sustainable Economy Business Enterprise
Sales		Sales
Less socially incurred costs net product		Less socially necessary costs* net product§
Less returns to labour economic surplus	Itemised proposals	Less socially desirable labour cost‡§ economic surplus
Less external redistribution corporate income		Less external redistribution corporate income
Less internal consumption ie managerial discretionary expenditure		Less internal consumption‡§ eg socially desirable costs – anti-pollution etc
saving		saving§

NOTES:
* to provide for 'fair working conditions'
† to ensure 'everyone who works has the right to just and favourable remuneration ensuring for himself and his family an existence worthy of human dignity'. P. Sieghart, *The Lawful Rights of Mankind* (OUP, 1985) p. 128
‡ expressed as a set of programmes
§ performance indicators derived from income statement

other goals, and the progress towards their realisation achieved. With the exclusion of the portion of the economic surplus externally redistributed, the remaining expenditures (that is, the managerially administered discretionary expenditures) could be visualised as being incurred in pursuit of specific programmes. For each programme an appropriate performance indicator could be devised.

The general approach to the restructuring of the income statement may have relevance for nationalised corporations, co-operative undertakings, workers' co-operatives and business enterprises (for example, in the context of planning agreements). In addition, the general approach may have relevance for business enterprises in Third World countries, especially where there is a tradition of communal, rather than individual, endeavour. And, possibly, for worker representatives in the event of the CBI conceding to EEC proposals for worker participation in the running of business enterprises. That is, the present proposals may point in the direction of the objective 'everyone their own accountant' specified by Tomlinson (see Chapter 4).

TOWARDS A SOCIALIST ACCOUNTING?

Accounting for the business enterprise is based on the fallacious assumption that private costs and private benefits are identical with social costs and social benefits (that is, externalities are deemed to be nonexistent). Or, alternatively, if the existence of a discrepancy is acknowledged, it is presumed to be so neglible that it may be ignored. It has been observed that 'Externalities exist only because of the institutional limitations on the costs and benefits which the decision-makers choose to take into their reckoning' (Lichfield, 1965, p. 247).

Accounting, in conferring a utility to the business community, has deprived itself of a social, as distinct from business, legitimacy. Accounting as an expression of 'institutionalised egoism' is the 'negation of sociality'. In its power to provide an apparent legitimatisation for economic action 'accounting itself can become a form of ideology, in that it depicts systems, which may in fact be partisan, in terms apparently impartial. One might even propose that no reorganisation or reform can long exist in terms of an old accounting system, but must be accompanied by the kind of redefinition of the "rules of the game" that only an accounting reform can bring' (Merkle, 1985).

Concerning the direction in which such an accounting reform

should be sought, Palmer (1985) observed 'What has not been developed is a comprehensive social cost accounting system which can measure investment inputs and potential returns in terms of society's overall economic interests. As a result capitalist 'micro-efficiency' in terms of redundancies and plant closures are bought at the expense of massive macro-economic efficiency in terms of human, social and economic waste' (p. 24). Meszaros (1970), after remarking 'The only form of accountancy known to capitalism is a narrow monetary accountancy', continued 'the Marxian view . . . implies . . . the replacement of "piecemeal" monetary accountancy by a comprehensive social accountancy' (p. 306).

Only in the context of a comprehensive social accounting is there a promise of an approach in a consistent manner to an appreciation of socio-economic issues affecting significant segments of the national economy, such as were raised during the major disputes affecting the steel and coal industries. The attempt to represent sectional interests in the absence of a comprehensive social accounting is liable to degenerate into special pleading. The remarkable silence of the majority of the academic and non-academic leaders of the accountancy profession during the prolonged coal dispute, in which the relevance and appropriateness of a narrow accounting in monetary terms was a central issue, seems to have been a silent admission of accounting's lack of a social legitimacy.

Bibliography

Andors, S., *China's Industrial Revolution* (London: Robertson, 1977).
Armstrong, P., A. Glyn, and J. Harrison, *Capitalism Since World War II* (London: Fontana, 1984).
Arthur Andersen & Co., *Objectives of Financial Statements* (New York: Arthur Andersen & Co., 1972).
Bray, F. S., 'Review of Singer, H. W., "Standardised Accounting in Germany"', *Economic Journal* (1946), pp. 482–4.
Bray, F. S., *The Accounting Mission* (Cambridge University Press, 1951).
Bray, J. and N. Falk, *Towards a Worker Managed Economy* (London: Fabian Society, 1974).
Chambers, R. J. in W. E. Stone, (ed.) *Foundations of Accounting Theory*, (University of Florida Press, 1971).
Cowling, K., *Monopoly Capitalism* (London: Macmillan, 1982).
Desai, M., *Marxian Economic Theory* (London: Gray-Mills, 1974).
Fine, B. and L. Harris, *Rereading Capital* (London: Macmillan, 1979).

Forrester, D. A. R. (ed.), *Frank Sewell Bray* (Glasgow: Strathclyde Convergencies, 1982).

Godelier, M., *Rationality and Irrationality in Economics* (London: New Left Books, 1972).

Goldberg, L., *An Inquiry into the Nature of Accountancy* (Sarasota, Fl.: American Accounting Association, 1965).

Hendrikson, E., *Accounting Theory* (Illinois: Irwin, 1977).

Hicks, J. R., *The Social Framework* (Oxford: Clarendon, 1952).

Kuhne, K., *Economics and Marxism*, Vol. I (London: Macmillan, 1979).

Lasserre, G., 'An Exploration of the Concept of the General Interest', *Annals of Public and Co-operative Economy* (1967) pp. 71–92.

Lichfield, N., 'Spatial Externalities', in Margolis, J., (ed.), *Urban Public Expenditure: a Case Study in The Public Economy of Urban Communities* (Baltimore: John Hopkins Press, 1965).

Marx, K., 'Critique of the Gotha Program', in K. Marx, and F. Engels, *Selected Works, Vol. II* (Moscow: FLPH, 1951).

Marx, K., *Capital, Vol. I* (Moscow: FLPH, 1954).

Merkle, J. A., *Management and Ideology* (University of California Press, 1980).

Meszaros, I., *Marx's Theory of Alienation* (London: Merlin, 1970).

Nove, A., *The Economics of Feasible Socialism* (London: Allen & Unwin, 1983).

Palmer, J., *Guardian* (1 October 1985).

Paton, W. A., *Accounting Theory* (Lawrence, KS: Scholars' Book Co., 1963).

Porritt, J., *Seeing Green* (Oxford: Basil Blackwell, 1984).

Scott, D. R., *The Cultural Significance of Accounts* (Lawrence, KS: Scholars' Book Co., 1973).

Seidler, L. J., *The Function of Accounting in Economic Development* (New York: Praeger, 1967).

Sombart, W., *Der Moderne Kapitalismus* (Leipzig: Duncker & Humblot, 1922).

Sowell, T., *Marxism – Philosophy and Economics* (London: Unwin, 1986).

Stone, R., *Functions and Criteria of a System of Social Accounting, Income and Wealth, Series I* (Cambridge: Bowes & Bowes, 1975).

Thomas, H., *Guardian*, 30 January 1986.

Turk, I., 'Analysis of Efficiency by Means of Interrelated Indicators: a Yugoslav Approach', *International Journal of Accounting* (1982) pp. 89–102.

Vanek, J., *The Economics of Workers' Management: A Yugoslav Case Study* (London: Allen & Unwin, 1972).

Wheeler, J. T., 'Comment on paper of Bedford, N.', in W. E. Stone (ed.), *Foundations of Accounting Theory* (University of Florida Press, 1971).

Williamson, O. E., *The Economics of Discretionary Behaviour* (London: Kershaw, 1974).

11 A Marxian Analysis of National Income and Expenditure

Jon Gubbay

As both a socialist and a university lecturer my interest in National Income and Expenditure derives equally from political agitation and academic research.

Over the years, I have written quite a lot of leaflets designed to stir up discontent and handed them out at workplace entrances. Typically, they used company accounts to show profit per worker, capital accumulated in recent years, return on capital, shareholders' capital gains, directors' salaries and perks, and so on. However, such leaflets are more difficult to write for hospital workers, local authority employees or university staff, since the categories of profit and capital appear inapplicable to their situation. A further embarrassment becomes more prevalent in a period of economic recession. Suppose that workers' capacity, and right, to improve their wages and conditions is seen solely in terms of cutting into their particular employer's profits; if the accounts show the firm is unprofitable it is not then clear what the workers should do, at the very time when their livelihoods are at stake.

Such confusions can be compounded by the socialist accountant unless attention is shifted from the individual enterprise or institution considered on its own to its location within anarchic market relations and class exploitation in the whole system. 'To those capitalists . . . who . . . offer to throw open their books to the workers – usually to demonstrate the necessity of lowering wages – the workers answer that they are not interested in the bookkeeping of individual bankrupts or semi-bankrupts but in the account ledgers of all exploiters as a whole. The workers cannot and do not wish to accommodate the level of their living conditions to the exigencies of individual capitalists, themselves victims of their own regime." (Trotsky, 1970, pp. 14–15). Unfortunately, Trotsky's opinion of working-class consciousness at the time was wishful thinking, though he was quite right to point out that class interests are defined beyond the bounds of the enterprise.

The more academic interest in National Income and Expenditure comes from research in class theory, in particular a polemic against the Weberian conception of class situation as opportunities for gain in the market – and advocacy of a 'sophisticated' Marxist model (Crompton and Gubbay, 1977). In my view, class positions are defined by the part they play in the generation, distribution and consumption of value; in effect, a Marxist system of accounts is a model of class structure. The extent to which the working class is exploited is the quantity of surplus value they create and that is taken from them by the capitalist class; this is the total number of hours they labour minus the amount of labour time equivalent to their wages, that is unpaid labour. Now, this is a definite quantity of hours of work per annum, although there are immense difficulties in actually measuring it. If its size and the way it changes can be indicated, then it should be possible to construct an economic history on genuinely Marxist lines, showing how economic and social changes parallel the conflicts within and between classes. It is argued that, although the National Income and Expenditure accounts mystify the real economic relationships in capitalist society, they are a valuable resource that can be reworked to estimate Marxist aggregates.

Thus, bringing together the study of national accounts and class inequality can provide a sound basis on which to criticise capitalist exploitation and a cogent way of describing economic change and crisis.

ASSUMPTIONS IN THE OFFICIAL ACCOUNTS

Measures of national product, conceived of as total annual production of marketable goods and services, are calculated and published by most governments in industrialised societies – in the case of the UK as the Blue Book, *National Income and Expenditure*. This document contains a great body of information by which politicians, the media and various experts assess the failure or success of economic policy with regard to the balance of payments, profitability, investment, employment, inflation and economic growth.

However, the reliability of the estimates in the Blue Book is deeply suspect, and there are some quite arbitrary judgements about what aggregates to include and how to classify them, especially with regard to imputed values for non-marketed goods. These problems are not merely technical in the sense that improved data sources and more consistent application of a given conceptual scheme would achieve an adequate set of accounts. Indeed, the very validity and intellectual coherence of concepts of national product is in dispute.

The official accounts should not be seen as a scientific record of economic achievement, or lack of it, but rather as constructions employed by the state for several, partly contradictory, but quite practical purposes. Firstly, examination of the amount of goods and services produced is vital for assessing the potential for capital accumulation and how it might be raised. Secondly, reckoning up the incomes of households, firms and the state is necessary for devising suitable policies for regulating aggregate demand with minimal inflation and unemployment. Moreover, measures of *national* product fulfil a crucial ideological role in representing the whole nation, regardless of conflicting class interest, as pursuing the common goal of economic growth to which the state is committed.

It is true that the accounts give a breakdown between profits and employment incomes, though not between wages and managerial salaries, but this appears within a framework where the only meaningful area of conflict can be over shares of a cake whose growth in size serves everybody's interests. Even then, the way the accounts are constructed constricts the scope of opposed interests by presenting, at least implicitly, the engine for growth of national product as the rate of investment. Thus, it is not a matter of capital accumulation reproducing the domination of one class by another but rather the gross domestic fixed capital formation promoting a universally desired goal. In reality, the competitive relationship between capitals and the division of interests between classes results in the improvement in the quality of working-class consumption, if at all, only as a by-product of capital accumulation. For this fundamental reason, national income cannot be validly taken as an index of common welfare. What meaning can there be in the nation's welfare when the nation is split by opposed class interests? From a Marxist perspective, it is quite fruitless to attempt to construct a more valid measure of welfare by modifying national product to exclude diswelfares and include imputations for non-marketed goods. To take an extreme case, is workers' acquisition of food, housing and entertainment to be regarded as part of total consumption or as investment by the capitalist class in human capital? Again, if such a profoundly ambiguous concept as welfare is to be the touchstone for assessing contributions to national product, there seems to be no good basis for deciding whether health and education contribute to consumption or intermediate goods. There is no escape from arbitrariness. Nordhaus and Tobin (1971) have provided an ambitious and influential construction of a net welfare index which values leisure time as a contribution to welfare, according to the wage rate. Unfortunately, this procedure has the fatal flaw of reckoning welfare as unaltered *both* when people choose increased leisure and when they are sacked.

There is a profound ambiguity about capitalists' viewpoints on state activities such as subsidising industry, administration, distribution of social security, provision of education and health services, maintaining courts, police, prisons and military defence. On the one hand, the fact that they do not make a profit and are financed by taxation makes them appear as an economic burden, so they are defined as 'expenditure'. On the other hand, they provide essential conditions for capital accumulation or directly promote it, so that the 'output' of these activities cannot be ignored. The procedure adopted in the official accounts is to value these activities at factor cost even though, by estimating this as proportional to the wage bill or size of the labour force, there is the perverse effect of making an increase in labour productivity appear as a fall in output. (Hall, 1983, p. 16). It is, of course, quite inconsistent to value state provisions at factor costs while other output is reckoned at market prices. Although this procedure is generally defended in terms of the practical problem of imputing market prices to non-marketed goods and services, the lack of theoretical justification reflects the ambiguity referred to above. In short, there is an irresolvable conceptual confusion in constituting national product as the sum of heterogeneous economic categories.

With the exception of housing, the official accounts take the viewpoint of the capitalist class in a quite accurate and consistent fashion when dealing with the household economy, though largely for practical rather than theoretically well-grounded reasons.

All housing is treated as a type of capital which generates rent for its owners and, accordingly, repair and purchase of new houses is taken as contributing to gross domestic fixed capital formation. Consistent application of this procedure is not extended to all consumer durables because of difficulty in obtaining suitable data. However, from a Marxist standpoint, a more important criticism is the failure to distinguish between ownership of commodities as possessions for personal consumption and as bases for appropriating profit or rent. In obscuring this distinction, the Blue Books place owner-occupiers in the same category as landlords and, in a bizarre further confusion, treat house ownership as a sector of production.

No attempt is made to impute values for domestic production, even though such activities are vital for sustaining conditions for the reproduction and maintenance of labour power. From the capitalist's perspective, this is quite logical, since the way domestic labour operates and how much it produces can be largely left to the devices of households without supervision or comparison with marketed production. To make this point is not to ignore or devalue domestic labour, but rather to recognise that the national accounts take the viewpoint of the capitalist class, and to criticise the notion that they can be rendered acceptable to Marxist political economy by simply extending the scope of what counts as production.

MARX'S ANALYSIS OF VALUE FLOWS

Although I would certainly wish to discredit the official conceptions of national product and the various ways of modifying it in the literature (Nordhaus and Tobin, 1971; Kendrick, 1979; Kuznets, 1951) this is not the prime purpose of this paper. Rather, the concern is to find a way of properly posing certain questions characteristic of the Marxist tradition. The central question I should eventually like to see answered is whether post-war prosperity and subsequent economic crisis can be adequately analysed in terms of initially high but then declining rates of surplus value. If this is the case, then an explanation for such a decline is also required, tying in abstract with a concrete historical account. There have been some very thoughtful and informative essays along these lines (Mandel, 1980; Armstrong et al., 1984; Kidron, 1974; Gillman, 1957; Harman, 1984), but it is not clear that the various statistical series these authors utilise are appropriate indices of rate of surplus value, organic composition of capital and other variables in their theoretical schemes. Thus there is an uncomfortable sense of a gap between abstract theorisation and descriptive material so that their series of statistics illustrate a point rather than provide firm evidence. This situation could, in my view, be improved if the available conventional statistics were fully re-worked in terms of a sufficiently sophisticated version of Marxist class theory. It is the aim of this paper to outline a model of class structure adequate for this purpose and indicate how the Blue Book statistics can be used as a resource for estimating the value flows in the model.

There is no space here to demonstrate the complex series of accounting equations needed to reorder the system of accounts, though they are implicit in the diagrammatic representation of class structure (Figure 11.1). A technical paper is available on request.

Marx himself provides two useful starting points for constructing a model of the overall flows of value in a capitalist economy, by firstly defining departments of production, and secondly, analysing different sequences where capitalists start and finish with money. Unfortunately, he does not bring these two approaches together.

Three departments are distinguished – for production of means of production (I), for production of means of consumption of the working class (II) and for production of means of consumption of the capitalist class (III). Clearly there are various mathematical identities as conditions for equilibrium, whether with growth, stability or contraction, such as that the demand for means of production in all three departments must be satisfied by the output of department I, and the demand for means of working-class consumption in all three departments must be satisfied by the output of department II. This sort of approach has been a considerable inspiration, though in very different ways, to Liontieff in his devising of input/output tables and to the Sraffians. As far as I know, although a number of Marxists have been able to gain considerable insight into the logic of the accumulation process through analysis of the three departments, they have not sought to provide empirical quantification of the elements in these accounts.

It is quite true, though also quite unhelpful, to be told that the conventional way of accounting cannot be validly taken directly into the Marxist system, especially as calculations are carried out there in terms of labour values rather than market prices. An obvious reason why one cannot even begin to rework the official accounts into the format of the Marxist departmental analysis is because that analysis only relates to a small part of the total flows of value in the capitalist system. What is needed for empirical quantification is division of the departments between capital and labour, and the addition of new departments for banking, commerce, property and certain state functions. Also, since in actual capitalist societies there are petty businesses, professionals working for a fee, charities and other nontrading private enterprises, we need a further petty and miscellaneous department. Finally, if we are to examine the flows of value within a particular territorial section of the world economy, we need a way of analysing value flows across national boundaries by having departments for assets owned abroad by residents and assets owned within the country by non-residents.

Marx's other cue for the sort of model I wish to construct is his schema for circuits of capital. For example he writes the circuit of productive capital as:-

$$\text{Money} \rightarrow \text{Commodities} \begin{cases} \text{Labour power} \rightarrow \\ \\ \text{Means of production} \nearrow \end{cases} \text{Commodities} \rightarrow \text{Money}$$

He also constructs similar 'diagrams' for commerce and banking, though these are often presented in a rather confusing fashion and discussed in an unnecessarily complicated way. In fact, it is quite possible to simplify Marx's diagrams and combine them with one another to show how the articulation of two sorts of capital transfers surplus value between them. Each diagram can be taken not as a representation of a typical banking or commercial capital or whatever, but rather as an aggregate of all banking or commercial capital. Then the flows of value between all capitals of one sort and all those of another sort can be seen as a palimpsest of diagrams representing the articulation of each capital of the first sort with each of the second (Gubbay, 1980, 1981).

Marx's circuits of capital can be paralleled by circuits for the state, the working class, the petty and miscellaneous sector, and so on. Each circuit can then be extended by adding in phases for taxation, payment of subsidies, payment and receipt for dividends, transfers abroad and so on. By showing the articulation of all these circuits through the transfers of value between them, we effectively construct the sort of elaborated departmental analysis advocated above.

A SIMPLE BUT INCORRECT REWORKING OF THE OFFICIAL ACCOUNTS

It might seem as if an unnecessarily complex calculation is being demanded when it would be sufficient, on the one hand, to use abstract arguments, say, about the tendency of the rate of surplus value to fall and, on the other hand, *careful* use of the conventional categories to illustrate the empirical manifestation of these underlying processes. This is surely an unsatisfactory position, damaging to the very plausibility of Marxian political economy. If the key concept of that theory, surplus value, is not quantifiable, at least in principle, then doubts are justifiably raised about whether it is meaningful and, indeed, whether the whole theory has any intellectual coherence. Conversely, if a clear and explicit quantity of surplus value produced annually can be specified, the charge of obscurantism levelled against Marxism from both Ricardians and neo-classicals loses much force. In short, quite major issues are at stake in the success or failure of the effort to quantify surplus value.

An easy shortcut to arriving at the Marxian aggregates is to add up various categories from the official accounts – constant capital used up equals depreciation minus value of physical increase in stocks and work in progress; variable capital equals employment incomes, and surplus value equals profits of companies and trading surpluses of public corporations. Unfortunately, this neat and convenient calculation is seriously flawed. It might have some validity if owners managed their enterprises, virtually all of which were engaged in commodity production, if there were very low numbers of people working on their own account or for unincorporated businesses, and if general government activities were very small. Under these circumstances, we would be entitled to ignore such elements as the surplus value appropriated by salaried managers, by the state as taxation and the wages of unproductive workers. Inclusion of depreciation by the personal sector and general government would then be acceptable. The fact is, however, that the conditions for such identities do not and never have prevailed. Consequently, it is impossible to evade a decision on how to account for a number of quantitatively large and economically significant transactions, such as payment of expenditure taxes. Should they be regarded as an indirect appropriation of surplus value by reckoning wages as net of such taxation, or should they be treated as a special form of expropriation by state controllers on a par with surplus value taken by capitalists, or should they simply be seen as an undefined arbitrary category of price increases? (Mandel, 1971, p. 315). Another problem with this oversimplified calculation of the Marxian aggregates is how to deal with incomes, other than employment incomes, in the petty sector. Neither lumping them all into surplus value nor all into variable capital could be justified, but then it is unclear how to split them up and whether any other theoretical category is also needed. In conclusion, there is no way of avoiding a rather complicated calculation on the basis of a sufficiently elaborate model of class structure.

VALUE FLOWS AND CLASS STRUCTURE

The considerable debate in recent years over the definition of productive and unproductive labour has provided a distinction which is essential for my model (Fine and Harris, 1979). In this paper a sharp line is drawn between productive labour, labour power hired by capitals to produce commodities whether or not they take physical form, and all other labour. The central Marxist presumption is that capitalists employing such productive labour are able to obtain profits because the value of labour power is less than the value created by it, the difference being referred to as surplus value. By definition and hypothesis, productive workers are precisely wage labourers who produce commodities and are thus exploited, that is create surplus value. The distinction between productive and unproductive labour is drawn *within* the category of wage labour, so that capitalists, the self-employed, domestic labourers and personal servants are neither productive nor unproductive. All and only capitalists employing productive workers are exploiters. As we shall see, unproductive workers perform necessary functions for the capitalist system and receive incomes as a part of surplus value – but are neither exploited nor exploiters.

With regard to productive labour, I construct an idealised sequence of transformations corresponding to the values possessed by the employing capitalists, the core phases of which are as follows:-

(1) Initial value possessed by the capitalists equivalent to the wage bill, fixed capital and raw materials.

(2) Reduction in cash balance equal to wages laid out by acquisition of labour power of equal value.

(3) Fixed capital used up (depreciation), so corresponding reduction in the value possessed.

(4) Raw material used up, so corresponding reduction on the value possessed.

(5) Labour power 'consumed', that is labour carried out under the capitalists' direction, resulting in a corresponding reduction in value possessed by them.

(6) Production resulting in the formation of commodities (product and fixed capital) of greater than the initial value. This difference, measured in units of labour time, is surplus value.

It is convenient for reworking the official accounts to distinguish each of these phases although, in reality, production is the *simultaneous* use of labour power to convert raw materials into the finished product while depreciating fixed capital.

These phases involve a series of interactions between productive workers and their employing capitalists by which the former labour and receive wages while the value of the latter's money and commodities increases; the value owned by the workers is unchanged but they have created surplus value which their employers have appropriated.

Although these core phases are the key to understanding class exploitation, there are other components of the class structure which interact in prior and subsequent phases with productive workers and their employing capitalists – and each other. Some of the most important phases are consumption, hiring, buying and selling, borrowing and lending, paying and receiving benefits, rent, interest, taxes and dividends. Accordingly, additional phases can be defined and, at each one, transactions and changes in value possessed by each component can be stated.

At those phases where, on theoretical grounds, an increase in the value possessed by some components is balanced by a decrease in the value possessed by others, an accounting equation can be constructed. Thus, by working through the phases, it is possible to build up a system of accounting equations to represent the transactions between all the components of the class structure. The value flows corresponding to these equations can be indicated diagrammatically (Figure 11.1).

CLASS ACCOUNTS

Some further explanation needs to be given for the components in this model of class structure.

There are three types of capitalist which, directly or indirectly, reappropriate portions of the surplus value initially appropriated by capitalists employing productive workers. They are banking capitalists obtaining interest, property capitalists obtaining rent and commercial capitalists obtaining profit on the difference between their buying and selling prices.

The unproductive workers employed by such capitalists receive in wages part of the surplus value that their labour enables their employers to acquire. Since they do not create surplus value, by definition, they

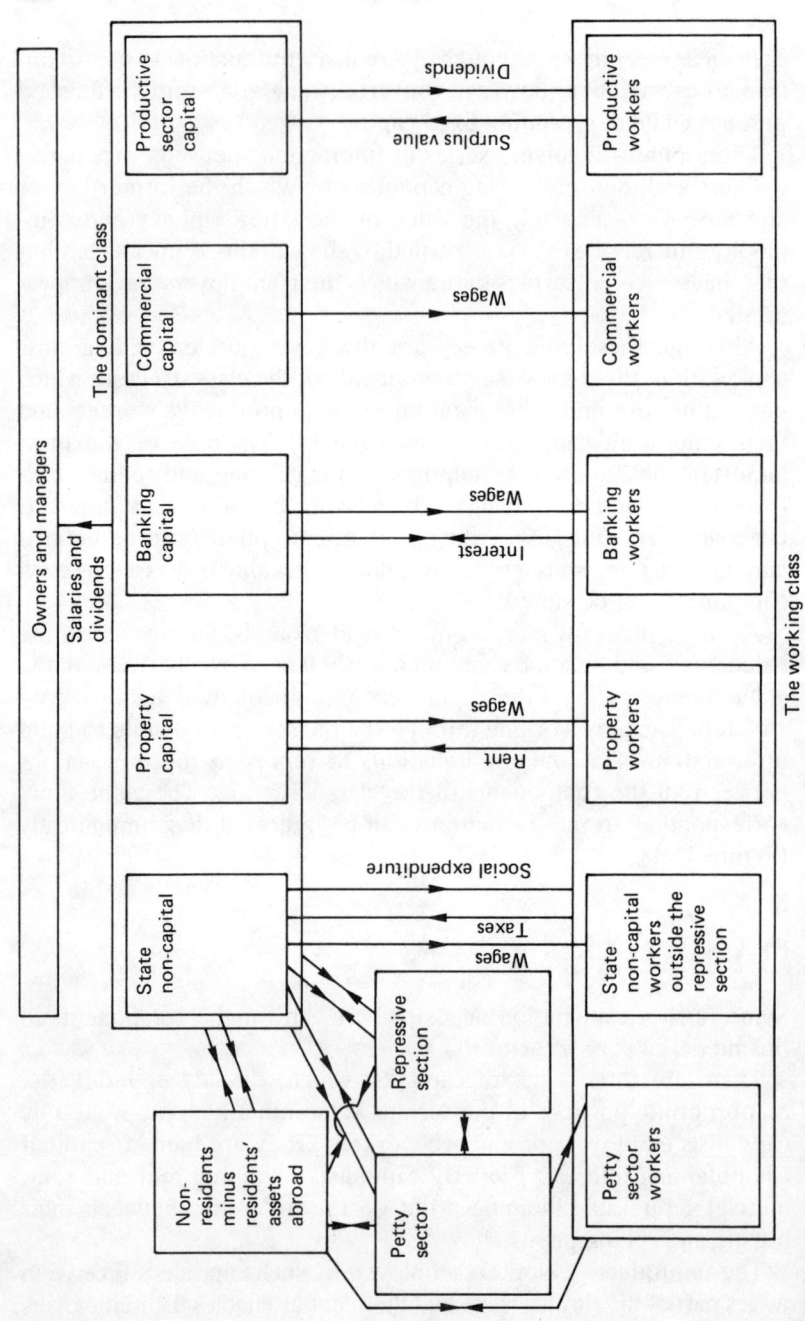

FIGURE 11.1 *A Model of Class Structure*

are not exploited. However, unproductive and productive workers are equally propertyless wage labourers, similarly paid and subject to direction in their work and, for this reason, share common class interests.

'Capitalists' are taken here in a rather abstract sense as one or more roles, such as owners and managers, which, in combination, direct wage labourers in appropriating and investing surplus value, whether created under their own aegis or under that of other capitalists. Enterprises are 'capitalist' as long as there are mechanisms, ultimately responsive to the market, which drive their managers to accumulate capital – and this includes state-owned businesses. Thus no distinction is drawn between nationalised and private business in my accounts and the corresponding diagram.

However, there *is* a vital distinction between capitalist enterprise and activities, largely carried out by the state, which provide *conditions* under which capital accumulation can take place. There are two major state non-capital functions, namely social expenditures which promote a compliant working class, and non-capital investment, which lowers investment costs to capitalists. Social expenditures are of two sorts, firstly promotion of social harmony such as state pensions and secondly 'repressive' aspects such armed forces, police, courts and prisons. Actually, it is often difficult to distinguish expenditures which promote social harmony from those which feed in to capital accumulation by making labour power available – so that unemployment benefit, for example, is both a social expenditure and a non-capital investment. Non-capital investment can be divided by two cross-cutting distinctions, firstly according to whether it subsidises constant or variable capital and, secondly, according to whether it is generally available infrastructure or is engrossed by particular companies as income to them in money or in kind. Thus, state schooling, subsidies to particular firms, general availability of depreciation allowances and the New Workers Scheme have to be recorded differently in the system of accounts being constructed. The state élite which jointly controls the state machine, though not acting as a capitalist, is committed to those functions which promote conditions for capital accumulation. It directs the work of those carrying out these activities and also of those who collect taxes to finance both these functions and payment of managerial salaries and workers' wages. Although not capitalists themselves, and divided though they may be on how best to carry out their functions, they are so intertwined with the capitalists that, together, they constitute the 'dominant class'. Figure 11.2 gives a Marxist account for the dominant class.

FIGURE 11.2 *Dominant Class Accounts*

Income

Tax from non-residents, petty and miscellaneous sector, repressive
   section, working class, owners and managers.

Surplus value from productive workers

Net dividends from abroad

Net interest from abroad

Rent from petty and miscellaneous sector, working class, repressive
   section, owners and managers.

Expenditure

Dividends to petty and miscellaneous sector, working class, repressive
   section, owners and managers

Rent to petty and miscellaneous sector

Charity to petty and miscellaneous sector

Wages to repressive section, and to commercial, banking property and
   other state non-capital workers

Transfers to non-residents

Social expenditure to the working class and repressive section

Increase in state non-capital assets at constant prices

Capital accumulation at constant prices

In analysing the situation of state employees, it will be important to
distinguish between the repressive section and the rest. The repressive section workers lack the power and economic privilege of the
state élite but are specially responsible for coercion, surveillance and
social control functions of the state – the ranks of the armed forces,
the lower levels of the police and prison officers, court officials, and
so on. Characteristically, such employees are tied into these activities
by a hierarchy of control, special codes of discipline, lack of trade
union rights, privileged pension entitlements and management efforts
to inculcate an occupational *esprit de corps*. The ambiguity of their
social position is that, although not part of the ruling class, they are
especially closely bound to it both by the terms and conditions of
their employment, and the central function they perform in sustaining the social order.

All other state employees are wage labourers enjoying similar
wages and conditions to those employed by capitalists, similarly
lacking power in their workplaces and similarly subject to managerial
efforts to cut costs and raise 'output'. For these reasons, Marxist
accounts should treat all these wage labourers as constituting the
'working class', even though some sections may be subject to ideo-

logical attack as unproductive employees of parasitic capital or servants of the busybody state.

It is possible to treat the value of labour power as wages *after* the deduction of taxation and *after* the addition of subsidies. In that case neither of these elements would appear as flows of value between the dominant and the working classes. Such a procedure might have been very plausible in the past, when taxation was a low proportion of working-class incomes, because the range of state non-capital activities was much less than today. This seems to have been the approach adopted by Marx. However, the very scale of tax levied on the working class suggests that a more realistic treatment is to take the value of labour power as wages *before* tax and subsidies, and then treat the balance of these payments as a form of state non-capital expropriation from the working class. Rent can be regarded in a similar way. No crucial theoretical issue hangs on the decision about how to treat taxes, subsidies and rent as long as a convention, once adopted, is held to consistently. What is important is to identify the total effect of all appropriations on the working class's capacity to purchase commodities, and this requires investigating, for example, whether or not rising taxes or rents are 'passed on' by the working class in higher wages. This is an empirical matter.

With regard to working-class income in the form of interest and dividends, it is again an empirical matter as to whether this is positive or negative. Such property income may well be interpreted as spreading earnings over lifetimes though it is a matter of fact rather than theory as to whether there is any additional gain or loss.

Figure 11.3 gives an account for the whole working class in the light of the above points.

An account has to be constructed for all those people who are self-employed, work in partnerships, employ few people or manage private non-profit-making organisations like churches, charities, clubs and pressure groups. I refer to this as the petty and miscellaneous sector.

A further account can be constructed for wage labourers employed by small businesses or private non-profit-making organisations.

Finally, the whole system of accounts can be completed by the addition of a sector to represent non-residents' assets in the UK minus residents' assets abroad.

* * *

FIGURE 11.3 *Working-class Accounts*

Income
Wages of the working class
Net interest from banking capital
Dividends from dominant class
Dividends from non-residents
Social expenditure from state non-capital

Expenditure
Transfers to non-residents
Rent to petty sector
Tax to state non-capital
Rent to property capital
Consumption
Saving at constant prices

There is a further important issue that needs to be addressed now even though there is no space to develop it here (see Crompton and Gubbay, 1977, Ch. IX). The model presented so far focuses on the distinction between the ruling class and the working class, with only the repressive section of the state and the petty and miscellaneous sector being left out of this dichotomy. However, control in organisations actually runs down in a complex hierarchy rather than across a clear line of cleavage to the workers. How, then, should the class position of technical experts, middle managers, supervisors, and foremen be characterised? They do not, in my view, constitute a middle *class* with identifiable class interests but rather a set of positions which are quite literally *ambivalent*, that is attached to two opposing class interests. Drawing attention to these middling positions does not invalidate a model based on class dichotomy, but it does pose a difficult accounting problem about how to make the demarcation. It is not a matter of drawing a line in the managerial hierarchy such that all jobs above it are concerned solely with control and all those below it solely with executing given tasks; there is no such line for the very good reason that job specifications in the hierarchy typically involve both control and execution. Rather, the problem is to estimate for each of these jobs the proportions in which these two functions are combined. The problem is thus to partition the activities carried out by people occupying middling positions rather than partition the positions themselves. It is supposed that analysis of salary differentials might yield the required partition on the hypothesis that a manager's payments for control correspond to the excess of his or her salary over wages for workers of similar skills.

* * *

It might be objected that the sorts of calculations envisaged here are flawed because of a false identification of values with market prices. There is certainly an argument of impeccable logic which applies to capitalists organising commodity production, to the effect that equality of market profits and variation in organic composition of capital implies disproportion between values and prices. Effectively, the total of surplus value is redistributed among capitalists in proportion to the size of their capital. This important fact is not, however, destructive of my model, since it aggregates all capitalists organising production and thus nets out this effect. A more intractable problem arises for this and other reasons in accounting properly for the flow of surplus value across national boundaries.

QUANTIFYING THE MARXIAN MODEL

A 'sophisticated' Marxist model of class structure has been constructed for which each component element has an income/expenditure account. These accounts were derived, for each component, from an idealised sequence of transactions between them.

Now, it is possible to construct from each of these sequences current and capital accounts in a similar form to those found in the Blue Books. However, it is necessary to combine some of these accounts and divide up others in order to identify them precisely with the official accounts. For example, accounts for commodity-producing capitalists have to be combined with those of banking, commerce and property, and then divided into private and state ownership to correspond to 'Companies and Financial Institutions' and 'Public Corporations' respectively.

All accounts for the various components of the working class have to be combined with the repressive section, managers and owners and the petty and miscellaneous sector to yield the 'Personal' sector.

By working back to reconstruct the official accounts, comparing them with figures in the Blue Books and then working forward to the Marxist accounts, it should be possible to estimate the size of its major categories.

Much work remains to be done before this calculation can be adequately achieved. Other sources of statistics must be used in conjunction with the Blue Books if the information available in them is to be properly reorganised as a set of accounts which can provide a basis for Marxist economic history.

Bibliography

Armstrong, P., A. Glyn, and J. Harrison, *Western Capitalism Since World War II* (Data Appendix) (London: Fontana, 1984).
Central Statistical Office, *National Income and Expenditure* (London: HMSO, 1982)
Crompton, R. and J. Gubbay, *Economy and Class Structure* (London: Macmillan, 1977).
Fine, B. and L. Harris, *Rereading Capital* (London: Macmillan, 1979).
Gillman, J., *The Falling Rate of Profit* (London: Dobson Books Ltd., 1957).
Gubbay, J., 'Types of Capital and Value Schema', *Economics Discussion Paper 59*, University of East Anglia, 1980.
Gubbay, J., 'Capital and the State', *Sociology Discussion Paper*, University of East Anglia, 1981.
Hall, D., *The Cuts Machine: The Politics of Public Expenditure* (London: Pluto, 1983).
Harman, C., *Explaining the Crisis* (London: Bookmarks, 1984).
Kendrick, J., 'Expanding Imputed Values in the National Income and Product Accounts', *Review of Income and Wealth* (1979) pp. 349–363.
Kidron, M., *Capitalism and Theory* (London: Pluto Press Ltd., 1974).
Kuznets, S., 'Government Product and National Income', *Income and Wealth* (Series I) (1951) pp. 178–244.
Mandel, E., *Marxist Economic Theory* (London: Merlin Press Ltd., 1971).
Mandel, E., *Late Capitalism* (London: Verso, 1980).
Nordhaus W., and Tobin J., 'Is Growth Obsolete?', in M. Moss (ed.), *The Measurement of Economic and Social Performance* (Princeton, University Press, 1971) pp. 509–32.
Trotsky, L., *The Death Agony of Capitalism and the Tasks of the Fourth International* (New York: Pathfinder, 1970).

12 Measuring the Performance of Worker Co-operatives

Keith Jefferis and Alan Thomas[1]

The producer co-operative sector in the UK is, by European standards, relatively small, but it has in recent years demonstrated a remarkable capacity for growth. The number of co-operatives has increased rapidly, from around 300 in 1980 to 1000 by 1986 (CDA, 1980; London ICOM, 1986), but knowledge of co-operative performance is largely based upon case studies (for instance, see Cornforth, Thomas, Lewis and Spear, 1988) rather than on aggregate data covering a broad range of co-operatives. General perceptions are still influenced by the experience of the three 'Benn co-ops' in the mid-1970s (Triumph Meriden, KME and the *Scottish Daily News*) as lame ducks supported by public funds. While no serious attempt was made to assess the value of such spending in job creation terms compared to other publicly-supported ventures (hence leading to under-funding and eventual collapse), they are not typical of the majority of co-operatives today. The sector now consists largely of small co-operatives, started from scratch (Jefferis, 1986), providing less than 9000 jobs in total, and receiving relatively little support from public funds.

The ability of these newer co-operatives to succeed has not yet been fully tested; many are still in the process of becoming established. But what is also open to debate is the way in which success for co-operatives should be perceived (see, for example, Thomas, 1982). Our position is that co-operatives should be viewed as a radical alternative to a conventional company, with different aims and objectives, offering the potential for at least a partial escape from the exploitation of wage labour in the existing economic structure. While there is clearly a requirement to survive in the market, we believe that success for co-operatives cannot solely be judged in the conventional manner, in terms of profitability. There are many aspects of performance which can be considered important; different co-

233

operatives, and different members within any one co-operative, may be motivated by one or more of a variety of factors (Paton, 1978; Wajcman, 1983). These may include employment creation or job-saving; participation and internal democracy; growth; profitability; the provision of good pay and conditions; a new approach towards the labour process; technology and the division of labour; or the fulfilment of community or social needs for products and services provided. Others may consider that working in a co-operative is in itself a political statement. Much of the recent local authority support for co-operatives is based on their pursuit of social objectives as part of a wider strategy of restructuring the economy in favour of labour rather than capital. The notion of 'success' can be applied to the achievement of any or all of these objectives.

Our aim is to examine theoretically the measurement of co-operative performance, and suggest some measures which can be practically applied. Ideally these should allow:

(1) comparability between co-operative ventures;
(2) assessment of the performance of individual co-operatives over a number of years;
(3) judgements to be made by public bodies and others on effectiveness of investments in co-operative enterprises;
(4) some degree of comparability with performance measures for conventional small businesses.

We are currently establishing a data base of financial information on UK co-operatives. This will supplement the existing worker co-operative data base (London ICOM, 1986) with financial and trading information, thereby assisting other researchers and the co-operative sector itself. This data base will use the measures as they are developed and in turn provide a basis for testing them. In this paper we take a preliminary look at a range of possible financial measures and apply them to the first few years of some co-operatives in two sectors (clothing and printing) where we have carried out pilot studies for the data base project. This leads to two sets of conclusions: first on the relative merits of ratio measures based on value added, as opposed to profitability; second, some preliminary findings on different possible and viable types of co-operative.

THE CHOICE OF PERFORMANCE MEASURES

Co-operative Performance

The underlying motivation and rationale of many co-operatives is implicitly a rejection of the existing capitalist system. This rejection can take a variety of forms, and in assessing co-operative performance any one of a number of different variables could be chosen, each giving a different 'ordering' of co-operatives depending on their chosen policies and objectives. To choose any one objective as the means of measuring success is to a certain extent arbitrary but also potentially dangerous, as the choice made will tend to reflect a certain perspective of what is important.

Whatever their objectives, co-operatives must survive by operating in a market economy. Whether as independent entities or with external support, commercial performance is crucial for survival. In this paper we concentrate on the measurement of financial performance, reflecting both their need to survive and the ready availability of financial data. We attempt to do this without losing sight of the other achievements made by co-operatives.

Profit for Co-operatives

For capitalist firms, performance is assessed on the basis of profitability and related measures. Given the role of profit in the maintenance of the capitalist system this is entirely logical. Orthodox conceptions of profit maintain the belief that profit maximisation is a commendable, socially responsible activity (rather than a measure of the degree of exploitation of one class by another). Such conceptions are easily demolished (Fine, 1977; Howard, 1983) and profit is revealed not as the result of a situation of equality between capital and labour, but the result of 'the appropriation of the surplus product by one class through its monopolisation of the means of production and of the system of wage exploitation' (Fine, 1977, p. 113).

Co-operatives represent an attempt to move away from the exploitation of labour by capital. They should be wary of the use of profit; the surplus which remains within a co-operative is often termed profit but is not conceptually the same as profit in a capitalist company.

On an empirical level, the use of profit as a measure of performance may underplay the performance of co-operatives relative to other businesses. Some commentators (Oakeshott, 1978; Bradley and Gelb, 1983) envisage the benefits of co-operatives coming from higher productivity and profitability (and therefore being more successful in capitalist terms) because the conflict beween management and workforce has been removed. But there are other factors which come into play. The removal of conflict in this form is part of the non-capitalist nature of co-operatives. However, conflict will remain in some form, either between different members holding conflicting objectives for their co-operative, or, more fundamentally, between the interests of the co-operative as an entity and the interests of the members, particularly within the capitalist environment.

Even if co-operative members are united in what objectives they wish to pursue, it is likely that these will conflict with profitability. By their very nature, internal democracy, employment maximisation, job rotation, alternative forms of technology and the division of labour, and production for social need all tend to conflict with profitability – they have only been undertaken by capitalist firms in unusual circumstances precisely because they do in general conflict with the objective of profit maximisation and control.

A final argument against using profit as a measure of performance for co-operatives is that even when a given surplus is earned, the 'profit' figure will depend on the decision taken by the co-operative members as to the division of that surplus between wages and earnings retained in the business. A decision to take low wages (and then vote themselves a bonus out of the profits) would lead to a higher profitability figure than the payment of high wages to start with, yet there is no particular reason to assume a different performance in each case.[2]

The conceptually different role of the surplus can be illustrated as follows. Rather than acting as profit maximisers, co-operatives must make a minimum surplus to survive, that is, the claims of capital (interest, rent) and of the state (taxation) have to be met. The co-operative may decide to earn and set aside a surplus for investment. Once this has been achieved, the co-operative can consider its other objectives. The conflicts between the different aims of co-operatives reflect the contradictory position of co-operatives within the capitalist system – the desire to pursue various aims is always constrained by the need to survive in the market. The earning of a surplus can be seen as giving the flexibility to pursue these policies.

Value Added

Is there an alternative measure which can be used for the financial performance of co-operatives? Such a measure (or measures) must reflect the characteristics of co-operatives, as represented by the slogan 'Labour hires capital rather capital hiring labour'. These characteristics include the following:

(1) In a co-operative, labour is not a cost incurred by capital. Instead, labour owns the means of production and so the surplus accrues to labour.

(2) To a capitalist, labour appears as a cost, even though it is the source of value. In a co-operative, capital appears as a cost, even though this is a result of capital's remaining hold over the means of production, through finance capital.

A quantity which encompasses the concept of this surplus in a co-op is value added, suitably defined. Value added includes wages as well as profit, and therefore does not depend on the distribution between the two of the surplus which results from production.

There may appear to be a danger in the use of value-added accounting. When in the 1970s it became fashionable for companies to present value-added accounts to their employees, this was widely criticised as a means by which management further manipulates the workforce (Hird, 1983; Labour Research, 1978). Value added presents a 'picture of a unity of interests in the financial performance of a given business organisation, whereas in fact there exists a basic conflict of interests' (Burchell, Clubb and Hopwood, 1985, p. 17). However, co-operatives are an attempt to break away from the relationship between labour and capital which gives rise to this conflict (although other, different, conflicts may arise in the process). To the extent that co-operatives do represent a co-operative effort by the workforce, then perhaps value added can provide a suitable representation of performance.

Williams, Haslam, et al. (1986) advocate the use of value-added criteria in assessing investments in industry. This is claimed to be a better measure of wealth creation, and in a similar argument to our own, they note that labour has the major interest in modern manufacturing industry.

In a co-operative, value added records a meaningful quantity, that is, the surplus which remains from revenue once costs have been deducted. If capital is treated as an input like any other, then its cost (interest) can be treated in the same way. Thus value added is the quantity which accrues to labour; labour then takes the decision as to the distribution of this surplus between current payments such as wages, bonuses and so on, and retained earnings for investment. The important role of value added for co-operatives has been noted by Marris (1984, p. 19), who states that 'Value added is the true contribution of the business to its worker members'. Value added does appear to have more relevance to co-operatives than profit, and is additionally useful because the same measure can be derived for the performance of conventional companies.

Ratio Measures based on Value Added

In order to make comparisons between co-operatives some form of rate of return is required.[3] Customary accounting measures are centred on return on resources (the ratio of operating profit to net assets), with a variety of other ratios contributing to this. Analysis of contributory ratios can assist in a diagnosis of reasons for good and bad performance of a firm, and furthermore are useful for making comparisons between different firms (see for instance Harper, 1977, for a typical pyramid of ratios based on return to capital).

It may be possible to develop a similar set of measures for co-operatives. Suitable diagnostic tests would enable the early identification of co-operatives likely to run into difficulties. Support agencies – organisations such as GLEB in London, various CDAs around the country, and even a hypothetical investment bank for co-operatives (Labour Party, 1985, p. 16), could pick up on these early warning signals (as of course could the co-operative members themselves).

Moving from a diagnostic to an explanatory perspective, it should be possible to identify some of the factors which contribute to a successful co-operative. In particular, the effectiveness of particular support strategies could be assessed, for instance, testing hypotheses as to whether co-operatives assisted by grants or wage subsidies are less likely to succeed than those receiving 'soft' loans.

Such a set of measures of performance for co-operatives cannot necessarily be derived from conventional measures simply by substituting value added for profit wherever it occurs. For a capitalist company, the ratio [profit: net assets] makes sense, as it measures the rate at which the resource (capital) generates a return to itself. In the case of co-operatives, the situation is different. While a ratio [value added: net assets] can be calculated it is meaningless once labour has been identified as the source of value.

One of our aims is to find a measure of the efficiency with which a co-operative's labour force generates its output. While in a sense this is measuring the extent of 'work-intensity', we believe that higher productivity (that is, output or value added per labour unit input) is beneficial, at least to the extent that we elevate the financial aspect of performance to primacy over the other objectives.

Problems with Measuring Return to Labour.

The key problem faced is therefore one of deriving a measure of the rate of return to labour, rather than capital, with the return defined as value added rather than profit. But on what basis is the labour input to be calculated? The simplest approach is to use value added per worker, a measure which is easy to calculate but which suffers certain drawbacks. Firstly, labour input varies according to the length of the working week or year (although account could be taken of this if sufficient data were available). More importantly, it neglects differences in the skill composition of the workforce, and in the level of technology employed. Value added per head will be higher if a given output is produced by a small number of skilled workers rather than a large number of unskilled workers, without implying any difference in efficiency. A co-operative which 'undervalues' its skilled workers will demonstrate an artificially high value added per head in the same way that a firm with undervalued assets will demonstrate a high rate of profit. Similarly, a co-operative with more capital-intensive technology will have higher value added per head even if there is a less capital-intensive option with similar levels of skills and profitability.

These points will certainly be less important in making comparisons between co-operatives in similar activities, where skills and technology may not vary a great deal between co-operatives.[4] However, effective and useful comparisons across co-operatives in different sectors and with different technologies requires some alternative method of measurement of labour.

The problem of taking account of skill differences is one of measuring non-homogeneous labour in a way that will enable aggregation. The analogous problem – measuring the rate of profit on physically different types of capital – is solved by the monetary valuation of different capitals (even if such valuations are arguably inaccurate, particularly during periods of inflation). For labour of different skills there is no simple equivalent.

One possible solution is to measure labour by *wages/salaries* paid. On the (somewhat tenuous) assumption that wage differentials reflect relative skills, the total wage bill would therefore reflect the total endowment of skills which the co-operative has. This leads to a ratio such as [value added: total wages], or inverting it, wages as a percentage of value added, which is relatively easy to obtain from available data. This ratio also fulfils a direct function, as a measure of the distribution of surplus between immediate renumeration and reinvestment or other non-wage objectives. Clearly if the ratio is greater than one over a prolonged period, a need is indicated for some form of external subsidy if the co-operative is to continue in operation.

A major difficulty with this measure is the relationship between skills and wages. It could be argued that in the economy in general, wage differentials reflect skill structures, but this is unlikely to be true in co-operatives. Many adopt a policy of narrow or no wage differentials, whatever the workers' skills. Co-operatives are frequently forced to pay low wages as a result of their peripheral position in the economy, in common with some other small businesses. But the extent to which low wages are necessary varies from co-operative to co-operative, and so the wage structure in an individual co-operative cannot necessarily be said to reflect the skills of its workers. Furthermore, if the ratio [value added: total wages] were adopted as a measure of productivity, a co-operative would apparently improve its performance by reducing wages, which is clearly incorrect and illogical.

An alternative method of using wages to measure skill differences would be to use an external scale of differentials – for example, union rates or national wage levels for the relevant skills. However, this would require data on the physical skill structure of each co-operative and on external wage rates. There is a clear trade-off here between simplicity and theoretical rigour.

Mondragon – Index of Value Added

As for comparability between co-operatives with different levels of technology, a partial attempt to face this problem has been made at Mondragon, a town in the Basque country of Spain which is renowned as a centre of a well established regional co-operative economy. The financial aspects of co-operation are administered by a credit co-operative, the Caja Laboral Popular (CLP), whose research department has developed measures of co-operative performance (Thomas and Logan, 1981). The most interesting of these is an 'Index of Value Added', which is defined as follows:

$$IVA = \frac{GP}{W + (C/E)}$$

where
GP = gross profit (sales-cost of sales)
W = no. of workers
C = annual cost of fixed and working capital
E = average annual earnings.

The denominator is therefore a composite number comprising the annual cost of capital divided by the average wage and the number of workers. The contribution of capital is thus measured in terms of equivalent 'labour units', and the ratio computes the return to capital and labour combined. (Gross profit is used rather than our Value Added, but the principle is similar.) In this it is something of a halfway house between a return to capital and a return to labour. IVA does take account of different capital resources in different co-operatives, but it still fails to allow for differences in workers' skills. In making comparisons between co-ops and other businesses in the UK, the problem of low wages in co-operatives reduces the usefulness of comparability. However, Thomas and Logan (1981, p. 108) report that the problem identified above, of wages not reflecting skills because of reduced differentials or low wages all round, does not apply. In Mondragon the level of earnings is linked to that of similar branches of economic activity, and so there is no downward bias as a result of using co-operative earnings. The same authors report, however, that the Mondragon co-operatives tend to invest heavily in education and training, and so their workforces tend to be more highly skilled than those in comparable firms. Thus co-operative performance would tend to be overestimated by this measure, because of the undervaluing of the skilled labour input into the co-operatives.

The Role of Value-Added Measures in Assessing Performance

Any measure based upon value added will be playing a very different role to one based on profit. For conventional enterprises, performance can be encompassed by the one measure because of the role which profit plays in a capitalist economy – that is, the rate of profit is a means by which investment is directed and capital allocated to different firms and activities. Profitability can be used as the firm's judgement of performance because it is the economy's judgement of performance. A firm has other activities in addition to making a profit – it produces output and employs workers – but these are irrelevant in the capital market, except insofar as they contribute to profit. They are not important aspects of performance in their own right.

We do not expect to be able to replace the rate of profit with any single value-added-based measure for co-operative performance, for two reasons. Firstly, value added does not have the particular role of profit in the economy at large. Secondly, objectives vary between co-operatives and between members, and so a variety of different measures would be used to assess different aspects of co-operative performance.

Nevertheless, value-added-based measures can be very useful. These measures are an indicator of relative strength to pursue broader objectives, subject to the need to survive commercially. Once a co-operative has met its external obligations, it will hopefully be left with a surplus to pursue a range of objectives – paying bonuses to members, making political or charitable contributions, employing more staff, and so on. It is in the interest of co-operatives to earn a large surplus (that is, to maximise value added), giving the flexibility, or slack, to pursue these objectives.

Alternatively a co-operative may distribute its *potential* surplus rather than its *actual* surplus – effectively distributing the surplus before earning it. This could be by pricing policy, or by adopting a division of labour or technology which is not value-added maximising. It is illustrated in the following example (Cockerton et al., 1980, p. 74), describing the work of a printing co-operative, Calverts North Star Press:

> At present we are earning £70 for a 35-hour week or £85 for 42 hours, but are aiming for the average industrial wage in the short term. All workers earn equal wages. Some of our potential earnings (maybe £15 a week each) goes towards subsidies on jobs whose publishers have no printing budgets e.g. community groups, campaigning organisations, etc. We operate three price scales depending on the size and financial position of the customer.

Such achievements will escape value-added measures and these objectives will be relegated in importance. Although adequate financial performance is a constraint, can it be elevated to the sole criterion of success?

This question is indicative of a wider problem – that of assessing achievements which are not quantifiable in monetary terms, many of which are felt outside of the co-operative itself. How do we take account of the benefits to consumers of socially-useful products (more exercise and less pollution from bicycles, better health from wholefoods), which would not necessarily be provided on the basis of profit rather than need. Indeed, one could argue that as the existing economic system acts to exploit and oppress the vast majority of people, then *any* co-operative activity which rejects existing reactionary practices is advantageous and socially desirable.

One conventional response to these externalities is the cost-benefit approach of the social audit. This attempts to put a monetary valuation on externalities, including wider costs and benefits in a calculation. In different circumstances, this is adopted by Rowthorn and Ward (1979) and Nove (1973); they aim to quantify the wider impact of decisions taken by nationalised industries. A similar exercise could be undertaken by a government interested in the macroeconomic impact of co-operative development as an employment creation strategy. The shadow cost of investment in co-operatives would then be much less than the monetary cost, reflecting the relatively low net cost to the state of publicly-funded employment creation.

For many, however, co-operatives are part of a wider strategy of restructuring the economy in favour of labour, rather than simply employment creation. Generally the 'social benefits' involved cannot be valued in a monetary way. Unfortunately the concept of 'social returns' to social investments, as an analogy to financial returns to financial investments, is relatively undeveloped (but see Jefferis & Robinson, 1986).

PERFORMANCE OF PRINTING AND CLOTHING CO-OPERATIVES

Following on from our theoretical analysis, we have used the measures derived there in an empirical analysis of the performance of worker co-operatives in the UK clothing and printing sectors.

Scope of the Study

The first of our pieces of empirical work was a pilot project (Thomas, 1985) on co-operatives in clothing, footwear and textiles (although the majority are co-operatives of sewing machinists). This sector was chosen because the Co-operatives Research Unit collectively has firsthand knowledge of several such co-operatives through case studies (see Lockett, 1978; Cornforth, 1981; Emerson, 1983), so that interpretation of data could be checked. Furthermore, the sector has been in decline in Britain for many years, and is characterised by low pay and poor working conditions. If co-operatives are to have a beneficial impact on the conditions of labour, then this is one area where they are needed. Finally, worker co-operatives had traditionally been active in this sector, and several survive from the nineteenth century, although our analysis is limited to those founded more recently.

Following our work on clothing co-operatives, our attention has recently turned to the printing sector. In 1984 there were sixty co-ops involved in this sector (CDA, 1984), and as with clothing, there has been a notable co-operative presence since the nineteenth century. Furthermore, there has been a substantial growth and printing co-operatives were amongst the earliest to emerge in the 'new wave' of worker co-operatives since the mid-1970s. But there are additional reasons why printing is interesting, and appropriate for co-operative activity. Firstly, employment has been dominated by skilled work, for craftsmen, giving the workforce a high degree of control over the labour process. Associated with this has been a high degree of unionisation and politicisation. Printing has, however, been in decline for some time, particularly in traditional centres of the trade such as London, and is facing major problems with the introduction of new technology. In addition, the nature of the product (producing to individual customers' specification rather than mass production) means that there is ample opportunity to cater for sectors of the market with which co-operatives have some sympathy – as a result many printing co-operatives specialise in work for trade unions, black, feminist and left-wing groups, and community organisations. Given this background, there would appear to be a potential for worker co-operatives to organise in printing and ensure that the restructuring that does take place is for the benefit of those working there. In this, co-operatives have a role to play as part of the wider labour movement; in London for instance the GLEB introduced a strategy for the London printing industry as the first of its sector initiatives (GLEB 1985). The combination of GLEB's co-operative strategy and printing sector strategy led to the formation of the London Co-operative Printers Association by a group of established printing co-operatives, as a collective effort to compete more effectively and strengthen their position.

Use of Financial Indicators

Following on from our theoretical analysis, the centrepiece of the empirical analysis is the testing of the following measures of co-operative performance: *value added per head, wages as percentage of value added*, and *average wage*. We also consider the Mondragon-inspired *index of value added*. Appendix 12.1 shows the results of these ratios for a number of printing and clothing co-operatives for 1982 and 1983.

Monitoring

At this stage the use of these measures is geared towards the *monitoring* of co-operative performance. That is, they can tell us how well a co-operative is achieving a return to labour (at least to the extent that this can be expressed in financial quantities). The three measures combined give an indication of survival strength in expressing the extent to which members' personal financial needs are covered and value retained for co-operative maintainance, security and the pursuit of other objectives. The wage measure indicates relative stress on the wages satisficing objective. These measures parallel the conventional use of profitability as a measure of company performance. We envisage these measures being used by co-operatives and public authorities to assess co-operative performance. They could provide *comparisons* between co-operatives, particularly in the same sector of business.

We have used relatively old data (four years old or more); for realistic monitoring purposes, co-operatives' internal information systems would need to be much improved, with the introduction of a management accounting framework based on these measures.

Prediction

It may be possible to use these and other measures for *prediction* of co-operative evolution. By examining the past experiences of both successful and failed co-operatives, it should be possible to recognise patterns of co-operative development. In considering the results in this paper we will later suggest a number of alternative paths which appear to characterise the majority of co-operatives studied.

Explanation

Eventually we aim to use some of these measures in an analysis of the causes of varying financial performance among co-operatives. For example, reliance on internal or external loans for capital funding; revenue or capital support, and assistance from CDAs are factors which we believe are important in determining co-operative perform- ance. The central measures we have derived would either individu- ally or as a composite be the dependent variable denoting co-operative performance.

Classification and Usefulness of Co-operative Financial Indicators

The empirical measures fall into three groups:

(1) descriptive (classificatory) measures;
(2) secondary (internal) performance indicators;
(3) primary performance indicators

The first group consists of factors which give an indication of the type of co-operative. Degree of capitalisation and degree and form of integration into the market are examples of descriptive factors that can be indicated at least in part by financial ratios. These descriptive measures are useful but limited. If they are to be used as part of a set of explanatory variables, they need to be supplemented by other data sources if the full range of factors influencing performance are to be covered. Conditions of start-up (rescue, new start or 'phoenix') and the political and work orientations of the members cannot be derived from financial data, but are important. Easily quantified factors such as industrial sector, geographical location (or those related to loca- tion, such as presence or absence of a local co-operative support organisation, or the level of unemployment) are more readily avail- able.

The second group consists of factors which give an indication of the internal operation of the co-operative. They could include efficient use of material assets; increased turnover per head or in relation to overheads; or a liquidity ratio. These are examples of internal factors contributing to overall performance. For co-operatives which are similar in descriptive terms, one can expect to look to these internal factors for a diagnosis.

The third group consists of the three related measures of value added per head, wages as a percentage of value added and average wage, plus the index of value added.

The division into descriptive and performance measures is by no means clear-cut, and it is possible for a measure to undertake both functions in different circumstances. For instance, the ratio of value added to turnover can be descriptive, distinguishing a printing co-operative from a typesetting co-operative, or a Cut, Make and Trim clothing co-operative from one making to own designs. However, once the classification into type has been made, then the same ratio is a good indicator of performance, an increasing figure showing that a greater part of the turnover generated by the co-operative is accruing to and at the disposal of labour.

Deriving the Measures in Practice

The first problem with calculating performance measures loosely based upon a *return to labour* is that conventional financial reporting is not geared in this direction. In Chapter 10 of this volume, Bailey notes that 'from a Marxian point of view the accounts of an enterprise contain a jumble of heterogeneous items that prevent wages and profits, as defined by Marx, from being distinguished properly'. Major difficulties from this source are:

(1) separating outgoings into returns to labour and capital – such as rent, rates, and interest, particularly that part of interest incorporated in HP and lease payments. Direct wages are often lumped together with production costs;

(2) Obtaining accurate information on labour input. This covers basic information such as the size of the workforce,[5] plus whether full- or part-time, hours worked etc. Also important is the skill structure of the workforce, and individual wage rates and differentials.

If we wish to make any calculations based on the measurement of capital, we encounter particular problems. Frequently a co-operative's *net assets* are negative, implying that the co-operative is accumulating losses and relying on its creditors for short-term financing. In such cases it is clearly meaningless to use this figure to measure, say, capital employed in a ratio of rate of return on capital.

However, even then it is useful to have a material measure of the means of production in use. Perhaps for this purpose it is better to use *fixed assets*. This situation can obviously apply to any business, but co-operatives in particular suffer from problems of undercapitalisation (Thornley, 1981, p. 12; GLEB, 1984). Balance-sheet valuations may also be inaccurate; fixed assets can be undervalued, as when a rescue co-operative succeeds in buying machinery from the receiver very cheaply. The cheap sale of machinery, for example, could partly be due to the unique position of a potential rescue co-operative *vis-à-vis* any other business trying to obtain the wherewithal to start trading.

There is also an important question about how co-operatives themselves view their capital and valuation of assets. They may, for example, regard external loans as burdens to be repaid rather than looking on successful debt servicing as a way of improving external confidence with a view to future growth. Again, if the co-operative's reserves are held in common with a prohibition on the distribution of assets to individuals, then there is no motive for ensuring that the co-operative's worth on paper accurately reflects the value of its assets.

Primary Performance Measures

Appendix 12.1 shows the results of applying various measures to the performance of printing and clothing co-operatives[6] for 1982 and 1983. It includes the three primary measures Value Added per Head (VA/H), Average Wage (W/H) and Wages as a percentage of Value Added (W/VA), and in addition, Index of Value Added (IVA) and Profitability (P/NA). Co-operatives are presented in ascending order of value added per head for 1983.

We have not yet carried out a rigorous statistical analysis of these data, but some interesting points do emerge from an inspection of the results.

Value Added Per Head   (VA/H) covers a fairly broad range, from 166 to 10 824 in 1982 and 20 938 in 1983. It is noticeable that the ordering of co-operatives does not vary a great deal from 1982 to 1983, suggesting that the measure provides a fairly good indication of the underlying state of affairs in co-operatives' trading positions.

Average Wage   measures the extent to which the objective of paying a reasonable wage level is being met. With one or two exceptions, the wage level is closely related to VA/H. That is, as VA/H rises, so does the wage level; the relationship is particularly marked in 1983. This is not particularly surprising – one would expect wages to rise with productivity.

Wages as a Percentage of Value Added. It is also clear that the more successful co-operatives, where value added is higher, are also more successful at retaining a surplus for reinvestment or meeting other objectives. The less successful co-operatives are forced by low value added and by the need to pay a reasonable level of wages, to pay out more in wages than they are generating. This is shown by a figure of over 100 per cent, and manifested in increasing accumulated losses with a co-operative living off reserves or borrowing, or leading to failure/collapse or dependence on subsidies.

Index of Value Added appears to follow the average wage level, with one or two exceptions. It is likely that when used by the CLP at Mondragon, the calculation is based upon appropriate financial reporting. In our work there are likely to be inconsistencies in the data used which will affect the results. The use of 'soft' loans will distort the relationship between interest payments and capital used; similarly, wages payments will not truly reflect labour input. Other payments to capital (rent, lease payments) are difficult to isolate.

Profitability (rate of return to capital) varies wildly from year to year, much more than value added per head. These results support our earlier contention that profitability is not a particularly relevant or good indicator of co-operative performance – certainly it does not appear to pick up *underlying* trends in performance, prospects and the trading position of co-operatives, which are unlikely to move so erratically.

Types of co-operative

Obviously in the early years any business expects to make losses while establishing itself. What is interesting is to look at the conditions under which co-operatives can grow to become self-sustaining, independent entities. Other work which we have carried out (Jefferis and Thomas, 1986) suggests that there are several distinct pathways.

Firstly, many co-operatives appear to labour under adverse conditions in early years. They are characterised by low wages, long hours and poor conditions of work necessary to overcome initial undercapitalisation. Building up the business in this way can be called 'sweat equity'. Gradually they acquire the reserves and security to take on loans, and can increase wages. After three to four years, they reach a point of financial security and independence. In terms of the above analysis, this could mean that the low value-added-per-head figure is a correct indicator of poor initial performance, but that this performance improves before money and commitment run out.

Alternatively, the value-added-per-head figure may be low but sustainable. Many clothing co-operatives are marginal, but offer better opportunities than the alternatives, particularly in terms of flexibility and the provision of childcare facilities for women.

Others remain small and technically loss-making (and possibly insolvent), but have a high degree of external revenue support. Many are subsidised from public funds – grant aid, wage subsidies or training grants – or from other sources, to support their other valuable but non-financial benefits.[7] This might be purely for reasons of job creation, or for providing a particular community service. Many loss-making co-operatives of course do not receive subsidy and eventually collapse.

A final group appears to be those with a mixture of internal and external finance, which may be able to perform similarly to conventional small companies. To date the only examples which we know of are 'rescue' clothing co-operatives, although in principle this could also apply to new co-operatives.

There appears to be little movement between the groups – those co-operatives starting with subsidy only rarely manage to become self-sufficient and independent of that external support.

Qualitative case-study research to date suggests that a crucial element is the type of support which co-operatives receive – whether capital support (soft loans) or revenue support (subsidy). Capital support could be particularly important in assisting the establishment of 'sweat equity' co-operatives as viable businesses, and further work is needed to ascertain the impact of these alternative policies.

Two Printing Co-operatives

At this stage the classification is intuitive, and not conclusive, and the next stage of our work is to carry out an analysis of explanatory factors. Two alternative pathways for surviving co-operatives are illustrated in Appendix 12.2, where examples of the evolution of two printing co-operatives are given.

In the first example, the co-operative has operated for seven years, with an increasing turnover but continued dependence on external sources of finance. Perhaps as a result of the uncertainty of that support, wages have remained low and even so have been in excess of value added generated. The co-operative remains undercapitalised and is clearly not generating a sufficient surplus for reinvestment. External borrowing is low.

The second co-operative starts from a similar turnover, but is better capitalised and has demonstrated sustained growth. Internal efficiency has improved (TO/FA), (VA/TO). Wages have risen, and at the same time the proportion of value added devoted to wages has declined. The co-operative has now achieved the position of paying reasonable wages at the same time as retaining part of the surplus for the repayment of the borrowings necessary to finance capital growth.

Further work is necessary to evaluate the non-financial or social achievements of co-operatives. In the example the first co-operative is probably making sufficient gains (it is a feminist co-operative) to justify continued support from grants and donations. Co-operative Two is active in the 'alternative' movement, and may have used its relatively strong financial position to achieve other benefits (such as job rotation/skill sharing). The nonformalised nature of social returns compared to financial returns means that such evaluation requires additional sociological research.

Comparison between Sectors and with Capitalist Companies

Clearly clothing co-operatives have performed less well in absolute terms than printing co-operatives. Both value added and wages are lower in clothing, suggesting that the experience which workers have in a co-operative will vary significantly depending on which sector they are in. However, it is also interesting to compare the experience of co-operatives with those of capitalist companies. Comparative figures for some indicators for the two industries as a whole are given at the bottom of Appendix 12.1. It is apparent that conditions of work are worse in the clothing industry as a whole, and the imbalance is not specific to co-operatives. Looked at in this way, both sectors display common features. The majority of co-operatives perform less well than capitalist industry, with lower value added per head and lower wages than the industry averages. However, it is essential to remember that all the co-operatives considered are relatively young, which could explain a large part of the poorer performance of co-operatives.

There is one interesting contrast between the two sectors, however. For printing co-operatives, the product can easily marry with the motives of many of those who are attracted to co-operatives; because of the relationship between the product and the customer, and the function of the product, an explicit political commitment is easy to maintain. In clothing, however, this is not the case, and the product is relatively 'neutral'. An interesting question which arises from this is whether printing co-operatives find it easier, as a result, to maintain commitment and hence success in maintaining the co-operative form rather than degenerating into a typical small capitalist business.

CONCLUSION

We draw two sets of conclusions, relating to the various measures employed to assess co-op performance, and to the actual records of the co-ops in the study.

Firstly, measures based on value added appear to reveal substantially more about co-op performance than does the rate of profit. The latter appears to be particularly unhelpful; in addition there are conceptual problems involved in its application to co-ops. While no one measure can act in the same way as return on capital for conventional firms within a capitalist economy, a combination of ratios can be very revealing. In particular, value added per head, wages as a proportion of value added, and the average wage, can tell us a great deal about co-ops' relative performance, and the performance of a particular co-op over time.

There is a need for more detailed research into which measures in fact inform co-operatives' decision-making and how they are computed internally. This relates to Marris's (1984) concern to promote the use of value added as opposed to profit-related measures. At the same time we note that for many co-operatives, however, information systems and decision-making are immature, particularly in the early phases of the struggle to survive, and there may well be no measures informing the process. While we feel it is premature to make suggestions about accounting practices, this is an area where our research could be of use in future.

Secondly, there appear to be a number of distinct types of co-operative, with very different long-term prospects. In particular, there are some co-ops which may seem to have a precarious existence in their early years, but through hard work and commitment achieve success as co-ops and as businesses. Furthermore, during the most difficult and risky period of the first few years, the chances of this success can be increased and accelerated by the provision of 'soft' loans. Conversely, co-ops which appear to be heavily dependent on grants or subsidies may be able to achieve their own objectives – perhaps providing facilities to groups who would otherwise not get them – but undoubtedly suffer from low wages. There is also little evidence of these co-ops transforming themselves into the first type; their flexibility and ability to achieve desired policies may be severely hampered by the level of subsidy or grant they receive, and their continued existence subject to the uncertainties of prolonged funding.

It is encouraging that for some co-ops there is a possibility that co-ops can escape from the low wage-low productivity trap that many find themselves in, as typical small firms on the periphery of the capitalist economy. The final word shall rest with a member of Calverts: 'As a result of our fight at our previous firm there has been a great feeling of solidarity amongst the members of the co-op, resulting in a strong determination to make a genuine co-operative succeed. We have progressed from being on the dole, through earning pitiful wages to a situation where we now work normal hours for acceptable money in the sort of workplace we can enjoy. There is no denying it has been hard work on the way, but well worth it'.

Notes

1.   We would like to acknowledge the helpful advice and comments of our colleagues at the Open University. All opinions, errors and omissions are of, course, our own. Some of the work for this paper was carried out as part of the project 'Creating a Successful Co-operative Business,' funded by the Leverhulme Trust. We are grateful to both Leverhulme and the ESRC for financial support.
2.   This argument also applies to family firms and partnerships. It is

customary to draw up accounts showing 'profit before partners' drawings' (which is close to value added).

3. It is relatively straightforward to compile data on value added across a range of co-operatives and other businesses, and figures for value added in clothing and printing co-operatives are presented later in this paper. Comparison of absolute magnitudes is not in itself particularly useful for assessing performance, however. To do this we can either use a production function or a ratio analysis approach. The former can lead to some interesting and useful results – particularly in identifying the factors which determine performance (see for example, Estrin, Jones & Svejnar, 1984) – and it is one of our longer-term aims to undertake such analysis. However, there are both theoretical and empirical problems – the assumption of constant production function parameters across firms and industries, and the availability of adequate data – and for the moment we are concentrating on developing a ratio analysis which is particularly applicable to co-operatives.

4. This is akin to the assumption of equivalent parameters in a production function across firms.

5. It is interesting to note that reporting under the Industrial and Provident Societies (I&PS) Acts – legislation designed specifically for co-operatives – *does* require this, in contrast to the Companies Acts. Over recent years the majority of new worker co-operatives have registered under the Companies Acts.

6. We have excluded those co-operatives which are very small (turnover less than £10 000), or are 'CPF' co-operatives surviving from the nineteenth or early twentieth century, and are not part of the 'new wave' of worker co-operatives to emerge since the 1970s.

7. Mellor (1986) has suggested that co-operatives be treated as part of the social economy; their wide range of social objectives, their frequently strong links with the community, and, for some, dependence on local authority funding, distance them from the conventional capitalist economy.

Bibliography

Bradley, K. and A. Gelb, *Worker Capitalism – The New Industrial Relations* (London: Heinemann Educational, 1983).

Burchell, S., C. Clubb, and A. Hopwood, 'Accounting in its Social Context: Towards a History of Value Added', *Accounting, Organisations and Society* (1985).

CDA (Co-operative Development Agency), *Directory of Workers' Co-operatives*, (London: CDA, 1984).

Cockerton, P. et al., *Workers Co-operatives. A Handbook.* (Aberdeen Peoples Press, 1980).

Cornforth, C., *The Garment Co-operative, Case Study No. 5*, (Milton Keynes: Co-operatives Research Unit, Open University, 1981).

Cornforth C., J. Lewis, R. Spear and A. Thomas, *Developing Successful Worker Co-operatives* (London: Sage Publications Ltd., 1987).

Emerson, T., *The Story of Neighbourhood Textiles, Case Study No. 6*, (Milton Keynes: Co-operatives Research Unit, Open University, 1983).

Estrin, S., D. C. Jones, and J. Svejnar, *The Effect of Participation on Productivity in Worker Co-operatives* (London: London School of Economics mimeo, 1984).

Fine, B., 'The Concept and Origin of Profit', in F. Green and P. Nore (eds) *Economics: An Anti-Text* (London: Macmillan, 1977).

GLEB (Greater London Enterprise Board), *A Strategy for Co-operation – Worker Co-ops in London* (London: GLEB, 1984).

GLEB (Greater London Enterprise Board), *Printing Matters – Towards a Strategy for the London Printing Industry* (London: GLEB, 1985).

Harper, W. M., *Management Accounting, 2nd ed.* (London: M&E Handbooks, 1977).

Hird, C., *Challenging the Figures* (London: Pluto Press Ltd., 1983).

Howard, M., *Profits in Economic Theory* (London: Macmillan, 1983).

Jefferis, K. 'Worker Co-operatives in Britain – 1986' *The New Co-operator* (Leeds: ICOM, September 1986).

Jefferis K. and M. Robinson, 'Social Investment in Production' *Proc. Conference on Local Economic Strategies* (London: Open University, December 1986).

Jefferis K. and A. Thomas, 'Conditions for financial viability in workers' co-operatives: the case of UK clothing and printing co-ops', *Annals of Public and Co-operative Economy* (vol. LVII No. 1, 1986) pp. 79–102.

Labour Party, *Labour's Charter for Co-ops* (London: Labour Party, 1985).

Labour Research, 'Value Added', *Labour Research* (February 1978).

Lockett, M., *Fakenham Enterprises, Monograph No. 1* (Milton Keynes: Co-operatives Research Unit, Open University, 1978).

London ICOM, *Workers' Co-operative Database* (London: London ICOM, 1986).

Marris, T., 'Worker Co-operatives', *Accountants' Digest* (No. 162, 1984).

Nove, A., *Efficiency Criteria for Nationalised Industries* (London: Allen & Unwin, 1973).

Oakeshott, R., *The Case For Workers' Co-ops* (London: Routledge and Kegan Paul, 1978).

Paton, R. C. F., *Some Problems of Co-operative Organisation, Monograph No. 3* (Milton Keynes: Co-operatives Research Unit, Open University 1978).

Rowthorn, R. and T. Ward, 'How to run a company and run down an economy: the effects of closing down steel-making in Corby', *Cambridge Journal of Economics* (1979) pp. 327–40.

Thomas, A. R., 'What is Meant by "Success" for Workers' Co-operatives?' *Seventh Co-operative Seminar Papers* (Oxford: Plunkett Foundation, 1982).

Thomas, A. R., *Clothing Co-ops: Interim Report of a study of the economic performance of Clothing, Textiles and Footwear Co-ops in the UK since 1975* (Milton Keynes: Co-operatives Research Unit, Open University, 1985).

Thomas, H. and C. Logan, *Mondragon: An Economic Analysis* (London: Allen & Unwin, 1981).

Thornley, J., *Workers' Co-operatives – Jobs and Dreams* (London: Heinemann Educational Books, 1981).

Wajcman, J., *Women in Control. Dilemmas of a Workers Co-operative* (Milton Keynes: Open University Press, 1983).

Williams, K., C. Haslam, A. Wardlow, and J. Williams, 'Accounting for Failure in the Nationalised Enterprises – Coal, Steel and Cars since 1970', *Economy and Society* (1986) pp. 168–219.

Appendix 12.1

Financial Indicators for Selected UK Printing Co-operatives 1982 & 1983							
Co-op	Year	Age	VA/H	W/H	W/VA (%)	IVA	P/NA (%)
PR	1983	3	76	274	362.6	1 255	−12.3
WO	1983	7	423	1 529	361.5	6 424	−13.8
AM	1982	6	166	380	229.3	1 776	−12.2
AM	1983	7	1 054	1 098	104.2	4 631	−106.2
CF	1982	2	1 865	1 728	92.7	3 594	−3.6
CF	1983	3	1 698	1 690	99.5	4 060	−20.2
OP	1983	5	2 445	1 797	73.5	4 750	10.6
KE	1982	2	2 738	4 216	154.0	8 720	−6392.7
TP	1982	3	1 612	1 262	78.3	4 164	40.6
TP	1983	4	3 374	1 814	53.8	7 145	65.5
MA	1982	3	2 878	894	31.1	10 052	33.8
MA	1983	4	3 490	1 512	43.3	11 998	29.8
FL	1982	4	3 022	2 364	78.2	9 540	8.0
FL	1983	5	3 595	2 672	74.3	9 425	81.5
BR	1982	1	3 336	2 555	76.6	4 766	19.6
BR	1983	2	3 921	3 832	97.7	5 305	−6.7
SW	1982	1	2 032	2 032	100.0	4 816	−10.4
SW	1983	2	4 196	3 748	89.3	7 737	10.0
TY	1983	8	4 700	4 911	104.5	15 627	−0.5
CA	1982	5	5 913	5 270	89.1	12 143	−51.7
LE	1982	5	3 688	4 049	109.8	10 994	7.6
LE	1983	6	6 114	4 428	72.4	12 985	18.7
PA	1982	3	7 444	6 485	87.1	10 241	0.6
PA	1983	4	7 211	6 816	94.5	9 615	−109.6
BL	1982	4	7 377	4 606	62.4	23 041	33.0
BL	1983	5	8 159	6 831	83.7	27 481	5.3
SP	1982	2	8 331	7 039	84.5	19 559	−14.5
SP	1983	3	10 655	7 882	74.0	24 119	26.9
LI	1982	3	10 824	8 201	75.8	23 842	24.9
LI	1983	4	20 938	10 300	49.2	39 230	65.0

Financial Indicators for Selected UK Clothing Co-operatives 1982 & 1983

Co-op	Year	Age	VA/H	W/H	W/VA (%)	IVA	P/NA (%)
HA	1983	2	1 007	1 057	104.9	1 157	−2.0
GR	1982	4	1 157	1 038	89.8	1 348	0.0
WR	1982	2	3 757	3 569	95.0	4 448	30.0
WR	1983	3	2 880	3 062	106.3	3 335	−9.9
BA	1982	2	2 805	2 625	93.6	3 076	0.0
BA	1983	3	3 114	3 015	96.8	3 732	0.0
RR	1982	3	1 408	1 717	122.0	4 264	0.0
RR	1983	4	3 245	2 978	91.8	7 532	0.0
RL	1982	2	2 308	2 828	122.5	5 173	−89.6
RL	1983	3	3 778	2 955	78.2	9 866	39.6
TR	1983	1	3 927	3 237	82.4	8 138	0.0
LO	1983	2	7 445	6 366	85.5	7 604	129.9

Comparative Results for Capitalist Firms
Clothing

Year	VA/H	W/H	W/VA (%)
1982 a	5 740	3 784	65
1982 b	5 451	3 695	−
1982 c	−	3 233	−
1983 a	6 242	4 043	64
1983 b	7 885	3 906	−
1983 c	−	3 453	−

Printing

Year	VA/H	W/H	W/VA (%)
1982 a	13 314	8 043	59
1982 b	12 441	7 130	−
1982 c	−	6 784	−
1983 a	14 424	8 845	61
1983 b	13 276	7 827	−
1983 c	−	7 433	−

a – figures for industry as a whole
　(clothing – SIC 453; printing & publishing – SIC 475)
b – small firms in the industry (<100 workers)
c – wage levels for production workers (i.e. excludes administrative & management workers)

SOURCE:　Companies House; Registry of Friendly Societies; *Business Monitor*.

Appendix 12.2
Financial Indicators for two Printing Co-operatives

Co-op	Year	Workers (H)	Turnover (TO)	TO/H	TO/FA	NA/H	FA/H	Value Added
AM	1977	3.0	5 136	1 712	12.5	188	137	869
AM	1978	3.0	6 546	2 182	3.5	945	627	1 458
AM	1979	3.0	6 458	2 153	4.1	502	520	645
AM	1980	3.0	8 381	2 794	6.2	580	450	1 316
AM	1981	3.0	10 646	3 549	4.0	936	883	1 774
AM	1982	4.0	11 076	2 769	6.4	625	435	663
AM	1983	4.0	18 525	4 631	7.7	303	600	4 216
LE	1978	1.0	7 425	7 425	5.1	2 694	1 470	972
LE	1979	1.0	8 610	8 610	1.3	8 786	6 552	2 410
LE	1980	3.0	19 113	6 371	3.3	1 883	1 911	6 730
LE	1981	4.0	29 511	7 378	2.1	2 594	3 546	11 753
LE	1982	4.5	49 471	10 994	2.2	3 946	5 110	16 596
LE	1983	5.0	64 481	12 896	2.9	3 311	4 476	27 515

KEY:	VA – value added	H – no. of workers
	TO – turnover	P – profit
	NA – net assets	IVA – index of value added
	FA – fixed assets	W – wages

VA/TO %	VA/H	Wage W/H	W/VA %	IVA	P/NA %	Reserves	Internal Loans	External Loans
16.9	290	271	93.6	984	−10	−1 383	0	1 940
22.3	486	599	123.3	1 554	100	1 329	0	1 500
10.0	215	776	360.8	1 692	−90	−2	0	1 500
15.7	439	631	143.9	2 068	10	232	0	1 500
16.7	591	402	68.0	2 306	40	1 300	0	1 500
6.0	166	380	229.3	1 776	−10	994	0	1 500
22.8	1 054	1 098	104.2	4 631	−110	−294	0	1 500
13.1	972	1 357	139.6	7 365	10	1 883	400	210
28.0	2 410	2 784	115.5	8 503	10	2 465	300	5 424
35.2	2 243	3 657	163.0	6 358	−60	−738	1 292	4 232
39.8	2 938	4 204	143.1	7 237	−50	−5 702	2 920	12 015
33.5	3 688	4 049	109.8	10 994	10	−4 352	2 750	19 343
42.7	5 503	3 985	72.4	11 686	20	−1 249	3 000	14 784

13 Consequences of the Failure to Account for Externalities

Martin Freedman and A. J. Stagliano

In many ways the conventional accounting and reporting model is limited by its focus on private costs and benefits. Inclusion of only these factors is, to some degree, a reflection of a reliance on traditional micro-economic theory for the underpinnings of accountancy. A justification for much of the current accounting model is its relationship to this theory.[1] This supposedly value-free functional structural world view has recently come under increasing criticism, but it continues to represent the 'mainstream' status quo position of accountancy today.

For the contemporary model, nonprivate (or social) costs and benefits are generally ignored because they are assumed to be immaterial, thought to be unmeasurable, or deemed to be nonquantifiable. There may be at once both a mistaken and harmful idea that anything that exists ought to be measured, and whatever we cannot count is not meaningful. As McHarg (1968) has expressed this problem:

> Neither love nor compassion, health nor beauty, dignity nor freedom, grace nor delight are true unless they can be priced. If not, they are described as nonprice benefits relegated to inconsequence, and the economic model proceeds towards its selffulfillment – which is to say more despoliation. The major criticism of that model is not that it is partial (which is conceded by its strongest advocates), but more that the features which are excluded are among the most important human values, and also the requirements for survival.
>
> (pp. 214–215)

Implicit in a free-market capitalistic production and trading system is a mechanism which allows costs to be borne by third parties rather than either the producer or consumers of the firm's products. The accounting system generally fails to recognise such costs whenever the 'market' does not incorporate them into its pricing model. Employees, for example, form one group that may bear a disproportionate amount of these costs. Occupational safety and health costs is the broad classification used to describe this type of externality. By not including in the firm's reckoning of product cost the harmful effects of production on workers, outputs can be sold at a relatively lower price. In normal circumstances, this leads to excessive demand (Mansfield, 1970, p. 429; Stigler, 1966, pp. 22–23). A larger margin is then available because workers bear part of the costs without compensation.

In general, accounting has supported a positivist view of society that is associated with both capitalistic production schema and marginalist economics. That it is not informed by the problematic is a stultifying consequence of a dependence on a physical/objective reality that exists independently of societal participants.

If, instead, accountants could include some of these 'social costs' in their model (as both inputs and outputs), a fairer and more efficient allocation of resources might be possible. The interrelatedness of the world economy suggests that this is a global problem. Unless accountants in all countries include these factors as part of the costs of production, some countries may bear an inordinate amount of the burden. In this regard, we will examine the situation of cotton dust in the textile workplace as a prototypical example of the difficulty in accounting for externalities, and the problems and consequences engendered by our failure to deal explicitly with them. In addition, certain concerns about the interactions of social, political, and economic aspects of accounting will be explored briefly.

EXTERNALITIES IN COTTON TEXTILE MANUFACTURING

During the manufacturing process in a cotton textile mill, dust is emitted into the air. Inhalation of ambient air contaminated with cotton dust can lead to byssinosis, the so-called brown lung disease (National Institute of Occupational Safety and Health, 1974). The cleaner the factory (in terms of dust) the less likely it would be for workers to become sick. Reducing dust emissions to a safe level may require a large capital outlay by the mill operator.

Alternative Accounting Calculations

In the United States, the Occupational Safety and Health Administration (OSHA) recognised the medical problems caused by cotton dust. After some prodding by the Congress, this government agency issued a health standard to limit the amount of dust permitted in a factory over the working day (OSHA, 1976). OSHA set the standard at 0.2 mg/m^3, despite union criticism that the standard was at too high a contaminate level, and textile firms' belief that meeting such a low level would cause significant financial hardship for the industry.

Textile manufacturers, through their trade association, brought a suit to block implementation of the OSHA standard (*American Textile Manufacturers Institute, Inc., et al.* v. *Raymond J. Donovan, Secretary of Labor, United States Department of Labor, et al.*, 617 F.2d 636, USCA-DC, 1979). The case eventually reached the US Supreme Court. There, the Reagan Administration sided with the manufacturers and filed a brief *opposing* OSHA's action on the grounds that it was economically infeasible.[2] Thus, economic issues became the primary argument for overriding the medical evidence on the effects of cotton dust on workers in the industry.

The US Supreme Court upheld the cotton dust standard (101 S.Ct. 2478, 1981), finding that the sole limiting criterion for rule-making implementation was technological feasibility. The Court determined that cost-benefit analysis, an economic procedure, was not required. In an examination of the history of the enabling legislation, the Court noted that the Congress recognised occupational safety and health regulations might create substantial financial burdens for employers. It was clear, though, that imposition of these explicit costs was necessary to create a safe and healthful workplace. Social policy, forged in the political arena, was applied to correct a perceived failure in the free-market production process and, at the same time, convert previously unpriced externalities into factor costs. This would appear to be an interpretive paradigm adjustment to the extant economic model.

The impact of this regulation on the US textile industry is that a detriment previously borne by workers (and their families) is now partially included as a cost of manufacturing. Workers who contracted brown lung disease, an irreversible occupational illness, became sick, then disabled, and ultimately died from its effects. These individuals might have been compensated through worker insurance, but not to the extent of covering all medical costs, lost wages, and certainly not for the pain and hardship suffered by themselves and their families. The only 'accounting' for these costs would consist of expensing the insurance premiums. Now, a larger portion of the impact, in the form of maintenance and depreciation on the new equipment needed to clean up the mills (and any external financing costs on the purchase of equipment), will be included in product cost. Thus, some of the externality is being internalised (Mishan, 1973, p. 91). The role of the sociopolitical mechanism in bringing about this change should not be overlooked.

Internalisation of social costs also occurs when other techniques are applied to reduce unwanted spillover effects of production. Taxing, fining, and shutting down facilities all impose additional marginal costs on the producer. Unless technological change occurs which enhances production efficiency, product price must increase to account for these items or profit will fall (Mansfield, 1968). Firms internalising social costs of this nature will find it difficult to compete with those in the industry who do not have to deal with such costs.

EFFECTS OF THE CLEAN-UP ON THE US TEXTILE INDUSTRY

Subsequent to the Supreme Court decision, there have been a number of mergers in the cotton textile industry, but no major shake-up has occurred. It was originally predicted that the cost of cleaning up the mills would drive marginal firms out of business (NIOSH, 1974). This was expected because additional capital investment was required to meet the 0.2 mg/m^3 cotton dust standard. Such a financial commitment causes increased production costs, reduces mobility of existing resources, creates higher barriers to entry, and forces an overall upward shift in the long-run average cost curve. These conditions presumably will lead marginal firms into bankruptcy or merger with more profitable ones. However, since this pessimistic scenario has not occurred, it can either be because marginal firms have not yet made the investment in new equipment, or because the demise of these firms was exaggerated. An accurate assessment probably should include a little of both reasons.

If American firms invest in new equipment, this may lead to greater productivity. To some extent, also, capital will be substituted for labour, making it easier for US manufacturers to compete with firms from the Far East.[3] Internalisation of controllable social costs provides the general impetus for this capital-labour substitution.

In the short run, substitution of capital for labour creates higher unemployment levels among textile workers.[4] Just as mechanisation in farming, mining, and basic-metals production paved the way for greater efficiency at the expense of jobs, this same phenomenon should be expected in the case of upgraded mechanical operations placed in service to meet more stringent occupational health standards. This short-term consequence is presumably one of the major reasons the cotton textile industry has not been held to stricter in-plant clean air standards sooner. The functionalist nature of the neo-classical micro-economic model, then, is not all pervasive. Workers, especially disadvantaged ones, will often choose unhealthful jobs to no jobs at all (Shue, 1981).

Textile workers, even those who are unionised, are a relatively powerless body of employees in their dealings with management. There is a historical reason for this. This US textile industry was initially located in New England. It was one of the original 'cottage industries'. Most firms of any size shifted their operations to the Southern States to take advantage of the abundant pool of cheaper, nonunion labour. It has only been within the past dozen years that union organisers have made meaningful inroads into these textile mills.

While unions have been effective in enhancing wage levels, they have had little impact on improving working conditions. Even though the textile workers' union was instrumental in the political and legal battles to tighten the cotton dust emissions standard, the issue of cleaning up the mills has never been a part of any negotiated contract agreement. The OSHA standard is a government-imposed one. Mandating improvements in workplace conditions in this manner is not atypical of the way in which change is effected. To negotiate health and safety standards, workers will usually have to trade immediate private material benefits (that is, wages and/or fringes) for a better work environment. Adding to that the historically-demonstrated prospect of worker layoffs caused by greater mechanisation, it was not unexpected that the relatively weak textile unions sought present benefits and tended to disregard detriments embodied in unhealthy working conditions. The trade-off of current economic welfare for future physical well-being was simply not faced. It was left for government to mandate cleaner and safer cotton mills.

In the alternative, if technological improvements are not made by the US textile industry, it would appear to be increasingly difficult for these companies to compete, in the longer term, with firms from the Far East whose labour costs are relatively so much lower. Ironically, although the needed substitution of capital for labour will cause short-term unemployment increases, without this shift of input factor mix there may well be no viable American cotton textile manufacturers to employ workers in the long run.

It is possible, though, that this added investment will increase the price of US products relative to those of the Far East, thereby making these firms less competitive in both the domestic and world markets. In the absence of restrictions on finished goods imports, US textile manufacturers may suffer irreparable damages. Under these circumstances, it would not be unreasonable to expect American textile firms to export more raw cotton for mill consumption in developing countries and to step up importation of both intermediate and finished cotton products. In effect, this is an alternative to changing productive facilities or systems to comply with health standards: when restrictions are imposed at home, companies simply exploit their poorer trading partners by exporting environmental problems. A secondary consequence of such a corporate policy is that internalising of social costs may not occur in any degree. An insidious result is that moving these costs outside the firm's own accounts simply extends the profitable life of technology that is known to be physically harmful, but for which an alternative exists.[5]

GLOBAL NATURE OF THE PROBLEM

The internalisation of a social cost will initially raise the explicit cost of production. For a country that exists in isolation (that is, has no foreign trade) this 'fuller' accounting for product cost will lead to a fairer, more efficient domestic market-based allocation of resources.[6] In the world trading system, this result may not hold. The effects that occur when one nation's producers choose (or are 'forced') to include these costs in product price – and others do not follow suit – may not be so positive. The domestic industry, by producing goods at a higher nominal cost, will be unable to compete in the world market unless it becomes more efficient.[7] Otherwise, the industry and its workers will suffer financially: (1) its higher-priced goods are not exchangeable in the world market; (2) in a reasonably free-trade world economy, lower-priced foreign-produced goods will supplant domestic output.

Instead of being internalised, the social cost may be exported.[8] This is not an uncommon occurrence. Production of pesticides, chemicals, asbestos products, and other products that result in major social cost have all been exported when compliance with government regulations was deemed to be too expensive. By exporting the hazardous production process, its externalities are visited upon workers in other nations. Although this action may benefit the population of the exporting nation (which will no longer be exposed to dangerous processes), it does nothing to encourage the elimination of harmful technologies or reduction in the number of unhealthy or unsafe work-places in the world. The problem is, as Coase (1960) has noted, to devise practical arrangements which will correct defects in one part of the system without causing equivalent harm elsewhere.

Another fundamental problem with the exportation of troublesome production functions stems from the various stages in which industrialisation has taken hold throughout the world. Considering the whole of the globe's diverse economic entities, a few are highly developed, many are well along in the transformation from agrarian-based to industrial societies, most continue to be underdeveloped or deindustrialised (Worsley, 1980). A potentiality, therefore, is that the developed (or core) countries might transmit their social-cost-generating industrial problems to those on the periphery. These poorer countries might, in fact, welcome such a transference. Industrial catastrophes (for instance, the chemical plant leak which killed thousands in Bhopal, India, and Mexico City's gas storage tank explosion tragedy) in Third World countries stemming from transferred technology lend credence to this possibility. Some observers (for example, Robert Wasserstrom of the World Resources Institute) see this as the single most important long-term health threat to the world's developing societies.

On one hand, there is belief in an equivalency of the sanctity of life and the environment throughout the world. This argues for global worker protection standards. On the other hand, many business groups have railed against 'regulatory imperialism' and 'international nannyism' which would impose one country's standards on others. To a developing nation, the trade-offs on this matter are little different from those, described above, that were faced by US cotton textile workers and their unions: current economic welfare must be weighed against future physical well-being. Notwithstanding all the arguments, though, it appears that the core countries will have to lead the way in setting criteria for worker protection throughout the world. This is essentially the case because (1) industrialised states are the usual beneficiaries of socialisation of externalities, and (2) they alone have the power, ability, resources, and knowledge to change the existing system. It is unfortunate that no universally accepted mechanism now exists to achieve agreement in this area (Wallerstein, 1976, p. 230). The dynamics by which this change might be brought about are not in themselves known either.

THE POTENTIAL FOR SOLUTION

From a global perspective it may not be advantageous for any one nation or small group of nations to regulate and internalise social costs. What is called for is a global solution. The divergence between private and social products requires an approach that transcends narrow economic analysis (Coase, 1960). It may well be that a movement from the functionalist to the interpretive, or even radical, viewpoint will be needed to deal with such a change. In essence, this revision may be the type of 'paradigm shift' necessary for scientific progress that is suggested by Kuhn (1970). The current model appears to lead to an equilibrium position in which net externalities are imposed on the weakest parties (Ratliff and Merino, 1983).

An accounting system can do much more than simply act as a repository for financial effects of the production process.[9] Accounting is not devoid of value judgments (Laughlin, 1985; Chua, 1986). Industrial policy reflects the broader-scale political climate. Accounting systems embody the operationalisation of both current financial goals and overarching societal aims. If the actors in the system, rather than 'market forces', are expected to determine the allocation of society's resources, then a nonconventional world view may be needed to reframe and prescribe the input of accounting. Just as Lakatos (1970, p. 136) has argued that every model will be replaced by higher levels of development, O'Leary (1985) posits a need for redrawing the boundaries between accountancy and the extant sociopolitical arena.

In Batstone's (1979, pp. 256–9) terminology, systems of accounting are 'vocabularies of motive'. Societal controls operate through such devices. In other words, by setting the terms of debate and defining the targets of organisational procedures, systems of financial reckoning can actually change, direct, and legitimate industrial operations. The economic and social priorities of the global productive enterprise are reflected in accounting procedures. Through the continual feedback mechanism of this system, the way in which we account for activities will generate modifications in the way we go about achieving societal goals (Watts and Zimmerman, 1978). Internalising instead of externalising, socialising, or exporting social costs can have a powerful impact on the means we use to control the negative aspects of the production process.

Some industrialised nations have taken major strides in internalising social costs through mandated abatement of air and water pollution, product design control, and occupational safety and health regulation. When there is a concerted effort by most of the nations of the world to internalise or reduce social costs, the initial actions of the core countries can be effective. Further leadership in this area can be exerted, though, in adopting a revised and greatly expanded view of the uses of accounting systems. Dealing with accounting as an active, not passive, component of industrial policy seems appropriate. This argues for accounting to assume a political role. As Cooper and Sherer (1984) have noted, it may well be that a 'political economy' framework for accounting is needed. The contemporary debate and emerging literature on this subject will provide guidance as the institution of accounting changes.

A broad-based effort by the nations of the world could lead to internalisation of many social costs. By including all impacts of production in the accounting for product costs, those who generate negative outputs will be more clearly charged with the responsibility for their abatement and financial impacts. Otherwise, it would appear that the poor and powerless will continue to bear the brunt of these untoward products of industrialisation.

CONCLUDING COMMENT

It should be obvious that the analysis of the problem presented and the solution described are drawn from but one perspective for dealing with externalities. As Laughlin (1985) has remarked, there are many ways of viewing nonprivate costs and benefits – each dependent upon an alternative value system. By choosing other than the conventional approach to evaluate these negative outputs, a 'better' solution for dealing with them might be uncovered. Both Tinker (1985) and Chua (1986) believe that a different perspective (especially one that critically handles the problematic) might lead to real change. Although it is readily acknowledged that competing solutions abound for the externalities issue, and that the 'best' one is that which brings about needed change rapidly, there is no 'right' way to go about choosing among the alternatives. A good solution is one that is workable and translates words into action.

By debating these issues and bringing the problem before those who have the ability to effect meaningful change, it is possible to hasten the actual implementation process. Either end of the continuum for analysis, the marginalist economic framework within the functionalist context of a historical case review, or critical social theory applied in the radical-humanistic perspective, should yield the same view of the environment: some workers will be at risk, without adequate compensation, from controllable health hazards on the job. Doubtless, change can come about to ameliorate these circumstances. A pro-active stance made to be an integral part of the accounting methodology can be of use. Externalities might be eliminated through changes in the workplace or adjustments in the systems linked to it in the production-distribution process. It is possible that a change in the system will precipitate a change in the workplace itself.

Notes

1. Although historically the development of the *practice* of accountancy has been a political and social process, the most direct *conceptual* linkages have been to economic theory. On the issue of the sociopolitical processes involved, see Tinker, Merino, and Neimark (1982).
2. OSHA is part of the US Department of Labor and, therefore, in the executive branch of government. In effect, President Reagan opposed his own subordinate Department in this case.
3. The fibre-textile-apparel industry complex is highly labour-intensive. As such, it is quite sensitive to changes in nominal wage rates and other employee costs. It is also very susceptible to price competition from nondomestic producers.
4. Employment in US cotton weaving mills, which exceeded 200 000 just 20 years ago, has fallen to below 100 000 production workers. In fact, the American textile industry shrank by almost 20 000 employees during 1984 alone.
5. While it is true that the number of spillover effects that can be internalised into the pricing mechanism or the costing systems of firms is limited, the instant case of cotton dust does exhibit the characteristics of a social cost that can both be controlled and given explicit factor cost treatment. On this matter, see Mishan (1973, p. 93).
6. The argument here is that the market pricing mechanism will enhance the overall resource allocation process. That a Pareto-optimal allocation may not occur in these circumstances is taken up by many authors; see Burkhead and Miner (1971, pp. 97–141) for an excellent review of the problem.

7. We do not consider here the possibility of government intervention through a subsidy arrangement. Nor, on the other hand, do we take up the question of 'protection' by way of import restrictions.

8. It is the harmful or unsafe production process, and its attendant technology, which is exported. The social-cost-generating activity itself is sent beyond national borders. The net private cost of doing this may be lower than either the previous domestic production cost or the projected costs after implementing new technology. At any rate, there is a further domestic externality created if workers lose jobs because of production process exportation; this consequential, or second-round, impact is not taken up here.

9. For the strong view that accountancy should maintain its neutral measurement focus and *not* do more, see Solomons (1978).

Bibliography

American Textile Manufacturers Institute, Inc., et al. v. *Raymond Donovan, Secretary of Labor, United States Department of Labor, et al.*, 101 S.Ct. 2478 (1981).

Batstone, E., 'Systems of Domination, Accommodation and Industrial Democracy', in T. R. Burns and V. Rus (eds) *Work and Power* (New York: Russell Sage Foundation, 1979).

Burkhead, J. and J. Miner, *Public Expenditure* (Chicago: Aldine Publishing Company, 1971).

Chua, W. F., 'Radical Developments in Accounting Thought', *The Accounting Review* (1986), pp. 601–32.

Coase, R., 'The Problem of Social Cost', *Journal of Law and Economics* (1960), pp. 1–44.

Cooper, D. J. and M. J. Sherer, 'The Value of Corporate Accounting Reports: Arguments for a Political Economy of Accounting', *Accounting, Organizations and Society* (1984), pp. 207–32.

Kuhn, T. S., *The Structure of Scientific Revolutions*, 2nd ed. (University of Chicago Press, 1970).

Lakatos, I., 'Falsification and the Methodology of Scientific Research Programmes', in I. Lakatos and A. Musgrave (eds) *Criticism and the Growth of Knowledge* (Cambridge University Press, 1970).

Laughlin, R. C., 'A Comment on "Accounting and the Exportation of Externalities"', paper presented at the Interdisciplinary Perspectives in Accounting Conference (University of Manchester, 1985).

McHarg, J. L., 'Values, Process, and Form', in W. Johnson and J. Hardesty (eds), *Economic Growth and the Environment* (Belmont, CA: Wadsworth Publishing Co., 1971).

Mansfield, E., *The Economics of Technological Change* (New York: W. W. Norton & Company, Inc., 1968).

Mansfield, E., *Microeconomics: Theory and Applications* (New York: W. W. Norton, 1970).

Mathews, M. R., 'Towards Multiple Justifications for Social Accounting and

Strategies for Acceptance', Discussion Paper Series No. 35 (Massey University, 1985).

McHarg, I. L., 'Values, Process and Forum', in *Fitness of Man's Environment*, Smithsonian Annual II: Papers Delivered at the Smithsonian Institution Annual Symposium (Washington, D.C.: Smithsonian Institution, 1968) pp. 207–27.

Mishan, E. J., *Economics for Social Decisions: Elements of Cost-Benefit Analysis* (New York: Praeger Publishers, 1973).

National Institute of Occupational Safety and Health, *Occupational Exposure to Cotton Dust* (Washington: US Government Printing Office, 1974).

Occupational Safety and Health Administration, *Cotton Dust: Technological Feasibility Assessment and Final Inflationary Impact Statement* (Washington: US Government Printing Office, 1976).

O'Leary, T., 'Observations on Corporate Financial Reporting in the Name of Politics', *Accounting, Organizations and Society* (1985), pp. 87–102.

Ratliff, J. R. and B. D. Merino, 'Administrative Theory Versus Interest Group Pluralism – An Analysis of Alternative Public Interest Frameworks', paper presented at the American Accounting Association Annual Meeting (New Orleans, 1983).

Shue, H., 'Exporting Hazards', in P. G. Brown and H. Shue (eds), *Boundaries: National Autonomy and Its Limits* (Totowa, NJ: Rowman and Littlefield, 1981).

Solomons, D., 'The Politicization of Accounting', *The Journal of Accountancy* (1978), pp. 65–72.

Stigler, G. J., *The Theory of Price*, 3rd edn. (New York: Macmillan, 1966).

Tinker, A. M., *Paper Prophets* (New York: Holt, Rinehart and Winston, 1985).

Tinker, A. M., B. D. Merino, and M. D. Neimark, 'The Normative Origins of Positive Theories', *Accounting, Organizations and Society* (1982), pp. 167–200.

Wallerstein, I., *The Modern-World System: Capitalist Agriculture and the Origins of the European World-Economy in the Sixteenth Century* (New York: Academic Press, 1976).

Watts, R. L. and J. L. Zimmerman, 'Towards a Positive Theory of the Determination of Accounting Standards', *The Accounting Review* (1978), pp. 112–34.

Worsley, P., 'One World or Three? A Critique of the World-System Theory of Immanuel Wallerstein', in R. Miliband and J. Saville (eds), *The Socialist Register* (London: Merlin Press, 1980).

14 Corporate Social Accounting and the Capitalist Enterprise

T. Colwyn Jones

CORPORATE SOCIAL ACCOUNTING: THEORY

Since 1970 some accountants have shown an interest in new forms of corporate reporting which differ markedly from traditional practices. What characterises Corporate Social Accounting (CSA) is its concern with a widening of both the content of accounting reports and the audience at which they are aimed. The view taken by supporters of CSA is that modern business enterprises have responsibilities which are wider than their legal obligations to shareholders, and encompass social obligations to other 'stakeholders'. The ASSC (1975) lists the stakeholders of a firm as: equity investors; loan creditors; employees; analyst-advisors; business contacts; and the government. Others have widened the list to include consumers and the community or neighbourhood (Ramanathan, 1976). These stakeholders are seen as actual or potential users of information to be provided by accountants. Following this redefinition of 'users' the content of accounting reports is redefined. For external reports on business to the wider society, accounts should include the 'social contribution of an individual firm' (Ramanathan 1976; Council for Economic Development, 1971; Estes, 1976). This form of CSA, Social Responsibility Accounting, deals with 'externalities' and attempts to account for the impact that a company has on society-in-general. For internal accounting, Employee Accounting is suggested as part of an overall strategy of 'open management', with reports to include information on job satisfaction and career opportunities as well as existing management information which could be used by trade unions (Ramanathan, 1976; Owen, 1982).

The detail in which these prescriptions are advanced differs quite widely. Owen (1982, p. 6), for example, states that, 'until the concept of social accountability is accepted it is fruitless to search for developments in social accounting' but others have generated fairly elaborate schemes and have occasionally used them in preparing reports (Marlin, 1973). In whatever detail the proposals are advanced, their advocates clearly see CSA as a very significant development, perhaps even amounting to a revolution in accounting, (Flint, 1980; Glautier and Underdown, 1974). What has brought accounting to the brink of such fundamental change?

CSA and Social Change

Advocates of CSA present differing accounts of the nature of social change, the way it produces a wider scope of business responsibility, and hence a 'need' for new forms of accounting. Broadly, three views may be identified:

Moral imperative Some advocates of CSA view businesses as insufficiently aware of the social consequences of business activity and as being unwilling to acknowledge, and be held accountable for, their social responsibilities (Dierkes and Bauer, 1973). The solution to this moral problem is that accountants should take the lead in changing the views of management. 'Is it asking too much for accountants, just for once, to take an initiative!' (Owen, 1982, p. 6). Accountants might achieve this by developing CSA and then imposing it on companies by changing the legal requirements of businesses (Monsen, 1973, p. 107).

External pressure Others consider that there already exists a high level of social pressure which forces a higher level of social responsiveness on firms, and that this has been recognised by management. For some writers, this social pressure is highly diffuse. Ramanathan quotes, with approval, one formulation of this view. 'Any social institution – and business is no exception – operates in society via a social contract, expressed or implied, whereby its survival and growth are based on: (i) the delivery of some socially desirable ends to society in general and, (ii) the distribution of economic, social, or political benefits to groups from which it derives its power.' (Shocker and Sethi, 1974, p. 67). Ramanathan uses this as a basis for his definition that, 'the purpose of social accounting is to help evaluate how well a firm is fulfilling its social contract.' (Ramanathan, 1976, p. 519).

Other writers have pointed to more particular pressure coming from central and local governments, public pressure groups and large institutional investors such as churches, foundations, and universities (Estes, 1976; Parker, 1986). In this view management are increasingly aware of the voices from certain quarters for more information. Failure to accede to these demands may challenge successful business operation.

Internal change   The boldest argument on social change emphasises changes which have taken place within the business enterprise itself and have resulted in internally-generated demands for CSA. In this view a decline in the power of ownership has led to a reduction in the importance of profit as a company goal, which is now seen as only one goal among many. Thus the ASSC (1975, p. 32) quotes the ICA's 1952 definition – 'the primary purpose of the annual accounts of a business is to present information to the proprietors, showing how their funds have been utilised and the profits derived from such use' – but then comments 'this statement was no doubt correct at its time of issue, but with the passage of time it has become increasingly clear that it is incomplete and unsympathetic to modern needs . . . distributive profit can no longer be regarded as the sole or *premier* indicator of performance' (ASSC, 1975, p. 38, emphasis added). This view is found again in the Flint Report: 'the primacy of the position of the owners or shareholders has gone and the current philosophy is to recognise as stakeholders all those with interest in business performance or conduct . . . Responsibility to and accountability to the stakeholders is . . . a fact' (Flint, 1980, p. 4).

Each of these three approaches seeks to demonstrate a need for new forms of accounting, and to argue that CSA must be developed in order to satisfy this need.

Accounting and Social Responsibility

Much criticism of CSA has been concerned with the technical difficulties in developing such accounts (Perks and Gray, 1979; Benston, 1982) and whether or not accountants have, or can hope to develop, the relevant skills to undertake the task (Perks and Gray, 1981; Gambling, 1974). These considerations lead Benston (1982, p. 102) to conclude that 'the social responsibility of accountants can be expressed best by their forebearing from social responsibility accounting'. In addition, criticism has been directed at the explanation of the 'need' for CSA.

Criticism of moral imperatives The argument that accountants should take an initiative in imposing upon companies a more socially responsible framework within which they ought, or may be forced, to operate may be challenged on the grounds of accountants' own moral position. Perks and Gray (1979, p. 22) point out that accountants may well have a vested interest in CSA: 'accountants within a company see the opportunity to expand their horizons by producing social reports. Auditors see the opportunity for increased fees in return for checking and putting their name to such reports'. Or accountants might find themselves used as pawns by other interested parties in presenting partial and politically-orientated images of enterprises. 'Anti-Capitalists' or 'Corporate Defenders' may seek to use the prestige of accountancy to support their own interests. In this way the objectives of CSA would not be to report on companies' activities in respect of social responsibilities, but to serve the interests of particular groups within society. As Puxty (1986) argues, this raises severe problems about the moral desirability of CSA.

Criticism of 'external pressure' approach The view that business enterprises have to be responsive to society-in-general in order to survive appears to have close links with Functionalist Theory in sociology. This theory states that each 'part' of a social system can be understood in terms of its 'function' (that is, the needs it satisfies) in relation to the 'whole' of society. Apart from severe methodological problems with this approach, a major difficulty with the 'theory' is that it requires that society be viewed as a highly unified structure so that 'needs' can be identified unproblematically. Where different 'parts' of society have different, perhaps conflicting 'needs', the theory offers no explanation of the way in which some needs come to be dominant. (Cohen, 1968; Lee and Newby, 1983). In order to understand business enterprises it is necessary to examine the specific groups which sustain them and which exercise influence over their activities.

It is far from clear that, for Britain at any rate, pressure from external interest groups is strong and that managers feel a need to respond to it. As Benston (1982) notes, social reporting in the UK has been rather limited and, in 1979, the ICA survey of 300 companies showed only thirteen with any form of social accounts (quoted in Perks and Gray, 1981, p. 29). In the 1980s there have been occasional specific and strong demands that corporations show themselves to be socially responsible – as in the cases of British Nuclear

Fuels Limited after Chernobyl, and Barclays Bank on South African investments. However there is little evidence that more general external pressure for CSA, either from interest groups or the government, has been increasing on the managements of British enterprises.

Criticism of 'internal change' approach   The strongest of the arguments for the introduction of CSA come from those who argue that the demand for new forms of accounting are generated within the firm by managers who are now pursuing wider corporate objectives than before, and who seek means of reporting on these activities. Some support for this view appears to come from various business organisations. The ASSC (1975, p. 32) cites a 1973 CBI report suggesting there should be legislative encouragement for companies 'to recognise duties and obligations . . . arising from the company's relationship with creditors, suppliers, customers, employees and society at large'. The (then) Director-General of the Institute of Directors, Hildreth (1976, p. 80) asserted that 'in directing the company's affairs the director must strike a balance between the demands of all those with a rightful interest in it', and that these rightful interests could be identified as those of the shareholders and other investors; creditors; employees; the public; and the company and its future. The BIM report (Melrose-Woodman and Kverndal, 1976) found 'a surprisingly high number of companies that had made a positive commitment to social responsibility both through statements to philosophy and concrete actions'. These statements, however, present the 'public face' of business, and in doing so may be concerned more with appearance than reality. They also, in some degree, reflect a view from 'the top' which may not correspond to actual management practices below board level. Even so, they show more caution than many CSA advocates in discussing the importance of profitability. The CBI report declares that profits must be the main objective of a company and Hildreth (ibid., p. 80) emphasises 'wealth creation' and reminds his readers that, at present, 'company law recognises explicitly that the shareholder's primary interest is the security and effective deployment of their funds and in the resulting prospects for distributed profits'. The BIM reports that the consensus among UK business people is that profit is the company's most important objective, and adds that most of the business reasons for social responsibility are based on enlightened business self-interest in the maintenance of profitability. Whether social responsibility is extended into business activities which divert resources from directly or indirectly profitable avenues is clearly much more problematic, since as Benston (1982, p. 92) argues 'corporate managers have little discretion to act other than in the interests of shareholders'.

The Need for CSA

Advocates of CSA have variously identified a 'need' to change accounting theories and practices. Others have questioned whether such a need exists and whether accountants can respond to it. To what extent is the CSA view of this need reflected in the way that accountants who work in companies perceive the existing requirements for accounting information and the way these may change?

CORPORATE SOCIAL ACCOUNTING: PRACTICE

The views reported here are those of fifty-seven 'accountants' in six large manufacturing and merchanting firms in Avon, interviewed in 1979 and 1980. The term 'accountant' is used broadly (in a similar manner that used in the companies) to cover both qualified and unqualified accountants from the level of 'Financial Director' to 'Assistant Accountant' and 'Trainee Accountant'. (See Tables 14.1 and 14.2) A fuller account of these interviews is given in Jones (1986), from which the extracts quoted below are taken.

Social Responsibility Accounting

Discussion of SRA usually began with some difficulty, since none of the firms published any form of corporate social report (with the exception of employee reports which are discussed below) and few accountants had much awareness of the discussions which had taken place. The initial reaction to questions about SRA was, typically, puzzlement. Most accountants were unwilling or unable to make comments beyond, 'I wouldn't know about that', 'We don't do that here', 'That's a new one on me!'. Many of the comments which were volunteered by the remaining accountants indicated a low degree of priority placed on social responsibility reporting by the company and, more particularly, by the interviewee. Only one thought that social responsibility reporting might be important for accountants.

TABLE 14.1 *Job levels of accountants*

Company	Level of post					All
	Senior		Middle		Junior	
	I	II	III	IV	V	
A	1	2	3	7	6	19
B	2	2	4	1	2	11
C	1	2	1	4	2	10
D	1	2	2	0	1	6
E	1	1	2	1	1	6
F	1	0	0	2	2	5
	7	9	12	15		
TOTAL	16		27		14	57

I = Finance Directors, Financial Controllers, Company Secretaries.
(Pay range £12,000 and above)

II = In large units – Finance Managers, Chief Accountants, Management and Financial Accountants. (£10,000 – 12,000)

III = In small units – Finance Managers, Management and Financial Accountants. (£8,000 – 10,000)

IV = Accountants, Production/Product/Cost Accountants (£6,000 – 8,000)

V = Assistant/Trainee Accountants, Management Trainees (Accounting), Finance Officers, Financial Clerk. (£3,500 – 6,000)

NOTE: This classification covers the most common job titles used in the companies. The pay range is based on information provided by the respondents in 1979/80 and covers nearly all the accountants in each category. In a few cases however the pay lies outside the ranges indicated where the respondent was in an unusually large or small unit. In April 1980 for all GB adult males the mean earnings in non-manual occupations was approximately £7,300 and in accounting £8,150 (DoE; New Earnings Survey 1980 Part D).

I think that [SRA] is beginning to be more important. It's still very early days. Particularly in the plastics field most of the products we make are disposed of and go into the earth rather than being re-used and I suppose one should say that that's not a terribly responsible use of resources. Pollution is not exactly the word . . . I suppose control and measurement of what you emit into the atmosphere. What you emit into the water system, that sort of thing will be becoming more important. And obviously that sort of

TABLE 14.2 *Company location of accountants*

| | Company Location* | | |
COMPANY	Head or Group Office	Divisional or Regional Office	Operating Unit
A		3	16**
B	7	2	2
C		10	
D			6***
E			6
F			5
TOTAL	7	15	35

NOTES:
*   Not all locations were visited in each company. In those locations which were visited, all accountants were interviewed.
**   5 units visited, only 1 in other companies.
***   Head Office combined with main factory.

area if figure work and measuring actual amounts and working out ratios and percentages and things, so that will come into the role of the accountant. So SRA I would say, is on the up.

(Financial Accountant – Company A)

No other accountant expected any impact on accounting work, and even this view seems to suggest that in order to be socially responsible, the company would have to alter the way in which it operated.

Most of the other respondents who saw a need for changed company policies which would be more in line with social responsibility stressed the conflicts between socially-responsible policies and the company's need for profit, or at least that profit was a strong constraining force.

The conflict you have all the time is between the social responsibility and profit – in the sense that some items of social responsibility don't seem to generate profit and there's a query as to whether our company ought to spend money if there aren't any returns.

(Finance Director – Company F)

This was true even in one company which enjoyed a local reputation as a 'responsible employer':

> There is conflict between your social conscience and profit – it is a tremendous struggle. It gets harder and harder all the time. We're getting tougher.
>
> (Finance Director – Company E)

All those who spoke on the social responsibility of companies had a firm conviction that making profit was the purpose of management in companies as they exist at present (rather than in hopes for the future). This was most strongly expressed by the Financial Director of a company which subsequently withdrew from the research:

> Look here, Mr Jones, I've read these business studies textbooks which talk about various priorities in business. I'll tell you our priorities. One is profit; two is profit; and three is profit.

A similar view was expressed in all the companies studied in terms of 'profit' or 'money' or 'contribution' or 'wealth' or 'targets'. Even if some other managers in the company occasionally lose sight of this prime goal, it is considered the responsibility of accountants to put a check on activities which might divert attention to some subordinate (or even irrelevant) goals:

> The engineers are designing an all-singing, all-dancing machine – the best that they can design. Very often they don't look at the financial side of things. Their job is to design a damn good machine – that's what they want to do. They get upset when we come back and say 'this machine is too expensive – can you cut down this? Can you select a cheaper material?' They get very upset.
>
> (Management Accountant – Company F)

> You have to make sure that salesmen sell the product at a price which is going to pay the company to sell it and that they don't let themselves get into fierce price cutting wars just so they can say they've sold £X,000 this month.
>
> (Financial Accountant – Company B)

Each manager's performance is monitored and levelled as against

TABLE 14.3   *Summary of attitudes of accountants to SRA*

Attitude	Level of post			
	Senior	*Middle*	*Junior*	*All*
Full support	0	1	0	1
Partial support	3	2	1	6
Neutrality/No comment	13	24	13	50
TOTAL	16	27	14	57

Full support = SRA is important in the company and for accountants.
Partial support = Interested in Social Responsibility but gives it low priority or sees it as unrelated to accounting.
Neutrality = No real interest in SRA or scepticism about its relevance and applicability.

his budget. If he beats his budget he's a good bloke – if he doesn't beat his budget then he's not such a good chap (unless outside influences – say a strike at a supplier's factory or something like that – affects him) . . . you've got to stand back and say 'well, is this guy doing his job properly? Is this department a profitable investment or not?'

(Finance Manager – Company B)

The majority of accountants, however, saw little gap between their own profit-orientated views and those of other managers.

Accountants showed little interest in SRA, with fewer than a third of them willing (and/or able) to make any comment about it. (See Table 14.3.) Profitability was seen as the central managerial purpose, and it was not clear to these accountants how the question of social responsibility was related to this purpose. Some saw a strong and direct conflict between the two and thus considered that companies could not afford to look too carefully at the issue. A very few vaguely hoped for changes in business policy which would increase the emphasis on social responsibility and might change the way in which companies operated, but there was little sign that any of the companies might voluntarily move towards some kind of social report – and no one had considered the possibility that such a report might be imposed on companies by external pressure. In short, SRA was seen as having no managerial purpose.

Employee Accounting

Discussion of EA provided a marked contrast. All the respondents had heard of it, and no explanation or examples were needed. Although some accountants declined to make comments about it, the majority of accountants were willing to discuss it, and many spoke at length about it. Each of the six companies produced some kind of employee report and in most a fairly considerable amount of time and effort seemed to be devoted to it, and strong support was expressed by accountants at senior management levels.

> We've got an educational task with these [shop-floor] employees. You may find a man's a good accountant, a good manager, but a poor teacher. It's a bit worrying . . . If people don't understand what you're trying to do they may resist it with a certain amount of teeth.
>
> (Finance Director – Company C)

> I think all employees have the right to influence decisions before they're made. To do that they've got to be aware of all the facts and they've got to be briefed properly.
>
> (Financial Controller – Company B)

For senior managerial accountants, EA is concerned with getting 'the facts' across and that this is linked to some definite pay-off – the employees will be 'briefed properly' and less likely to resist, more likely to give what is wanted. This senior managerial support for EA was shared by a number of accountants at middle- and junior-managerial levels who often expressed themselves more forcefully. Some supported a passive kind of EA – reporting the true facts in a neutral manner – but others espoused a more active role in changing attitudes. In particular, trade unions were seen as important, and a more favourable climate of opinion might be achieved either by bypassing trade unions and speaking directly to 'the individual' or by influencing trade-union representatives.

> It's [EA] an attempt to confront trade-union pressure in a way because I don't think companies would do it if they didn't think it was of benefit to them. The reason why it's of benefit to them is that it gives them a chance to talk to the individual – to put their

TABLE 14.4   *Summary of attitudes of accountants to EA*

Attitude	Level of post			
	Senior	*Middle*	*Junior*	*All*
Full support	10	7	0	17
Partial support	1	3	3	7
Neutrality/No comment	4	13	10	27
Skepticism/Opposition	1	4	1	6
TOTAL	16	27	14	57

Full support	= EA is important in the company and for accountants.
Partial support	= Reporting to employees is important but is not being successfully carried out at present.
Neutrality	= No clear support or opposition to EA.
Skepticism	= Strong doubts about the usefulness of EA.
Opposition	= EA seen as dangerous disclosure of information.

point of view – in a way it's a propaganda exercise – but it isn't opposed to the current reporting to shareholders.

(Financial Manager – Company B)

Support for EA 'in principle' was tempered at all levels by concerns that the objectives of EA were not being achieved fully in the company. There were many reasons suggested for this failure: the inability of employees to understand reports; the lack of seriousness or rigour with which EA was conducted; employees' lack of interest in the reports; and, in one company, the lack of trust shown by employees. A final reservation expressed by some supporters of EA about its success was that senior management showed reluctance in disclosing enough information, whereas for two accountants the view of EA as a potentially dangerous opening-up of information was the basis of their opposition to it (see Table 14.4).

EA was seen as important, not because of a generalised sense of business responsibility, but because a clear managerial purposes had been identified at senior management level. In particular it was seen as a way of influencing employees' attitudes to managerial decisions. In this way, accounting may serve to legitimise the profit-making goals and activities of managers (Knights and Collinson, 1987; Berry et al., 1985).

CSA in practice

A survey of practice and opinion in six companies and involving only fifty-seven 'accountants' can give, at best, only a partial insight into a very limited area of CSA practice. Thus these comments should be treated as tentative initial attempts to portray the views of practitioners after a decade of academic interest in CSA.

Very little interest was expressed, at any managerial level, in ideas of reporting on the social responsibilities of business to an audience outside the firm. Objections were raised, not only about the technical difficulties of creating such reports, but also about the status (and even existence) of social responsibility as a business goal. The relationship between social responsibility and profitability was frequently questioned, and the central importance of profit was asserted. No threat was seen to the long-term prospects for profitable trading from demands for more socially-responsible business policies, and no likelihood of SRA being imposed by outside pressure. Only a few felt any moral imperative to change business towards more socially-responsible policies, and these felt there was little likelihood of change occurring.

In contrast, EA received widespread (but not universal) support from accountants, especially at higher managerial levels. This makes it difficult to explain lack of interest in SRA as simply caused by 'traditionalism' or 'conservatism' (Hastings and Hinings, 1970) on the part of accountants. The difference in the reaction of accountants in these large corporations to SRA and to EA seem to stem from the clear managerial purpose identified for EA, where the goals of social responsibility and profitability are seen as compatible. Indeed, it was widely believed that there is a direct relationship between increasing disclosure of information and increasing (or at least maintaining) profitability. For SRA no such managerial purpose has been identified, and social responsibility is seen as irrelevant, of very low importance, or in conflict with the central goal of profitability.

ACCOUNTING AND THE CAPITALIST ENTERPRISE

There is clearly a considerable gap between the view taken in the Corporate Report (ASSC, 1975) that profit is no longer the sole or premier indicator of performance, and the views of accounting practitioners reported here. Their response closely mirrors that found by

Nichols and Beynon (1977, p. 31) in a study of one large British firm: 'none of the managers we talked to there [a chemical plant] is in any doubt that his job was to make profit and that if he failed in this his future with ChemCo [pseudonym] was in jeopardy'. Indeed, in their comments about other managers, some accountants stressed that it was their job to ensure that managerial performance was monitored in this way. What explanation can be given of the gulf between CSA supporters' view of business enterprises, and the views of accountants who work in them?

In the 1970s there were two common assumptions underlying each of the three approaches to CSA. The first assumption was that the power of owners is no longer such that their interests dominate business enterprises. Thus it was seen to be possible for non-owners – accountants, external pressure groups and/or managers – to create or identify new corporate goals. The second assumption was that these new objectives could be generally classified as 'social responsibility', which was seen as displacing 'profitability' as the prime enterprise goals. What theoretical justification is there for such assumptions?

Managerialism and Social Responsibility

The argument that owners have 'surrendered' control over modern corporations to managers, and hence that the objectives of these corporations have changed, has its origin in the work of Berle and Means (1932). The ideas they put forward have become known as 'The Managerialist Thesis', and were so widely accepted in social science by the end of the 1960s that Means was able to introduce their second edition by stating, 'The fact of the corporate revolution is now so widely accepted that statistical evidence is no longer needed to establish its occurrence'. (Berle and Means, 1968, p. xxix)

The Managerialist Thesis, in its original form, was based on large-scale business enterprises in the USA. Berle and Means argued that there was a tendency to a wider distribution of share ownership, and that such large numbers of small individual owners were unable to control the business activities of the enterprises they 'owned'. They saw control of large-scale (modern) enterprises devolving into the hands of managers who were 'a neutral technocracy' pursuing company objectives which were different from the objectives of owners. The dominance of the 'rights of the community' in creating such objectives meant that 'public need' would replace 'private greed' as the prime enterprise goal. So 'soulful corporations' become the central feature of a new form of society labelled 'People's Capitalism' (Berle, 1960).

Critique of Managerialism: Goals

Although Managerialism seemed to be widely influential, by the start of the 1970s there was already a strong body of criticism which presented quite different views of the consequences of change in modern corporations. Galbraith (1972) argued that managers had gained power in companies and that they used this power, collectively, to pursue their own interests. The prime managerial goal is the survival of the organisation itself, which depends on the preservation of corporate autonomy. Once this is achieved, the goals of growth and technological virtuosity/innovation become important. Only after the satisfaction of these goals do corporations pay attention to other, lesser, objectives which can be categorised as social responsibility goals. For Galbraith, however, corporations are socially responsible only to the extent that management itself defines this social responsibility and has the power to impose its definitions on wider society. Managerial Economists share Galbraith's emphasis on the pursuit of managerial interest constrained by fear of takeovers, mergers and other forms of market pressure (Baumol, 1959; Williamson, 1966; Marris, 1964, 1972; Simon, 1959. Reviewed in Curwen, 1974). Until the 1980s, accounting theorists largely seem to have ignored this version of Managerialism in favour of the original emphasis on social responsibility. In an alternative approach, Nichols (1969) argued that the motives of managers are unlikely to be very different from those of owners. The background ('social experience') and values of managers closely resemble those of owners, and we should not expect that the objectives they choose will be significantly different from, let alone hostile to, the interests of owners. Thus even if managers are in a position to 'choose' the goals of their companies, these goals will still be centred around profitability. Others have argued that managers have little scope to make any other 'choice'. De Vroey (1975b) sees objectives being imposed on companies by 'the logic of capitalism', and Zeitlin (1974, p. 1097) argues that profitability is 'both the only unambiguous criterion of successful managerial performance and an irreducible necessity for corporate survival'. Even if the power of owners has been significantly reduced, the ultimate necessity for 'long-term profit seeking' (Scott, 1979) or 'profitable growth' (Child, 1985) is seen as placing severe limits to any possible change in corporate objectives.

Critique of Managerialism: Ownership and Control

In the 1970s a more fundamental critique of Managerialism gained ground. It was argued that owners had not surrendered control of modern corporations. Managerialism was rejected on grounds of: the inadequacy, or falseness, of the statistical findings and the methods used to identify management control (Chevalier, 1969; Burch, 1972; Zeitlin, 1974; Nyman and Silberston, 1978); the applicability of the theory outside a limited historical period in the US and UK (Scott, 1979; 1986); and the inadequate concepts of 'ownership' and 'control' used by Managerialists (De Vroey, 1975b). Critics limited the claim that ownership had been separated from control to a minority of large companies and, even for these companies, 'managerial control' was redefined so that managers were seen as having merely delegated authority which could be reclaimed following owners' direct interventions in business decision-making, or by the use of their power to replace top executives (De Vroey, 1975a; Zeitlin, 1974; Nyman and Silberston, 1978). Ultimate power was seen as resting with a core group of 'economic owners' but this power was seen as usually hidden or potential and only disclosed when some particular crisis of unprofitability triggered an intervention (Zeitlin, 1974; Nyman and Silberston, 1978).

Further, this ownership power was seen as concentrated in an owning/controlling class. This class was variously identified on the basis of: its wealth (Atkinson, 1972; Westergaard and Resler, 1975); its social ties of family, education and marriage (Lupton and Wilson, 1959; Zeitlin, 1974; Scott, 1982); its social cohesion through interlocking directorships (Barratt Brown, 1968; Stanworth and Giddens, 1975; Scott, 1979); and its essentially capitalist economic functions and interests (Dr Vroey, 1975b). Although owners of companies, if seen as isolated individuals, would appear to have little power to set the goals of 'their' companies, viewing them as members of a distinctive class reveals a basis for collective power. The possibility of managers setting and pursuing business goals other than those of capital accumulation is seen to be limited, not simply by some abstract 'market regulation' or 'logic of capitalism', but by the intervention (or potential intervention) of individual, family and institutional owners.

Finance and Impersonal Capitalism

In the 1970s much of the work of the critics of Managerialism was aimed at 'de-bunking' the existing orthodoxy. In the 1980s there have been attempts at constructing a new general theory of change in capitalist enterprises. The earlier emphasis on the importance of banks and other financial institutions (Fitch and Oppenheimer, 1970; Zeitlin, 1974; Nyman and Silberston, 1978) has been developed into a theory of historical development from entrepreneurial capitalism to impersonal/financial/institutional capitalism. Francis (1980) suggests that, to the extent to which owners actually lose control to managers, this is merely a transitional stage between individual/family control and institutional control. Scott (1982) shows the historical develop-ment of a 'business class' divided into different fractions of financial, entrepreneurial and internal capitalists represented by financiers, shareholders and executives. These fractions constitute 'constella-tions of interests' which control modern corporations and are con-nected together by networks of interlocking directorships, at the centre of which are major banks (Scott, 1979). The US and UK are seen as having a 'financial hegemony' in which 'banks, insurance companies and pension funds are crucial in the availability of capital to enterprises, their collective control over capital giving them the power to determine the general conditions under which other enter-prises must make their corporate decisions' (Scott, 1986, p. 28). Of course, even 'impersonal capitalism' is subject to human agency (Schuller and Hyman, 1984) but in Scott's view it produces a frame-work of financial targets within which 'operational managers are com-mitted to the forms of calculation and monetary accounting, criteria of profitability and growth, and so on which are required by modern capitalist production' (Scott, 1982, p. 129).

Organisation, Goals and Accounting

This view may be criticised as an overly rational depiction of business enterprises. Firstly, writers in the 'Organisation Theory' tradition have seen goals of organisations as problematic. People, rather than organisations, are seen as having goals, and in attempting to achieve these goals corporate objectives are produced which are multiple, changing, vague and often conflicting (Perrow, 1970, 1972; Pfeffer, 1981). Thompson (1982, p. 248) argues that firms should be regarded as dispersed social agencies in which 'there is no 'essential function' of the firm which subordinates all others'. Instead there are coalitions of interest whose heterogeneity prevents the emergence of 'a set of more or less unambiguous objectives towards which an institution, firm or enterprise might be working' (p. 234).

Secondly, accounting theorists in the 1980s challenged the view that accounting produces profit measures which are the 'unambiguous criterion of successful managerial performance' (Zeitlin, 1974, p. 1097). Mitchell (1985) argues that the accounting profession has simply allowed a mystique to develop which promotes a view of accounting as creating objective, undeniable, unavoidable truth. Other authors have seen the accounting profession implicated in the production of this mystique through: its presentation in accounting textbooks (Hopper et al., 1987); rationales of objectification and abstraction of accounting knowledge (Burchell et al., 1980); and the professionalisation of accountancy and accounting knowledge (Loft, 1986; Armstrong, 1985). Tinker (1985) shows how the acceptance of accounting reports as unambiguous and valid knowledge of business has a powerful influence on even the apparently most astute financial institutions.

Both these views highlight dangers in a simplistic approach to financial control of enterprises by institutions and point to some unresolved issues. The view that managers hold power only to the extent that it is delegated to them and may be withdrawn, leaves open the possibility of considerable variation in the use of this managerial power. Evidence that, in the long term, extreme cases of low profitability lead to ownership intervention tells us little about the short-term discretion which managers may exercise or about the levels of profit which prompt owner intervention. Evidence that accountants attempt to restrict other managers' pursuit of non-profit goals is not evidence that they are successful in this. Evidence of interlocking directorships and an ownership class does not demonstrate a unity of interest and purpose among owner-controllers. Although owners may have a common general interest in 'profitable growth', there is scope for considerable variation in specific objectives which may weaken the collective power of owners to intervene.

Despite these unresolved issues, what the critique of Managerialism has done is to place discussion of corporate objectives in the context of the ultimate power of owners to intervene in the affairs of their enterprises, even though this may be resisted by other parties, and even if one of the fundamental tools, accounting, is (like any form of control) less than perfect.

CONCLUSION: PROSPECTS FOR CORPORATE SOCIAL ACCOUNTING

CSA may be seen as 'a child of the 1970s' (Puxty, 1986, p. 107) or 'an indulgent fad of an affluent society' (Gambling, 1978, p. vii). However, academic interest in CSA has not disappeared in the 1980s (Parker, 1986; Gray et al., 1986). For CSA to be anything more than an academic pursuit (in the perjorative sense) requires recognition of the centrality of profitability to the capitalist enterprise and location of pressure for 'social responsibility' in this context. Failure to do so will lead either to CSA being merely a utopian dream, or to its being part of corporate public relations, offering the mystique of accounting as an ideological cloak for business practices. To avoid these alternatives, CSA supporters need to place themselves in the political arena (Cooper and Sherer, 1984).

Radical accountants may decide either that social responsibility cannot be imposed on business enterprises short of revolution, or instead that there is scope for limited reform within the confines of capitalist enterprise. 'Revolutionaries' probably will have despaired of this essay already. For 'Reformers', there are some mildly encouraging prospects. Given that the power of capital and its control of management (let alone labour) is not absolute, some scope for changing business practices is available. Some allies may be found among accountants in industry – a few of whom indicate a willingness to explore the social responsibilities of firms (in relation to SRA) and more who show flexibility in accounting practices (in relation to EA). These prospects should not be exaggerated, but for any radical development of CSA, some optimism is required. Radical accountants may be able to construct measures which expose the activities of capitalist enterprises and assist social reform. Even if failing to do this, they can help to demystify the conventional accounting practices which currently produce 'knowledge' of the capitalist enterprise. The publication of this book, along with other critiques of accounting in the 1980s, suggests that this is not a wholly unrealistic vision.

Bibliography

Armstrong, P., 'Changing Managerial Control Strategies: The Role of Competition Between Accountancy and Other Organisational Professions', *Accounting Organizations and Society* (1985) pp. 129–48.

ASSC, *The Corporate Report* (London: Accounting Standards Steering Committee, 1975).

Atkinson, A. B., *Unequal Shares: Wealth in Britain* (London: Allen Lane, 1972).

Barratt Brown, M., 'The Controllers of British Industry', in K. Coates (ed.), *Can the Workers Run Industry?* (London: Sphere Books Ltd., 1968).

Baumol, W. J., *Business Behaviour, Value and Growth* (New York: Macmillan, 1959).

Benston, G. J., 'Accounting and Corporate Accountability', *Accounting Organizations and Society* (1982) pp. 87–105.

Berle, A. A., *Power Without Property* (New York: Harcourt Brace, 1960).

Berle, A. A. & Means, G. C., *The Modern Corporation and Private Property* (New York: Macmillan, 1932, 1968).

Berry, A. J., T. Capps, D. Cooper, P. Ferguson, T. Hopper, and E. A. Lowe, 'Management Control in an Area of the NCB: Rationales of Accounting Practices in a Public Enterprise', *Accounting Organizations and Society* (1985) pp. 3–28.

Burch, P. H., *The Managerial Revolution Reassessed* (Massachusetts: Lexington, 1972).

Burchell, S., C. Clubb, A. Hopwood, J. Hughes, and J. Nahapiet, 'The Roles of Accounting in Organisations and Society', *Accounting Organizations and Society* (1980) pp. 5–27.

Chevalier, J. M., 'The Problem of Control in Large American Corporations', *Anti-Trust Bulletin* (1969), pp. 163–80.

Child, J., 'Managerial Strategies, New Technology and the Labour Process', in D. Knights, H. Wilmott and D. Collinson (eds), *Job Redesign: Critical Perspectives on the Labour Process* (Aldershot: Gower Press, 1985).

Cohen, P. S., *Modern Social Theory* (London: Heinemann, 1968).

Council for Economic Development, *Social Responsibilities of Business Corporations* (New York: CED, 1971).

Cooper, D. J. and M. J. Sherer, 'The Value of Corporate Accounting Reports: Arguments for a Political Economy of Accounting', *Accounting Organizations and Society* (1984) pp. 207–32.

Curwen, P. J., *Managerial Economics* (London: Macmillan, 1974).

De Vroey, M., 'The Owners' Interventions in Decision-Making in Large Corporations', *European Economic Review* (1975a) pp. 1–15.

De Vroey, M., 'The Separation of Ownership and Control in Large Corporations', *Review of Radical Political Economics* (Summer, 1975b), pp. 1–10.

Dierkes, M. and A. A. Bauer (eds), *Corporate Social Accounting* (New York: Praeger, 1973).

Estes, R., *Corporate Social Accounting* (New York: Wiley 1976).

Fitch, R. & Oppenheimer, M., 'Who Rules the Corporations?' *Socialist Revolution* (Volume 1, Nos 4, 5, 6; 1970).

Flint, D., *The Impact of Change on the Accounting Profession* (Edinburgh: ICA Scotland, 1980).

Francis, A., 'Families, Firms and Finance Capital: The Development of UK Industrial Firms with Particular Reference to their Ownership and Control', *Sociology* (1980) pp. 1–27.

Galbraith, J. K., *The New Industrial State* (Harmondsworth: Penguin, 1972).

Gambling, T., *Societal Accounting* (London: George Allen and Unwin, 1974).

Gambling, T., *Beyond the Conventions of Accounting* (London: Macmillan, 1978).

Glautier, M. W. E. and B. Underdown *Accounting in a Changing Environment* (London: Pitman, 1974).

Gray, R., D. Owen and K. Maunders, 'Corporate Social Reporting: the Way Forward', *Accountancy*, (December 1986) pp. 108–9.

Hastings, A. and C. R. Hinings, 'Role Relations and Value Adaptation: A Study of the Professional Accountant in Industry', *Sociology* (1970) pp. 353–66.

Hildreth, J., 'The Role of the Board', *Director* (October 1976) pp. 79–80.

Hopper, T., J. Storey and H. Willmott 'Accounting for Accounting: Towards the Development of a Dialectical View', *Accounting, Organization and Society* (1987) pp. 437–56.

Jones, T. C., 'Corporate Social Accounting: the Gulf Between Theory and Practice', *Occasional Papers in Sociology*, No 3 (Bristol Polytechnic, Department of Economics and Social Science, April 1986).

Knights, D. and D. Collinson, 'Disciplining the Shopfloor: A Comparison of the Disciplinary Effects of Managerial Psychology and Financial Accounting', *Accounting, Organizations and Society* (1987) pp. 457–77.

Lee, D. and H. Newby, *The Problem of Sociology: An Introduction to the Discipline* (London: Hutchinson, 1983).

Loft, A., 'Towards a Critical Understanding of Accounting: the Case of Cost Accounting in the UK, 1914–1925', *Accounting, Organizations and Society* (1986) pp. 137–69.

Lupton, C. and C. Wilson, (1959) 'The Social Background and Connections of "Top Decision Makers"' in J. Urry and J. Wakeford (eds) *Power in Britain* (London: Heinemann, 1974).

Marlin, J. T., 'Accounting for Pollution', *Journal of Accountancy* (1973) pp. 41–6.

Marris, R., *The Economic Theory of 'Managerial Capitalism'* (London: Macmillan, 1964).

Marris, R. 'Why Economics Needs a Theory of the Firm', *Economic Journal* (March 1972, special issue) pp. 321–52.

Maunders, K. T., 'Employee Reporting', in T. A. Lee (ed.) *Developments in Financial Reporting* (Oxford: Philip Allen, 1981).

Melrose-Woodman, J. and I. Kverndal, 'Towards Social Responsibility: Company Codes and Ethics of Practice', *Management Survey*, No 28 (London: British Institute of Management, 1976).

Mitchell, A., 'NCB Lesson for the Profession', *Account* (7 November 1985) p. 7.

Monsen, R. J., 'Is Social Accounting a Mirage?' in M. Dierkes and A. A. Bauer (eds), *Corporate Social Accounting* (New York: Praeger, 1973) pp. 107–12.

Nichols, T., *Ownership, Control and Ideology* (London: Allen & Unwin, 1969).

Nichols, T. and H. Beynon, *Living with Capitalism* (London: Routledge, 1977).

Nyman, S. and Silberston, A., 'The Ownership and Control of Industry', *Oxford Economic Papers (New Series)* (1978) pp. 74–101.

Owen, D., 'Why Accountants Can't Afford to Turn Their Backs on Social Reporting', *Accountancy* (January 1981) pp. 44–5.

Owen, D., 'Social Accountability: A Role for Accountants', *Accountants Record* (July 1982) pp. 4–6

Parker, L. D., 'Polemical Themes in Social Accounting: A Scenario for Standard Setting', *Advances in Public Interest Accountancy* (1986) pp. 67–93.

Perks, R. W. and R. H. Gray, 'Beware of Social Accounting', *Management Accounting* (December 1979) pp. 22–3.

Perks, R. W. and R. H. Gray, 'What is Social Accounting?' *Management Accounting* (July-August 1981) p. 29.

Perrow, C., *Organisational Analysis* (London: Tavistock, 1970).

Perrow, C., *Complex Organisations* (Brighton: Scott Foresman, 1972).

Pfeffer, J., *Power in Organisations* (London: Pitman, 1981).

Puxty, A. G., 'Social Accounting as Immanent Legitimation: A Critique of Technicist Ideology', *Advances in Public Interest Accounting* (1986) pp. 95–111.

Ramanathan, K. V., 'Toward a Theory of Social Accounting', *The Accounting Review* (1976) pp. 516–28.

Schuller, T. and J. Hyman, 'Forms of Ownership and Control: Decision-Making Within a Financial Institution', *Sociology* (1984) pp. 51–70.

Scott, J., *Corporations, Classes and Capitalism* (London: Hutchinson, 1979).

Scott, J., *The Upper Classes: Property and Privilege in Britain* (London: Macmillan, 1982).

Scott, J., 'The Debate on Ownership and Control', *Social Studies Review* (1986) pp. 24–9.

Shocker, A. D. and S. P. Sethi, 'An Approach to Incorporating Social References in Developing Corporate Action Strategies', in S. P. Sethi (ed.), *The Unstable Ground: Corporate Social Policy in a Dynamic Society* (Los Angeles: Melville, 1974) pp. 67–80.

Simon, H. A. (1959) 'Theories of Decision-Making in Economics and Behavioural Science', *American Economic Review* (1974) pp. 253–83.

Stanworth, P. and A. C. Giddens, 'The Modern Corporate Economy', *Sociological Review* (1975) pp. 5–28.

Thompson, G., 'The Firm as a "Dispersed" Social Agency', *Economy and Society* (1982) pp. 233–50.

Tinker, A. M., *Paper Prophets: a Social Critique of Accounting* (Eastbourne: Holt Rinehart and Winston, 1985).

Westergaard, J. and H. R. Resler *Class in a Capitalist Society: A Study of Contemporary Britain* (London: Heinemann, 1975).

Williamson, J. H., 'Profit, Growth and Sales Maximisation', *Economica* (1966).

Zeitlin, M., 'Corporate Ownership and Control', *American Journal of Sociology* (1974) pp. 1073–1119.

15 Value for Money Auditing: Some Observations on its Origins and Theory

Brendan McSweeney and Michael Sherer[1]

In both academic discourse and political debate, increasing reference has been and is being made to 'value for money' as a benchmark against which the performance of local authorities, and other parts of the public sector, can be judged. The phrase, value for money, implies that there exists a knowable and appropriate, even ideal, relationship between the inputs a local authority consumes and the outputs it provides, between its accomplishments and the monetary expenditure incurred in achieving them.

The Audit Commission for Local Authorities in England and Wales (the Audit Commission) defines value for money (VFM) in terms of: economy, efficiency and effectiveness (the three 'Es'), and external auditors appointed by the Audit Commission are required under the 1982 Local Government Finance Act (the 1982 Act) to give an opinion on whether local authorities have made appropriate arrangements for securing the three 'Es' in their operations. Whilst an appropriate external evaluation of the operations of organisation may, at times, be beneficial, with the potential for enhanced accountability and accomplishments, we shall argue that there are both theoretical and implementation deficiencies in the main espoused VFM auditing theory. Stated theories and theories in action may differ. The gap between the general and the specific may be very large; the consequences of VFM audits may or may not articulate closely and automatically with their stated aims (Hopwood, 1984). Reforms are often promoted in the name of their potential rather than their practical possibilities or actual accomplishments (Pressman and Wildavsky, 1979; National Consumer Council, 1986). However, because of the virtual absence of studies of VFM auditing in action, we do not examine the execution of such audits or their short-or longer-term consequences here. Instead, this paper has two main aims: first, to place the recent interest in VFM auditing for local authorities within a context; and second, to critically evaluate some of the major assumptions and characteristics of the espoused theory of VFM auditing. We examine the publications of some of the large accounting firms and the Audit Commission, with particular emphasis on the implicit and explicit assumptions made about organisational goals, the measurement of performance and the relationship between arrangements and outcomes.

EXTENSION OF THE LOCAL AUTHORITY EXTERNAL AUDIT

The 1982 Act heralded a major change in the audit requirements of local authorities in England and Wales. In addition to the auditor's established responsibility for assessing the credibility of authorities' accounts and the detection and reporting of fraud, the 1982 Act imposes a duty on the auditor to consider the value for money of an authority's activities and operations. Specifically, the 1982 Act requires the auditor to satisfy himself or herself that the authority has made proper arrangements for securing economy, efficiency and effectiveness in its use of resources. The auditor must verify that such arrangements are in place and are effective, (Audit Commission, 1984a). Although auditors of local authorities already had a nominal responsibility to disclose instances of 'poor value for money', that requirement was merely mentioned in a Department of the Environment circular (Department of the Environment, 1973); no guidelines were issued on how this might be assessed, and little emphasis was given to it in practice. In contrast, the Audit Commission now requires that about 40–50 per cent of an external audit of a local authority must now be concerned with issues of value for money; evaluating arrangements and undertaking studies of particular activities chosen by the Audit Commission (Audit Commission, 1983).

This increasing scrutiny and standardisation is not restricted to local authorities, but is occurring, at a time of economic restraint and changing conceptions of the State and its activities, elsewhere in the public sector (Department of Health and Social Security, 1983; RIPA, 1983; Hopwood, 1984; Likierman, 1984; Sherer, 1984; HM Treasury, 1986; Meyer, 1986). Here we focus our study on local authorities.

The 1982 Act also transferred the District Audit Service from the Department of the Environment to the quasi-independent Audit Commission, which has the sole authority for appointing and setting the fees of local authority auditors in England and Wales. It prescribes the way in which audits are to be conducted. (Jones, 1985). For some years before the 1982 Act, local authorities were given the choice of using the District Audit Service or appointing an 'approved' auditor (a private-sector accounting firm), but very few authorities chose this second option (Fielden, 1984). One of the most immediate consequences of the 1982 Act was the appointment by the Audit Commission of thirteen private-sector accounting firms as auditors to 117 (out of 456) local authorities, with staff from the District Audit Service (DAS, now officers of the Audit Commission), auditing almost all of the remaining authorities. In a few cases joint auditing is undertaken.

It is the intention of the Audit Commission to eventually increase to one-third the proportion of local authorities audited by private-sector accounting firms, although the number of firms appointed to undertake the enlarged number of audits may be reduced (Audit Commission, 1985b).[2]

Relative Emphasis

Each year the Audit Commission selects particular services or costs upon which value-for-money audits should be performed by the auditor of an individual authority (Audit Commission, 1983). In the first year, 1983–4, that VFM audits were undertaken, particular attention was paid to Purchasing; Refuse Collection; Council Tenants' Arrears, Further Education and the Use of Civilians in the Police Force (Audit Commission, 1984b).

The VFM reports on individual authorities are not publicly available unless the members of the council decide to make them so.[3]

Publicity for the recommendations of VFM audits is provided by the Audit Commission, which publishes summaries of the results of individual studies. For the year 1983–4, over 1800 individual VFM projects were undertaken (74 per cent by the District Audit Service and 26 per cent by outside firms) on the services and costs selected by the Audit Commission.

The emphasis of these published summaries is predominantly on the cost savings that could be made if all authorities conformed to the practice of the 'best' authorities if external standards were adhered to. For example, the report on purchasing (Audit Commission, 1984c, pp. 13–14) states that a gain of £200 million a year could be achieved if prices paid for purchases were closer to those secured by the more successful authorities; while the report on refuse collection showed that 'if all authorities were willing to adopt the lowest refuse collection methods (and accept the service standards involved)', total savings of £70 million a year could be achieved (Audit Commission, 1984d, pp. 14–15).

Many of the reports published thus far demonstrate an asymmetry in the recommendations of VFM auditors. A great deal of attention is given to possible cost savings that can be made (Kline and Mallaber, 1985; Barker, 1986). In contrast, much less attention is given to an evaluation of the effectiveness of local authority activities, although one report from the Audit Commission showed concern that the present low levels of capital spending were weakening the effectiveness of housing, schools and roads policies (Audit Commission, 1985b; Kline and Mallaber 1986). This imbalance in the recommendations is not consistent with a stated equal concern for each of the three components of value for money: economy, efficiency and effectiveness (Audit Commission, 1984a; National Consumer Council, 1986). The three 'Es' are not discrete aspects of organisational activity. To the extent that they can be distinguished, they are often inter-related – sometimes conflicting, sometimes reinforcing each other (McSweeney, 1984; Pollitt, 1986). Emphasising one or two components whilst neglecting the other(s) can have distorting consequences, for example, increasingly focusing organisational attention on some activities and values to the detriment of others.

VFM Audits and Accountability

In addition to judging whether each local authority has made proper arrangements for securing economy, efficiency and effectiveness in its use of resources (Audit Commission, 1984a) VFM auditing is being advocated as a means of enhancing the accountability of local authorities to their ratepayers and/or electors (Audit Commission, 1985b). This aim was not a significant part of the discourse that preceded and surrounded the statutory requirement for audits of local authorities, nor indeed the early period of these audits (Hopwood, 1982; Audit Commission, 1984a; Audit Commission, 1984b).

If VFM audits disproportionally concentrate on economy, as the limited evidence available suggests, to the neglect of the effectiveness

part of the audit (Grimwood and Tomkins, 1986; Kline and Malle-
bar, 1986) the selective scrutiny and consequent limited visibility can
result only in inadequate and partial accountability. Without proper
attention to effectiveness, and indeed to other criteria which may be
equally important to the consumers of services (for example, equity
(McSweeney, 1983) quality, predictability (Pollitt, 1986) and availability, awareness and user satisfaction (Clarke, 1984)), VFM auditing cannot create a means by which recipients of services can hold
members to account, nor can it attempt to improve the quality of
information about the potential outcomes of alternative programmes
(Holtham and Stewart, 1981). Information on the opportunity costs
of political judgements will, in general, not come from VFM audits.
VFM auditing may be advocated as a means of enhancing public
accountability, but it is questionable whether the accounts that will
be rendered under its name will provide the kind of information
adequate or appropriate to the bonds of accountability that are to be
found in local government.

VALUE FOR MONEY THEORY: THE ACCOUNTING FIRMS AND ORGANISATION THEORIES

How do auditors approach the complexity and diversity of local
authorities? As yet, very few independent and rigorous studies of
VFM have been undertaken. However, an examination of the major
assumptions in some of the large accountancy firms' VFM manuals
and other documents provide some insights. These assumptions we
have called VFM Theory.[4] A wide range of interpretations have
emerged to describe or alter organisations (Morgan, 1986). That
diversity and controversy is unrecognised in the large accounting
firms' manuals we have examined. Instead, they confidently assert an
undisputed knowledge of the one best way of assessing and changing
organisations, including local authorities.

VFM theory is influenced by a particular set of organisation theories which may be loosely grouped together under the heading of
Management by Objectives (MBO), (Dirsmith and Jablonsky, 1979).

It is based on a taken-for-granted image of how organisations do,
or should, function. The determining metaphor or ideal pattern of
organisation is that of a machine and is based on classical management theory. The first and most essential requirement of VFM is a

formal statement of unambiguous goals by organisations for each of their activities.

These goals then become the targets towards which organisational activity is directed and provide the benchmarks against which accomplishments are assessed. That model of how local authorities do, or should, operate is deceptively and seductively simple.

Organisational objectives are often vague, ambiguous, and change with time. They are often set by ill-defined processes and are multiple and partially conflicting. Life would be easy for the value-for-money auditor if complex organisations' explicit, operative, real, overall, implied component parts, and individual participants' objectives, were all the same; if they did not conflict; if they were clear, agreed, unambiguous, simple, few and capable of easy definition and measurement. Unfortunately, in the real world, organisations are not like that (Etzioni, 1964; Gross, 1969; Georgiou, 1973; Wildavsky, 1978).

In politically-dominated environments, such as local authorities, there is the additional pressure to declare publicly-acceptable goals, and indeed different goals may be declared in different subenvironments (McSweeney, 1985a). VFM theory assumes that explicit statements and ranking of goals can and should be achieved before determining what actions should be taken to achieve these goals. However, the concept of organisational goals is elusive and controversial. Human-choice behaviour is often at least as much a process of discovering goals as acting upon them (March, 1971).

Ends and means are often chosen simultaneously. What life has joined together, VFM Theory tries to render asunder. It is quite common for local authority members (of the same or different parties) to agree on actions despite different, indeed conflicting, intentions (Majone and Wildavsky, 1979; Ring and Perry, 1985). VFM Theory is not rich enough to cope with the political characteristics of local authorities, and consequently views 'politics' as a negative influence to be reduced as much as possible (Audit Commission, 1983; Butt and Palmer, 1985).

There is a considerable and diverse literature rejecting the view that the pursuit of explicit goals is the critical variable determining organisational behaviour (Warner and Havens, 1968; Georgiou, 1973; Morgan, 1986). We have not here provided an extensive description or evaluation of that literature but merely identified its existence as the contested nature of the discourse on organisational goals is effectively ignored in VFM Theory (Butt and Palmer, 1985). One perception of organisation alone is influential in VFM Theory, the others are unknown or ignored. Organisations know more, depend on more, are influenced by more, and are attentive to more than they are able to articulate or reflect on (Smith, 1982).

Quantification, Multiplicity and Ambiguity

VFM Theory places considerable emphasis on quantification – both of goals as preludes to action and as means of assessing the outcome of such actions. Quantification is regarded as the ideal representation of goals and the quintessential indicator of effectiveness. From the commencement of local authority VFM audits, some of the large accounting firms, faced with the diversity, ambiguity, and sometimes intangible nature of many local authority outputs, have sought to discover quantifiable 'performance indicators' as surrogate output measures. There are circumstances in which quantified indicators are the appropriate primary or supplementary effectiveness indicators. However, there is often an inadequate understanding of the limitations and misleading nature of such measures in many circumstances (Long, 1985). Many VFM auditors use the term 'quantified' as synonymous with 'objective' or 'scientific' or 'factual'. By contrast non-quantified or qualitative measures are often described as 'soft' or 'subjective'. In practice, so-called hard or quantified data themselves usually turn out to be quite soft, in the sense of subjective and value-laden. In almost all cases, the selection of priorities, weights and standards are decisions that rest on subjective, normative assumptions. In order to quantify, many aspects of the area which the measure is supposed to illustrate may have to be suppressed or drastically simplified, thus significantly reducing the fidelity of the data. There is no absolute refuge in quantification. It is not superior to other types of information when it is inappropriate, or when relevant qualitative data is ignored or neglected (Holtham and Stewart, 1981). An associated error is the assumption that quantified indicators are continuous and linear, yet it may be difficult to find a measure that even points consistently in the right direction (Quade, 1982).

The emergence and characteristics of contemporary cultural rationalisation (especially performativity and standardisation, in part facilitated, generated and represented by increasing quantification) has been discussed elsewhere (Weber, 1961; Habermas, 1984;

Hoskin and Macve, 1986; Lyotard, 1986). The pervasively inferior status of the non-quantified in VFM Theory (Roberts and Scapens, Chapter 6), combined with the comparative studies of local authorities undertaken by or on behalf of the Audit Commission, are possibly powerful forces for increasing the 'coercive' and 'normative' homogenisation (DiMaggio and Powell, 1983; Meyer, 1986) of local-authority functioning, making them not only more uniform in themselves but increasingly moving them to greater conformity with the dominant image of how the private sector operates (the machine metaphor of VFM Theory) – an image whose realism and appropriateness for the private sector is increasingly being questioned (Morgan, 1986). However, public-sector reorganisation has often confronted considerable constraints and uncertainties, frequently accomplishing far less than the originators' wishes (Olson and March, 1983). Current and potential changes in local authorities, and the wider public sector, require considerable exploration.

Ambiguity

A prior problem to the question of whether outputs of a particular activity are in fact measurable is the extent to which objectives can be identified in an unambiguous manner.[5] There are several reasons why objectives may be ambiguous, including:

(1) conflicts of perceived interest or values;
(2) lack of knowledge about means-ends relationships;
(3) turbulence in the organisation's environment.

(Hofstede, 1981)

Considering the first cause only, if a local authority has a department which can be evaluated using three criteria, then clearly (2:2:2) is better than (0:0:0), assuming a goal of maximisation; but is (2:1:0) better than (1:1:1) or is (2:1:0) equal to (1:0:2) (Goodman and Pennings, 1974; Quade, 1980)?

However, even when ranking problems can be solved, Lindblom (1959) points out that social objectives do not always have the same relative value. One objective may be highly prized in one circumstance, another in a different circumstance. That one value is preferred to another in one decision situation does not mean that it will be preferred in another decision situation in which it can be achieved only at great sacrifice of another value. Even if all local-authority

officers had at hand an agreed set of values, objectives, and constraints, their actual choices in specific situations would be impossible
to formulate. Preference ordering of goals is unstable (Lindblom,
1959).

In auditing (in the sense of examining or interrogating) an organisation, or group of organisations, the use of a specific form of
rationality for particular activities may be adequate. However, VFM
Theory is based on one form for all circumstances and purposes.
More importantly, the aim of VFM audits is not solely to assess but
to change local authorities also, by attempting to make them increasingly function according to that narrow rationality. There is a significant literature which argues that an excessive emphasis on formal,
quantified goals as preludes to planning and action, and/or as yardsticks for evaluation, can have undesirable consequences when output uncertainty is significant – for example, a decline in organisations'
ability to be flexible, adaptable and able to learn (Weick, 1979;
Landau and Stout, 1979) – and/or an increase in the efforts of
organisational participants to accomplish the readily quantified to the
detriment of other less easily quantified or unquantifiable, but no less
relevant, tasks (Dornbusch and Scott, 1975).

The Transformation Process

In addition to the above issues of valid performance indicators, goal
ambiguity and context-influenced priorities, there is also the problem
of identifying which factors have, are, and will influence outputs.
VFM auditors are required to satisfy themselves about the economy, efficiency and effectiveness of local authorities' arrangements
(Audit Commission, 1984a). This assumes an ability to know what
the consequences of existing arrangements are, and also the ability to
predict what the consequences of those, or altered arrangements,
could be. VFM Theory does not recognise the uncertainty that often
characterises such means-ends relationships in local authorities. Instead, it assumes that there is a clear relationship between structure,
process and output. However, as with many other organisations,
local authorities are characterised by both causal (cause/effect) and
output uncertainty, as shown in Figure 1, which is adapted from
Thompson (1967) and Thompson and Tuden (1959).

The four-cell model of local-authority decision-making shown
there, based upon the two dimensions of uncertainty of output and
uncertainty about the transformation process, is an overtly simple

Uncertainty of Outcomes

		Low	High
	Low	(1)	(2)
Uncertainty about cause and effect	High	(3)	(4)

FIGURE 15.1   *Dimensions of Local Authority Uncertainty*

representation of decision-making in complex organisations. Nevertheless, it does reflect a complexity and realism beyond that presently incorporated in VFM Theory (Markus and Pfeffer, 1983).

In VFM Theory, local authority activities are assumed to fall into Cell 1. It assumes both crystallised standards and knowledge of outputs, and complete knowledge of the effects of actions. When objectives are clear and undisputed, and the consequences of actions are known, it is relatively easy to determine whether the results of actions will or will not satisfy the objectives laid down and agreed beforehand (Simon, 1960). A school heating system, but not education in the school, may be considered to be a good example of this; both the outcomes and the transformation process are readily identified (Jones and Pendlebury, 1983). But VFM Theory encourages the adoption of approaches suitable for appraising 'Cell 1'-type activities also for activities that are better characterised by one of the other cells. The consequences of assuming certainty where it does not exist, and the extension of certainty-relevant controls into the domain of the judgemental is not fully charted. However, research both in the public and private sectors point not to positive, though less potent, results than achieved with 'Cell 1'-type activities, but rather to the strong possibility of unintended and dysfunctional consequences (Landau and Stout, 1979; Burchell et al., 1980; Hofstede, 1981).

There are tasks which are amenable to standard procedures where deviations from such arrangements almost certainly leads to ineffeciency. But as Hofstede (1981) argues, such tasks must have four characteristics:

(1) unambiguous objectives;
(2) identifiable outputs;[6]
(3) known effect of intervention; and
(4) repetitive.

In other areas, examples of grossly inappropriate procedures or practices may be apparent. VFM Theory assumes that there are universal arrangements (known to auditors), and that the production of a given quantity of output is a known function of linear combinations of input, equivalent to the economic concept of technical or productive efficiency (Sen, 1975). However, this excludes a considerable domain of local-authority activities. Neither management nor auditors know master arrangements applicable for every task (Simon, 1960; Birnberg et al., 1983; Landau and Stout, 1979).

As Hopwood (1982) states:

> Evidence from elsewhere suggests that the relationship between . . . routine and organisational performance is far more equivocal than is being presumed. Not only does their effectiveness depend upon the existence of far more subtle organisational processes than can be encapsulated in organisational manuals and reports, but also such procedures invariably have consequences that are unanticipated as well as anticipated.

The pervasiveness of the unintended and unanticipated (Giddens, 1979) is a world inconceivable within the narrowly rational VFM Theory.

Effectiveness – Failure to Fit

The large accounting firms' manuals and documents we have examined acknowledge only one significant difficulty in the application of VFM Theory (both as a method of evaluation and the basis upon which organisations should function). That problem is the considerable difficulty they have encountered in identifying for some local-authority activities quantifiable performance criteria.

The assumed availability of such criteria is the bedrock of the theory, providing both performance targets and evaluation yardsticks. The advocates of VFM Theory do not regard the quantifiable criteria problems they are encountering as a fundamental defect in the theory. The theory's failures result largely from the process- and output-uncertainties of many local-authority activities (discussed above). However, as VFM Theory is based on the assumption of certainty, the problems encountered in trying to identify quantifiable outcome criteria for the contested, the ambiguous, and the intangible, is seen merely as a data problem (Kuhn, 1970) to be dealt with in two ways. First, the use of often crude criteria, and secondly, the confident belief that the problems will be overcome in the very near future (Price Waterhouse, 1983). VFM Theory works within the framework of the conceivable, but as yet unreached, exact knowledge through quantification. But the quest is not ultimately limited by cost, time or limited expertise, but by the very nature of profound uncertainty.

Efficiency – Achieving Optimality

Despite the often equivocal relationship between inputs and outputs, the large accounting firms' literature we have examined ignores this problem and confidently asserts their absolute ability to evaluate and advise on the efficiency of all local-authority activities. If the criterion for efficiency was simply a good or satisfactory relationship between inputs and outputs, the problems discussed above (of first, the uncertain and unpredictable links between arrangements, actions, and outputs, and secondly, the indefinite, uncertain, contested nature of some of these outputs), would prevent auditors from evaluating, advising or changing local authorities in a manner consistent with that definition of efficiency. However, the efficiency definition problem is even greater within VFM Theory, as assessment of efficiency requires knowledge, not simply of an acceptable relationship between inputs and outputs, but of an optimum one.

The definitions used by the large accounting firms are similar, or identical, to that of the Audit Commission:

> An efficient operation produces the maximum output for any given set of resource inputs; or, it has minimum inputs for any given quantity and quality of service produced.
>
> (Audit Commission, 1984a)

This definition assumes the existence of maximum/best/optimum criteria against which known outcomes of specific local-authority outcomes – which are themselves the direct and known consequences of local-authority arrangements/actions/inputs – can be compared.

Such criteria rarely exist. Verification of optimality is, with a few low-level exceptions, fundamentally impossible. Hence VFM Theory's definition of efficiency is not operational for many managerial and auditing purposes. The efficiency definition used by VFM auditors must therefore differ from the espoused definition. What it is, and what the consequences are, requires studies of VFM audits in action.

SUMMARY AND CONCLUSIONS

This chapter has considered VFM auditing in local authorities in England and Wales. We briefly described its emergence and its legal and institutional characteristics. Primarily, we focused on the espoused approach to such audits in the VFM auditing manuals and other literature (some published, some unpublished) of most of the large accounting firms, who in addition to the District Audit Service, undertake such audits. When we wrote the paper (of which this chapter is a revised version) for the Interdisciplinary Conference in Accounting Conference (July 1985), there was limited experience of VFM audits in English and Welsh local authorities, and no significant empirical research of such audits. We concentrated our analysis on the espoused approach of the large accounting firms to determine whether there was a common descriptive and prescriptive model, and if so, to compare it with our understanding of local authorities.

We found in the available large firms' literature a consistent model of how organisations, such as local authorities, ought to and can function, and be audited. That stated view we have called VFM Theory. It is characterised by assumptions of unrestricted rationality and certainty. Prior specification of a few uncontested, unambiguous and tangible goals for each local authority task and a local authority as a whole is regarded as both always feasible and always highly desirable. These stated goals should be used to plan and control local-authority activities, and their accomplishment (or not) should be regularly determined and represented by quantified performance indicators. Causal as well as output certainty is also assumed: that is, that it is always feasible to know the relationship between inputs and outputs (like causes always produce like effects, and like effects necessarily follow from like causes) (Popper, 1979), and, thus, that there are procedures (arrangements) known to auditors which, when implemented, always and everywhere ensure a knowable, consistent and optimum relationship between actions and intended results.

However, we have argued that many local-authority activities are characterised by uncertainty and a lack of unanimity of (1) goals, (2) causal relationships, and (3) accomplishments.

Theories (including VFM Theory) of auditing, analysing, evaluating organisations must inevitably be simplifications of a more complex organisational reality. Nevertheless, the differences between VFM Theory's characterisation of local authorities and ours are so fundamental that they necessarily lead to different explicit or implied, predictions about VFM auditing.

Differences as regards Effectiveness: in VFM Theory, high levels of certainty about local-authority accomplishments are assumed, and thus auditors should have few problems in identifying, measuring and attributing the realisation (or not) of intended accomplishments (effectiveness). By contrast, we argued that many local-authority aims and outcomes are characterised by uncertainty, ambiguity and are often contested. This suggests that the effectiveness aspects of VFM auditing would be neglected or inadequately treated. The empirical evidence (albeit limited) available since the Interdisciplinary Conference (referred to above) suggests that the prediction that flows from our analysis of partial rather than comprehensive VFM audits is correct. The strongest evidence of the gap we anticipated between VFM Theory and VFM Audits is the Audit Commission's recently completed assessment of three years of such audits.[7] Little attention, it says, 'has been paid to considerations of effectiveness'.

Differences as regards Arrangements: VFM Theory asserts the existence of known organisational arrangements which will always produce intended and attributable results. Thus it predicts that auditors, knowing the optimum operational methods, will have few difficulties in evaluating existing local-authority arrangements. We rejected that universality and causal certainty. Again, the Audit Commission's assessment of local-authority audits supports our prediction (in contradiction to that of VFM Theory) that auditors, not knowing 'one best way', would find the evaluation of local-authority arrangements very difficult. 'Few auditors', it states, 'have come to grips with the problems of assessing authorities' overall management arrangements' (ibid.). This failure to 'come to grips' is likely to be the main focus of the Audit Commission within the next few years, with greater emphasis on attempting to change many local authorities' arrangements and on regularly monitoring the maintenance of the alterations and changed emphases (McSweeney, 1988). The stated mission of the Audit Commission is not merely to describe or evaluate local authorities but to change them. These changes should not be explored exclusively from a positive perspective (they 'modernise', they 'reduce waste'), nor from a purely negative perspective (they 'cut services', they 'reduce democracy'). There will be unintended and unacknowledged consequences as well as the intended and acknowledged ones. We must seek to explore the reality they actually produce.

Notes

1. We would like to acknowledge the helpful comments and criticism of Andrew Coulson, Clive Holtham, Anthony Hopwood, Rowan Jones, and participants at an accounting and finance seminar at the University of Warwick.
2. Indeed, one of the original private sector firms of accountants has decided not to continue to undertake this type of audit work.
3. The implications for public access to these reports of the Local Government (Access to Information) Act 1985, which came into force on 1 April 1986, are not yet clear.
4. The observations in this and subsequent sections are restricted to the dominant view in most of the large auditing firms' VFM manuals (referred to as 'VFM Theory'). Some of the firms may have a different perspective but the theory considered below is overwhelmingly the main model.
5. 'In most policies of interest objectives are characteristically multiple (because we want many things, not just one), conflicting (because we want different things), and vague (because we can agree to proceed without having to agree also on exactly what to do)' (Pressman and Wildavsky, 1979).
6. Hofstede's second characteristic is 'measurable outputs', but we consider this to be too restrictive and have substituted 'identifiable outputs'.
7. The Audit Commission's review of three years of local authority audits: 'Audit Commission Strategy Review' was completed in late 1986. Though unpublished, it was circulated in early 1987, without restrictions on quotation, to a limited number of institutions and individuals, including one of the authors of this chapter.

Bibliography

Audit Commission, *Handbook on Economy, Efficiency and Effectiveness* (London: The Audit Commission for Local Authorities in England and Wales, 1983).

Audit Commission, *Code of Local Government Audit Practice for England and Wales*, (London: HMSO, 1984a).

Audit Commission, *Report and Accounts year ended 31st March 1984*, (London: The Audit Commission for Local Authorities in England and Wales, 1984b).

Audit Commission, *Reducing the Costs of Local Government Purchases*, (London: HMSO, 1984c).

Audit Commission, *Securing Further Improvements in Refuse Collection*, (London: HMSO, 1984d).

Audit Commission, *Capital Expenditure Control in Local Government in England*, (London: HMSO, 1985a).

Audit Commission, *Report and Accounts year ended 31st March 1985*, (London: The Audit Commission for Local Authorities in England and Wales, 1985b).

Audit Commission, Audit Commission Strategy Review, (unpublished), completed: November 1986.

Barker, K., 'Auditing the Effectiveness of Local Authority Spending', *Accountancy Age*, 4 December 1986, p. 17.

Birnberg, J. G., L. Turopolec, and S. M. Young, 'The Organizational Context of Accounting', *Accounting Organizations and Society* (1983) pp. 111–29.

Burchell, B., C. Clubb, A. Hopwood, J. Hughes, and J. Nahapiet, 'The Roles of Accounting in Organizations and Society', *Accounting Organizations and Society* (1980) pp. 5–27.

Butt, H. and B. Palmer, *Value for Money in the Public Sector: The Decision-Maker's Guide*, (Oxford: Basil Blackwell, 1985).

Clarke, P. J., 'Performance Evaluation of Public Sector Programmes', *Administration* (1984) pp. 294–322.

Department of Health and Social Security, *Report of the DHSS/NHS Audit Working Party*, (Stanmore: DHSS, 1983).

Department of the Environment, *Local Government Audit Code of Practice*, Circular 79/73, (London: HMSO, 1973).

DiMaggio, P. J. and W. W. Powell, 'The Iron Cage Revisited: Institutional Isomorphism and Collective Rationality in Organizational Fields', *American Sociological Review* (1983) pp. 147–60.

Dirsmith, M. W. and F. S. Jablonsky, 'MBO, Political Rationality and Information Inductance', *Accounting Organizations and Society* (1979) pp. 39–52.

Dornbusch, S. and W. R. Scott, 'Evaluation and the Exercise of Authority' (San Francisco: Jossey-Bass, 1975) pp. 28–43.

Etzioni, A., *Modern Organizations* (Englewood Cliffs, NJ: Prentice Hall, 1964).

Fielden, J., 'A Consultant's Experience in Undertaking Value for Money Review', in J. J. Richardson (ed.) *Value for Money and Effectiveness Auditing in the Public Sector: A Symposium*, Strathclyde Papers on Government and Politics, No. 30, (Glasgow: University of Strathclyde, 1984), pp. 36–46.

Georgiou, P., 'The Goal Paradigm and Notes Towards a Counter Paradigm', *Administrative Science Quarterly* (1973) vol. XVIII, pp. 291–310.

Giddens, A., *Central Problems in Social Theory*, (London: Macmillan, 1979).

Goodman, P. S., J. M. Pennings, and Associates, *New Perspectives in Organizational Effectiveness*, (San Francisco: Jossey-Bass, 1974).

Grimwood, M. and C. Tomkins, 'Value for Money Auditing – Towards Incorporating a Naturalistic Approach', *Financial Accountability and Management* (Winter 1986) pp. 251–72.

Gross, E., 'The Definition of Organizational Goals', *British Journal of Sociology* (1969) pp. 277–94.

Habermas, J., *The Theory of Communicative Action, Vol. 1: Reason and the Rationalization of Society*, (London: Heinemann, 1984).

HM Treasury, *Output and Performance Measurement in Central Government: Progress in Departments*, (London: HM Treasury, 1986).

Hofstede, G. H., *The Game of Budget Control*, (Assen: Van Gorcum, 1967).

Hofstede, G., 'Management Control of Public and Not-for-Profit Activities', *Accounting, Organizations and Society* (1981) pp. 193–211.

Holtham, C. and Stewart, J., *Value for Money: A Framework for Action*, (Birmingham: Institute of Local Government Studies, 1981).

Hopwood, A. G., *Value for Money: Practices in Other Countries in VFM: Proceedings of A Seminar*, (London: Royal Institute of Public Administration, 1982).

Hopwood, A. G., 'Accounting and the Pursuit of Efficiency', in A. Hopwood and C. Tomkins (eds), *Issues in Public Sector Accounting* (Oxford: Philip Allan, 1984).

Hoskin, K. and R. Macve, 'The Power of Accounting', paper presented to the Interdisciplinary Perspectives on Accounting Conference, University of Manchester, 8–10 July 1985. Revised edition published in: *Accounting, Organizations and Society*, ('Accounting and the Examination: A Genealogy of Disciplinary Power') (1986) pp. 105–36.

Jones, R., *Local Government Audit Law*, 2nd ed. (London: HMSO, 1985).

Jones, R. and M. Pendlebury, *Public Sector Accounting* (London: Pitman Books, 1983).

Kline, R. and J. Mallaber, *Whose Value? Whose Money?* (Birmingham: Trade Union Resource Centre/Local Government Information Unit, 1986).

Kuhn, T. S., *The Structure of Scientific Revolutions*, 2nd ed., enlarged (Chicago University Press, 1970).

Landau, M. and R. Stout, 'To Manage Is Not to Control: or The Folly of Type II Errors', *Public Administration Review* (1979) pp. 148–56.

Likierman, A., 'Planning and Control – Development in Central Government', in A. Hopwood and C. Tomkins (eds), *Issues in Public Sector Accounting* (Oxford: Philip Allan, 1984).

Lindblom, C., 'The Science of Muddling Through', *Public Administration Review* (1959), pp. 79–88.

Loasby, B. J. , *Choice, Complexity and Ignorance*, (Cambridge University Press, 1976).

Long, A. F., 'Effectiveness: Definitions & Approaches' in A. F. Long and S. Harrison (eds), *Health Service Performance: Effectiveness and Efficiency*, (London: Croom Helm, 1985).

Lyotard, J., *The Postmodern Condition: A Report on Knowledge*, (Manchester University Press, 1986).

McSweeney, B., 'Accounting for the Audit Commission', *The Political Quarterly* (Spring, 1988), pp. 28–43.

McSweeney, B., 'The Rise of UK Public Sector Accounting', *World Accounting Report* (May 1983) p. 2.

McSweeney, B., 'Can Auditors Put a Price on Democracy?' *Guardian*, 25 April 1984, p. 17.

McSweeney, B., *Value for Money Audits: Some Defects in the Theory*, Chartered Association of Certified Accountants Discussion Paper (1985a).

McSweeney, B., 'Case Studies from the Public Field', *Certified Accountant* (September 1985b) pp. 24–25.

Majone, G. and A. Wildavsky, Appendix, in J. L. Pressman and A. Wildavsky (eds), *Implementation* (University of California Press, 1979, 2nd ed.).

March, J. G., 'The Technology of Foolishness', *Civilokonomen* (May 1971) pp. 7–12.

Markus, M. L. and J. Pfeffer, 'Power and the Design and Implementation of Accounting and Control Systems', *Accounting Organizations and Society* (1983) pp. 205–18.

Meyer, J. W., 'Social Environments and Organizational Accounting', *Accounting Organizations and Society* (1986) pp. 345–56.

Morgan, G., *Images of Organization* (Beverly Hills: Sage, 1986).

National Consumer Council, *Measuring Up: Consumer Assessment of Local Authority Services: A Guideline Study* (NCC, London, 1986).

Olson, J. P. and J. G. March, 'Organising Political Life: What Administrative Reorganisation Tells Us About Government', *American Political Science Review* (1983) pp. 281–95.

Otley, D. T. and A. J. Berry, 'Control, Organizations and Accounting', *Accounting Organizations and Society* (1980) pp. 231–46.

Pascale, R. T., 'Perspective on Strategy: The Real Story Behind Honda's Success', *California Management Review* (1984), pp. 155–70.

Pollitt, C., 'Beyond the Managerial Model: the Case for Broadening Performance Assessment in Government and the Public Services', *Financial Accountability and Management* (1986) pp. 155–70.

Popper, K. R., 'Normal Science and its Dangers', in I. Lakatos, and A. Musgrave (eds), *Criticism and the Growth of Knowledge* (Cambridge University Press, 1970).

Popper, K. R., *Objective Knowledge: An Evolutionary Approach*, Rev. ed. (Oxford University Press, 1979).

Prakash, P. and A. Rappaport, 'Information Inductance and Its Significance for Accounting', *Accounting Organizations and Society* (1977) pp. 29–38.

Pressman, J. L. and A. Wildavsky, *Implementation: How Great Expectations in Washington are Dashed in Oakland* (University of California Press, 1979).

Price Waterhouse, *Value for Money Auditing Manual* (London: Gee & Co, 1983).

Quade, E. S., 'Pitfalls in Formulation and Modelling', in G. Majone and E. S. Quade (eds), *Pitfalls of Analysis* (Chichester: John Wiley, 1980).

Quade, E. S., *Analysis for Public Decisions* (New York: North-Holland, 1982).

Ring, P. S. and J. L. Perry, 'Strategic Management in Public and Private

Organizations: Implications of Distinctive Contexts and Constraints',
Academy of Management Review (1985) pp. 276–86.

RIPA, *Management Information and Control in Whitehall* (London: Royal
Institute of Public Administration, 1983).

Sen, A., 'The Concepts of Efficiency', in M. Parkin and A. R. Nobay (eds),
Contemporary Issues in Economics (Manchester University Press, 1975).

Sherer, M. J., 'Current Cost Accounting as an Instrument of Government
Policy', *British Accounting Review* (Spring 1984) pp. 3–12.

Shortell, S. M., S. W. Becker, and D. Neuhauser, 'Effects of Management
Practices on Hospital Efficiency and Quality of Care', in S. M. Shortell
(ed.), *Organisational Research in Hospitals* (Chicago: Blue Cross Association, 1977).

Simon, H. A., *The New Science of Management Decision* (New York:
Harper & Row, 1960).

Smith, K. K., in P. S. Goodman, and Associates, *Change in Organizations*
(San Francisco: Jossey-Bass, 1982).

Thompson, J. D., *Organizations in Action* (New York: McGraw-Hill, 1967).

Thompson J. D. and Tuden, A., 'Strategies, Structure and Process in
Organisational Decisions', in J. D. Thompson et al. (eds), *Comparative
Studies in Administration* (University of Pittsburg Press, 1959).

Vuori, H. Y., *Quality Assurance of Health Services*: Concepts and Method-
ologies (Copenhagen: World Health Organisation, 1984).

Warner, W. K. and E. A. Havens, 'Goal Displacement and the Intangibility
of Organisational Goals', *Administrative Science Quarterly* (1968) pp.
539–55.

Weber, M., *General Economic History*, (New York: Collier Books, 1961).

Weick, K., *The Social Psychology of Organising*, 2nd ed. (Reading: Addison
Wesley, 1979).

Wildavsky, A., 'Policy Analysis Is What Information Systems Are Not',
Accounting Organizations and Society (1978) pp. 77–88.

Part IV
The Accounting Profession and Power

16 Serving the Public Interest? A Critical Analysis of a Professional Claim

Hugh C. Willmott[1]

In advanced capitalist societies, accounting plays an important role in the calculation, organisation and regulation of processes of production and exchange. In addition to supplying investors and creditors with data on corporate performance, technologies of accounting are used for purposes of taxation assessment and macro-economic planning (Burchell et al., 1980). Accounting is perceived to present information in a reliable and comparable form by quantifying and reporting the basic facts of economic life, thereby monitoring past performance and facilitating rational, efficient decision-making in respect of the generation and allocation of resources. In performing this role, accounting is widely understood to serve the public interest.

The view that accounting serves the public interest is not derived purely from its technical content. In the UK context, the self-regulation of accounting practice by professional bodies is founded upon a commitment to act independently of any sectional interests, including their own self-interest. Lord Benson, a most highly regarded and influential spokesman for the profession, and a former president of the English Institute, recently outlined 'the responsibilities of the profession to the public we serve'. With respect to independence, he has asserted:

> the members of the profession, whether in practice or employment must be independent in thought and outlook. They must be willing to speak their minds without fear or favour. They must not allow themselves to be put under the control and dominance of any person or organisation which could impair this independence.
>
> (Benson, 1984, p. 18)

Lord Benson alludes to the possibility that accountants may be influenced or even corrupted by those whose self-interest is affected by the contents of accounts, the most publicly visible target being the auditor of company accounts, who may lose repeat business or lucrative consultancy work if too exacting a scrutiny is imposed upon the client. In this light, the contribution and value of the professional accountant is said to reside in the training and discipline which underpins confidence in their ability to report the facts 'without fear or favour' (ibid.).

By formulating the issue of 'control and dominance' in this way, the question of whether accounting itself serves the public interest is excluded from consideration. In focusing attention upon the potential corruptability of the individual accountant, appreciation and discussion of the possible institutional loading or partiality of accounts is effectively silenced. Public perceptions of the failure of accounting to serve the public interest are thus limited to an examination of the regulation of practitioners (cf. Hoskin and Macve, 1986), thereby denying the relevance of any deeper, critical investigation of the claim that accounting practices serve the public interest.

A central objective of this paper is to stimulate reflection upon the neutrality of accounting practice and, in particular, the basis and plausibility of its claim to be independent in thought and outlook. In pursuing this objective, it is argued that the study of the 'behavioural aspects' of accounting must include, yet go beyond, a concern to reveal how the apparent precision and objectivity of accounting techniques and standards may be compromised in practice.

In common with a number of other recent critical commentaries found in this book and elsewhere (for instance, Burchell et al., 1980, 1985; Tinker, 1982, 1984, 1985; Tinker, Merino and Neimark, 1982; Merino and Neimark, 1982; Cooper and Sherer, 1984; Hopwood, 1984), the chapter seeks to illuminate the relationship between accounting practices, the self-regulation of accountants and the institutional contexts through which accounting has taken shape. The first section explores the meaning of the public interest, and suggests that its roots lie in political debates over alternative structures for organising human action. It concludes with a sketch of the relevance and contribution of critical analysis for examining the claim that the public interest is being served by, in this case, the accounting profession. The second section addresses the profession's conception of itself as a medium and outcome of inexorable human progress, as a prelude to examining how the profession's claim to serve the public interest is articulated. This claim is critically examined in the third section. There the independence of the profession is questioned by attending to the historical constitution of the structure of social and economic relations that accounting represents and reproduces. In exploring the connection betwen the practices of the profession and the structure of capitalist social and economic relations, the claim to represent the public interest is seen to rest upon a naturalisation of the status quo.

Overall, the chapter is premised upon the notion that, fundamentally, there are two ways of interrogating the profession's claim to serve the public interest (although there is plenty of room for diversity with these two perspectives). One approach assumes that capitalism provides an efficient, effective and free mechanism for generating and allocating resources and/or to argue that issues of politics are properly discussed and resolved outside of civil society, in the political sphere. From within this perspective, it is logical to contend that accounting serves the public interest simply by facilitating the smooth operation of the capitalist economy; and debate is readily confined to consideration of essentially *technical* questions about, for example, the appropriateness of particular practices and modes of regulation for maximising objectivity and minimising individual incompetence and corruption. The alternative is to be attentive to 'the contested nature of *the accounting problematic* and indeed the concept of what is or is not in the public interest' (Cooper and Sherer, 1984, p. 222). In which case, it becomes possible to explore the extent to which the existing structure of social and economic relations may be *institutionally loaded* in favour of the private interests of capital. In this light, accounting practice and regulation may be revealed as a medium as well as an outcome of the institutionalised control and dominance of these private interests – a dominance which is invisible as long as the neutrality of the status quo is naturalised. In promoting the second of these perspectives, the chapter is informed by the belief that an important and legitimate task for the academic, rather like that of the court jester, is to stimulate reflection and debate by scrutinising the authority of conventional wisdom (cf. O'Leary, 1985).

THE DISCOURSES OF 'THE PUBLIC INTEREST'

There is no universal agreement on the meaning or measure of 'the public interest' (Held, 1970, appendix). This absence of consensus has prompted some commentators (for instance, Schubert, 1960) to describe it as slippery, value-laden and vacuous, and to call for its rejection as an analytical concept. The chief limitation of this counsel of despair is that it refuses to confront the connection between the empirical-analytic problems surrounding the concept and the practico-moral problems that the concept has emerged to address. The fact that operationalising the concept of 'public interest' proves difficult, if not impossible, does not of itself provide a sufficiently strong rationale for its erasure from the analysis of politics. This is a point well made by Flathman (1966, p. 13) who observes that

> The much discussed difficulties with the concept are *difficulties with morals and politics*. We are free to abandon the *concept*, but if we do so we will simply have to wrestle with the *problems* under some other heading (first emphasis added).

The practical value and significance of the concept of 'public interest' resides precisely in its capacity to stimulate and articulate debate upon some of the most fundamental of political issues (cf. Connolly, 1974). It begs what is perhaps the most central question of politics: do the objectives, procedures and policies embodied in the structure and regulation of social and economic relations benefit the 'many'; or do they, in the name of the public interest, disproportionately advantage a minority of unnecessarily privileged individuals, members of powerful interest groups or a dominant class?

Answers to such questions depend upon the set of assumptions that guide political analysis. If it is believed that human beings are essentially self-interested, then the service of the public interest is equated with the development of a structure of relations that defends the right of the individual to pursue his or her material self-interest without unnecessary restriction. This structure then comes to be viewed as an expression of individual freedom and/or as a condition of the efficient production and allocation of scarce resources. As Held (1984, p. 354, emphasis added) has remarked of this discourse,

> The structure of the economy is regarded as non-political, such that the massive division between those that own and control the means of production, and those who must live by wage labour, is regarded as *the outcome of free private contracts*.

If, on the other hand, human nature is taken to be fundamentally open, and therefore historical and relational in constitution, it may be argued that the public interest is served only when 'the many' join together to determine and control the structures that shape their wants. This second perspective places in question the view that assumptions about human interests are 'free floating' ideas voluntarily accepted or rejected by individuals. This is because ideas are seen to be articulated and reinforced *within* asymmetrical relations of power and control (Henriques et al., 1984; Beechey and Donald, 1985).

Any blindness or insensitivity towards the construction and colouring of the reality of the public interest within particular structures of social relations, makes of the analyst of politics a mere apologist and legitimator of established interests (cf. Lindblom, 1982). Yet, whether any analysis can ever be wholly successful in steering a course between the Scylla of 'contamination' by commonsense reasoning, on the one hand, and the Charybdis of ensnarement in the illusion of objectivity is, of course, questionable. Critical analysis is inevitably a prisoner of the language and conventions of commonsense reasoning while, at the same time, seeking to be heard as something more than an idle opinion (O'Neill, 1975). More specifically, it relies upon the capacity of human beings to reflect upon their situation, and thereby to recognise that the world-taken-for-granted is not 'given' but, rather, a tapestry of conventions unstably bound together by relations of power. In this light, 'factual reporting' of these conventions is not objective, but highly partial – and doubly so if it does not register the power-invested relations that constitute and sustain their plausibility.

PUBLIC INTEREST IN PROFESSIONAL PRACTICE

There is little argument that the accounting profession is a product of particular historical circumstances in whose development it has played a not insignificant part (Worthington, 1895; Brown, 1905; Carey, 1969; Macdonald, 1984; Willmott, 1986). What is in doubt, however, is the character of the historical circumstances, the influence that accounting has had on their development and, in particular, the role of the profession as protector of the public interest.

That accounting is a product of historical circumstance is directly acknowledged by the profession:

it was the burgeoning of the industrial revolution that created the demand for accountants . . . The new works were much more labour-intensive than the craft workshops that preceded them and in many cases the investment needed was too large for an individual or small group. These new companies needed more sophisticated bookeeping and also since numbers of shareholders were involved, an independent audit'.

(ICAEW, 1980, p. 8)

In this history, the development of the profession is seen to emerge spontaneously from the growth in size of organisations – growth that is itself understood to be stimulated by advances in technology. Because firms grew in size, more sophisticated methods of internal accounting were needed; while, at the same time, the diffusion of share ownership required by the expansion of industry created a demand for an independent audit. In this light, accounting is characterised as a technically necessary agent of an inevitable progress from less efficient craft production, to more efficient, machine-based technologies.

Conspicuously absent from such a history is any consideration of the social relations of production through which change is accomplished (Braverman, 1974; Hopwood, 1984; Tinker, 1985) – a point to which I shall return. There is no recognition of a struggle between competing classes or groups over the historical development of accounting practice. Any awareness that history might take shape through a process of conflict and bargaining is displaced by the assumption that impersonal, universally beneficial forces dictate the course of social development; that dominant groups are merely the agents of inevitability; and that resistance to their destiny is selfish and irrational because it is contrary to the collective interest in human advancement.[2]

In this account of the formation and growth of accounting practice, the very depth of involvement of the profession in the institutions of modern society is itself taken as evidence of its service of the public interest, evidence that is confirmed within the constitutions of the major professional associations representing accountants in the UK. For example, when successfully petitioning for a Supplemental Charter to the one originally granted in 1880, the 1948 proposal of the English Institute is couched in terms of its relevance for serving the public interest:

the furtherance of the objects for which the Institute was originally constituted and incorporated has become increasingly desirable in the public interest . . . the furtherance of the aforesaid objects would be facilitated and the public interest served if certain limits upon the operations of the Institute were extended and further powers and privileges granted to the Institute.

(ICAEW)

Through the granting of a Royal Charter, an official seal of approval at the very highest level of the British state is conferred upon occupational associations. As Chartered Associations,[3] the six major accountancy bodies are each bound by the terms of their charters to exclude from their purposes all selfish objects (Millerson, 1964). The obligation to serve the public interest is also written into the terms of reference of subcommittees of the Coordinating Committee of Accountancy Bodies (CCAB). So, for example, the members of the Accounting Standards Committee are required not to regard themselves as 'representing sectional interests' but to be 'guided by the need to act in the general interest of the community and the accountancy profession as a whole' (ICAEW, 1979, p. 15). In a similar vein, when responding to those who have suggested that the professional ethos is 'for the benefit of members of the professions at the expense of the public' a senior member of the accounting profession has retorted recently that

It is strange that this situation has come about since most of the major professions are incorporated by Royal Charters and are obliged under the terms of those Charters to operate in the public interest.

(Sharpe, 1984, p. 3)

From this perspective, the means of serving the public interest are defined in terms of the application of impartial principles through the exercise of independent judgement on the part of the professional person. This is an argument powerfully made by Stamp (1979, p. vi) who appeals to members' shared interest in defending their autonomy:

Selfishness, self-interest, and a lack of genuine professionalism, are the root causes of many of the things that are wrong with the profession today . . . If profound changes are indeed necessary to preserve the independence of our profession then let us hasten to make them. Because one thing is certain. Once we lose our freedom from government interference and control we shall never recover it. It will be too late then to realise how precious is the freedom and independence of the true professional man.

As Stamp (1969) argues elsewhere, he believes that the public interest as well as the standing of the profession is best protected by safeguarding its members' independence. However, in common with the vast majority of other commentators of the accounting profession and the public interest (for instance, Tricker, 1983, p. 64, p. 145), Stamp offers little illumination of what he takes to be 'in the public interest'. Instead, it is simply assumed and asserted that the public interest will be served by a profession capable of voluntarily and impartially generating, applying and enforcing reliable principles and standards. Or, to be more precise, it is assumed that accountants safeguard the public interest by dispassionately providing users of accounting information with the quality and reliability of service required to maintain 'the stability of our economic system' (Stamp, 1979, p. 3; cf. Stamp, 1969, p. 32).

PRIVATE INTEREST IN PROFESSIONAL PRACTICE

When examining alternative methods for ensuring a reliable and economical supply of accounting information, the leadership of the accounting profession has shown little enthusiasm for any proposal that removes or dilutes its formal control over accounting practice. So, on the one side, the 'efficient markets' approach to accounting regulation is rejected on the grounds that it cannot be depended upon to supply the quality and quantity of information necessary for reliable decision-making. And, on the other side, spokesmen of the profession have argued that regulation by Parliament is not wanted by the preparers and users of accounting information; and that, in any case, it would overload government with a task that is better left in the hands of the experts.

Arguably, what such defences of 'self-regulation' reflect, yet conceal, is the dependence of the standing and privileges of the profession upon maintaining the *idea* that it serves the public interest. Confirmation of this contention is offered, quite inadvertently, by Watts (1983, p. 15) in a revealing section of a lecture on the role of the Accounting Standards Committee. Having first asserted that accounting standards 'have to be generally acceptable', he then adds that 'there must be *at least* broad general acceptance *by the business community*' (emphasis added). Why is this necessary? Watts explains: 'otherwise standards will not be observed to a satisfactory degree and the system will break down' (ibid.). Thus, 'general acceptance' would seem to be a euphemism for 'found to be agreeable to business interests'. Because business interests are unproblematically equated with national interests, the form and content of accounting and auditing is regarded as nonpartisan or apolitical.

In enabling private and corporate investors to make 'rational choices in allocating their necessarily limited investment resources' (Stamp, 1980, p. 33), it is understood that accounting necessarily acts in the public interest – with the proviso, of course, that it is safeguarded by the independent, professional ethos of accountants (cf. Briloff, 1986). Thus, with specific reference to accountants' service of information to private investors, Stamp (1980, p. 34) takes it for granted that

> it is in the general economic interest that their needs should be properly looked after if the primary and secondary security markets are to function effectively. The efficient operation of these markets is in the national interest since they are so important in the continuing health and strength of the operations of the private sector of the economy.

The principle of private ownership, combined with the 'free' and reliably-informed operation of markets, are here assumed to provide *the* unquestionably rational means of securing 'the general economic interest'. It is taken as self-evident that the only condition for achieving the public interest is that the markets be allowed to work effectively by providing private, individual decision-makers with a supply of reliable and comparable information, an understanding that has been echoed in a forthright manner by a past enforcement director of the US Securities and Exchange Commission. In answer to the rhetorical question 'Do we (i.e. the SEC) have any special responsibility for the public interest?', he observed how 'At the SEC, by Charter, we only had the one interest, which was namely the interest of investors' (Sporkin, 1984, p. 114). And then, revealingly, he continues,

> But, when you really look to the interests of investors, I would

dare say there are very few other constituents that would not be similarly protected. Even the company and its directors are protected if they abide by the rules because they will not be sued or thrown into jail.

The accounting profession has generally accepted and elaborated this line of argument. Accordingly, debates over accounting and the public interest have, at best, been confined to arguments over the appropriate balance of control between the profession, the state and (other) users of accounting information (Willmott, 1985). Excluded from such debate is any sustained reflection upon the more critical and fundamental issue of whether the prevailing economic system, and accounting's role within it, is itself 'in the public interest'. The accounting profession has thereby contrived to fulfil its espoused commitment to the public interest by assuming and upholding the legitimacy of the private interests of investors and business.

ACCOUNTING AS INTERESTED PRACTICE

It has been noted that the profession's definition and defence of its service of the public interest is underpinned by the assumption that the prevailing structure of social relations embody, albeit imperfectly, a universal, public interest. By attending to social and economic relations from this perspective, the presence of any real or potential conflicts of interest, or structural contradictions, within society are effectively defined out of existence (Hines, 1988). Or, as Hopwood (1985, p. 11) puts it,

> By appealing to an abstract, organisationally detached, technical essence of accounting, conventional discourses endow their subject with a metaphysical existence that is difficult to ground in or relate to the specifics of the organisational and social functioning of the craft.

Only when the social and organisational grounds of accounting are remembered is accounting shown to be shaped by the contexts that it seeks to report. Seemingly authoritative accounts of these contexts are then seen to reflect highly selective or partial methods of disclosing, representing and interpreting the world of its accounts. A similar argument is made by Lindblom (1984, p. 25) who, in commenting upon the inadequacy of public regulations over the operation of business activity, has observed that 'the tradition of proprietor privacy and of trade secrets has militated against disclosure of the information that we need for regulation'.

However, despite the reference to 'proprietor privacy', Lindblom appears to believe that the need for regulation can be satisfied within the context of capitalist societies – for example, by requiring business enterprises to reveal information that has relevance for the welfare of the community, such as indicating and controlling its impact upon the environment, or monitoring its noneconomic contributions to the community. Absent from his analysis, however, is any deep appreciation of the *structural* divisions and contradictions of advanced capitalist society that systematically invite and impede such reform. The idealism of Lindblom's radical liberal perspective prevents him from recognising how resistance to disclosure is not simply the outcome of a secretive, competitive 'tradition' but is central to the preservation of asymmetrical relations of power and control.

The selectivity of accounting and its service of particular 'interests' has been highlighted by Tinker (1980, 1982, 1984, 1985; Tinker, Merino and Neimark, 1982). A distinguishing feature of this analysis is its focus upon the historically distinctive structures of social relations wherein accounting is constituted and practised. The understanding that interests are defined and organised within these structures is central to the argument of this chapter.

> Social systems, such as slavery, feudalism, mercantilism and capitalism differ in terms of the . . . social categories to which individuals are assigned. Master and slave, feudal lord and serf, and labourer and capitalist, are different social structures reflecting different relations of power, rights, obligations, beliefs, inequality, customs, traditions, modes of conflict and exploitation . . . They shape the character of emerging interest groups and structure the form of social conflict that ensues.
>
> (Tinker, 1984a, p. 66)

From this standpoint, the accounting profession is seen to play an historically reactionary role in the defence of capitalism, as it accepts and legitimises the equation of the private interests of investors or 'business' with the interests of the public. Accounting is shaped above all by a systematic tendency to privilege the interests of capital relative to labour (cf. Johnson, 1980, 1982). Instead of advancing forms of practice that serve to expose the limitations and contradictions of the capitalist structure of social and economic relations (cf. Cooper and Sherer, 1984), the profession is seen to promote and exploit the understanding that professionalism ensures an objective, independent representation of the economic facts of life.

However, while it may be accepted that, above all, it is the political economy of capitalism that shapes accounting practice, there is a danger of relying too heavily upon such one-dimensional explanations when it comes to appreciating the complexity of accounting practice and regulation. For even if it is agreed that accounting is broadly *compatible* with the requirements of capital, it is necessary to appreciate that those involved in developing accounting practice and regulation are not blessed with perfect knowledge of how to act in its 'interests'. On the contrary, their practices are frequently structured by concerns and priorities that bear only a tenuous relationship to what might, rationally and abstractly, be calculated to be in capital's best interests. Accounting *is* valued because it serves to discipline, lubricate and dissemble the contradictory and conflict-ridden structures of the capitalist system. But this 'function' is largely an unanticipated consequence of the loosely coordinated, historically-conditioned efforts of individuals and groups (such as accountants) who seek to define, secure and advance their interests within capitalist structures of power and control, whose historical identity they both shape and reproduce (cf. Burchell et al., 1985).

CONCLUSION

A central theme of this chapter has been that accounting practice and regulation is forged within distinctive historical contexts whose features accounting itself shapes, solidifies and reconstitutes (Hines, 1988). In scrutinising the claim that the profession serves the public interest, it has been suggested that the apparent neutrality of accounting is underpinned by a prior naturalisation of the value and rationality of capitalism as a provider and allocator of wealth. In this light, it is seen that

> Not only is accounting policy essentially political in that it derives from the political struggle in society as a whole but also the outcomes of accounting policy are essentially political in that they operate for some groups in society and to the detriment of others.
> (Cooper and Sherer, 1984, p. 208)

To date, the insulation of the UK accountancy profession from sustained public criticism and enquiry has been remarkable. Conceivably, this is because accounting and accountants have acted in ways that are unequivocally 'in the public interest'. Alternatively, it may be that the technical and conservative image of the profession, combined with the slightness of public accountability for their actions, have served to disarm or suspend the critical faculties of clients, politicians and academics alike (Sikka, Willmott and Lowe, 1988). As Schmitter (1985, p. 43) has observed of other 'private interest governments', much of their power depends upon 'invisibility and ignorance'. He continues: 'If their processes and consequences were better known and rendered accountable to the wider public, their legitimacy would, no doubt, suffer'.

Not that the accounting profession should be made a scapegoat for the distortion and frustration of public interests that is built into the political economy of capitalism. As sellers of intellectual labour, accountants have struggled to create and expand a privileged niche for their services (Willmott et al., 1988). This they have done by responding to, and exploiting the demand for, techniques and services that are valued by fractions of capital and/or agents of the state in the mediation, regulation and legitimation of the contradictions within and between the formally separated economic and political spheres of society. Rewarded by their compliance with, and advocacy of, ideologies which naturalise the status quo, they are disinclined to suspend belief in the notion that 'the institutional context and other aspects of the prevailing social order' are 'ineluctable and immutable' (Tinker, 1982, p. 31). Paradoxically, it is this unacknowledged investment in the status quo which enables accounting to appear as an independent observer and monitor of the political economy in which it moves, and from which it draws its rationale and privileges. For this reason, it has been argued, the profession's powers of surveillance are focused upon the potential incompetence or corruptability of *individual* accountants, and not upon the historical and *institutional conditioning* of the scope and effects of accounting practice.

Finally, if it is accepted that an important role of the academic is to enrich and extend public debate, this must include scrutiny of the claims of powerful groups, including the professions. A primary objective of such research is to deconstruct the authority of accounting in order to facilitate alternative contexts of accounting in which existing means of producing and allocating scarce and valued resources are superceded by more democratic, publicly accountable forms of practice.

Notes

1. I would like to thank members of the Accounting Regulation Study, especially David Cooper, and members of the Public Interest Section of the American Accounting Association, in particular Marilyn Neimark, for their support and stimulation.
2. On this account, it is not necessary to deny that some groups (for example, accountants) are more advantaged by existing structures and institutions than are other groups. Nor is it denied that progress may be painful, and that there is always room for further improvement. However, inequalities are understood to be functionally necessary for progress and improvement to be made. Likewise, it is anticipated that those deficiencies in the status quo which are not attributable to the shortcomings of human nature or the complexity and flux of modern living are remediable in due course.
3. In the UK, Associations are formed by depositing a 'Memorandum of Association' with the Register of Companies. In this memorandum are set out the aims of the association and its structure, together with an indication of how its objectives are to be fulfilled. Once established, professional associations of accountants have sought to enhance their status and authority by petitioning the Queen, through the Privy Council, to obtain a Royal Charter. An *ad hoc* committee of Privy Councillors, comprising the Establishment 'great and good' is then formed to investigate the proposal. At this time, there may be counter- and cross-petitioning from existing Chartered bodies seeking to resist an application. After due consultation with other influential parties (e.g. relevant departments of state), the petition is either rejected (without explanation or right of appeal), or associations are invited to submit a draft Charter which, after further consultations may eventually be accepted (Millerson, 1964; Willmott, 1985).

Bibliography

Beechey, V. and J. Donald, *Subjectivity and Social Relations* (Milton Keynes: Open University Press, 1985).

Benson, Lord, 'The Nine Obligations of the Chartered Accountant' in Institute of Chartered Accountants in England and Wales, *Proceedings of the Conference on the Accountancy Profession and the Public Interest* (London: ICAEW, 1984).

Braverman, H., *Labor and Monopoly Capital* (New York: Monthly Review Press, 1974).

Briloff, A. J., 'Accountancy and the Public Interest', *Advances in Public Interest Accounting* (1986) pp. 1–14.

Brown, R., *A History of Accounting and Accountants* (Edinburgh: Blackwood, 1905).

Burchell, S., C. Clubb, A. Hopwood, J. Hughes, and J. Nahapiet, 'The Roles of Accounting in Organisations and Society', *Accounting, Organizations and Society* (1980) pp. 5–27.

Burchell, S., C. Clubb and A. Hopwood, 'Accounting in its Social Context:

Towards a History of Value Added in the United Kingdom', *Accounting, Organizations and Society* (1985) pp. 381–413.

Carey, J. L., *The Rise of the Accounting Profession* (New York: American Institute of Certified Public Accountants, 1969).

Connolly, W. E., *The Terms of Political Discourse* (London: D. C. Heath, 1974).

Cooper, D., 'Discussion of Towards a Political Economy of Accounting', *Accounting, Organizations and Society* (1984) pp. 161–6.

Cooper, D. J. and M. J. Sherer, 'The Value of Corporate Accounting Reports: Arguments for a Political Economy of Accounting', *Accounting Organizations and Society* (1984) pp. 207–32.

Flathman, R. E., *The Public Interest; An Essay Concerning the Normative Discourse of Politics* (New York: John Wiley & Sons, 1966).

Held, V., *The Public Interest and Individual Interests* (New York: Basic Books, 1970).

Held, D., 'Power and Legitimacy in Contemporary Britain' in G. McLennan, D. Held and S. Hall (eds), *State and Society in Contemporary Britain* (Cambridge: Polity, 1984).

Henriques, J., W. Hollway, C. Urwin, C. Venn and V. Walkerdine, *Changing the Subject* (London: Methuen, 1984).

Hines, R., 'Financial Accounting: In Communicating Reality, We Construct Reality', *Accounting, Organizations and Society* (1988) pp. 251–61.

Hopwood, A. G., 'Accounting Research and Accounting Practice: The Ambiguous Relationship Between the Two', New Challenges for Management Research Conference, Leuven, Belgium, May 1984.

Hopwood, A. G., 'Accounting and the Pursuit of Social Interests', mimeo, London Business School, 1985.

Hopwood, A. G., 'The Archaeology of Accounting Systems', *Accounting Organizations and Society*, forthcoming.

Hoskin, K. W. and R. H. Macve, 'Accounting and the Examination: A Genealogy of Disciplinary Power', *Accounting, Organizations and Society* (1986) pp. 105–36.

Institute of Chartered Accountants in England and Wales, *The Making of a Profession* (London: Penshurst Press, 1980).

Johnson, T., 'Work and Power', in G. Esland and G. Salaman (eds), *The Politics of Work and Occupations* (Milton Keynes: Open University Press, 1980).

Johnson, T., 'The State and the Professions: Peculiarities of the British' in A. Giddens and G. Mackenzie (eds), *Social Class and the Division of Labour*, (Cambridge University Press, 1982).

Knights, D. and H. C. Willmott, 'Power and Identity in Theory and Practice' *Sociological Review* (1985) pp. 22–46.

Lindblom, C., 'Another State of Mind', *American Political Science Review* (1982) pp. 9–21.

Lindblom, C., 'The Accountability of Private Enterprise: Private – No. Enterprise – Yes', in A. M. Tinker (ed.), *Social Accounting for Corporations* (Manchester University Press, 1984).

Macdonald, K. M., 'Professional Formation: the Case of Scottish Accountants', *British Journal of Sociology* (1984) pp. 174–89.

Merino, B. and M. Neimark, 'Disclosure Regulation and Public Policy: A Socio-historical Reappraisal', *Journal of Accounting and Public Policy* (1982) pp. 33–58.

Millerson, G., *The Qualifying Associations: A Study in Professionalization* (London: Routledge and Kegan Paul, 1964).

O'Leary, T., 'Observations on Corporate Financial Reporting in the Name of Politics', *Accounting, Organisations and Society* (1985) pp. 87–102.

O'Neill, J., *Making Sense Together* (London: Heinemann, 1975).

Schmitter, P. C., 'Neo-Corporatism and the State', in W. Grant (ed.), *The Political Economy of Corporatism* (London: Macmillan, 1985).

Schubert, G., *The Public Interest*, (Glencoe, Ill.: Free Press, 1960).

Sharpe, K., 'Introduction and Conference Aim', in Institute of Chartered Accountants in England and Wales, *Proceedings of the Conference of the Accountancy Profession and the Public Interest* (London: ICAEW, 1984).

Sikka, P., Willmott, H. C. and Lowe, E. A., 'Guardians of Knowledge and the Public Interest: Evidence and Issues of Accountability in the UK Accountancy Profession, *Accounting, Auditing and Accountability Journal*, forthcoming.

Sporkin, S., 'Introduction to a Discussion of Sporkin's Accounting and Realism', in A. M. Tinker (eds), *Social Accounting for Corporations* (Manchester University Press, 1984).

Stamp, E., 'The Public Accountant and the Public Interest', *Journal of Business Finance* (1969) pp. 32–42.

Stamp, E., 'The Future of Accounting and Auditing Standards', International Centre for Research in Accounting, University of Lancaster, Occasional Paper no. 18, 1979.

Stamp, E., *Corporate Reporting: Its Future Evolution*, Canadian Institute of Chartered Accountants, 1980.

Tinker, A. M., 'Towards a Political Economy of Accounting', *Accounting, Organizations and Society* (1980) pp. 147–60.

Tinker, A. M., 'The Naturalization of Accounting: Social Ideology and the Genesis of Agency Theory', Working Paper #67, New York University, Faculty of Business Administration, 1982.

Tinker, A. M., 'Theories of the State and the State of Accounting: Economic Reductionism and Political Voluntarism in Accounting Regulation Theory', *Journal of Accounting and Public Policy* (1984a) pp. 55–74.

Tinker, A. M., 'Accounting for Unequal Exchange: Wealth Accummulation versus Wealth Appropriation', in A. M. Tinker, (ed.), *Social Accounting for Corporations: Private Enterprise v. The Public Interest* (Manchester University Press, 1984b).

Tinker, A. M., *Paper Prophets* (New York: Praeger, 1985).

Tinker, A. M., B. D. Merino, and M. Neimark, 'The Normative Origins of Accounting Theories: Ideology and Accounting Thought', *Accounting, Organizations and Society* (1982) pp. 167–200.

Tricker, R. I., *Governing the Institute* (London: The Institute of Chartered Accountants in England and Wales, 1983).

Watts, T., 'The Role of the Accounting Standards Comittee', Deloitte, Haskins and Sells Lecture, University College Cardiff, 1983.

Willmott, H. C., 'Setting Accounting Standards in the UK: The Emergence of Private Accounting Bodies and their Role in the Regulation of Public Accounting Practice', in W. Streeck and P. C. Schmitter, *Private Interest Government* (London: Sage, 1985).

Willmott, H. C., 'Organising the Profession: A Theoretical and Empirical Examination of the Development of the Major Accountancy Bodies in the UK', *Accounting, Organizations and Society* (1986).

Willmott, H. C., D. J. Cooper, A. G. Puxty, K. Robson and E. A. Lowe, 'Organising Professional Labour: The Case of Accountancy in the UK', mimeo, Manchester School of Management, UMIST, 1989.

Worthington, B., *Professional Accountants: An Historical Sketch* (London: Gee, 1895).

17 The Accountancy Profession in the Class Structure

Anthony G. Puxty[1]

The framework of research into the social context of the accountancy profession has in the past been socially functionalist (Montagna, 1974; Groves et al., 1984), frequently with implications of political pluralism (Hope, 1979; Hope and Gray, 1982; Benston, 1985; Zeff, 1978). Since such research has been concerned with the profession in society, due consideration of the theory of the professions should be had: yet until recently no regard has been had to the multiplicity of theories of the professions that have been developed in sociology and economics (recent works repairing this omission include Willmott, 1984, 1985; Cooper, chapter 18; Loft, 1985; Armstrong, 1987; Macdonald, 1984; Cooper et al., 1989). This paper argues that to understand the relationship of accountancy to society it is necessary to understand the position of the accountancy profession in the class structure.

Stinchcombe has remarked that sociology 'has only one independent variable – class'.[2] Now much scholarship has been invested in the nature of social class. It has been central to the work of Marx and Weber, and consideration of its nature has been more recently the subject of major work by, among others, Dahrendorf (1959), Aron (1964), Ossowski (1963), Poulantzas (1975), Giddens (1973) and Wright (1985). These authors differ from each other in many basic respects, but common to most is the recognition that society is constituted by several classes, that the nature of these classes is such as to set them in conflict with each other, and that the most fundamental of these classes are the working class, or proletariat, and the capitalist class, or bourgeoisie. Despite much criticism of Marx's original formulation[3] most writers accept that these two classes exist and are in opposition.[4]

The sociology of the professions has been heterogeneous in its interpretation of the class nature of the professions. Moreover, while

332

some have argued that the professions are members of, or allied to, one of these principal classes, others have taken the professions to be linked to, and to have a function similar to, the State, itself a social institution that has been taken to link itself in various ways to the class structure.

This paper examines existing theories of the professions, and proposes an alternative theory. This is applied to accountancy specifically, and illustrated by a particular development in accounting thought and practice, the rise of decision-usefulness as a criterion for financial statements. This development is analysed historically, and then used to enrich the theory of the professions proposed.

THE CLASS LOCATION OF THE PROFESSIONS

Some writers have taken professions to either be in potential alliance with labour or to constitute part of labour. It has been suggested, for instance, that 'elements of the professional middle class like scientists and physicians (may) form part of a diverse group with interests objectively opposed to the bourgeoisie' (Saks, 1983, p. 11, on Baran). Although supported by the economic surplus formed in capitalist society, they are not *per se* linked to the interests of capital, and would persist in alternative social formations. Others focus on the deskilling of occupations (Braverman, 1974) which include professions, as part of the continued fractionalisation of the labour force carried out by the interests of capital as part of the technological imperative of the developing forces of production.

For our present purposes neither of these is persuasive or helpful: insofar as there is a feature of the professions that is exploited or the object of power structures, it may be subsumed under Wright's notion of a contradictory location.[5] Hence in the main, for the remainder of this paper, we shall focus on the profession's relation to capital, the fractions of capital, and the State, although in doing so we cannot omit its functions in relation to capital and State that themselves are in contradiction to the interests of labour.

A second possibility is that the professions are agents of the state apparatus that perform two tasks which serve capital by aiding the repression of the masses: ideological inculcation on the one hand, and the reproduction of class relations on the other (Ehrenreich and Ehrenreich, 1977; Navarro, 1976, 1978). In this view, although professional workers are not recipients of surplus value themselves, they are in a contradictory role to the working class proper, since the functions they perform is in opposition to the interests of the working class.

To claim that professions are the agents of capital requires a specification of the linkages. Now certainly there is a common educational background and other links such as common clubs and job exchanges (Miliband, 1969, 1983) among members of the professions, senior management of industry and finance, and government service. For many professions there is direct employment at the top of large organisations: for example the in-house corporate legal advisor, chief engineer, financial director and so on. Yet to view professions unequivocally in this way is untenable. It is overdeterministic; it does not discriminate between different professions (do they all necessarily relate in just the same way?). It says nothing about the way the state articulates to society, that is, to the forces and relations of production.

Cain, based on her empirical study of sectors of the legal profession, suggests that conceptualising the professions as undertaking 'social control' can be misleading. She contends that 'controlling is not what British solicitors – even those at the bottom end of the market – spend most of their time doing' (Cain, 1983, p. 111) since 'in sixty-seven of the eighty-two cases which I observed . . . the client announced his need and set the objective for the solicitor' whereas 'the specific practice of lawyers which was identified was that of translating' by which she refers to the translation from lay to legal terms of the problem. She argues instead that 'lawyers are *conceptive ideologists* . . . who think, and therefore constitute the form of, the emergent relations of capitalist society' (ibid., pp. 111–12, emphasis in the original). There are tasks for such agencies other than repression, one of which is 'that of formulating and constituting new forms of relation appropriate to this expanding reproduction'. She names accountants in her list of conceptive ideologists.

Cain, then, differentiates the professions. An alternative approach to differentiation of professions and their roles is taken by Johnson (1977), who is interested in the internal differentiation within professions. He employs Carchedi's (1975) analysis which provides 'a theoretical basis for the identification of the new middle class in terms of their production relations rather than their distributive characteristics' (Johnson, ibid., p. 101). This distinguishes the labour process from the surplus-value-producing process, and enables Johnson to see parts of the professions as working class, where their work is routinised, and parts as intrinsic to the global functions of capital which 'are dispersed to agents who are not themselves owners of the means of production' (p. 103).

Other writers have specifically linked the professions to the state (Johnson, 1982; Fielding and Portwood, 1980; Larson, 1977). This relation is undeveloped, since the conception of the State has not been explicitly tackled within this literature. Theories of the state have however been extensively reviewed by Jessop (1982), and some have been analysed in an accounting context by Tinker (1984). We take this to be a particularly promising approach: and the theory of the state to be employed here will rely particularly on the approach proposed by Offe and Habermas. Because the particular nature of the state theory is important to the subsequent argument, it will be presented in some detail.

The Basic Thesis: The Functions of the State in Late Capitalism

Three aspects of most Marxist theory are rejected from the first (Offe and Ronge, 1982): that the state is an instrument of the ruling class, that it is merged with the interests of monopolies, and that its actions can only be understood in negative terms, that is, as supportive of the ruling class against the masses. Instead it is proposed that

> the state does not patronise certain interests, and is not allied with certain classes. Rather, what the state protects and sanctions is a set of rules and social relationships which are presupposed by the class rule of the capitalist class. The state does not defend the interests of one class, but the common interest of all members of a capitalist class society.
>
> (pp. 249–50)

Such a notion of common interest has been continually disavowed by Marxists. Yet certain actions can be in the interests of labour as well as capital: for example, trade barriers can protect jobs as well as profits.[6] The state is dependent on the capital accumulation process for its own existence, being funded by taxes. It is thus in the state's interest to support that mode of production which it sees as being most likely to continue to provide those funds. This is why the capitalist mode of production (CMP) is promoted: not because of an alliance between the state and capital, but because it is in the interest of the state itself. This state of affairs creates contradictions at three different levels: the economic, the political and the ideological.

In economic terms, taxation is necessary to support the state apparatus and to take regulatory actions: yet this takes away the freedom of the individual capitalist to use his or her funds as he or she thinks best: to sustain the free-enterprise system this freedom must to some extent be removed. A second contradiction is the political, because to support the commodity form of production it is necessary to expand the state sector, which is not the commodity form: state support at the same time supports and restricts it. A third contradiction is the ideological, since for the commodity form to work an ideology must be propagated of possessive individualism – yet the state is obliged to intervene and subvert this in the 'common interest'.

All of these contradictions are sources of tension. The tension is managed by state regulatory action in order to avoid crisis. Habermas (1976, pp. 48–50) defines four types of crisis (economic, rationality, motivation and legitimation crises). He defines a crisis in these terms:

> In classical aesthetics, from Aristotle to Hegel, crisis signifies the turning point in a fateful process that, despite all objectivity, does not simply impose itself from outside and does not remain external to the identity of the persons caught up in it. The contradiction, expressed in the catastrophic culmination of conflict, is inherent in the structure of the action system and in the personality systems of the principal characters . . . Crises in social systems are not produced through accidental changes in the environment, but through structurally inherent system-imperatives that are incompatible and cannot be hierarchically integrated.
>
> (1976, p. 2)

Crisis Management

Two concepts of crisis will be considered. The first is the economic. Given the instability of capitalism, it is necessary for the state to intervene to prevent the system entering a crisis stage, through adjustment of taxes, of money supply, changing interest rates, and so on. The intervention takes place to continue the long-term viability of the CMP from which the state gains its revenues. Arguments such as this have now gone beyond the boundaries of neo-Marxism, and have more recently been employed by the conservative historian Keith Middlemass (1979) who has depicted almost the whole of twentieth-century British history as being one of crisis avoidance.

A second type of crisis is legitimation crisis (Habermas, 1971, 1976, 1979). Without state intervention, the workings of the market are seen as the workings of fate, which cannot be altered. However, as the state does become involved, for reasons outlined above, this changes, and such things are demystified. Not only is the state seen to take actions: the state actions are more visible then the invisible hand previously. As state intervention becomes institutionalised and expected, it also becomes expected that the state can achieve more and more. Increasingly, more areas of life are seen as political and subject to choice. This leads to more demands upon the state, which then needs to fulfil these demands to avoid a crisis of legitimation. This basic mechanism is based on class contradictions because the underlying reason for the problem is the contradiction of capitalism. The system, which is fundamentally zero-sum in terms of class interests, must be supported by the state while at the same time seeking to hide the fact that its actions bolster the interests of that class.

Now distinguishing between conceptions of the professions as 'part of' the State and as 'captured by' it, seems on the face of it important yet problematic: for, insofar as the state is concerned with regulation of some kind over the capitalist production process, the professions tend to be drawn in. Examples have already been given of ways in which such regulation occurs. Yet given that the state itself is not monolithic, and different interest and power struggles may take place within it, then the problem of whether to conceptualise professions as part of, or as captured by (in the corporatist mode) the state loses urgency. This means that we might envisage the state function of the professions, insofar as its exists, to be one of either being relatively independent actors seeking to bolster the interests of capital, perhaps by unifying fractions of capital (or fractionalising labour) or as an autonomous set of institutions which act on their own behalf to smooth crises which arise from capitalist economic phenomena or the legitimation crises which arise from the contradictions of the spread of state action in a world of atomistic liberal ideology.

Toward a Theory of the Professions

On the basis of the above discussion we reject invariant typologies, and developing the ideas sown by Cain and Johnson we propose a more organic alternative: that the professions, or parts of the professions, will take on characteristics of each of these aspects of society, depending upon the situation in which they are placed. In the case of accountancy, for example, the supervisor changes from bolstering capital to forming part of labour, and the senior partner may sit on the Accounting Standards Committee, thus switching from capital to State and back again. We may also find that certain parts of the professions favour different fractions of capital with, for instance, small practitioners favouring non-monopoly productive capital, while large firm partners favour either finance capital or international monopoly capital.

The circumstances faced by a profession will have different characteristics at different times. Different organisations, institutions, and so on, will affect the profession at different times. In addition the underlying fabric of society, which may include values, ideology, attitudes, and other such variables, will also change. All of this is the temporal aspect. Similarly, the significance of these different environmental interests will change over time. Some will be important to the profession at one point in time, but will recede in importance later: and at one point in time, some will be more salient than others. This is the spatial aspect. Thus the circumstances facing the profession may be more rigorously and technically defined in terms of the structures which are defined by these two aspects, and we propose the term 'temporal-spatial structural matrix' (TSSM) to define these circumstances.

A second term is required to define the feature of the profession under discussion. We are concerned with the way in which a profession, or a part of a profession, may be understood as relating to interests in society, depending upon the TSSM. It is cumbersome to refer constantly to the fact that what might be involved could be the whole profession or only one part or aspect of it. A term is needed which encompasses both this and the fact that the feature involved must be seen in its context. This will be referred to the 'objective professional function' (OPF).

The definition given earlier can now be refined for professions in general: The objective professional function will be contingent upon the nature of the temporal-spatial structural matrix of society.

A term such as 'contingency theory' has been proposed in the past in organisation theory to suggest an objective change in an organisation's circumstances depending upon the environmental, or other independent circumstances. The latter is the independent variable, the former the dependent variable, and each is a straightforward measurable feature. This is not what is being proposed here. Although in the main the TSSM is an independent variable at a point in time, the state it has reached may well be the result of previous TSSM-OPF relationships, and to treat it as fully independent would be a distortion. The OPF should not be understood as the 'state' of the profession at a point in time. It refers instead to the way that professional features might best be understood in relation to the TSSM. The 'objective' in the nomenclature does not refer to measurability or independence, but to the fact that the theoretical framework involves aspects of materialism and the OPF is not in itself a subjective construction of the observer only.

Sole, Joint and Conflictual Aspects of the OPF

Observation of a particular OPF in the context of a given TSSM will lead to one of three results which are mutually exclusive and exhaustive:

(1) there may be a sole OPF relating to the TSSM. For example, consider the labour process. The TSSM is defined in terms of current work technology; belief structures of management concerning the optimal structuring of jobs; current types of work which have to be carried out by the profession, and the current ideology of the workforce of audit clerks. The OPF is a matter of labour only, and has no aspect of the state or capital.

(2) there may be more than one OPF given a particular TSSM which are in harmony with each other. Consider the audit function. This is in global capital's interest because it legitimates the capitalist system. Since the state also desires the continuation of that system, the audit function is an OPF which is jointly in harmony in terms of the TSSMs of state and capital.

(3) there may be more than one OPF, given a particular TSSM, which is in conflict with another. An example is the accounting standard referring to depreciation. The state and global capital support it (for reasons of legitimation); some individual capitals (property companies) do not, because of perceived wealth-transfer-effects on profits. Thus the OPF serves the first two, but not the third. In such a case a conflict-resolution process is necessary.

CLASS FUNCTIONS AND AFFILIATIONS OF THE ACCOUNTING PROFESSION

We turn now to an analysis of the accounting profession in the context of the three class affiliations discussed above. The structure of the argument is summarised in Table 17.1. We define a state function for the accountancy profession in the following circumstances: if, for reasons related to the state's operations in society, some members of the state apparatus would feel it necessary to undertake a function which the profession currently undertakes, were the profession not to operate that function, then the profession is acting on behalf of the state with respect to that function, and hence is affiliated to it.

Auditing

Being required by corporate legislation, it is clear that the state considers auditing important for three of its own purposes: first, it requires an attestation that the accounting figures which are used for government statistics are correct; second, it is in the interests of the state directly that the market stability which arises from the trust engendered by an unqualified audit certificate should exist; third, the state benefits from a supposed improvement in resource allocation which might be supposed to arise from the good decisions which arise from trustworthy historical records of comparative success (but see Puxty and Laughlin, 1983; Puxty, 1984).

A second aspect of auditing is the uniformity in methods which has resulted from the audit and accounting standards developed in the past few years by the accounting profession. Since these are considered by the state to be important for financial reporting, the state would undertake these regulatory functions itself were they not administered by the profession. Such standards are supplementary to corporate legislation and may thus be considered 'quasi-legislatory'.

Tax work

Like audit, this is undertaken directly for the client, and paid for by the client. It might be supposed therefore that the revenue authorities would view with some suspicion the profit estimates produced by firms' accountants, and undertake safeguards such as demands to check the results – in effect, auditing the auditors. This is rare, because the integrity which is supposed to attach to the accounting

TABLE 17.1 Structural Affiliations of Accountancy Functions

		Audit	Tax	Liquidition
State		1. Government statistics 2. Market stability 3. Resource allocation 4. Standards: as above, emphasised	Save State effort.	none
Capital	GLOBAL	1. Facilitates operation of capital markets 2. legitimation (a) directly: audit certificate (b) indirectly: apparent smooth capital markets	none	legitimation: orderliness and efficiency
	INDIVIDUAL	reduces agency costs	minimises tax liability	reduces monitoring costs when capitalist is a creditor
Labour		Separate Conceptual Approach		

profession is normally seen by the Inland Revenue as a basis for trusting the estimates produced by them. This provides grounds for arguing that by the very nature of their professionalisation, the accountants are acting on behalf of the state.

Liquidation

It is not suggested that this is a state function. The liquidation of a company will be financed by the parties involved, and the terms under which it takes place are a matter for them, subject to legislation concerning creditor preference which ensures uniformity and settles potential disputes. There is no reason to suppose that in the absence of the accounting profession, this would be undertaken by the state. Indeed, many liquidators are not accountants, but may be creditors or their representatives.

Turning from the State to the interests of capital, two aspects must be distinguished following Müller and Neusüss (1978): the interest of global capital and the interest of the individual capitalist. The audit function is in the interest of global capital because, firstly, it facilitates the operation of capital markets by increasing the reliance which can be placed on the published results of the firms traded in the markets, thus reducing transaction costs. Secondly, it provides a source of legitimation for capitalism in two ways: directly, through certifying that accounts are describing the entity appropriately (through the 'true and fair' criterion), thus adding legitimation to the notions of profit, cost, efficiency and so on, which constitute the backbone of capitalist accounting; and indirectly, through contributing to the resulting picture of the efficient and smooth operation of capital markets which helps lead observers to conclude that the system is indeed efficient in resource allocation for society. It is in the interest of individual capitals, because for each of them it reduces the agency costs of monitoring management activities in the conditions of the separation of ownership and control which are characteristic of managerial capitalism.

The more general accounting aspect of the profession contributes to capital, as Sombart and others have pointed out, by making the abstract concrete and enabling complex entities to be manageable by reducing the essential control information to a summarised homomorphic financial matrix. This is helpful to capital both globally and individually: the former because it means that the system as a whole, with both internal and external reporting, can function with some degree of efficiency as defined by capital, and the latter because the individual capitalist will gain from such a picture being available. There are no grounds for arguing that the tax function of the profession is helpful to global capital. However it helps individual capitals because the tax slice taken by the state is a zero-sum game, and the independent accountant who is paid by the firm can be trusted, if competent, to ensure that the minimum of tax is paid to the state.

Next, we consider the liquidation function of the accounting profession. As with the audit function, this is helpful to global capital in terms of legitimation, and for the same reason: that the profession provides a source of trustworthy liquidators who will dispose of assets in an orderly fashion and minimise the questioning of such sensitive matters, thus contributing to the belief that the market system functions efficiently. It is helpful to the individual capitalist who finds himself or herself to be a creditor in a winding-up by reducing his or her monitoring costs over the process of liquidation.

Finally we turn to labour. Based on the earlier argument, we consider two ways in which the accountancy profession might be considered part of labour. The first is that the profession is not *per se* linked to the interest of capital, and would be necessary even in a different social formation. The first part of this may be rejected, the second accepted or rejected based upon a distinction.

Although some professions may not be considered directly linked to the interests of capital, this cannot be said of the accounting profession: it is almost uniquely linked to it. Unlike the ancient professions, it grew only under capitalist conditions, and it did so in almost every aspect of its·functioning linked to the CMP. Liquidation, audit, corporate tax, accounting standards, are all linked to business. Some minor functions (in terms of fee income) such as personal tax computation and executorship are not directly linked to and supportive of financial or productive capital: but even here, we see them in most cases linked to the wealthy, and many of the wealthy are in that position as a result of owning capital rather than the more ancient income source of land.

The second part requires a distinction. The experience of socialist countries suggests that accounting is still necessary without the CMP. It is a different form of accounting however: thus the accounting profession might well continue to exist under a different social formation, but with a greatly altered nature. The second aspect concerns the deskilling argument of the labour process debate. To what extent is this true of the accounting profession? There has always been a considerable amount of routine work, and the apprenticeship system of articles of clerkship has (*inter alia*) provided the independent professional firm with a supply of labour to undertake this. There is thus no reason to suppose that the quantity of routine work is higher today than in the past. Hence the conclusion must be that there has been little if any deskilling in the accountancy profession.

We now concretise the theory by reference to a particular empirical case in detail. In the next section we analyse the development of the idea that accounts should be designed on the basis of the needs of whose who use them. This is referred to as the 'user criterion' or 'decision-usefulness'.

A HISTORICAL PERSPECTIVE ON THE USER CRITERION

The notion that accounts should be useful is not one many would dispute. From this simple starting point however two misunderstandings have grown up: first, that usefulness as a general term can be defined more specifically as 'useful for decisions', inferring in turn that this means that the wishes of either specified users or some general notion of an ideal-type user should be built into the criterion for accounting; and second, that usefulness for individual decisions has historically been a basis for providing external financial information. The argument here is concerned to refute the latter supposition: and we begin by defining more carefully what we understand 'decision-usefulness' to mean.

The Meaning of Decision Usefulness

Accounting information is concerned with the financial representation of a subset of the events which concern the reporting entity, with the intention that it will be used by one or more classes of people who have some interest in the results.

This simple statement breaks down into two parts. The first concerns the relationship between the underlying events and the accounting information, and the second concerns the relationship between the accounting information and the interested parties who use it. This is depicted in Figure 17.1. We call the first relationship R (representation), the second U (usefulness).

We call those who see the purpose of accounting in terms of the proper mapping of the events which affect the entity, 'mapping proponents': they emphasise the propriety of relationship R. Those

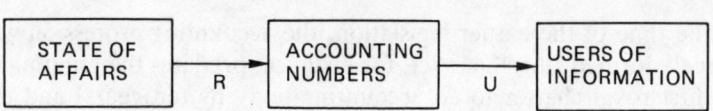

FIGURE 17.1 *The Accounting Process*

who see the purpose of accounting in terms of the use to which the information is put emphasise relationship U, and these we may call 'usefulness proponents'. In effect, the former is predicated on a very weak notion of use: specifically, that good representation is all that is needed to satisfy any possible user. There is no suggestion that the parties involved have seen matters in this light.

The History of the Accounting Criterion

The criterion laid down by the Joint Stock Companies Act, 1844, was that a balance sheet should be 'full and fair'. The Companies Clauses Act, 1845 included the criterion that accounts should be 'full and true', adding that there should be an 'exact balance sheet' which showed 'a true Statement of the (assets and liabilities) . . . and a distinct View of the Profit or Loss of the (period)'. Chastney (1975) comments:

> the true balance sheet perceived in the 1845 Act could mean no more than an accurate representation of the state of the books of account at a particular point in time. Full and fair, on the other hand, seems to have a much wider interpretation: not only is the balance sheet to present all the facts as they appear in the books but also display these facts such that anyone reading the balance sheet would get as good an idea of the state of the company as can be obtained from the information revealed on a company's balance sheet.
>
> (p. 6)

Thus the latter Act 'could be seen as looking for little more than an enumeration of the financial facts': and similarly the 1900 Companies Act referred to a balance sheet being

> properly drawn up so as to exhibit a true and correct view of the state of the company's affairs as shown by the books of the company.

At the time of the earlier legislation, the accounting profession was scarcely formed (the 1844 Act, for instance, predates the granting of the first royal charter to an accounting body by ten years) and the wording of the legislation was that of the lawyers and laymen who drafted, amended and passed the Bill into law.

The quotation from the 1900 Companies Act is significant because it requires, not that accounts represent the underlying state of the company, but merely that they represent the account balances in the books. This was 'weak decision-usefulness': the belief that unique representation was possible, and that good representation in itself would be appropriate to any user.

Use could be omitted from the framing of legislation at this time because legislators supposed representation to be the nature of financial statements. It is true that disclosure provisions were inserted into the 1844 Act in order to provide some monitoring of corporate affairs by those not involved in the day-to-day operations of the company: but such use was not strongly user-orientated in the sense that particular users' needs were considered in the framing of particular disclosures. Supportive evidence for this is the repeal of such disclosure in the 1856 Act.

The Early Twentieth Century

This approach was defensible because of a second feature of contemporary thought: the entity was separate from its shareholders (Salomon v. Salomon and Company, Ltd (1897)). The corollary of this was that the welfare of the company and the welfare of the shareholders were carefully distinguished. Thus the foundation of non-disclosure in the nineteenth century was the belief that the company was an entity separate from the shareholders, and that actions had to be for the good of the company (NOT any individual shareholder). So long as this underpinned thinking, user sovereignty could not intrude. As late as 1935 a textbook stated

> the duty of directors is, primarily, to the company as a company and not to the shareholders of to-day or to-morrow as individuals.

and

> The interests of the company as a continuing business are paramount, the interest of the temporary or speculative shareholder being strictly subordinate thereto.

However, by the turn of the century there had been a growing realisation that some user need should be incorporated more explicitly into the criterion used. In 1906 this was recognised in the judgment of Newton v. Birmingham Small Arms Company, Ltd that

> The purpose of the balance-sheet is primarily to shew that the financial position of the company is at least as good as there stated, not to shew that it is not or may not be better.

Hence the judgement recognised use, supplying a conservative criterion as a guide which would lead to the most appropriate accounts for the use envisaged.

Secret Reserves and Consolidations

Further evidence that it was the good of the company rather than individual users that was the underlying philosophy behind financial statements comes with two significant aspects of early twentieth-century accounts: secret reserves and consolidations. Yamey writes that

> The creation of secret reserves, and their resurrection to augment the recorded profits in subsequent periods, were important features of company accounting in the second half of the nineteenth century and for several decades later . . . Provided it was done in good faith *and in the interests of the company* the directors could, within wide limits, present final accounts embodying deliberate and material deviations from the application of the accounting conventions.
>
> (Yamey, 1977, p. 29, emphasis added)

The significant phrase appears in the italicised passage: it was the good of the company which was deemed to be important in the retention of secret reserve accounting.

Similarly Sir Robert B. Finlay in Newton v. Birmingham Small Arms advocated that

> Many companies and commercial houses find the necessity of keeping a secret reserve fund . . . If its position is disclosed, and the public get information about it, a great injury may be done to the business. Difficulties may be caused between rival traders or between capital and labour. The common way to create a secret

reserve fund is by undervaluing the assets of the company, and we are only trying to do the same thing with the knowledge and consent of the shareholders.

Next, consider consolidations. If one is to understand properly the state or the progress of a company, then its consolidated accounts are fundamental. Yet, although techniques of consolidation were known (in Britain, the first published consolidated balance sheet came from Nobel Industries in 1922, and in 1919 the New York Stock Exchange had tried to encourage reporting through consolidated accounts), it was not until 1934 that Dunlop's accounts were published in group form, and described as a 'landmark in accountancy history' (Jones, 1981, pp. 153–5).

No doubt there is some truth in the standard interpretation of this – that corporate managements were reluctant to expose their performance to scrutiny, and any method such as unconsolidated accounts, where profits could be moved around without this becoming obvious, would have been helpful – but this in turn implies more fundamentally the belief that the good of the company as a company should be foremost. Had this not been accepted, then consolidation would have been required much earlier than The Companies Act, 1948.

True and Fair as a Transitional Criterion

Thus the criterion for accounting until the Companies Act, 1948 varied, but almost exclusively concerned itself with the representation only. Accounts only came to be published at all, in many cases, as a result of legal compulsion. Because accountants were obliged to comply with the law in presenting published accounts, the frame of reference that underlay corporate legislation came to influence strongly the accountant's own view of his duties. These were to 'state whether in (the auditor's) opinion the Balance Sheet referred to in the Report is a full and fair balance sheet, properly drawn up so as to exhibit a true and correct view of the state of the company's affairs as shown by the books of the company' (Whinney, 1891). The idea of 'fair' implied in this passage, which actually uses the term, was, it is suggested, that accounts represent book balances correctly. The term did not at that time imply what it was later to imply as part of the expression 'true and fair'.

'True and correct', then, relates the financial statements to the books of account. 'True and fair' may not have been carefully thought out as an exact expression (cf. Chastney, 1975, pp. 12–13) but it was rightly seen as a broader expression than 'true and correct'.[7]

The meaning of 'true and fair' has never been fully settled. Yet the change from 'true and correct' was pivotal, because the new expression had within it the seeds of a strong user-orientation. It 'implies that all statutory and other essential information is not only available but is presented in a form in which it can be properly and readily appreciated' (Sir Russell Kettle, 1948). Writing at the time of the Act which introduced the criterion, Kettle recognised that it implied a user 'appreciation'. The word 'true' still incorporated a representative role, but this was now supplemented by a user criterion.

The Genesis of the User-Orientation Proper

In analysing the development of the user criterion, we add to the three parties considered so far – those who developed corporate law, those who made decisions on disclosure (the directors of companies), and the professional accountants – a fourth, the academic writer, who has cross-fertilised with the profession both through personal contact (more recently being involved with research for the regulating bodies) and through writing in the many professional journals.

By the fifties and sixties the accounting profession was coming to recognise that there were problems in accounting. One reaction was to give at least some consideration to the overall purpose of accounting. Purpose is fundamental to any activity, yet it had hardly exercised the minds of accountants. Curiously (to the outsider) the profession had never felt it necessary to ask itself either about its own function as a profession or about the function of the accounts it produced.[8]

Staubus appears to have been the first to articulate a theory based upon decision usefulness, in a 1953 doctoral dissertation (subsequently published as Staubus, 1961). Soon after, Chambers published a classic 'Blueprint for a Theory of Accounting' (1955) and from then on the revolution was under way, in academic thought at least. There were hesitations in the progress of the idea (as in, for instance, Moonitz (1961 pp. 4–5) (see Staubus, 1977: p. 24) but

The turning point in the official and sponsored literature came in 1966. The AAA Committee to Prepare a Statement of Basic

Accounting Theory bought the decision-usefulness approach lock, stock and barrel.

(Staubus, op. cit., p. 25)

By the 1970s this was appearing in the professional literature. Staubus tells us that 'APB Statement No. 4 (1970) was the first AICPA document to recognise the decision-usefulness objective . . . This statement was a great leap forward for the accounting profession in the U.S. It was followed by the strongly decision-oriented statement of the Study Group on the Objectives of Financial Statements in 1973' (op. cit., p. 25). With another writer Staubus himself produced a statement for the Australian profession and noted happily that it was given 'a hospitable reception in 1972'. The UK discussion document *The Corporate Report* also seemed predicated on decision usefulness.

Thus the centre of the profession at least (that is, those who produced, or supported the publication of, statements giving a usefulness emphasis) appeared to have adopted usefulness as a criterion and, what is more, changed their frame of reference to accommodate it. We must now ask a critical question: why did decision usefulness come to prominence as it did? The suggested path is as follows.

Class Interests and the Change in the Accounting Criterion

In the mid-nineteenth century when corporate legislation was first developed in detail, financial disclosure to the owners and to the public more generally[9] had been developed in the context of stewardship. Uppermost in the minds of the representatives of the embryo state, as it passed legislation enabling incorporation of joint-stock companies to take place by registration under Acts of Parliament, were two conflicting pressures. One was a desire to liberalise the contemporary situation which left the question of incorporation highly uncertain – which meant the introduction of limited liability. The countervailing pressure was to monitor the activities of these new entities. The first was necessary because financial capital was finding difficulties in investing in production: no satisfactory vehicle was available. The second was necessary because it was well-known that unscrupulous promoters were active in floating worthless stock.

However in terms of an appropriate criterion for the resulting financial statements[10] there was no thought to anything except proper representation as a criterion. To understand why nothing more demanding than this weak mapping criterion existed, we must look more closely at the circumstances of the time. The early nineteenth-century State bore little relation to the interventionist State under late capitalism, being small with low revenues and restricted functions. Yet the threads of its relationship to capital are clearly visible: and even though at this early stage some legitimation devices were necessary in framing corporate legislation, and we find Gower referring to 'more than a slight whiff of Victorian humbug when one reads the evidence of Chancery barristers accepting the eager invitation of MPs to persuade them that limited liability was desirable in the interests of the poor' (1969, pp. 45–6) there is little doubt that the real impetus for corporate legislation was the need of finance capital.

It was this need on the part of finance capital which was fundamental to the development of a user orientation. Finance capital already had close links with the embryo state. The enactment of corporate legislation points to the influence of those who needed it to make profitable use of their funds. This was a result of the class hegemony between the state and finance capital. Gower remarks that

> it may be that the altruism of 1851 had been supplanted by more selfish fears for self-preservation; by this time the fortunes of the governing classes were in commerce rather than land.
>
> (ibid, p. 48)

and Macdonald comments, even more revealingly, that

> The work of Arnstein [1973] and Rubenstein [1977a, 1977b] show that the really wealthy were not in manufacturing, but in commerce and that they tended to be associated with the landed aristocracy, who continued to dominate the political arena: in the 60 years following the Reform Act only two cabinets had less than 50 per cent aristocrats (1868, . . . 1892).
>
> (Macdonald, 1984, p. 178)

A specific disclosure of corporate affairs aimed at finance capitalists was unnecessary because when promoting or otherwise investing in joint stock companies, they were sufficiently close to its directors for external financial information to be superfluous; and this situation continued so long as such capital tended to be in private hands. This situation is of course true only of disclosure; finance capital did need other aspects of the joint-stock companies acts, and as such, its interests coincided with those of the accountancy profession which from the first, therefore, was linked closely to the state (since it was state legislation that created the corporations) and finance capital (since it was this which benefited most from the formalisation of incorporation):

> 'global capital' required more 'control agents' as the industrialisation developed and accountants in England and Scotland managed to establish themselves as legitimate occupants of that role in a manner which has had consequences for the development of accountancy throughout the capitalist world. It should also be noted, with reference to the distinctions within the wealthy bourgeoisie just mentioned, that it was particularly the interest of 'finance capitalists' that was served by the passing of the Companies Act of 1856 and 1862, legislation which was crucial in the development of the accountancy profession.
>
> (Macdonald, 1984, p. 179)

Thus so far as the state and finance capital are concerned, the inadequacy of the weak mapping criterion only became evident as capital ownership became more widespread, and as managerial capitalism challenged the owner-manager's prevalence. As to the other parties we are concerned with, productive capital would clearly have been content with a representational criterion so long as its tenets did not extend to a high degree of disclosure: and the fledgeling accountancy profession appeared to see the nature of accounts as mapping representations in any case (for example, the true meaning of depreciation only slowly dawned upon the profession over the course of the century).

The proximate cause of the development of the user criterion was the demand of finance capital. Individual finance capitals are interested in allocation of resources rather than the total impact of any technical system in society on overall wealth: hence there was pressure by the various finance capitals to provide the accounting information wanted by them. This was of course opposed to some extent by productive capitals. In general, finance capitals won out in the approach taken by the Accounting Standards Committee. Despite opposition more than once, new exposure drafts continued to be framed in user-need terms. (Laughlin and Puxty, 1983).

Two principal reasons may be adduced for the profession's attraction towards a policy favouring finance rather than productive capital. First, there is the matter of social class in its ascriptive sense: accountants feel themselves to be closer to those working in the finance field, which has a higher status in the UK (cf. Weiner, 1982). Second, there is the matter of geographical location. The profession is centred in the City of London, and its leaders affiliate to the needs of those surrounding them (for survey evidence see Puxty, 1984).

A proposed model to explain the change in criterion is given in Figure 17.2. In stage I of this model, in the early stages of capitalist development and accountancy development, there was no pressure for anything other than a representational basis for accounting. Partly this was because any pressure which might have come was from finance capital, which had no need for anything else as described already: partly it was because most firms were small, and the complexity of their financial affairs was not such as to require any sophisticated accountancy practices. No alternative to representation, therefore, was either conceived of or needed.

The second stage developed over the course of the present century up to, perhaps, the nineteen-sixties. Industry was becoming increasingly concentrated, and the complexity of any given company's affairs was becoming such that users might have been expected to require something more than the simplest summarised results. At the same time, the increasing separation of ownership and control meant that outside finance capital was less likely to have privileged access to corporate results: those investing through the equity and loan capital markets were obliged to rely on published financial reports. The result was an apparent need for decision-useful accounts. The profession was slow to change its attitude to financial statements, relying principally on the Companies Acts together with (in the case of the ICAEW) nonmandatory Recommendations on Accounting Principles. These were based on the implicit belief that the 'true and fair' criterion was satisfactory for investment and disinvestment decisions by finance capital.

Stage III can be traced from the takeover and merger boom of the 1960s, both in its early stages, when it was the result of individual finance and productive capitals wishing to enhance their control and/or profitability by such action, and later, when it was also encouraged by the state itself in the Industrial Reorganization Corporation. The problems that arose, such as discovery by intending predators that victim companies' profits were fictitious in some sense (Leasco-Pergamon, for instance), or by selling shareholders that after sale the buyer was able to strip assets, and they had been misled

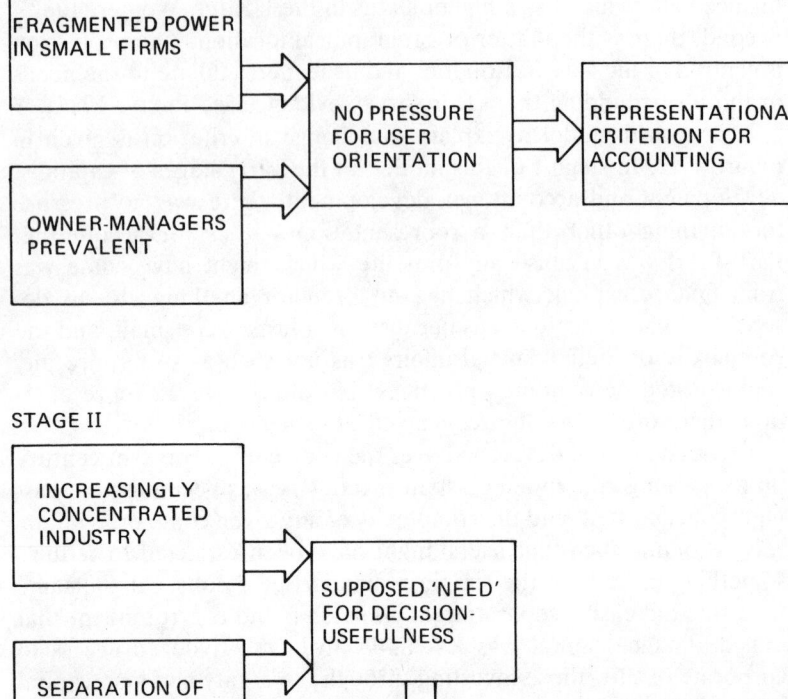

FIGURE 17.2 *Three Stages in the Development of the Accounting Criterion*

over the appropriate takeover price by misleading financial statements, led to pressure for a change in the profession's attitude to accounts users.

IMPLICATIONS FOR THE THEORY OF THE PROFESSION

The conclusions from the decision-usefulness case study have significant implications for the prosposed theory of the relationship be-

STAGE III

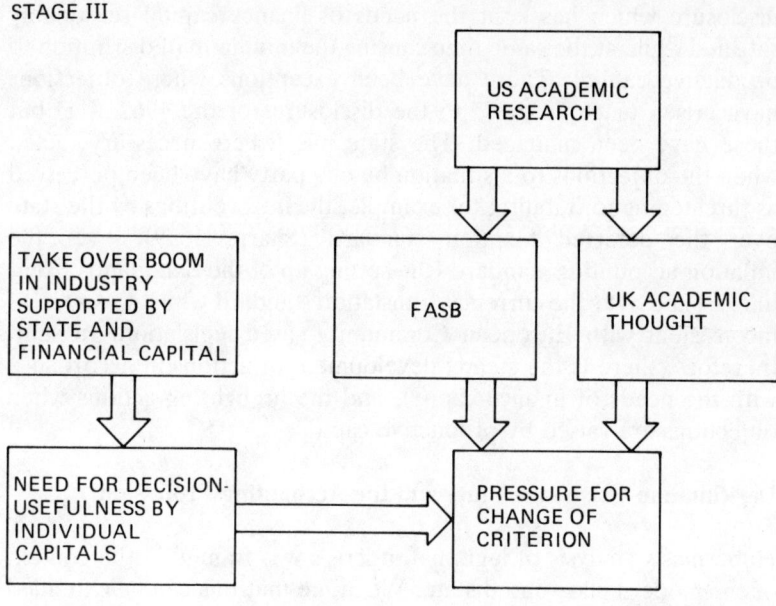

FIGURE 17.2 *(cont.)*

tween fractions of capital and the state in the context of professional action. We therefore return to the theory of the professions in order to see how the case of decision-usefulness gives more information about the workings of the accountancy profession and professions more generally. The argument will be couched in terms of finance capital, productive capital, the state, and the profession.

The State and Fractions of Capital

According to the Offe-Habermas theory of the state, the latter acts on its own behalf to regulate and sustain the capitalist system; and to do this it may have to antagonise certain fractions of capital if the system as a whole is to be maintained. In the case of published financial statements, there has been conflict between users and preparers of information, and these are effectively (respectively) finance and productive capital. Finance capitalists require better information to make investment decisions: productive capitals, in the form of individual firms, perceive this as threatening. The state has tended to take a midway course therefore: there has over the present century (as a user approach has taken hold) been a steady increase in disclosure which has kept the needs of finance capital reasonably satisfied while at the same time causing the minimum of disruption to productive capital. There have been exceptions where objections have arisen (such as those to the disclosures of the 1967 Act) but these have been managed. The state has, where necessary, acted when the objections to a situation by one party have been perceived as threatening to stability: for example, the interventions by the state over the deferred taxation standard (Sharp, 1979), over the inflation-accounting standard (the setting up of the Sandilands Committee) and over the currency-translation standard which was seen as inconsistent with European Community-based legislation. In sum, therefore, there is the steady development of actions in accordance with the needs of finance capital, and the firefighting actions when objections are raised by productive capital.

Legitimation Crisis, the State and the Accounting Profession

Habermas's analysis of legitimation crisis was framed in the context of the modern class-based state. We argue that this can be extended to the professions because, being institutions which can undertake quasi-state functions, they hold out contestable claims of legitimacy; they can also be adjudged legitimate or not independently of the contemporary state itself, since the state can alter its constitution to include or exclude them from such quasi-state functions. We may therefore proceed to analyse the legitimacy problems of both the accountancy profession and the state independently of each other, even though the validity of their legitimation claims may interact. We shall first consider how the profession has fitted in to the above process as an additional regulator, of which there are also expectations, and then go on to consider how the case of decision usefulness illustrates the way in which there is potentially immanent conflict in the OPF under these defined TSSM conditions.

Just as the state holds itself out increasingly as a regulator, so the accountancy profession has done so. Starting from a position where it made only Recommendations (and these by only one of the principal bodies) it has moved rapidly to a position, as the significance and scope of the ASC has increased, where it regulates an increasing number of aspects of corporate reporting. It has done this for just the same reasons as the state: because problems immanent in the capitalist process caused tensions, and regulation was deemed to be necessary. For the state, that regulation was a series of Companies

Acts. For the accountancy profession it was a series of accounting standards. This argument does not suppose that the profession has always been clearly aware of circumstances, or that it always acted swiftly or appropriately to curb the crisis tendencies with which it was faced. Indeed, the fact that bodies other than the ICAEW did not issue recommendations suggests no unanimous perception of socio-economic change. The long-term tendency to react to changing circumstances that affected the profession's interests did however lead to the changes observed.

In the same way that regulation resulted in increasing strains on the state as it held itself out to solve, and yet found increasing difficulty in solving, the contradictions caused by the accumulation process and the differences between fractions of capital, so the ASC found just the same problem; and yet as a result of its own internal dynamic, it had to find a means of solution. However, the profession is not the state: it is additional to it. This has meant that there are conflicts between the state and the profession as a result of these regulatory legitimising processes, and the efforts of each to sustain its legitimation has on occasion caused difficulty for the other.

This legitimacy however is, by the nature of the system, in a state of recurrent crisis. As a quasi-state regulator, the accounting profession is subject to the same crisis pressures as the state as a result of the contradictions within it. There is an economic contradiction in that professionalisation exists to protect the economic interests of its members (Carr-Saunders and Wilson, 1934), and yet to do this the individual profession must demand a substantial subscription. This is compounded by other rules which the profession has felt bound to make, such as a ban on all advertising until recently, and even now only restricted advertising. The individual member perceives this as a limit on his or her freedom to compete with the unqualified account-ant, and this again therefore constitutes an economic constraint. There is a political contradiction because any professional association is supposed to be owned by its members and exist only for them: yet members find themselves being controlled by the very people they elect – for example, through accounting standards, audit standards, and ethical committees. In particular, there is the contradiction of ideology: the institution which represents independent accountants, and is supposedly itself an independent actor, is obliged to take interventionist action which denies the legitimacy of the individual member to make the proper decisions over accounting reports. The profession claims strongly that professional accountants are independent, whether in public practice or within organisations: yet it intervenes with accounting and audit standards. Any environmental problem which arises, therefore, will be insoluble within the ideology the profession professes.

The Profession, Capital and the State

It is now possible to draw conclusions about the relationship between the accountancy profession, capital and the state. The basic question concerns the location of the accountancy profession in the class structure. We consider the implications of the evidence presented for the harmony or conflict of OPFs. Specifically, the actions of the profession in the particular circumstances of a given TSSM may serve both capital and the state, or the actions taken by it may be in favour of one and against the interest of the other. It may moreover be for or against particular fractions of capital as well as global capital.

In the case of decision usefulness generally there is evidence of harmony. As the separation of ownership and control, and the size and complexity of secondary capital markets developed, so the need of global capital was for accounts to be orientated more to the individual finance capitals that constituted the users of information in funding productive capitalist operations. Although there may have been conflicts between finance and productive capital over details of disclosure, the need of the capitalist accumulation process as a whole was served by the increase of information being made obligatory by the state through legislation.

In the general case, therefore, the interests of global capital and the state were in harmony. The accountancy profession acquiesced in developing its policies over the years, later than the state, but nevertheless in general harmony with it, as first Recommendations and then accounting standards were issued. The state found these in general to be a good thing – they supplemented the state's own legislation and reduced surveillance costs for the state – and capital, too, found them helpful since (*inter alia*) they reduced the level of controversy in accounting policies and hence led to the increased legitimation of the capitalist system as a whole.

In certain cases different capitals were in conflict in the policies they urged on the accounting regulators. Like the state, the profession had to act in ways that were not in the interest of individual capitals while at the same time acting in favour of the system itself. If the profession found it more difficult to hold out against pressure from aggrieved fractions, and succeeded less, for instance, than the state did when it forced through legislation to reduce factory hours, as discussed by Müller and Neusüss, this is evidence only that the profession had no ultimate power in the way that the state has through its political function. The profession must always rely in the last analysis on the state to give it such power. Its leaders did not, moreover, always appreciate what was in the interest of global capital (no theory should imply omniscience on the part of any social institution), and actions such as the issuance of a number of exposure drafts that were predicated on the needs of finance capital and viewed as hostile by productive capital (evidence for which can be found in Laughlin and Puxty, 1983), were only evidence of a lack of understanding in the individual case as to what should, within this framework, be done. One reason for this was the class-aspirational affiliation.

In cases of other user-based standards there has been evidence of conflict. One such is inflation accounting (for more detail of this case see Cooper, Puxty, Lowe and Willmott, 1989). It arose as a result of the very fact that the state is neither unchallenged as an institution nor solely acting in the interest of capital as a repressive agent. The state needs legitimation, and it found it could only retain that legitimation in the case of inflation by taking action which subverted the legitimacy of the accountancy profession (appointing the Sandilands Committee). In this case the action of the profession was, potentially at least, one of OPF conflict. On the one hand, its attempt to institute an initial inflation accounting standard based on ED8 was an action which was user-orientated. Moreover (although this is not to judge whether CPP fulfilled this function better than CCA-based methods) it was in capital's interest, whether because of legitimation of the capitalist system directly, or because the erosion of profits which had been observed as a result of over-high dividend distributions in some industries by researchers such as Baxter (1959) and Jones (1949) seemed to mean that in the longer term the erosion of the productive capital base would similarly have caused a crisis for the legitimacy of the capitalist system as a whole. On the other hand, that attempt subverted the state's legitimacy, because the institutionalisation of inflation was unacceptable to the state in its own attempt to retain legitimacy. Through its overt power, the state exerted pressure on the accountancy profession, and the profession was obliged to accommodate it (although it showed independence by not adopting the state's own – Sandilands – system in the way the state's own report had envisaged it).

Moreover, this latter signal of independence leads us to a final conclusion in this section. This concerns the question of whether the accountancy profession, as exemplified by the OPFs which have been analysed, might be considered 'part of' or only an instrument of, the state and capital. In order to be supportive of the Offe-Habermas thesis, evidence should weigh strongly towards the latter.

This is what we have observed. Simply stated, in order for the profession to regulate and adjudicate between different fractions of capital, it must have at least some independence from them, even though it may be, like the state in the Offe-Habermas position, dependent on the CMP. In other respects it may have the characteristics of a part of capital: as we argued in the exposition of the OPF-TSSM theory, that is entirely possible. But so far as the accounting criterion TSSM is concerned, the notion is not tenable.

The evidence presented has suggested that the profession is in principle independent of the state, although clearly many of its actions in the TSSMs we have observed have been evidence of a close relationship with, and in some cases a dominance by, the state. Yet the last observation concerning the inflation accounting debate – that the final form of SSAP16, and indeed, even the original draft ED18 were different from the State's own Sandilands recommendations – leads to the conclusion that it cannot be argued convincingly that the profession is an arm of the state.

CONCLUSION

This paper has argued that existing theories purporting to locate professions in the class structure are incomplete, since they are too rigid to accommodate the variety of relationships that professions have with other institutions in capitalist society. An alternative theory has been proposed, which takes the appropriate understanding of the class function of a particular profession in a particular situation to be situation-contingent. The case of the change from representation to the user as a criterion for financial information has been presented, and interpreted in terms of the state and capital fractions' interests it served. Finally, the case as a whole has been used to illustrate the proposed theory of the professions. The use of one case only has not been 'proof' for or against the framework proposed – nor could it be. It is hoped, however, that it will lead to further research which will uncover the tenability or otherwise of the suggested framework.

Notes

1. I should like to thank Richard Laughlin, Tony Lowe, and Marilyn Neimark for discussions and comments on the ideas contained in this paper. Thanks are also due to the University of Sheffield Research Fund for financial support of the research reported herein.
2. This is attributed to Stinchcombe by Erik Olin Wright (1979, p. 3) and dated 1973. No publication is cited.
3. This is itself a matter of dispute among scholars; for instance Ossowski has drawn attention to the difference between Marx's polemical propagandist writings, which use a dichotomous scheme, and his scholarly work, which takes account of intermediate classes.
4. Differences come in, for instance, treatment of the 'middle class' – which is crucial to our later discussions since accountants fall into this category – and the comparative importance of economic exploitation compared to other asymmetrical relationships such as authority structures. In general theories based on the latter are referred to as Weberian or Neo-Weberian. Whether Marx can be reinterpreted in terms of power rather than exploitation has been controversial but a legitimate argument of some writers.
5. Wright analyses in detail what he calls 'contradictory locations within class relations' (Wright, 1978; but see Wright, 1985). His analysis centres on those in the direct line of control over labour, and it is taken to be applicable to the present analysis. He correctly points out that a contradictory position can exist, his analysis centring on those people *as people* who have to take actions at different times that entail contradiction.
6. This is of course framed in the context of the individual nation-state. A conceptualisation of a worldwide working class being exploited internationally by multinational capital would be in conflict with this interpretation.
7. Jones (1981 p. 151–52) comments for instance that 'under the 1929 Act the auditor was merely required to say whether a balance sheet showed a "true and correct" view (as distinct from the "true and fair" view ordered by the 1948 Act) which the Royal Mail accounts satisfied, although they would not have complied with the later requirement'.
8. This was as true in the USA as in the UK: for instance Staubus concluded that 'we have seen that the public practice branch of the accounting profession had not articulated and utilised any fundamental objective of accounting prior to 1970' (Staubus, 1977, p. 20).
9. The Registrar of Companies was set up by the 1844 Act – see Gower, 1969, p. 42.

10. To the extent that they were compulsory. The 1856 Act's removal of compulsion bore witness to the willingness of the state to allow the extent of disclosure to be a matter of implicit negotiation between a company and its owners, and indeed in Gladstone's speech introducing the 1844 Bill there was no hint of publicity as a policing device, and certainly none of it as useful for interested parties.

Bibliography

Armstrong, P., 'The Rise of Accounting Controls in British Capitalist Enterprises', *Accounting, Organizations and Society* (1987) pp. 415–36.

Arnstein, W. L., 'The Survival of the Victorian Aristocracy', in F. C. Jaher, *The Rich, the Well Born and the Powerful* (Chicago: University of Illinois Press, 1973).

Aron, R., *La Lutte des Classes* (Paris: Gallimard, 1964).

Baxter, W. T., 'Inflation and the Accounts of Steel Companies', *Accountancy* (1959) pp. 250–7.

Benston, G., 'The Market for Public Accounting Services: Demand, Supply and Regulation', *Journal of Accounting and Public Policy* (1985) pp. 33–79.

Braverman, H., *Labor and Monopoly Capital* (New York: Monthly Review Press, 1974).

Cain, M., 'The General Practice Lawyer and the Client: Towards a Radical Conception', in R. Dingwall and P. Lewis (eds) *The Sociology of the Professions: Lawyers, Doctors and Others* (London: Macmillan, 1983) pp. 106–30.

Carchedi, D., 'On the Economic Identification of the New Middle Class', *Economy and Society* (1975) pp. 1–86.

Carr-Saunders, A. M. and P. A. Wilson, *The Professions* (London: Frank Cass and Co., 1964) (orig. pub. 1934 by Oxford University Press).

Chambers, R. J., 'Blueprint for a Theory of Accounting', *Accounting Research* (1955) pp. 17–25.

Chastney, J. G., 'True and Fair View: a Study of the History and Meaning of "True and Fair"', *ICAEW Occasional Paper No. 6* (London: Institute of Chartered Accountants in England and Wales, 1975).

Cooper, D. J., A. G. Puxty, E. A. Lowe, and H. C. Willmott 'The Accounting Profession, Corporatism and the State', in W. F. Chua, E. A. Lowe and A. G. Puxty (eds) *Critical Perspectives in Management Control* (London: Macmillan, 1989).

Dahrendorf, R., *Class and Class Conflict in Industrial Society* (London: Routledge and Kegan Paul, 1959).

Ehrenreich, B. and J. Ehrenreich, 'The Professional Managerial Class', *Radical America* (1977) pp. 7–31.

Fielding, A. G. and D. Portwood, 'Professions and the State: Towards a Typology of Bureaucratic Professions', *Sociological Review* (1980) pp. 25–53.

Giddens, A., *The Class Structure of the Advanced Societies* (New York: Harper Torchbooks, 1973).

Gower, L. C. B., *The Principles of Modern Company Law*, 3rd edn (London: Stevens, 1969).

Groves, R., M. Poole and P. L. Broder, 'Professional Commitments of the Practising Chartered Accountant in Modern Britain', *Accounting and Business Research* (1984) pp. 319–31.

Habermas, J., *Towards a Rational Society* (London: Heinemann, 1971).

Habermas, J., *Legitimation Crisis* (London: Heinemann, 1976).

Habermas, J., *Communication and the Evolution of Society* (London: Heinemann, 1979).

Hope, A., 'Accounting Policy: Theory or Pragmatism or Both, Submission on the Accounting Standards Committee's Document', *Setting Accounting Standards* vol. II (London: Accounting Standards Committee 1979) pp. 541–68.

Hope, A. and R. Gray, 'Power and Policy Making: the Development of an R & D Standard', *Journal of Business Finance and Accounting* (1982) pp. 531–58.

Jessop, B., *The Capitalist State* (London: Martin Robertson, 1982).

Johnson, T. J., 'The Professions in the Class Structure', in R. Scase (ed.), *Industrial Society: Class, Cleavage and Control* (St. Martins Press, 1977) pp. 93–110.

Johnson, T. J., 'The State and the Professions: Peculiarities of the British', in A. Giddens and G. Mackenzie (eds), *Social Class and the Division of Labour* (Cambridge University Press, 1982) pp. 186–208.

Jones, E., *Accountancy and the British Economy 1840–1980*, (London: Batsford, 1981).

Jones, R. C., 'Effects of Inflation on Capital and Profits: the Record of Nine Steel Companies', *Journal of Accountancy* (1949) pp. 9–27.

Kettle, Sir R., *Balance Sheet and Accounts under the Companies Act, 1948* (London: Gee and Co., 1948).

Larson, M. S., *The Rise of Professionalism*, (Berkeley: University of California Press, 1977).

Laughlin, R. C. and A. G. Puxty, 'Accounting Regulation: an Alternative Perspective', *Journal of Business Finance and Accounting* (1983) pp. 451–79.

Loft, A., 'Towards a Critical Understanding of Accounting: the Case of Cost Accounting in the UK, 1914–1925', *Accounting, Organizations and Society* (1985) pp. 137–69.

MacDonald, K. M., 'Professional Formation: the Case of Scottish Accountants', *British Journal of Sociology* (1984) pp. 174–89.

Middlemass, K., *Politics in Industrial Society* (London: Andre Deutsch, 1979).

Miliband, R., *The State in Capitalist Society* (London, Quartet, 1969).

Miliband, R., 'State, Power and Class Interest', *New Left Review* (1983) pp. 57–68.

Montagna, P. D., *Certified Public Accounting: A Sociological View of a Profession in Change* (Houston: Scholars Book Co., 1974).

Moonitz, M., *The Basic Postulates of Accounting*, (New York: American Institute of Certified Public Accountants, 1961).

Müller, W. and Neusüss, C., 'The Welfare State Illusion and the Contradiction between Wage Labour and Capital', in J. Holloway and S. Picciotto *State and Capital: A Marxist Debate* (London: Edward Arnold, 1978) pp. 32–9.

Navarro, V., *Medicine under Capitalism* (London: Croom Helm, 1976).

Navarro, V., *Class Struggle, the State and Medicine* (London: Martin Robertson, 1978).

Offe, C. and V. Ronge, 'Theses on the Theory of the State', in A. Giddens and D. Held (eds), *Classes, Power and Conflict* (London: Macmillan, 1982) pp. 249–56.

Ossowski, S., *Class Structure in the Social Consciousness* (London: Routledge and Kegan Paul, 1963).

Poulantzas, N., *Classes in Contemporary Capitalism* (London: New Left Books, 1975).

Puxty, A. G., *Decision Usefulness in Accountancy: A Contribution to a Critical Theory of the Professions*, unpublished PhD thesis (University of Sheffield, 1984).

Puxty, A. G. and R. C. Laughlin, 'A Rational Reconstruction of the Decision-Usefulness Criterion', *Journal of Business Finance and Accounting* (1983) pp. 543–59.

Rubenstein, W. D. 'The Victorian Middle Classes: Wealth, Occupation and Geography', *Economic History Review* (1977a) pp. 602–23.

Rubenstein, W. D., 'Wealth, Elites and the Class Structure of Modern Britain', *Past and Present* (1977b) pp. 99–126.

Saks, M., 'Removing the Blinkers? A Critique of Recent Contributions to the Sociology of Professions', *Sociological Review* (1983) pp. 1–21.

Sharp, K., 'The Whitehall Perspective: Government and Accounting Standards', *The Accountant*, 19 July 1979 pp. 67–9.

Staubus, G. J., *A Theory of Accounting to Investors* (Berkeley: University of California Press, 1961).

Staubus, G. J., *Making Accounting Decisions* (Houston: Scholars Book Co., 1977).

Tinker, A. M., 'Theories of the State and the State of Accounting: Economic Reductionism and Political Voluntarism in Accounting Regulation Theory', *Journal of Accounting and Public Policy* (1984) pp. 55–74.

Weiner, M., *English Culture and the Decline of the Industrial Spirit 1850–1980* (Cambridge University Press, 1982).

Whinney, F., 'Audits and Certificates', *The Accountant* 28 November 1891 pp. 836–42.

Willmott, H., 'The State, the Accountancy Profession and the Associative Model of Social Order', unpublished paper, Aston University, 1984.

Willmott, H., 'Setting Accounting Standards in the UK: the Emergence of Private Accounting Bodies and their Role in the Regulation of Public Accounting Practice', in W. Streeck and P. C. Schmitter (eds) *Private Interest Government: Beyond Market and State* (London: Sage, 1985) pp. 44–71.

Wright, E. O., *Class, Crisis and the State* (London: New Left Books, 1978).

Wright, E. O., *Class Structure and Income Determination* (New York: Academic Press, 1979).

Wright, E. O., *Classes* (London: Verso, 1985).

Yamey, B. S., 'Some Topics in the History of Financial Accounting in England 1500–1900', in W. T. Baxter and S. Davidson (eds), *Studies in Accounting* (London: Institute of Chartered Accountants in England and Wales, 1977) pp. 11–34.

Zeff, S., 'The Rise of Economic Consequences', *Journal of Accountancy* (1978) pp. 56–63.

18 Understanding the Development of the Accountancy Profession in the United Kingdom

Keith Robson and David J. Cooper[1]

The 'professional' basis of accountancy practice has only recently been subject to any serious analysis. Of course there has been traditional concern about the independence of accountancy and auditing, and this concern has been brought to public attention by the debates about accounting regulations and standard-setting, corporate financial scandals and the dominance of large accounting firms (Sterling, 1974; US Senate, 1978; Davidson, 1978). Much of the accountancy literature has regarded the 'professional' basis of accounting practice as relatively unproblematic. It has relied on the view of accountants and auditors themselves and their occupational institutions as to what it means to be professional.

This chapter offers an analysis of what it means to talk of the professional basis of accountancy and auditing in the United Kingdom (UK). The analysis places particular emphasis on accounting practices, their knowledge base, and the connections with the state and capital. In the first section, the accountancy profession's self-image is discussed and shown to be an inadequate basis for serious analysis, either of current arrangements or, particularly, of the possibility and desirability of change to those arrangements. In the second section, the meaning and significance of the term 'accountancy profession' is analysed, using the literature in the sociology of professions, particularly that literature which considers professions in their social context. Such an analysis places the accountancy profession and accountancy practices within modern British society.

The third section provides an assessment of the models of the profession offered and explores two particular issues, the role of the state, and the significance of accounting knowledge in the development of the UK accountancy profession (Hopwood et al., 1979;

Hopwood, forthcoming). This section of the paper identifies the role of the state in mediating between groupings of capital and locates accountancy within specific developments in British society. In so doing, it identifies how changes in the institutions of accountancy in the UK reflect and reinforce changes in capitalist development.

CONVENTIONAL APPROACHES TO PROFESSIONS

There have been a series of challenges to the accountancy profession and to the adequacy and accountability of its practices both in the United States and the United Kingdom. Criticism of the (lack of) independence of auditors and accountants, the (lack of) quality of audit work and the (weak) competition in the provision of accounting and audit services had, of course, been made many times before (for instance, cf. Scott, 1931; Briloff, 1972). In Britain, criticisms have tended to concentrate on accounting practices although such critic-isms have incorporated concerns about the organisation of the account-ancy profession itself (for instance, Stamp and Marley, 1970, Briston, 1979). Similar concerns about the independence of auditors has lead the European Commission to suggest restrictions in the activities of audit firms in its Eighth Directive on Company Law (1984).

There have been a variety of responses to such criticisms (Cohen Commission, 1978). One has been to challenge the observations concerning the power of the accounting establishment (Hussein and Ketz, 1980; Haring, 1979). A second response has been to challenge the observations about monopolistic concentration in the 'accounting industry' (Simunic, 1980; Moizer and Turley, forthcoming). A third response to criticism has been to strengthen and emphasise the knowledge base of accounting, in an attempt to demonstrate its scientific and neutral orientation (FASB, 1978 and 1980; Macve 1981; Solomons, 1986).

This chapter is interested in a fourth response to criticism of the accountancy profession. This response has been to emphasise the professional nature of the occupation of accountancy. Clearly these four responses (and others) are not independent and in discussing the professionalisation of accountancy practices, the other responses will be relevant. This section reviews the two conventional approaches to the analysis of professions which, whatever the source of their devel-opment, have been used in the implicit project of demonstrating the professional conduct of accountants.

The trait and functionalist approaches to professions have been used as a way of emphasising the service ethic of accountants and the legitimacy of self-regulation as a form of occupational control. These two conventional approaches have major weaknesses in that they are essentially ahistorical and asocial explanations of the nature and significance of treating particular occupations as professional. They offer an understanding of the nature of professions only in terms of current practices arising from the so-called needs of society. Variations between societies and over time are ignored.

The trait approach argues that professions possess some specific characteristics which distinguish them from other occupations. The trait approach seeks to identify core attributes and in Millerson's review (1964) he identified twenty-four items which had been suggested as essential elements of a profession. The traits include skills based on theoretical knowledge, provision of training, testing of competence of members, adherence to a professional code of conduct, and altruistic service.

The occupation of accountancy and audit has been analysed using the trait approach on a number of occasions. In a study of US accountancy, Roy and McNeil (1967) identified seven attributes which they suggested indicated that it was professional. Dyckman (1974), however, suggested that accountancy displayed the attributes of a guild rather than a profession. Groves et al. (1984) utilise the occupation-profession model of Pavalko (1971) to analyse the UK profession but identified 'different degrees of professionalism in each of the various characteristics'.

The confused nature of these studies should not be surprising, given the disarray of the trait approach. This disarray stems from three inter-related problems. Firstly, the trait approach is devoid of a theoretical basis. Accordingly the status and indeed nature of the suggested attributes is unclear. There is considerable difficulty in applying the lists of criteria to concrete situations. For example, how much theory is necessary as the authoritative basis of practice for accountancy to be regarded as a 'professional' occupation? If an accounting theory is sufficiently well developed to enable precise rules, does this undermine or enhance the professional nature of accountancy?

A second problem with the trait approach is its ahistorical character. There has been little concern within the approach to establish the time and social dimensions of the model. By searching for the correspondence between a particular occupation and a set of ideal-typical dimensions, the trait approach fails to deal with the dynamics of the process by which occupations become 'professional', the differentiation within existing professions and the challenges to professional status.

Instead of a historical analysis of professions, the trait approach offers a model of professionalisation (for example, Wilensky, 1964). This posits that occupations go through a series of stages which culminate in a profession that closely corresponds with the ideal type. But as Johnson demonstrates by comparing British and US experience 'there is no uniform or unilinear process of professionalisation which is of universal applicability . . . The trait approach . . . ignores variations in the historical conditions under which variant institutionalised forms of occupational activities develop . . . one of the underlying assumptions of the approach is that it is the inherent qualities of an occupational activity which autonomously determines the way in which institutional forms of control will develop'. (1972, pp. 29–30)

The problems of the atheoretical and ahistorical nature of the trait approach are symptomatic of a third difficulty. The trait approach is frequently based on studies of specific professions, and the traits identified are themselves derived from the characteristics of that specific profession, particularly the classical cases such as law and medicine. The difficulty with this approach to theorising is that the 'ideal' or 'ideal type' profession is depicted in terms of what is. A profession is defined as that which approximates to the current characteristics either of the classical professions, or to the occupational group which is currently striving for professional status. Further, professional claims about the characteristics of the occupation (for instance, service, knowledge basis, independence) is the basis of many of the traits identified. However, academics have a responsibility to critically evaluate professional claims, not treat them as unproblematic 'facts'; trait approaches have consequently been charged with taking professional ideologies on trust and 'legitimating professional privileges in advance of careful appraisals of the function and behaviour of professions in society'. (Saks, 1983, p. 3)

A functionalist analysis is the second conventional approach to the study of professions. A functionalist analysis attempts to provide a theoretical basis for the trait approach by identifying attributes which are alleged to be functional to either the wider social system (for instance, Parsons, 1954) or to specific professional-client relationship (for instance, Barber, 1963). For example, Parsons posits a relationship whereby society grants a privileged social and economic position (including the right of self-regulation) to an occupation which in return offers ethical and non-exploitative application of a complex body of knowledge to resolve social needs. It is suggested that the greater the importance of the application, the greater the privilege and position of the occupation in society.

This approach may appeal to the professions themselves in that it explains their privileges and position in terms of a rational solution to society's needs. A professional association is, in this view, seen to guarantee the trained competence and to maintain the service ideal of its members. But like the trait approach, the functionalist approach is seriously flawed. Before considering these problems, however, it is useful to illustrate its use in studies of accountancy.

The majority of studies that examine the development of the accountancy profession implicitly or explicitly adopt this approach. For example, Jones (1981) in a study of the evolution of Ernst and Whinney, traces the development of the accounting profession in relation to changing economic needs: 'the growth of the economy (and the prosperity of the nation) has been much dependent upon links between the growth of business and the professional services that support it' (p. 24). Accountancy firms are seen to evolve not so much because of their self-interest and desire for profit, but rather in terms of determinant pressures from the environment. For Jones (1981), the issues are to trace changes in the environment in terms of the growth and internationalisation of business and the increasing intervention of government in the economy. Accountancy firms are seen to merely respond to these social pressures and thereby to provide a service to the nation.

Most studies which consider the rise and significance of the accountancy profession focus on societal needs for co-ordination and resource allocation between enterprises and the role of accountants in preparing, auditing and regulating statements which are alleged to facilitate comparison between enterprises. The accountancy profession is regarded as a service function for society, utilising accounting knowledge to facilitate the stewardship of assets, the writing of financial contracts and the allocation of resources in society. It is, of course, not surprising that such statements underlie most of the pronouncements of the accountancy profession, particularly in relation to the setting of accounting standards (rules). The functionalist model also underlies the histories of Stacey (1954) and Carr Saunders and Wilson (1934) with regard to the English accountancy profession and Carey (1969 and 1970) and Littleton and Zimmerman (1962) for the US.

There are significant problems with the functionalist approach. It assumes a unitary model of society and its constituent enterprises. That is, the functionalist model assumes that there is a well-defined, uncontested and unproblematic set of needs, both within the firm and within society. To the extent that there may exist conflicts and dispute about society's needs, the functionalist model accepts the definition of need of those groups who are currently powerful in society. Indeed the problem with the functionalist analysis of professions is that it legitimates an occupation's own definition of needs. Not only does the approach dignify the statements of specialised occupational groups with legitimacy, but it also obscures the essentially contested nature of needs by positing the neutral, objective and rational application of scientific knowledge. The ideological nature of claims to objective knowledge has been well documented in accounting thought (for example, Tinker et al., 1982) – concepts such as efficiency, value and use(fulness) presume the dominance of specific interests in society.

The functionalist approach also tends to degenerate into a crude determinism. The accounting profession is seen to 'serve' the needs of society, including the need to coordinate the increasing division of labour in society. Its authority and influence is alleged to be determined by its ability to provide skills and competences that are highly valued and which maintain societal well-being. Professional and academic ideologies stress facilitating the allocation of capital around the economy, maintaining private property and determining the taxable capacity of individuals and enterprises. Questions about the need, origin, articulation and value of these services to society are not addressed. Accounting emerges as a benevolent rationalism. Questions concerning alternative ways of meeting the needs are likewise ignored. Instead, accounting is seen as reacting to society and to the extent that accounting practices survive, it is assumed that these practices are indeed functional to society. Functionalist analysis thus runs a serious risk of becoming tautological and of merely providing an elaborate justification for the status quo. In this view, professions are privileged occupations because they fulfil important social functions.

The failure to examine historical processes as anything other than the evolution of societal 'needs' leads the approach to ignore the possibility that social change might occur due to conflict. Changes in accountancy may be the result of unanticipated effects of other social developments (for example, in relation to the regulatory practices of the state and the financial sector). Burchell et al. (1985) indicate how accountancy practices may be caught in a web of other social developments. Further, the activities of accountants may not only be reflective of wider social practices, they may also help to make such practices possible and indeed constrain the precise nature of social practices. This is particularly evident in the changing management practices of the UK public sector, where the nature of managerialist practices is constrained and shaped by accounting knowledge and techniques.

PROFESSIONS IN THEIR SOCIAL CONTEXT

Critiques of the conventional approaches to professions have focused on the reasons why the professions might wish to conflate the two issues of the occupational activity and the particular institutionalised form of control of that activity. The essential issue in these critiques has been to examine the circumstances when claims for professional status are made.

The Internal Dynamic

One focus is on the 'internal dynamic' (Klegon, 1978) whereby practitioners attempt to raise their status, define the market for their own services, and achieve autonomy; 'the characteristics that have often been used to define professions can often be best understood as *strategies* for the achievement and maintenance of a particular type of occupational control – a particular type of social relationship, which grants power and prestige to the practitioners' (Klegon, 1978, p. 269).

Several issues arise out of studies of this internal dynamic, of what professions do in everyday life to negotiate and maintain their special position. They open up the issue of how the term profession is used as an 'honorific label which secures certain political advantages for its possession' (Becker, 1962, p. 39). Becker and his colleagues studied the practices of the medical profession, and demonstrate how doctors can use their professional status to enhance their position *vis-à-vis* other occupational groups. Although not a study of accountancy practices (of which there are lamentably few), Boland analyses how the institutions of the accountancy profession in the US use 'the myths of principle, the technology of standard setting and the myth of adequacy . . . as vehicles for the profession' (1982, p. 126). Boland traces the evolution of the institutions of US accountancy, and suggests that the American profession actively sought charters from collective authorities (for example, SEC) by stressing their service ideal and expertise, and thereby de-emphasising the possibility of external review of its outputs. His analysis adopts a view of an accountancy profession offering expert technology (even though it may not have a coherent body of knowledge) and thereby reinforcing its professional status and the rationality of self-regulation.

A focus on mechanisms in a professionalisation project alerts us to the variations in strategies between occupational groups; for example UK accountancy has not stressed the role of knowledge and expert technology to the extent evident for US accountants. Further, the approach undermines crude functionalist approaches because it challenges the rationality of current practices, recognising instead the importance of shared values and the use of symbols, myths and other means in the project to become professionalised.

Rosenberg et al.'s (1982) study of the accountancy profession is rooted in the day-to-day activities of accountants and is likewise concerned with the internal dynamic of change. However, they emphasise internal differentiation and segmentation as the dynamic for changes in the accountancy profession. For them, professions are constantly in flux, and Rosenberg et al. trace the origin and developments of one emerging professional segment in the public sector, namely accountants working for spending departments in local government. In a less detailed manner, Montagna (1974) adopts a similar approach in his analysis of changing activities within large accountancy firms in US. Such studies are invaluable both for their emphasis on professional dynamics and for understanding the precise mechanisms of change in accountancy.

Studies of the micropolitics of professions are relevant in tracing accountants' attempts to achieve control over their own occupational activities. In this regard it is important to recognise the UK accountancy profession as highly differentiated both hierarchically and horizontally. There are very real differences between the activities of an accountant in a small partnership; an accountant in one of the London offices of one of the 'Big Eight' accounting firms; an accountant working in local government, and an accountant working for a multinational manufacturing or service company. There are six major professional institutions and several more 'technical associations' in the UK and each one has differing privileges and attitudes to their own independence and activities. Indeed Macdonald's study (1984) of the formation of the Scottish accountancy profession demonstrates not only the differences in the patterns of formation compared to the English profession, but also highlights the variations between three local groups of practitioners (Edinburgh, Glasgow and Aberdeen) which all received legal recognition through charters from the Privy Council. These themes are developed in a later section of this chapter.

The External Dynamic

Yet the basic problem with studies which focus on the internal dynamic of occupational control is that the analysis offers no coherent explanation of why some occupations (or segments) successfully become accepted as professionalised whilst others do not. To resolve this problem it is necessary to locate the analysis more firmly in what Klegon (1978) refers to as the external dynamic, that is in social conditions. It is necessary to identify the sources of power that are available to an occupational group in their quest for professional status and the relationship of occupational organisations with other institutional forces. Saks (1983) identifies two general approaches used to locate professions in society. The first focuses on market conditions and is heavily influenced by Weber. The second approach focuses on the social relations of production and is influenced by Marxist political economy.

Weber (1968) refers to the notion of closure, whereby social groups seek to regulate market conditions in their favour, despite competition from others, by restricting access to opportunities. For Weberians, 'modern professions made themselves into special and valued kinds of occupations during the "great transformations" which changed the structure and character of European societies and their overseas offshoots. This transformation was dominated by the reorganisation of economy and society around the market (Polanyi, 1957). The characteristic occupational structure of industrial capitalism and its characteristic mode of distributing rewards are therefore based on the market' (Larson, 1977, p. xvi).

For Parkin (1974) professionalisation is a form of closure which is associated with the exercise of power to exclude or subordinate socially defined inferiors through the use of 'credentials'. Larson (1977) provides an elaboration of these processes:

I see professionalisation as the process by which producers of special services sought to constitute *and control* a market for their expertise. Because marketable expertise is a crucial element in the structure of modern inequality, professionalization appears also as a collective assertion of special social status and a collective process of upward social mobility. (p. xvi) . . . Professionalization is thus an attempt to translate one order of scarce resources – special knowledge and skills – into another – social and economic rewards . . . The focus on the constitution of professional markets leads to comparing different professions in terms of the 'marketability' of their specific cognitive resources.

(p. xvii)

The value of the market-based approach is that it highlights the importance of identifying groups external to the occupation which the aspiring profession can ally or attach itself to in the 'collective assertion of special social status and collective upward social mobility'. It also emphasises the signficance of strategies to legitimate the monopolisation of a particular market. Although economists have identified the monopoly power of professions (for example, Friedman and Kuznets, 1945) and analysed the barriers to entry created by the examination systems and training periods of various professions (for example, Pilcher's analysis of the US accountancy profession, 1974), they have not considered how professions might legitimate such practices. It is in this context that an analysis of the use of symbols and the celebration of technical rationality and knowledge takes on central significance (Becker, 1962; Meyer and Rowan, 1977).

Two studies of UK accountancy (Fielding and Portwood, 1981; Macdonald, 1984) examine the strategies for legitimising market control. They both use the concept of 'unresolved dialectic' to explain the changing structure and values of the accountancy profession. This concept suggests that succeeding phases of social development retain *central* characteristics of previous phases. Both studies suggest that in the emergence of accountancy as a profession, a crucial element was the emphasis on a gentlemanly image and respectability. These features are retentions of feudal society and do not seem to be central to a rapidly industrialising society (which is the feature emphasised in official histories). In the petitions for Charters from the Scottish societies, 'accounting skills receive scant attention' (Macdonald, 1984, p. 184). Indeed the emphasis seems to have been on the importance of the occupation, respectability and the close liaison with the legal profession which had already achieved higher social status.

Johnson (1972) examines variation in market forms of control. His analysis of accountancy within a social context is relatively well developed. Our subsequent analysis is intended to build upon, as well as critique, his work. The rest of this section explores his contribution.

Johnson concentrates on the relationship between the producer and consumer, locating in that relationship an element of uncertainty and tension due to the social division of labour. Dependence on the knowledge and skills of others reduces areas of commonality and thereby increases social distance yet also increases mutual dependence due to specialisation. For Johnson (1972) 'power relationships will determine whether uncertainty is reduced at the expense of producer or consumer' (p. 41). Johnson identifies three broad resolutions of the tension in producer-consumer relationships (namely, in favour of the producer, the consumer, or a resolution through third party mediation).

Professionalism is seen as being one particular means of controlling an occupation. It resolves the tension in the producer-consumer relationship in favour of the producer, relying on collegial forms of control. For Johnson, however, the development of accountancy illustrates a resolution in favour of the consumer. In particular, corporate patronage is seen to dominate. 'Occupations such as accountancy find themselves in present day industrialised societies, where a major part of the demand for their services comes from large corporate organisations' (1972, p. 46). The development of accountancy is seen as being the result of demands from business, both as a means of internal control and as a means of obtaining limited liability and funds. However, the interpretation of accounting history is not without its problems, as will be discussed later.

In his more recent work (1977, 1980, 1982) Johnson examines the structural conditions which underlie the relationships between consumers and producers, and outlines the broad mechanisms by which an occupational group may be associated with its clients. The structural conditions that Johnson examines are the classical Marxian contradictions between the producers and appropriators of surplus value in capitalist society. The distinguishing feature of capitalism is that surplus value is appropriated by non-producers and that this appropriation creates the conditions for the emergence of antagonistic social classes. In advanced capitalist society, both the appropriation and the surplus-value-producing processes require co-ordination. The appropriation process becomes fragmented, because capital is concentrated into larger units which themselves specialise in various activities associated with the appropriation and realisation of surplus value as well as the reproduction (maintenance) of capitalist relations of production.

Johnson (1977) links this analysis of society to an elaborated version of his earlier, market-based, analysis of professions (1972). He argues that there is an essential duality involved when knowledge is organised as work, and turns to the analysis of Jamous and Peloille (1970) to analyse this duality. Based on their study of French doctors, Jamous and Peloille identify two components of professional knowledge, technicality and indetermination. The former refers to the technical knowledge of the profession, which can be rationalised and codified. The greater the codification , the easier it is for another occupational group to capture or undermine the knowledge (as Armstrong, 1985, illustrates in his analysis of the rise of management accountants at the expense of industrial engineers) or the easier it is for the knowledge to be routinised and de-skilled (through the advent, for example, of computerisation). Indetermination refers to the unformulatable aspects of knowledge, the qualities which are necessary but not codifiable or rationalised. Examples include the bases of mystique, charisma and ascriptive qualities, such as social status and acceptability.

Johnson used the example of the UK accountancy profession to illustrate his analysis. He links technicality with the surplus-value-producing process and thereby suggests that the codifiable and potentially deskilled element of accountancy (book-keeping and routine processing of data) relate to the control and co-ordination of the labour process. 'Much of what is designated as accountancy work might be more validly characterised as book-keeping, that is to say, a purely technical function associated with the routine day to day implementation of systems of financial and stock control' (1977, p. 197).

Johnson links indeterminacy with the appropriation of surplus value. He identifies a second part of the accountancy profession whose knowledge is essentially unformulatable and nonprogramm-able, and whose activities are concerned with the co-ordination of capital. Whilst the bulk of routine accountancy work may be de-skilled and perhaps even deprofessionalised, there exists a small, high status, professional élite whose job is to design, instal and supervise systems of control and surveillance which sustain the administrative hierarchies of firms and the state.

As a result of his analysis, Johnson sheds useful light on certain features of accountancy as a practice and form of institutional control. First, recruitment is likely to be based on sponsorship; ascriptive criteria of evaluation will dominate recruitment and the orientation of the governing bodies of the accountancy profession will be orientated to the needs of business, particularly large companies. Second, patronage is also 'associated with a fragmented, hierarchical, locally orientated occupation group' (1972, p. 68). The accountancy profession is seen to respond to the particular consumer who is its patron and this leads to fragmentation and the pursuit of locally-based knowledge, specifically related to the needs of the client. The fragmentation, however, is limited by the widening of the consumer base, and Johnson recognises that corporate patronage of accountancy is modified by the extent to which the state and other consumers (for instance, financiers) became significant clients.

Finally, Johnson's analysis addresses the significance of accountants and accountancy. Conflicts about accounting relate not only to the production of surplus value, which is the concern of industrial accountants and the producers of accounts, but also to the global functions of capital, which concern an increasingly influential élite group of accountants involved in the allocation of surplus value between fractions of capital. Indeed Armstrong (1987) uses Johnson's analysis to examine the varying roles of accountants in Britain and West Germany.

Despite the value of this form of social analysis to illuminate features of British accountancy, there are several weaknesses with the form of Johnson's analysis. Most notably, it underplays the fragmentation within UK accountancy. A careful examination of the development of UK accountancy should attempt to explain the variation in its institutions of professional control and indeed the tensions within them. Recent studies both of the development of accountancy and its current form (for instance, Loft, 1986; Hopwood et al. 1979; Miller, 1987; Cooper et al., 1988) stress the range of conditions that have lead to the development of current practices and modes of organisation of accountancy. They emphasise the role of the state in providing the conditions for the development of particular forms of accountancy (notably insolvency, taxation, the management of war, the management of the economy, the control of the financial sector, and the management of the state sector, particularly local government and the nationalised industries). This suggests that the inter-connections between the state and corporations need to be more fully articulated in examining the development of accountancy. In the next section, we offer some suggestions towards such an articulation and in particular explore the role of accounting knowledge in the development of accountancy practice.

THE DEVELOPMENT OF THE UK ACCOUNTANCY PROFESSION

In exploring the development of accountancy in the UK and its emergence into what is conventionally seen as a 'professional' form, it is worthwhile examining a feature common to both conventional and social-contextual approaches to professions. This commonality revolves around the conception of functional efficiency.

The accounting profession would account for its existence in relation to the efficiency benefits for society as a whole, arising from the existence of an institutionally-organised body of accounting knowledge. This organisation into a professional form ensures the neutrality of the exercise of professional knowledge. A bargain is struck between society and accountants. In return for their monopoly position concerning the right to practise particular accountancy and auditing functions, accountants would see themselves as serving the public interest (Willmott, Chapter 16). The practice of accountancy implies 'efficiency' gains for the social system. Although the mechanism by which accountants calculate the public interest and formulate strategies is not explicated, the arguments often contend that the endurance of the professional form for the practice of accountancy bears testimony to this efficiency function.

Perhaps paradoxically, the approach to theorising professions associated with both Marx and Weber also embodies some similar conceptions of a functional efficiency. For example, Johnson considers accountancy to be efficient in the systematic realisation and appropriation of surplus value by capital or a fraction of capital. This process may encounter periodic 'crises', yet the outcome is a further impetus to the efficiency gains that propel accountancy.

In a sense, what unites the profession's self-image and the more structural of the contextual perspectives, is an explanation of the continued existence of a profession of accountants in terms of the functions they serve. The profession's image of itself serving the public interest, the continued existence of the profession therefore demonstrating this obvious truth, parallels Johnson's characterisation of accountancy increasing the efficiency of appropriation of surplus value, accountancy as an instrument of the rulers in the class struggle.

Both approaches suffer a similar teleology. Neither account for the development and maintenance of these functional mechanisms or indeed how, once established, their history and continued existence is linked to their functional contributions. One of the more crucial absences is the relationship of the knowledge base of the profession to society: how does it change, what links are there to practice, how does it relate to the normative category of efficiency? The latter part of this section offers some initial ideas in an examination of professional knowledges.

The Configuration of the Profession

Although our argument accepts that an understanding of the development of the accounting profession must appreciate its social and historical context, the approaches outlined in the previous section fail to capture distinctly the pattern of cross-national variations (Skocpol, 1985). The development of accounting practices will be partially bounded by the institutional configuration of the profession in each country. Within the UK, the existence of six professional bodies with claims to accountancy has provided a significant dimension.

It is difficult to understand the existence of the six professional bodies in the UK accountancy profession as somehow a response to the needs of the social. One is left pondering how it is that six quite specific 'needs' must have occurred at varying junctures, and indeed how it is that other extant segments of the profession did not appropriate the activity. Loft's account (1986) of the formation of the ICWA (now known as the Cost and Management Accountants), for example, presents aspects of a particular occupational grouping's appropriation of a series of cost-accounting techniques in competition with engineers. These are coupled with the state's management of a wartime economy providing a set of interlinked causal propositions, sometimes unintended, providing the conditions for a new professional institution. This historical outcome takes place within the context of a certain hostility and dismissiveness towards cost accountants by other existing professional bodies, challenging the entitlement of 'cost clerks' to professional status.

The continued existence of six professional bodies (as well as 'second-tier' and 'fringe' institutions) is itself a variable. Differences in status have been perceived by members of each of the six bodies and this has often constrained the capacity of the profession to act with unity. Attempts to integrate the profession have their own history which in part reveals the problematic relations between the institutes; the rejection of the scheme for integration by the members of the Institute of Chartered Accountants in England and Wales (ICAEW) in July 1970 reflects a view of their 'relative standing'. That particular episode also points to the difficulties in the management of a professional association where there are divergences in the orientation and practices of members (Cooper et al., 1988).

Part of this differential status perceived by members of the ICAEW highlights the dispersal of accountants among various organisational sites. The three national Chartered institutes (ICAEW, ICAS, ICAI) have provided the main site for the training of accountants in the UK who are qualified to pursue the audit function. The CACA is often seen as a lower-status body, partly due to its large overseas memberships and studentships. The status attached to training in practice outstrips that of the accountant trained in industry; the three national Chartered Institutes can stress this in recruitment.

The relative standing of the professional bodies also implies something of the differing organisational locations of accountants of the various professional bodies. The six accountancy institutes each maintain links with their sponsoring department in the British state, the Department of Trade and Industry. The ICAEW has, however, by far the greatest historical relationship, even though the Chartered Institute of Public Finance and Accountancy has the largest membership in government and public sector organisations. Yet the ICAEW has by far the strongest links with the state, often drawing upon its élite membership (particularly from the larger and increasingly multinational accounting firms) to advise in the drafting of Companies Acts, lobbying the EEC, legislation relating to financial regulation, and matters of taxation.

Although there exists a joint committee of the six major accountancy bodies (The Consultative Committee of Accountancy Bodies) and accounting and auditing standards are the province of that committee, it has been weak due to internal dissension and relies on a secretariat located in the ICAEW. This latter body, partly due to its location in the City of London, its status and its size, has interacted increasingly, particularly through the Parliamentary and Law Committee and its subcommittees, with the state on economic issues since the early 1960s (for evidence, see the Technical Release series). In part the relations between state and accountancy bodies has reflected the relative absence of accounting expertise within the state organisation. Although this is changing, in that accounting experts have been encouraged at the higher levels of the Civil Service, the emphasis has been in favour of the membership of the ICAEW (whose members, of course, also dominate the large auditing firms). The holders of the post of Head of the Government Accountancy Service have all come from the ICAEW.

The point here is that the existence of six bodies whose members operate in differing organisational forms (with overlaps) impacts upon the possibility of the profession developing standardised procedures. Occasionally this division of labour between six loosely coupled bodies can be a significant variable. One can, for example, point to the demise of Exposure Draft 35 relating to accounting for changing prices (Davison, 1985). Further the state itself has been involved in attempts to reorganise the profession into a more 'manageable' form for interchanges on accounting problems (Robson, 1987). Future research on the UK accountancy profession might find it useful to examine the intersections between the various professional bodies and the various branches of state administration. Our understanding of the history of UK accountancy is that these institutions critically mediate accountancy practices.

The Knowledge Base of Accountancy

It is common to dismiss accounts of institutional patterns as 'middle range'. To the extent that the existence of organisations are taken to embody interests and thus supply a general explanatory framework within which outcomes can be related, this attitude is justifiable. Organisations can rarely be conceived of in this way, and so to that extent the institutional dimension cannot stand on its own. Whist sensitive to the problematic nature of employing institutional categories, these do highlight the problem of the profession's self-management. The movements that create 'problems' which the élite members of the profession have to cope with can be coherently identified through an examination of the various sites within the social totality that are occupied by accountancy practices. While institutional forms that constitute the accounting profession present difficulties of co-ordination and control, particularly in the event of professional crises, tensions also emerge from the variety of practices accountants have now come to pursue. Difficulties in changing the knowledge or structure of the profession are intertwined with the variety of accountancy practices; e.g. in contrast to much continental European practice, membership of the ICAEW does not cease once a member moves outside of accountancy and auditing practice. This provides a particular condition within which the professional institutes may attempt to regulate its members' practices.

Within traditional areas of practice, the power associated with knowledge may be quite ambiguous. For example, in the audit task the expertise of the auditor is often confronted by members of the same profession, who are likely to have a strong overlap in technical competence and training experience. Insofar as professional expertise also incorporates judgemental factors or indeterminacy (Johnson, 1977), the ability of the auditor to draw upon this as a resource in the audit task is perhaps limited by a similar capacity on the part of the client's accountants responsible for producing an organisation's accounts. This presents an interesting structure of professional relations with implications for the possibility of the development of further regulatory procedures to 'strengthen' the audit. It also seriously complicates the analysis of occupations in the manner suggested by Johnson (1972), for, in the case of audit, producers and consumers (e.g. financial analysts) may belong to the same occupation.

There has been a significant movement of accountants trained in audit (in 'practice') into positions within industry or finance. Many tasks, including information systems, corporate treasury, planning and financial management, now come within the ambit of members of the accountancy profession. The knowledges which both are created and help inform such practices are only weakly reflected (if at all) in the examination systems of accountancy bodies. Although claims to experiential knowledge are commonplace in British society, the extent to which accountants move into new areas of managerial practice may undermine claims to professional expertise, knowledge and status.

Moreover, recognition of the variety of organisational settings which shape the practices of members of the profession has led to the commissioning of schemes for a more 'manageable' re-organisation of accounting bodies. Suggestions have come forward for the construction of sections or faculties within the ICAEW (Tricker, 1983).

In our discussion thus far we have concentrated on the variety of knowledges that inform accountancy practice, and the possibilities that ensue for the development of the organisation of the occupation of accountancy into a profession. We now turn to the way in which knowledge about the effects of accountancy influences the development of accountancy practices and the associated claims to accounting knowledge.

From beginnings in record-keeping and insolvency, accountancy has moved into the position of being a key mechanism by which economic organisations, both in the public and private sector, are interrogated. Sophisticated analyses of accounting numbers which help constitute those organisations have developed. As an instance, the Society of Investment Analysts, whose members are often accountants themselves, has grown around the analysis of company reports in a context where the management of stocks and shares is a crucial part of the *raison d'être* of an array of financial and commercial institutions. The propensity of the share form to facilitate the appropriation of economic control through takeover and acquisitions has further sensitised management to the signifying effects of accounting numbers such as EPS and P/E ratios. The concerns of corporate managers, the media, and financial regulators have all thus fed into the growing pressures for change in accountancy practices and measures. Auditing firms are now well aware of the responsibility imputed to their function by a range of 'users'. This has been particularly noticeable in relation to regulatory concerns in the UK regarding fraud and corporate failure. Accounting statistics have formed a basis for measuring the stability of banking and other financial institutions.

This expansion within the UK of accounting measures becoming a crucial site of society's regulatory process has at particular junctures crossed with the state's attempts at economic management. For example, in the 1980s concern at the level of R & D expenditure outside of defence spending has influenced the disclosure of R & D expenditure in the UK. But before the state can attempt to influence the quantity of R & D activity, it must first be revealed. Part of the impetus towards disclosure is the effect that this may have upon the object of measurement; the requirement to disclose R & D will serve as a sign for greater attention to be given to the development of innovation both within firms and by the Stock Market. Conversely, the reporting of R & D expenditure can be argued to penalise companies with comparatively high levels of research activity. Share prices may fall due to investor's beliefs about overinvestment, and such a fall could leave companies open to takeover. Thus the so-called rational economic consequences of the interest in accounting numbers and disclosures is not without ambiguity. The state may mediate in professional developments, as Johnson (1977) indicates, but the effects of so doing cannot be guaranteed (Thompson, 1987).

As struggles arise over the method through which particular key statistics pass into accountancy, so the knowledge base of that profession is called into question. The categories and terms of accounting knowledge organise particular economic and political conflicts into theoretical categories within which debates about accounting methods are then conducted. Johnson's identification of the duality of professional knowledge (1977) is helpful but perhaps insufficiently complex to understand the threats and opportunities to the profession's self-determination. Codification and standardisation of the accounting-knowledge base is often resisted as an affront to the qualities that define the professional person. Yet the increased exposure of the profession to the possibility of litigation or greater state regulation impels an exploration of the possibility of greater definition and standardisation of auditing and accountancy practices in the theoretical domain.

The investment in research to justify accountancy practices has significant effects. As crises emerge for the professions, so the impetus to examine and redefine the knowledge base is strengthened. The accountancy professions in various nations have shown differential willingnesses to invest in theory to justify, guide and perhaps even change practice. In the US, where the question of third-party liability for auditors is clearer than in the UK, the profession has been more prepared to invest resources into a 'conceptual framework' for accounting standard-setting (FASB, 1978 and 1980). Though the UK profession has so far been reluctant to take this option seriously (Macve, 1981), the conceptual framework option has arisen once again with a new author and new title to disguise the unpopularity of the old one (Solomons, 1989).

As the discursive possibilities of accounting numbers have expanded into the media and the state, and the risks attendant to the auditing process increased, so the larger auditing forms are beginning to change their orientation. The payoff from auditing is becoming a less significant proportion of the Big Eight firms' revenue. With the decline of UK manufacturing and the proliferation of financial services, so the larger firms have moved increasingly into the new areas, such as management consultancy, taxation and financial services. Also, not surprisingly, the significance of insolvency and receivership services has enlarged. It is certain that the shift of organisational sites of accounting practices will influence the future course of the accounting profession (Cooper et al., 1988), perhaps even threatening its existence, and most certainly threatening the corporate patronage model of Johnson's analysis (1972).

CONCLUSION

The literature on the development of occupations and professions has rarely seriously considered the knowledge base of the activity in question: how the knowledge emerges; the claims it makes, and the changing sites to which it is applied. Yet over time the specialisms that the accountancy profession is seen as encompassing have grown, most especially in the past two decades. Accountants have begun to assume a more prominent role in the conduct of local government (McSweeney and Sherer, Chapter 15); the NHS (Griffiths report, 1983); nationalised industries (Hopper et al., 1986), and the central state apparatus itself (UK Treasury, 1983). Management in the public sector, including the possibility of its deconstruction, now involves accounting knowledge and knowledges that are coming to be seen as accounting. Activity at many levels of social life is being defined in financial quantities, and these developments influence the development of the accountancy profession in both expected and unanticipated ways.

Accounting knowledges have moved with the dominant practices in society, and in particular the relation between financial institutions and the regulatory regime which is itself increasingly produced by calculative controls. This is not to assert that accounting knowledge reflects practice, but rather that the relationship between accounting theory and practice is likely to be complex. Furthermore, the continued expansion of the profession is as much an achievement of politics – in having its validity and relevance widely accepted, and also in having its end results acted upon by clients and regulators (Rueschemeyer, 1986).

These observations point towards the manner in which the particularities of the development of UK accountancy may begin to be understood. The earlier sections of this chapter which surveyed the literatures on the professions, ranging from the trait to the Marxian approaches, offers important pointers to understanding the broad sweep of professionalisation. But rather than apply these understandings of professions in general, we would urge critical accounting researchers to consider the development of a literature concerned to explain the specific development of accountancy practices and knowledges in their social context.

Notes

1. We have benefited from discussions with Anthony Hopwood, Tony Lowe, Peter Miller, Marilyn Neimark, Tony Puxty, David Rosenberg, Tony Tinker and Hugh Willmott. Neither they nor anyone else can be held responsible for any errors or views expressed herein. We are grateful for the support provided by the Research Board of the Institute of Chartered Accountants in England and Wales and the Economic and Social Research Council.

Bibliography

Armstrong, P., 'Changing Management Control Strategies: The Role of Competition between Accounting and other Organizational Professions', *Accounting, Organisations and Society* (1985) pp. 129–48.

Armstrong, P., 'The Rise of Accounting Controls in British Capitalist Enterprises', *Accounting, Organisations and Society* (1987) pp. 415–36.

Barber, B., 'Some Problems in the Sociology of the Professions', *Daedalus* (1963) p. 669–88.

Becker, H. S., 'The Nature of a Profession', in National Society for the Study of Education, *Education for the Professions* (University of Chicago Press, 1962).

Boland, R., 'Myth and Technology in the American Accounting Profession', *Journal of Management Studies* (1982) pp. 109–27.

Burchell, S., C. Clubb and A. G. Hopwood, 'Accounting in its Social Context: Towards a History of Value Added in the UK', *Accounting Organisations and Society* (1985) pp. 381–414.

Briloff, A., *Unaccountable Accounting* (New York: Harper & Row, 1972).

Briston, R., 'The UK Accounting Profession – the move towards monopoly power', *The Accountants Magazine* (November 1979).

Carey, J., *The Rise of the Accountancy Profession from Technical to Professional 1896–1936*, (New York: AICPA, 1969).

Carey, J., *The Rise of the Accounting Profession to Responsibility and Authority: 1937–1969* (New York: AICPA, 1970).

Carr Saunders, A. M. and P. A. Wilson, *The Professions* (London: Frank Cass and Co., 1964) (orig. pub. 1934 by Oxford University Press).

(Cohen), Commission on Auditors' Responsibilities, *Report, Conclusions and Recommendations* (New York: AICPA, 1978).

Cooper, D. J., E. A. Lowe, A. G. Puxty, K. Robson and H. Willmott, 'Regulating the UK Accountancy Profession', paper at ESRC Workshop, The State and the Professions in British Industry and Commerce: A Changing Relationship (London, Policy Studies Institute, 1988).

Davidson S. (ed.), *'The Accounting Establishment' in Perspective* (Reston, Virginia: Council of Arthur Young Professors, 1978).

Davison, I. H., 'The Accounting Standards Committee 1982–1984', Julian Hodge Accounting Lecture, University of Wales, 1985.

Dyckman, T, 'Public Accounting: Guild or Profession?' in R. R. Sterling (ed.), *Institutional Issues in Public Accounting*, (Houston, Texas: Scholars Book Co., 1974).

(Council of) European Communities, Eighth Council Directive based on Article 54 (3) (g), *Official Journal of the European Communities* no. L 126/20 (12.5.1984).

Fielding, A. G. and D. Portwood, 'Professions and the State – Towards a Typology of Bureaucratic Professions', *Sociological Review* (1981) pp. 23–53.

Financial Accounting Standards Board, *Objectives of Financial Reporting by Business Enterprises* (Stamford, Conn: FASB, 1978).

Financial Accounting Standards Board, *Qualitative Characteristics of Accounting Information* (Stamford, Conn: FASB, 1980).

Friedman, M. and S. Kuznets, *Income from Independent Professional Practice* (New York: National Bureau of Economic Research, 1945).

Griffiths, R., *The NHS Management Inquiry* (DHSS, 1983).

Groves, R., M. Poole and P. Broder, 'Professional Commitments of the Practising Chartered Accountant in Modern Britain', *Accounting and Business Research* (1984) pp. 319–32.

Haring, J. R., 'Accounting Rules and "the Accounting Establishment"', *Journal of Business* (1979) pp. 507–20.

Hopper, T., D. Cooper, T. Lowe, T. Capps and J Mouritsen, 'Management Control and Worker Resistance in the National Coal Board', in D. Knights and H. Willmott (eds), *Managing the Labour Process* (Aldershot, Hants: Gower Publishing, 1986) pp. 109–41.

Hopwood, A. G., 'Accounting Research and Accounting Practice: The Ambiguous Relationship between the Two', in A. G. Hopwood and H. Schreuder (eds), *Accounting Research and Accounting Practice: European Perspectives* (Hemel Hempstead, Herts: Prentice-Hall for ICAEW, forthcoming).

Hopwood, A. G., S. Burchell and C. Clubb, 'The Development of Accounting in the International Context: Past Concerns and Emergent Issues', in A. Roberts (ed.), *An Historical and Contemporary Review of the Development of International Accounting* (Atlanta, Georgia: Georgia State University, 1979).

Hussein, M. E. and J. Ketz, 'Ruling Elites of the FASB: A Study of the "Big Eight"', *Journal of Accounting Auditing and Finance* (1980) pp. 354–67.

Jamous, H. and B. Pelloile, 'Changes in the French University-Hospital System, in J. A. Jackson (ed.), *Professions and Professionalisation* (Cambridge University Press, 1970).

Johnson, T. J., *Professions and Power* (London: Macmillan Press, 1972).

Johnson, T. J., 'The Professions in the Class Structure', in R. Scase (ed.), *Industrial Society: Class, Cleavage and Control* (London: George Allen and Unwin, 1977).

Johnson, T. J., 'Work and Power', in G. Esland and G. Salaman (eds), *The*

Politics of Work and Occupation (Milton Keynes: Open University Press, 1980).

Johnson, T. J., 'The State and the Professions: peculiarities of the British' in A. Giddens and G. Mackenzie (eds), *Social Class and the Division of Labour* (Cambridge University Press, 1982).

Jones, E., *Accountancy and the British Economy 1840–1980* (London: Batsford, 1981).

Klegon, D. A., 'The Sociology of Professions: An Emerging Perspective, *Sociology of Work and Occupations* (1978) pp. 259–83.

Larson, M. S., *The Rise of Professionalism* (London: University of California Press, 1977).

Littleton, A. C. and V. Zimmerman, *Accounting Theory: Continuity and Change* (Englewood Cliffs, NJ: Prentice-Hall, 1962).

Loft, A., 'Towards a Critical Understanding of Accounting: The Case of Cost Accounting in the UK, 1914–1925', *Accounting, Organisations and Society* (1986) pp. 137–69.

Macdonald, K. M., 'Professional Formation: the Case of Scottish Accountants', *The British Journal of Sociology* (1984) pp. 174–89.

Macve, R., *A Conceptual Framework for Financial Accounting and Reporting* (London: ICAEW, 1981).

Meyer, J. and B. Rowan, 'Institutionalized Organizations: Formal Structures as Myth and Ceremony', *American Journal of Sociology* (1977) pp. 340–63.

Miller, P., 'On the Interrelationships between Accounting and the State', presented to European Accounting Association Congress, London, 1987.

Millerson, G., *The Quantifying Associations* (London: Routledge and Kegan Paul, 1964).

Moizer, P. and S. Turley, 'Concentration in the UK Audit Services market', *Journal of Business Finance and Accounting* (forthcoming).

Montagna, P., *Certified Public Accounting: A Sociological View of a Profession in Change* (Houston, Texas: Scholars Book Co., 1974).

Parkin, F., *Marxism and Class Theory* (London: Tavistock, 1974).

Parsons, T., 'The Professions and Social Structure', in T. Parsons *Essays in Sociological Theory* (Glencoe, Illinois: Free Press, 1954).

Pavalko, R. M., *Sociology of Occupations and Professions* (Illinois: Peacock, 1971).

Pilcher, J. A., 'An Economic Analysis of Accounting Power', in R. R. Sterling (ed.), *Institutional Issues in Public Accounting* (Houston, Texas: Scholars Book Co., 1974).

Polanyi, K., *The Great Transformation* (Boston: Beacon Press, 1957).

Robson, K., 'The Formation of the ASSC: A Study in the Relationship between Accounting and the Society in which it is located', unpublished paper, Dept. of Management Sciences, UMIST, 1987.

Rosenberg, D., C. Tomkins and P. Day, 'A Work Role Perspective of accountants in local government service departments, *Accounting Organisations and Society* (1982) pp. 123–38.

Roy, R. H. and J. H. McNeil, *Horizons for a Profession* (New York: AICPA, 1967).

Rueschemeyer, D., *Power and the Division of Labour* (Cambridge: Polity Press, 1986).

Saks, M., 'Removing the Blinkers? A Critique of Recent Contributions to the Sociology of professions', *Sociological Review* (1983) pp. 1–21.

Scott, D., *The Cultural Significance of Accounts* (Houston, Texas: Scholars Book Co., 1973, originally published H. Holt, 1931).

Skocpol, T., 'Bringing the State Back In: Current Research', in P. Evans, D. Rueschemeyer and T. Skocpol (eds) *Bringing the State Back In* (Cambridge University Press, 1985).

Simunic, D., 'The Pricing of Audit Services: Theory and Evidence', *Journal of Accounting Research* (1980) pp. 161–90.

Solomons, D., *Making Accounting Policy: The Quest for Credibility in Financial Reporting* (Oxford University Press, 1986).

Solomons, D. Guidelines for Financial Reporting Standards (London: ICAEW, 1989).

Stacey, N., *English Accountancy, A Study in Social and Economic History 1800–1954* (London: Gee and Co, 1954).

Stamp, E. and C. Marley, *Accounting Principles and the City Code* (London: Butterworths, 1970).

Sterling, R. R. (ed.), *Institutional Issues in Public Accounting* (Houston, Texas: Scholars Book Co., 1974).

Thompson, G., 'Inflation Accounting in a Theory of Calculation', *Accounting, Organisations and Society* (1987) pp. 523–44.

Tinker, A. M., B. Merino and M. Neimark, 'The Normative Origins of Positive Theories', *Accounting, Organisations and Society* (1982) pp. 147–60.

Tricker, R. I., *Governing the Institute* (London: ICAEW, 1983).

UK Treasury, *Financial Management in Government Departments*, Cmnd 9058 (London: HMSO, 1983).

US Senate, 'Report of the Subcommittee on Reports, Accounting and Management of the Committee on Governmental Affairs, Improving the Accountability of Publicly Owned Corporations and their Auditors', *Journal of Accounting* (1978) pp. 88–96.

Weber, M., *Economy and Society*, 2 vols. (New York: Bodminster Press, 1968).

Wilensky, H., 'The Professionnalization of Everyone?' *American Journal of Sociology* (1964) pp. 142–6.

19 Power and the Study of the Accounting Profession

Peter Booth and Neil Cocks

Social scientists have shown an enduring interest in the concept of power. The Community Power Debate has been at the forefront of arguments between 'élitist' and 'pluralist' scholars since the post-war period (Walton, 1966), and the concept is often used in the study of organisations (Golding and Jones, 1978). It is not surprising, therefore, that accounting researchers have also expressed such an interest.

The resulting studies of accounting have addressed power in its organisational and social context (Bartlett, 1983; Bougen and Ogden, 1981; Burchell et al., 1980; Cooper and Sherer, 1984; Gambling, 1977); information systems design (Bariff and Galbraith, 1978; Markus and Pfeffer, 1983); and the production of accounting standards (for example, Brown, 1981; Hope and Gray, 1982; Newman, 1981a, b).

But of these studies only Bougen and Ogden (1981), Burchell et al. (1980), Cooper and Sherer (1984), and Hope and Gray (1982) give explicit treatment to the radical writings on power in sociology and organisation theory. The remainder examine power from a perspective of who has it and how they use it during conflicts. They ignore the way in which such a capacity is created or its use to prevent conflict arising in the first place. Clegg (1975, 1979), Giddens (1976), and Lukes (1974) have all emphasised the need to extend such limited behaviourist conceptions of power to include the role of social structure.

This paper outlines such a conception of power and discusses its use for studying several facets of the accounting profession. First, we trace the development of power formulations from the early pluralists to Clegg (1975, 1979). Then we use Clegg's (1979) theory to explore standard-setting, professional socialisation, the production of accounting services, and professional domination as four such facets.

Although several of these have been considered indirectly in the accounting literature, a power framework provides a different research lens. It allows us to see the many facets of the profession, and within each to identify new issues and reconceptualise existing ones in an understandable and unified way.

THEORISING POWER

Dahl, originator of the pluralist view of power used by most accounting studies, defined power as a relationship between actors where 'A has power over B to the extent that he [sic] can get B to do something that B would not otherwise do' (Dahl, 1957, pp. 202–203). Dahl's commitment to a positivistic behavioural-science tradition led to the operationalisation of this definition through an emphasis on the concrete results of actions. This necessitates a conflict of interests between A and B over issues. A can hardly exercise power if A gets B to do something B would have done anyway, or does in consensus with A. Further, this conflict of interests must be overt: observable in the key issues over which such action (a decision) is taken.

Bachrach and Baratz (1962, 1963, 1970) criticised the pluralist view of power as unnecessarily confining analysis to overt conflict. They contend that this view ignores efforts by A to create or reinforce 'social and political values and institutional practices that limit the scope of the political process to public consideration of only those issues which are comparatively innocuous to A' (Bachrach and Baratz, 1962, p. 948).

By including A's efforts to limit the political process, 'non-decisions', that is 'decisions that result in suppression or thwarting of a latent or manifest challenge to the values or interests of the decision-maker' (Bachrach and Baratz, 1970, p. 44), can also be considered. But if 'there is no conflict, overt or covert, the presumption must be that there is consensus on the prevailing allocation of values, in which case non-decision-making is impossible' (Bachrach and Baratz, 1970, p. 49), and no power can be said to exist (Lukes, 1974).

Thus, as Lukes (1974) argues, Bachrach and Baratz ignore situations where non-decisions are not the result of conscious decisions, but the outcomes of some bias in power relations rooted in the existing social structure, and are thus unable to address critically questions of the production and effects of power. They also ignore the possibility that power acts to avoid conflict in the first instance. That apparent consensus may be a power phenomena where grievances are prevented by 'shaping . . . [individuals'] . . . perceptions, cognitions and preferences in such a way that they accept their role in the existing order of things, either because they can see or imagine no alternative to it, or because they see it as natural and unchangeable, or because they value it as divinely ordained and beneficial' (Lukes, 1974, p. 24).

Thus a theory of power must not only articulate how power operates at the level of social action, in both an overt and covert sense, but also how social structure plays a role in the production of power. One such theory is provided by Clegg (1975, 1979). He combines Giddens' (1976) notions of action, mediation, and structure with Weberian rationality and Gramscian hegemony (Gramsci, 1971) to develop a critical theory of power. Through his concepts of power, rule and hegemonic domination, Clegg develops a theoretical means to study 'issues' that are not individually based, but based on the rationality that actors use to orientate their actions and the 'structure of dominancy' that such orientation reflects.

Power

'Power' is used conceptually to designate the 'ability to exercise control over resources which, when subjects engage in practices, produce effects on other subjects' (Clegg, 1979, p. 95). Practices, at the level of action, represent visible social relations and their modification. In a modern organisational context this often relates to those social relations that are concerned with the control of the means and methods of production.

Rule

While individual practices may be treated as discrete events, they may also be constructed analytically as displaying a 'deep sameness', an underlying rule: the mode of rationality that subjects use in constructing the surface phenomena of visible social relations. The concept of an underlying mode of rationality provides the analytical concept for understanding the basis of actions which are possible within a given structural context. It is the means of mediating between this structural context and actions. Giddens (1976)[1] argued that action can only be understood as the continuous flow of social actors' 'lived-through experience'. As such it is a 'skilled performance' on the part of the individuals, not a mechanistic (or completely determined) response. Therefore, power, at the level of action, can only be understood via the modes of rationality used by such skilled actors in performing in their world.

Hegemonic Domination

At the level of structure, the achievement of domination is theorised using hegemony. Hegemony is 'an order in which a certain way of life and thought is diffused throughout society in all its institutional and private manifestations, informing with its spirit all taste, morality, customs, religions and political principles, and all social relations, particularly their intellectual and moral connotation' (Williams, 1960). It is the normal form of control in society, a subtle power that is not exercised as such, but provides the capacity for action (Clegg, 1979). Jessop (1976) suggests it is the means whereby the structure of a social formation limits the achievement of the interests of those who are dominated but does not totally determine such achievement. Finally, Johnson (1979) interprets Gramsci (1971) as saying that hegemony describes the interplay of the lived culture of a class, its organised conceptions (ideology and philosophy), and the 'educative' institutions through which these conceptions are modified and propagated. It is the extent to which common sense is made to conform to the necessities of production and to the construction of consent and political order.

By implication hegemony in modern Western society usually suggests the dominance of one class over others (for example, Femia, 1975). In such capitalistic social structures the underlying ideology embodies economic dominance. The concepts of private property and the market operate in favour of capital over labour, orientating and biasing much of the action in society towards that which furthers the ends of capital rather than labour. It is taken for granted that profit should be the yardstick of investment and that the living standard of workers should be set by the terms on which they sell their labour (Westergaard and Resler, 1975). The power of capital is therefore revealed more by the priority routinely given to private accumulation and market exchange, than in the conflict arising from positive acts of decision-making. Thus in any analysis of power within modern Western society, and especially corporations, how hegemony relates to the mode of production is a central concern.

Interaction of the Concepts

Power, in a total theoretical sense, is understood through the nested and dynamic interrelationship of these three concepts, power within rule within hegemonic domination. Hegemonic domination signifies what is seen as normal, proper, the everyday way of life that provides for certain actions and not others. It is to be understood in both a positive and negative sense. It is enabling in that it makes possible normal social relations by the reproduction of the social structure. But it is limiting in that these relations delimit and proscribe action in a form that provides for the domination of one class over others. Modes of rationality explain how individuals, as thinking, purposive social actors, act within the general possibilities of the social structure. Thus power, as the ability to exercise control over resources and produce effects on social actors, can be seen in everyday practices. The outcomes of which are made possible and acceptable by hegemonic domination, and are translated into normal social action via modes of rationality.

ISSUES OF POWER IN THE PROFESSION

The accounting profession is an area of increasing interest to critical scholars (Robson and Cooper, Chapter 18; Puxty, Chapter 17; Willmott, Chapter 16). This section uses the theory of power precised above to select and explore facets of the profession. First we critique the behaviourist orientation that has dominated standard-setting research. This highlights the need to broaden its focus to consider standard-setting as part of the wider social and institutional context. But standard-setting is only one facet of the accounting profession. Three others of interest to a power analysis are the socialisation of accountants, the production of accounting services, and professional domination. Our aim is not to develop definitive arguments about these, the lack of a relevant accounting literature prevents that, but rather to illustrate the potential of a power analysis for a critical understanding of the accounting profession.

Power Studies in Standard-setting

The acknowledged political nature of standard-setting (Horngren, 1973) has generated considerable research drawing implicitly or explicitly on the concept of power (Brown, 1981; Haring, 1979; Hope and Briggs, 1982; Hope and Gray, 1982; Hussein and Ketz, 1980; Meyer, 1974; Newman, 1981a, b; Rockness and Nikolai, 1977; Selto and Grove, 1982, 1983; Sutton, 1984).

The primary focus of this research has been the relationship between the voting behaviour of Accounting Principles Board (APB) and Financial Accounting Standards Board (FASB) members and the preferences of external groups. Meyer (1974) and Rockness and Nikolai (1977) considered APB voting on issued Opinions, and the members' group affiliations, to see if some group's preferences regularly prevailed. Neither report the dominance of any group across all Opinions or for a subset of more important Opinions (Key issues).

This approach displays a Dahlian concern with observable outcomes (votes) and conflict over issues (APB Opinions). It ignores the role of rationality in determining dominance as it assumes *a priori* differences between functional constituent groups (CPA firms, Commerce, Academe). If members and groups give one mode of rationality more legitimacy in standard-setting, then only issues consistent with it are likely to be on the agenda. Any conflict that does arise will involve competing options based on that rationality, thus making conflict resolution by final vote unimportant. Pluralistic voting does not, therefore, support the conclusion that dominance does not exist, as what is voted on is restricted to issues that already support a particular mode of rationality.

Haring (1979) investigated expressed preferences on FASB standards and, unlike the previous papers, found that outcomes favoured FASB sponsor organisations and accounting firms over commerce and academe. As preferences reflect the groups' modes of rationality, these results reinforce our argument above. However, by only examining final votes, Haring (1979) is forced to consider each member's behaviour as dichotomous (support or opposition). Compromise and influence are ignored. A study of rationalities would allow an examination of the variety of positions underlying the votes of each group. Also, like Meyer (1974) and Rockness and Nikolai (1977), Haring (1979) analysed a sample of those standards receiving a larger number of comments, that is, where overt conflict was greatest. As a mode of rationality is more dominant the fewer the comments standards elicit, his study is incorrectly biased towards concluding that plurality exists. The possible existence of such a dominance is indicated by the high number of FASB standards that elicit little comment.

Hussein and Ketz (1980) and Brown (1981) are also concerned with dominant coalitions. The former conclude that the Big Eight are not unified and are therefore not a ruling élite. Their framework again restricts domination to voting wins, and as such ignores any domination effected by influencing the rationality of the voting arena or the broader standard-setting arena. Understanding the significance of action in institutions, like the FASB, divorced from the institutional and social structure within which standard-setting takes place is problematic. Thus, when Brown (1981) uses responses to FASB Discussion Memorandum because they are 'neutral documents', he misses the point entirely. In the institutional context of standard-setting such documents place issues on the agenda, so they reflect power relations just as much, if not more, than voting outcomes.

While the work on voting power indices (Newman, 1981a, 1981b; Selto and Grove, 1982, 1983) attempts to address the issue of institutional arrangements, their very limited concern with abstract voting rules virtually ignores human agency. For example, an a priori group's *potential* as a winning bloc within certain voting rules takes no account of the blocks that are actually forged over time. As such they make little contribution to an understanding of actual power relations in a standard-setting arena.

Hope and Briggs (1982) and Sutton (1984) provide more useful analyses. The former ground their work in a historical review of the deferred tax debate. This allows them to consider a much broader range of influences and their context. Thus, they usefully consider agenda setting, the mobilisation of bias, and the use of a conceptual framework to justify partisan decisions. However, their analysis is limited by its view of standard-setting as a bargaining process. This presupposes compromise and rules out a consideration of the dominance of the bargaining arena through hegemony and modes of rationality.

Sutton's (1984) Downsian analysis of lobbying also recognises the importance of the institutional context. As standards differ in effect, he links lobbying to the consequence of a standard to the lobbyist's interests. He also recognises that some interests have greater legitimacy. However the analysis ignores social and political history, and limits interests to 'rational' economic costs and benefits. But modes of rationality may exist that construct interests on other grounds. For example, a 'professional rationality' may emphasis technical purity. Thus both Hope and Briggs (1982) and Sutton (1984) fail to broaden their analyses sufficiently.

Hope and Gray (1982) recognize this need theoretically but, as Cooper and Sherer (1984) note, their operationalisation of power is still narrow. This shortcoming parallels the restrictive definitions of key concepts like interests and democracy in the early empirical work on class. This social élites tradition therefore is restricted to considering who has power at some time, not the mechanisms that give rise to it, and a discussion of what constitute interests without a critical purpose. As élitism is a static theory that does little to explain the relationship between élites and masses it is unable to probe broader issues about the effects of particular social structures (see Bachrach, 1967; and Bottomore, 1966). Thus, Hope and Gray's (1982) approach may encourage the pursuit of an outdated tradition.

All these papers have approached the influence of standards promulgation from too narrow a perspective. From a broader power viewpoint they are deficient in two ways. First, they restrict their analysis to standard-setting. Drawing such boundaries is itself an exercise of power. It diverts attention from wider issues such as how the profession has sought, maintained, and profited from its license, towards the technical aspects of practice under such a license. Second, they isolate their explanations of standard-setting from its broader social and institutional context by ignoring the effects of hegemonic domination and modes of rationality. For example, they use restrictive views of human agency that do not adequately relate action in a standard-setting arena to this context.[2]

The Socialisation of Accountants

The discussion of hegemony and accounting modes of rationality leads us to consider how accountants come to embrace these. As Gramsci (1971) stressed the role of institutions, especially educational ones, in establishing hegemony, we will consider the general nature of accounting education, the problem-solving methods and accounting procedures taught, and the form of the explanatory theoretical models used.

Accounting, like most other professions, requires a long period of study in school and at a tertiary institution before gaining employment as a professional. Such study is almost entirely conducted within the confines of these educational institutions with very little, if any, contact with a practical work environment. This means that students are isolated from the social and political aspects of realistic work environments and the poorly defined and contested nature of decision-making in these contexts.

Instead they repeatedly solve problems with reference to prescribed accounting methods and solutions. There is little room for alternative conceptualisations of problems and their resultant solutions. This encourages students to accept their solutions as objective and absolute, instead of acknowledging that objectivity is only possible through ideological bias (Tinker et al., 1982) and that these solutions are inherently relative, not absolute.

Such views are strengthened by the nature of the problem-solving methods taught and the accounting procedures portrayed as appropriate for professional work. Heavy emphasis is given to the concepts of systematic critique and scientific evidence. In auditing, for example, the collection of evidence is directed at evaluating the faults in an accounting system objectively. The grounds for critique are largely defined as departures from accounting rules per se, rather than the effects of such indiscretions. The resulting attestation as to whether the financial reports are 'true and fair' thus assumes an air of absolutism far beyond that likely if a judgement of their communicative potential was required. Also the process of collecting data assumes great importance. Devices such as statistical sampling, detailed procedures manuals, and extensive proforma working papers are therefore used, and reinforce the portrayal of the collected data as objective, especially in retrospect.

Following from the narrowness of accounting problem-solving, an accountant's perception of what constitutes a problem becomes restricted. The same information about labour turnover, for example, may cause an accountant and a marketer to focus on completely different problems (Vernon, 1971). Accountants are conditioned by a technical reductionism to exclude social and political factors from consideration, and to define as problems only those things that are not technically correct or elegant. This orientation is further bolstered by the adoption of compatible values such as exactitude (Amernic et al., 1983; Hastings and Hinings, 1970), and acts as a power phenomena to exclude issues from the political agenda.

The form of the explanatory theoretical models brought into the curriculum also influences how students conceptualise. The loosely Popperian basis of most empirical accounting research produces explanations of phenomena according to individualistic and accounting causative agents rather than the social and structural factors they reflect. For example, the literature on small-company bankruptcy focuses on leverage, liquidity ratios, and management expertise as explanatory factors. The demise of such firms is often said to be a result of poor finance packaging, lack of working capital, and poor management generally (Argenti, 1976).

While such comments may be valid relative to ideal practice, they do not establish that the higher failure rate of small companies compared to their larger counterparts is due to differential financial structures or managerial expertise. They thus divert attention away from more fundamental explanations, such as the difficulties these small enterprises face in a capitalistic system characterised by cyclical and secular economic movements.

As ideological concepts such as objectivity, the legitimacy of law, and profit, are all occasioned by such socialisation, the effects of educational programmes previously regarded by most as an exercise in content, reasoning skills, or role creation, for example, a professional year, should be reconceptualised as part of the socialisation of accountants with a particular hegemony and modes of rationality consistent with it.

The role of education in spreading an accounting mentality consistent with the dominant world view throughout society is growing in importance as the proportion of professionals with substantial accounting training increases. The pervasiveness of such a hegemony is evidenced by the attempted extension of technical accounting rationality into areas of a complex social and political nature, for example human-resource accounting. Therefore, the education accountants receive is an important topic for critical research and should be considered with reference to the reproduction of a dominant hegemony.

The Production of Accounting Services

Public accounting is no longer the province of small-scale entrepreneurs. Paralleling the movement towards monopoly capitalism (Wheelwright, 1976) there has been a world-wide concentration of accounting services in the Big Eight. These firms have organised the production of accounting services around classic capitalistic principles of Tayloristic labour management, a significant measure of capital intensification, and the appropriation of surplus value. As a result accounting work is specialised, organised hierarchically, subject to stringent time constraints, standardised, increasingly automated, and facing proletarianisation. While these control relations are also evident to an extent in non-public accounting, our discussion deals with them mainly in the context of public accounting.

The specialised division of labour is reflected in the way in which the large audit firms organise audits. They are segmented into the sequential steps of pre-engagement activity, programme planning, programme execution, analytical review, and audit review and reporting (adapted from Robertson and Davis, 1985, p. 19). The more mechanistic execution function is almost exclusively conducted by audit juniors. Only audit seniors and partners consider the more abstract phases of the audit and direct the overall performance of it.

The strict audit hierarchy that results from this specialisation severely reduces the autonomy of those low in it. In response, auditors adopt a mode of rationality that abandons the consideration of broad conceptual or social issues, in favour of the technical aspects of tightly bounded problems. The exercise of power at an action level can therefore be seen in the day-to-day interactions of audit clerks with their seniors.

Further, the very notion of a hierarchy in professional practice helps to reinforce the importance of professional qualifications and experience. By ordering accounting labour according to these criteria rather than some more direct notion of capacity in the job, great importance is placed on professional values in achieving job status and worth. This defines the currency of success, subordinates those who lack it, and provides an incentive for them to pursue it in an effort to be upwardly mobile (see Larson, 1977; Johnson, 1980).

The organisation of audit time also encourages a technical orientation. Audits are conducted in concentrated bursts. A fairly large team is resident with each of several client organisations for only a few short periods every year. From this, auditors gain a broad experience of different accounting systems, but do not become intimate with the history of the client organisation and the subtleties of the social and political forces within it. They are thus encouraged to synthesise their experience on the basis of apparent technical factors, rather than the less tangible processes at work.

Further Tayloristic time-management principles are evident in the use of budgeting for audit work. All jobs have an overall budget which is closely monitored with penalties for exceeding it (see Burchell et al., 1980; Tricker, 1967). As part of this budget system, billing charges are calculated on very small periods of time and are used to collect a detailed breakdown of where audit effort has been spent. In concert these procedures stress a requirement for the effective utilisation of time and the primacy of the profit motive over audit excellence.

Another aspect of time management is the practice of allowing time in lieu instead of overtime. The direct effect of this is that a significant portion of the cost of cyclical audit work is borne by the audit workers. They absorb this unevenness by working longer hours in busy periods for an entitlement to a corresponding amount of time off in the less busy periods. But given the strict and often punitive nature of the hierarchical control structure, this time off is rarely taken in full. The tension inherent in such a practice is diffused by the lax accounting for this time. This is a paradox, given the strict audit billing system. The resulting vagueness about entitlement compounds the guilt often felt by employees in taking it, and discourages the issue of any residual claim from being raised.

Standardised work practices also have implications for the organisation of accounting services. In large audit firms, the ultimate responsibility for any legal penalties arising from negligent audit work falls on a few partners. To reduce this risk, firms could increase the comprehensiveness of the audit. Doing so may, however, lead the client to regard the fee as excessive and seek another auditor. While a new auditor would receive the fee, they would also face the same risk as the previous one and nothing would be gained.

As Western legal systems rely quite heavily on the opinions of other professional auditors to determine whether there has been a neglect of duty in audit work, there is a strong economic incentive for audit firms to co-operate to standardise audit procedures. This would provide substantial protection from prosecution by allowing accountants to argue that their opinions were based on universal professional practice.

It would be erroneous though to theorise that standardisation will occur in a mechanical form. If accounting procedures were completely mechanised then no ambiguity would exist about the proper accounting method. But situational ambiguity over method contributes substantially to the need for professional judgement. Any reduction in the judgement required would diminish the professional standing of accountants and would therefore not be encouraged by them.

To a large extent the profession has avoided this by constructing standards to preserve the need for judgement. The appearance of objectivity in standards is generated through the use of professional rhetoric to redirect lay attention to the lauded intent of the standards rather than their more flexible content. Thus the role of standards as a universal referent for proper practice is diluted by the need to preserve professional judgement. In this way we can view standard-setting from a power perspective as a device for accountants to influence the legal definition of appropriate audit procedures and rationality, rather than a determined attempt to rigidly codify rules of practice. This offers accountants some protection from legal action while preserving a division of labour favourable to themselves.

With the advent of data-processing equipment and the development of computerised judgement models, accounting in both public and private practice is increasing in capital intensity. It is conceivable that just as automated book-keeping systems largely displaced accountants from basic book-keeping functions in organisations, expert systems may alter auditing and tax work. Contrary to Puxty's conclusion in Chapter 17, this represents the deskilling of this work (see Young and Davis, Chapter Five).

But although the way technology influences the nature of accountants' work is an interesting research topic, one cannot simply ascribe the changes to technology per se. Reifying technology in this way obscures the social relations that are a part of it. For example, commenting that new technology has displaced the accountant from much of the routine book-keeping work does not explain why the people who operate this technology are mainly lowly-paid women working under the supervision of predominately male accountants (Macintosh, Chapter 8; Miller and Garrison, 1982). Thus the forces produced by new technology may well encourage the further division of labour, but to view this only as a technical phenomena would be to ignore the issues of power and control in the relations of production that are generated (Braverman, 1974; Buchanan and Boddy, 1982).

Public accounting firms are not only similar to modern corporations in terms of their labour management processes and use of technology, but also in the way they generate surplus value from an increasingly proletarianised workforce. A large proportion of the accountants employed by the Big Eight perform largely deskilled and fragmented tasks for small wages, while a small élite group of partners oversee the generation of surplus value which they then appropriate. This structure, of itself, is a power phenomenon worthy of study.

Professional Domination

Both the trait orientation to professions inspired by Durkheim (1957) and the functionalist orientation of Parsons (1964) encourage the view that professional jurisdiction is uncontested. In contrast, a power perspective directs us to consider how a profession gains a licence (Bucher and Strauss, 1961) over a particular type of work. Freidson (1977) argues that in the pursuit of this licence, professions are distinguished by their legitimate and organised autonomy. He suggests that such autonomy has the dual and related foundations of esoteric knowledge and state patronage.

The role of esoteric knowledge has already been canvassed in regard to standards, socialisation, and the production of accounting services. But in addition to studying such knowledge in relation to the practice of accounting work, a power perspective directs us to consider it as a resource in the competition between various parties over the jurisdiction of this work (see Armstrong, 1984). A history of accounting informed by this perspective would therefore include an account of the emergence of certain forms of knowledge during the conflicts over the control of occupational territory, and their use as political tools in the subordination, limitation, and exclusion of some groups in favour of others (see Willis, 1983).

The concern to maintain state patronage is evident in the scurry of professional bodies to introduce accounting standards prior to the state mandating them. To fail in such an endeavour would reduce the claim to professional self-control (Willmott, Chapter 16), and thus the right to exclusive or near exclusive licence over the accounting function (Bucher and Strauss, 1961). Therefore standard-setting can be seen as part of justifying a claim to professionalism that is, more accurately, an occupational ideology that legitimates autonomy (Larson, 1977). Gramsci (1971) argues that this in turn reproduces aspects of the dominant ideology and thus promotes hegemony. Such technological rationality, or an ideology of expertise (Habermas, 1970), supports the claim of beneficent power yet legitimates inequality and élitism (Larson, 1977).

CONCLUDING COMMENTS

This paper outlines a theory of power that allows a more critical analysis of accounting phenomena than the impoverished behaviourist traditions generally employed. We discussed four facets of the accounting profession; standard-setting, the socialisation of accountants, the production of accounting services, and professional domination. Our aim has been to illustrate the potential of a power analysis for a critical understanding of the accounting profession.

A consideration of hegemony and modes of rationality emphasises the need to study accounting phenomena in context. The dimensions of power and conflict would thus extend beyond simple economic interests to more fundamental social, historical, and institutional factors. Consistent with the tenets of a political economy of accounting (Cooper and Sherer, 1984), critical research should investigate the nature of the prevailing hegemonies that support, and are supported by, accounting. This draws our attention towards the dialectical relationship between hegemony, modes of rationality, and action.

Some of the examples of these relations we have discussed are: how accountants are educated, the Tayloristic organisation of accounting work, the concentration of accounting services in the Big Eight, and the use of state patronage to gain a licence over the accounting function. Others that could be studied include the role of modes of rationality in industrial conflicts involving accounting calculation (Owen and Lloyd, 1985; Neimark and Tinker, 1986); the relationship between the implementation of accounting standards and the governance of auditing practice; how a conceptual framework may act as a resource to give pre-eminence to the profession's mode of rationality in standard-setting.

Overall, this would enable the study of accounting phenomena to be more fully linked to the wider social structures of power and influence in which they are enmeshed.

Notes

1. While Giddens and Clegg exhibit similar heritages in phenomenology and Weber, and thus Giddens's discussion of action can be useful in understanding this portion of Clegg's analysis, it is critical to note that Giddens's commitment to voluntarism leads to an unsatisfactory discussion of power in relation to structure.

2. The application of a power framework to standard-setting research issues is considered in more depth in Booth and Cocks (forthcoming).

Bibliography

Amernic, J. H., R. Kanungo and N. Aranya, 'Professional and Work Values of Accountants: A Cross Cultural Study', *International Journal of Accounting* (1983) pp. 177–92.

Argenti, J., *Corporate Collapse, the Causes and Symptoms* (London: McGraw Hill, 1976).

Armstrong, P., 'Competition Between the Organisational Professions and the Evolution of Management Control Strategies', in Thompson K., (ed.), *Work, Employment, and Unemployment: Perspectives on Work and Society* (Open University Press: Milton Keynes, 1984).

Bachrach, P., *The Theory of Democratic Elitism: A Critique*, (Boston, Mass: Little, Brown and Company, 1967).

Bachrach, P. and M. S. Baratz, 'Two Faces of Power', *American Political Science Review* (1962) pp. 947–52.

Bachrach, P. and M. S. Baratz, 'Decisions and Nondecisions: An Analytical Framework', *American Political Science Review* (1963) pp. 641–51.

Bachrach, P. and M. S. Baratz, *Power and Poverty: Theory and Practice* (New York: Oxford University Press, 1970).

Bariff, M. L. and J. R. Galbraith, 'Intraorganizational Power Considerations for Designing Information Systems', *Accounting, Organizations and Society* (1978) pp. 15–27.

Bartlett, R. W., *Power Base Attribution and the Perceived Legitimacy of Managerial Accounting* (Ann Arbor: UMI Research Press, 1983).

Bottomore, T. B., *Ethics and Society* (Baltimore: Penguin Books, 1966).

Bougen, P. and S. Ogden, 'Power in Organisations: Some Implications for the Use of Accounting in Industrial Relations', *Managerial Finance* (1981) pp. 22–6.

Braverman, H., *Labour and Monopoly Capitalism* (New York: Monthly Review Press, 1974).

Brown, P. R., 'A Descriptive Analysis of Select Input Bases of the Financial Accounting Standards Board', *Journal of Accounting Research* (1981) pp. 232–46.

Buchanan, D. and D. Boddy, *Organisations in the Computer Age* (Farnborough: Gower Publishing Group, 1982).

Bucher, R. and A. Strauss, 'Professions in Progress', *American Journal of Sociology* (1961) pp. 325–34.

Booth, P. and N. Cocks, 'Critical Research Issues in Standard-Setting', *Journal of Business Finance and Accounting* (forthcoming, 1990).

Burchell, P., C. Clubb, A. Hopwood, J. Hughes and J. Nahapiet, 'The Roles of Accounting in Organizations and Society', *Accounting, Organizations and Society* (1980) pp. 5–27.

Clegg, S., *Power, Rule and Domination* (London: Routledge and Kegan Paul, 1975).

Clegg, S., *The Theory of Power and Organisation* (London: Routledge and Kegan Paul, 1979).

Cooper, D. J. and M. J. Sherer, 'The Value of Corporate Accounting Reports: Arguments for a Political Economy of Accounting', *Accounting, Organizations and Society* (1984) pp. 207–32.

Dahl, R. A., 'The Concept of Power', *Behavioural Science* (1957) pp. 201–15.

Durkheim, E., *Professional Ethics and Civic Morals* (London: Routledge Kegan Paul, 1957).

Femia, J., 'Hegemony and Consciousness in the Thought of Antonio Gramsci', *Political Studies* (1975) pp. 29–48.

Freidson, E., 'The Futures of Professionalism', in M. Stacey, et al. (eds.), *Health and the Division of Labour* (London: Croom Helm, 1977), pp. 14–40.

Gambling, T., 'Magic, Accounting and Morale', *Accounting, Organizations and Society* (1977) pp. 141–52.

Giddens, A., *New Rules of Sociological Method* (London: Hutchinson, 1976).

Golding, D. and D. Jones, 'Power and Control', in D. Ashton, (ed.), *Management Bibliographies and Reviews*, vol. IV (Bradford: MCB Publications, 1978).

Gramsci, A., *Selections from the Prison Notebooks*, edited and translated by Q. Hoare and G. Nowell-Smith (London: Lawrence and Wishart, 1971).

Habermas, J., 'Technology and Science as Ideology', in *Toward a Rational Society* (Boston: Beacon Press, 1970) pp. 81–122.

Haring, J. R., 'Accounting Rules and "The Accounting Establishment"', *Journal of Business* (1979) pp. 507–19.

Hastings, A. and H. R. Hinings, 'Role Relations and Value Adaptation: A Study of the Professional Accountant in Industry', *Sociology* (1970) pp. 353–66.

Hope, T., and J. Briggs, 'Accounting Policy Making: Some Lessons From the Deferred Taxation Debate', *Accounting and Business Research* (1982) pp. 83–96.

Hope, T., and R. Gray, 'Power and Policy Making: The Development of an R & D Standard', *Journal of Business Finance and Accounting* (1982) pp. 531–58.

Horngren, C. T., 'The Marketing of Accounting Standards', *Journal of Accountancy* (1973), pp. 61–6.

Hussein, M. E. and J. E. Ketz, 'Ruling Elites of the FASB: A Study of the Big Eight', *Journal of Accounting, Auditing and Finance* (1980) pp. 354–67.

Jessop, B., 'Power and Contingency', paper presented to the EGOS Symposium on Power (University of Bradford, 6–7 May 1976).

Johnson, R., in J. Clarke, C. Critcher and R. Johnson (eds), *Working Class Culture* (Hutchinson: London, 1979).

Johnson, T., 'Work and Power', in G. Esland, and G. Salaman (eds), *The Politics of Work and Occupations* (Milton Keynes: Open University Press, 1980) pp. 335–71.

Larson, M. S., *The Rise of Professionalism: A Sociological Analysis* (Berkeley: University of California Press, 1977).

Lukes, S., *Power: A Radical View* (London: Macmillan, 1974).

Markus, M. L. and J. Pfeffer, 'Power and the Design and Implementation of Accounting and Control Systems', *Accounting, Organizations and Society* (1983) pp. 205–18.

Meyer, P. E., 'The APB's Independence and its Implications for the FASB',

Journal of Accounting Research (1974), pp. 154–67.

Miller, J. and H. H. Garrison, 'Sex Roles: The Division of Labor at Home and in the Workplace', *Annual Review of Sociology* (1982) pp. 237–62.

Neimark, M. and T. Tinker, 'The Social Construction of Management Control Systems', *Accounting, Organizations and Society* (1986) pp. 369–95.

Newman, D. P., 'An Investigation of the Distribution of Power in the APB and FASB', *Journal of Accounting Research* (1981a) pp. 247–62.

Newman, D. P., 'The SEC's Influence on Accounting Standards: The Power of the Veto', *Journal of Accounting Research* (Supplement, 1981b) pp. 134–56.

Owen, D. L. and A. J. Lloyd, 'The Use of Financial Information by Trade Union Negotiators in Plant Level Collective Bargaining', *Accounting, Organizations and Society* (1985) pp. 329–50.

Parsons, T., *The Social System* (New York: Free Press, 1964).

Robertson, J. C. and F. G. Davis, *Auditing*, 4th edn (Texas: Business Publications, Inc., 1985).

Rockness, H. O. and L. A. Nikolai, 'An Assessment of APB Voting Patterns', *Journal of Accounting Research* (1977), pp. 154–67.

Selto, F. H. and H. D. Grove, 'Voting Power Indices and the Setting of Financial Accounting Standards: Extensions', *Journal of Accounting Research* (1982) pp. 676–88.

Selto, F. H. and H. D. Grove, 'The Predictive Power of Voting Power Indices: FASB Voting on Statement of Accounting Standards Nos 45–69', *Journal of Accounting Research* (1983) pp. 619–22.

Sutton, T. G., 'Lobbying of Accounting Standard-Setting Bodies in the UK and the USA: A Downsian Analysis', *Accounting, Organizations and Society* (1984) pp. 81–95.

Tinker, A. M., B. D. Merino, and M. D. Neimark, 'The Normative Origins of Positive Theories: Ideology and Accounting Thought', *Accounting, Organizations and Society* (1982) pp. 167–200.

Tricker, R., *The Accountant in Management* (London: Batsford, 1967).

Vernon, M. D., *The Psychology of Perception* (Harmondsworth: Penguin, 1971).

Walton, J., 'Discipline, Method and Community Power: A Note on the Sociology of Knowledge', *American Sociological Review* (1966) pp. 684–9.

Westergaard, J., and H. Resler, *Class in a Capitalist Society: A Study of Contemporary Britain* (Harmondsworth: Penguin, 1975).

Wheelwright, E., and K. Buckley, *Essays in the Political Economy of Australian Capitalism* (Sydney: Australia and New Zealand Book Company, 1976).

Williams, G., 'The Concept of "Egemonia" in the Thought of Antonio Gramsci: Some Notes on Interpretation', *Journal of the History of Ideas* (1960) pp. 586–99.

Willis, E., *Medical Dominance* (Sydney: George Allen & Unwin, 1983).

Willmott, H., 'Setting Accounting Standards in the UK: The Emergence of the Private Accounting Bodies and Their Role in the Regulation of Public Accounting Practice', in W. Streeck and P. C. Schmitter (eds), *Private Interest, Government and Public Policy* (London: Sage, 1985).

Index